Communications in Computer and Information Science 620

Commenced Publication in 2007
Founding and Former Series Editors:
Alfredo Cuzzocrea, Dominik Ślęzak, and Xiaokang Yang

More information about this series at http://www.springer.com/series/7899

Lorna Uden · Dario Liberona
Birgit Feldmann (Eds.)

Learning Technology for Education in Cloud

The Changing Face of Education

5th International Workshop, LTEC 2016
Hagen, Germany, July 25–28, 2016
Proceedings

Springer

Editors
Lorna Uden
Staffordshire University
Staffordshire
UK

Birgit Feldmann
FernUniversität
Hagen
Germany

Dario Liberona
Universidad Tecnica Federico Santa Maria
Valparaiso
Chile

ISSN 1865-0929 ISSN 1865-0937 (electronic)
Communications in Computer and Information Science
ISBN 978-3-319-42146-9 ISBN 978-3-319-42147-6 (eBook)
DOI 10.1007/978-3-319-42147-6

Library of Congress Control Number: 2016943464

Printed on acid-free paper

This Springer imprint is published by Springer Nature
The registered company is Springer International Publishing AG Switzerland

The 5th International Workshop on Learning Technology for Education in Cloud (LTEC 2016): The Changing Face of Education

July 25–28, 2016, Hagen, Germany

The rapid and constant pace of change in technology is creating both opportunities and challenges for education. The opportunities include greater access to rich, multimedia content, the use of online availability, the widespread use of mobile computing devices that can access the Internet, the expanding role of social networking tools for learning and professional development, the use of massive open online courses (MOOC), cloud computing, big data, and the growing interest in the power of digital games for more personalized learning. Besides technologies, there are also new pedagogical advances in learning and teaching.

The 5th LTEC (2016) examined these technologies and pedagogical advances that are changing the way teachers teach and students learn while giving special emphasis to the pedagogically effective ways we can harness these new technologies in education. Contributions address theory, research, practice, and policy, especially those can also be focused on particular approaches, technologies, and domains. LTEC 2016 presented work in the very broad area of educational technology.

This workshop presents academic research and practical applications in education from all areas, seeking to help practitioners finds ways of putting research into practice and for researchers to gain an understanding of additional real-world problems. It includes research papers and case studies from both industry and academia. The proceedings consist of 27 papers covering various aspects of technologies for learning including:

- Learning technologies
- Learning tools and environment
- MOOC for learning
- Problem solving and knowledge transfer
- Case study.

The authors of the papers come from many different countries, such as Chile, Colombia, Estonia, Finland, France, Germany, Greece, Guatemala, Japan, Mexico, Slovenia, Spain, Switzerland, Taiwan, the UK, and the USA.

We would like to thank our authors, reviewers, and Program Committee for their contributions and the FernUniversität in Hagen, Germany, for hosting the conference. Special thanks to the authors and participants at the conference. Without their efforts, there would be no conference or proceedings.

July 2016

Lorna Uden
Dario Liberona
Birgit Feldmann

Organization

Conference General Chair

Lorna Uden	Staffordshire University, UK

Program Chairs

Dario Liberona	Universidad Tecnica Federico Santa Maria, Santiago Chile
Birgit Feldmann	FernUniversität in Hagen, Germany

Local Chair

Tobias Augustin	FernUniversität in Hagen, Germany

Organizing Committee

Heike Brand	FernUniversität in Hagen, Germany
Franziska Demmer	FernUniversität in Hagen, Germany
Patric Albrecht	FernUniversität in Hagen, Germany
Sabine Siemsen	FernUniversität in Hagen, Germany

Conference Officials

Amanda Jefferies	University of Hertfordshire, UK
Birgit Feldmann	FernUniversität in Hagen, Germany
Carole R. Beal	FL Online Learning Institute, USA
D'Arcy Becker	University of Wisconsin, USA
Dario Liberona	Universidad Santa Maria, Chile
I-Hsien Ting	National University of Kaohsiung, Taiwan
Jane Sinclair	University of Warwick, UK
Jeremiah Sullins	University of Mobile, USA
Kyparisia Papanikolau	School of Pedagogical and Technological Education, Greece
Lorna Uden	Staffordshire University, UK
Luciana A.M. Zaina	University of São Carlos, Brazil
Manuel Santos-Trigo	Center for Research and Advanced Studies, Cinvestav-IPN, Mexico
Michael Vallance	Future University Hakodate, Japan
Richard Hartshorne	University of Central Florida, USA
Gunter Schlageter	University of Hagen, Germany

Contents

Learning Technologies

Revisiting Mathematical Textbooks Problems in a Technology Enhanced Learning Environment . . . 3
Matías Camacho-Machín, Mar Moreno, and Manuel Santos-Trigo

The Knowledge Management into Technology Based Firms (Model Proposal) . . . 15
Jorge Leonardo Puentes, Nancy Yurani Ortiz, and José Ignacio Rodriguez

Informational Technology Skills and Media Literacy in Students: A Case Study . . . 25
Jorge Chavez, Claudia Jaramillo, and Dario Liberona

A Case of Emotional Intelligence for Teachers' Professional Development: Emotions and Connections are Ubiquitous in Second Life . . . 39
Ioanna Giannakou, Fotini Paraskeva, Aikaterini Alexiou, and Hara Bouta

Using Games to Improve Learning Skills in Students with Cognitive Disabilities Through Kinect Technology. . . . 51
Dacarth Sarmiento, Yesid Díaz, and Roberto Ferro

Web Framework for Developing Real Time Applications for Education. . . . 61
Werner Creixell and Cristóbal Ganter

Learning Tools and Environment

Proposal of a Standard Architecture of IoT for Smart Cities . . . 77
July Katherine Díaz Barriga, Christian David Gómez Romero, and José Ignacio Rodríguez Molano

Investigating the Experience of Moodle Adoption Through Expert Voices . . . 90
June Sinclair and Anne-Maria Aho

Learning Strategies and Interpersonal Relationships of Students Learning Cooperatively Online. . . . 103
Jonathan Kaplan

Teaching Students to Learn IDEA: The Impact of Learner Attitudes . . . 112
D'Arcy Becker, Dawna Drum, and Aimee Pernsteiner

Emotion Determination in eLearning Environments Based on Facial Landmarks 122
Tobias Augustin

MOOC for Learning

A Practical Experience on the Use of Gamification in MOOC Courses as a Strategy to Increase Motivation 139
Miguel Morales, Hector R. Amado-Salvatierra, Rocael Hernández, Johanna Pirker, and Christian Gütl

From MOOC to GOAL: Ubiquitous Networked Learning in Higher Education 150
Sabine Siemsen

Case Study on Using MOOC Materials in a Small Private Online Course . . . 162
Whai-En Chen

Open Education – A Challenge for E-training. 168
Viktorija Florjančič

Problem Solving and Knowledge Transfer

Designing Technology-Based Tasks for Enhancing Mathematical Understanding Through Problem Solving 183
Fernando Barrera-Mora and Aaron Reyes-Rodriguez

Digital Technologies and a Modeling Approach to Learn Mathematics and Develop Problem Solving Competencies 193
Manuel Santos-Trigo, Isaid Reyes-Martínez, and Daniel Aguilar-Magallón

Knowledge Transference and Management Model for MSMEs Through the Pedagogical Strategy of Simulated Companies 207
Sandra Bonilla Cely, Leonor Rojas Marmolejo, and Victor Hugo Medina García

Knowledge Management Metamodel from Social Analysis of Lessons Learnt Registered in the Cloud 219
José López Quintero, Víctor Hugo Medina García, and Cristina Pelayo García

Case Study

Teaching Information Literacy in Secondary Education: How to Design Professional Development for Teachers? 235
Sabine Seufert, Nina Scheffler, Katarina Stanoevska-Slabeva, and Severina Müller

Can K-12 Students Learn How to Program with just Two Hours? 250
Kadri Umbleja

Course Implementation: Value-Added Mode. 265
Vello Kukk

Establishing Meta-Learning Metrics When Programming Mindstorms EV3 Robots 274
Michael Vallance

Three Curriculum Maturing Cycles in Academic Curriculum Management Systems 289
Kai Pata, Kairit Tammets, Vladimir Tomberg, Mohammad Al-Smadi, and Mart Laanpere

Is a Virtual Learning Environment a One-Size-Fits-All Solution? A Survey of Cognitive Styles Within a University Student Population 301
Russell Barton and Jonathan Foster

Author Index 309

Learning Technologies

Revisiting Mathematical Textbooks Problems in a Technology Enhanced Learning Environment

Matías Camacho-Machín[1(✉)], Mar Moreno[2], and Manuel Santos-Trigo[3]

[1] Universidad de La Laguna, San Cristóbal de La Laguna, Spain
mcamacho@ull.edu.es
[2] Universidad de Alicante, San Vicente del Raspeig / Sant Vicent del Raspeig, Spain
mmoreno@ua.es
[3] Cinvestav-IPN, Mexico City, Mexico
msantos@cinvestav.mx

Abstract. We analyse and discuss the extent to which the systematic use of digital tools offers prospective and practicing high school teachers an opportunity to construct and explore dynamic models of textbook problems in terms of visual, empirical, and geometric reasoning. In this context, the use of the tool not only offers them novel ways to think of the tasks, but also to engage in problem solving activities to extend and look for connections of the initial statements. Thus, the use of technologies provides learners a set of affordances to represent and explore dynamically textbook problems and to look for and support mathematical relationships.

Keywords: Digital tools · Mathematical problem solving · Dynamic Geometry Software (DGS)

1 Introduction

The availability of different types of technologies including multiple purpose and ad hoc designed technologies is challenging what students should learn and how learning environments should be organized and promoted. [4] pointed out that the incorporation of technologies in the students' mathematical learning implies discussing what types of transformations bring their use to mathematical knowledge. "[the uses of] digital technologies disrupt many taken-for-granted aspects of what it means to think, explain and prove mathematically and to express relationships in different ways" (p. 87). Likewise, the incorporation of digital technologies into mathematical lessons requires teachers to reorganize fundamental curriculum contents and to consider what challenges emerge during the technology implementation. How do teachers develop the experiences and expertise to incorporate the systematic use of technology in their actual

Partial results of this research were presented at the CERME 8 conference. This is an extended version from [12]

L. Uden et al. (Eds.): LTEC 2016, CCIS 620, pp. 3–14, 2016.
DOI: 10.1007/978-3-319-42147-6_1

practice? It is argued that digital technologies can provide an environment for teachers to share and collaborate with peers on the preparation of class material and ways to incorporate technology in problem solving approaches. Thus, one way for prospective and practicing teachers to recognize the potential associated with the use of a particular tool is to get them involved in problem solving experiences where the use digital technologies becomes important to work and extend routine problems found in regular textbooks [8, 9]. This study is part of a research project that aims to analyse and document ways in which the use of digital technology helps prospective and practicing teachers review and extend their knowledge and problem solving approaches. One essential phase during the development of the project was to characterize what ways of reasoning and problem solving strategies emerge when tasks or problems that appear in textbooks are approached through the use of digital tools. In this study, we focus on analyzing problem solving sessions that were part of a seminar that included the participation of mathematicians, mathematics educators and prospective and practicing secondary school teachers. During the development of the sessions, the participants used a dynamic geometry system (GeoGebra) to represent, explore, and solve a set of textbook problems, i.e., textbook problems were used as departure point to construct and explore dynamic models of the tasks.

Thus, the research questions that framed the development of the study included:

- *To what extent does the information that characterizes the use of the tool to approach textbook problems provide a basis to frame instructional routes to foster teachers and students' development of mathematical knowledge?*

2 Conceptual Framework

In order to frame the study, we relied on two complementary approaches to explain ways for people to take decisions during the development of their activities. Specifically, we recognize that prospective teachers, in their education, need to develop not only subject matter and pedagogic knowledge, but also strategic thinking to eventually take crucial decisions during the development of their teaching practices. Reflection, analysis, discussion, and informed decision-making are essential ingredients for teachers to frame their practices. Teachers' decisions involve the selection of problems, the introduction and discussions of concepts, the use of technology, ways to organize or structure learning activities, and ways to assess students' problem solving proficiency. How do teachers support and carry out choices and decisions related to the framing and development of a mathematical lesson? [11] proposes a framework to characterize and interpret ways in which people in different domains including teaching, shopping, automobile repair, electronic troubleshooting, and medical practice engage in, take decisions, and develop practices associated with their domains or fields. "People's decision making in well practiced, knowledge-intensive domains can be fully characterized as a function of their orientations, resources, and goals" (p. 182). Teachers' orientations involve their beliefs about the domain such as mathematics and how the discipline is learned; resources refer to their mathematical and didactical knowledge to frame and achieve their instructional goals. In a wider context, [5] identifies two systems to account for or explain the decisions and choices that people make: "System

1 operates automatically and quickly, with little or no effort and no sense of voluntary control. System 2 allocates attention to the effortful mental activities that demand it, including complex computations. The operations of System 2 are often associated with the subjective experience of agency, choice, and concentration" (p. 20). Hence, it is important to reflect on the extent to which the opportunities to use digital technologies and problem solving experiences that prospective teachers develop and encounter in their education permeate the development of their practices.

How do teachers construct their orientations or beliefs, dispositions, values and resources to pursue their goals? What is the role of the teachers' initial preparation and experience to achieve instructional goals that are consistent with mathematical practices? Delving into the teachers' preparation implies recognizing that there are multiple paths or programmes and traditions to prepare prospective teachers around the world. In some cases, the faculty of education and the mathematics departments jointly coordinate the teachers education; other programmes are part of a school or institutions (*e.g.*, teacher training colleges) exclusively dedicated to the education of teachers. Both models recognize the need and importance for prospective teachers to develop the mathematical and didactic knowledge that can help them structure and implement proper conditions for students to learn the subject. However, the extent to which prospective teachers develop the mathematical sophistication needed to structure a sound mathematical lesson, to interpret students' ideas or comments and to guide their learning has recently been questioned and thereby generating an ongoing debate. [2] states that the assumption that "advanced mathematics studies would enhance teachers' knowledge of mathematics, which in turn will contribute to the quality of classroom instruction" (p. 941) needs to be reexamined in terms of what it means for teachers to have enough subject-matter knowledge to become an expert teacher and how a teacher can develop and use that knowledge in his or her teaching.

To structure and organize the use of digital technologies to work on textbook tasks, we adjusted what [1] call a *Situation* that consists of three related parts: (a) the *prompt* in which we describe the textbook task; (b) the mathematical *foci* in which we examine mathematical features and ways of reasoning that appear as a result of using digital technology to approach the prompt and also, we identify contents and relevant strategies that extend paper and pencil approaches; and (c) we look for generalization or extensions of the initial tasks.

3 The Contexts, Participants and Methods

The tasks that provided the data in this study were discussed during problem solving sessions within a group that included two mathematics educators, two mathematicians, three high school prospective teachers and three high school in-service teachers. The group met once a week, three hours per session, and maintained discussion of the tasks and related themes via Internet (FaceTime). An important goal in the agenda was to discuss the types of changes that a teachers' educational programme needs to consider in order to incorporate the systematic use of digital technology to develop both mathematics and didactical knowledge. Our initial literature review allowed us to recognize that there is scant information on the characterization of ways of reasoning that subjects or learners can construct as a result of using a particular tool and how the use of several tools could help them enhance their problem solving approaches. There is abundant literature that recognizes the importance for teachers and students to use different digital tools in mathematics learning [3]; but there is little reflection on ways of reasoning that learners could consistently develop as a result of using several tools in problem solving experiences. In other words, prospective and in-service teachers need to discuss and reflect on what types of representations and explorations of tasks or problems could be constructed with the use of a particular tool and the kind of arguments, visual and empirical among others, that could be used to develop mathematical understanding and to support task solutions. Our point of departure was to work on mathematics tasks that appear in textbooks with the use of a dynamic geometry system and discuss, within the group, features of mathematical reasoning that characterize and are consistent with this approach. Thus, we focus on contrasting the tool approach that involves visualizing and supporting mathematical results through the use of empirical and geometric arguments with the analytic approach that relies on the use of algebraic models to represent and explore mathematical relations. In this process, the tool affordances become important to visualize the behaviour of particular parameters or relations without making the algebraic model explicit. According to ([6] p. 326) "affordance is of particular importance when considering mathematical tasks that involve the use of technology since interaction with the technology should be a critical epistemic element in such tasks".

The Problem Solving Sessions and the Unit of Analysis. For this study, we focused on analysing the group work exhibited during four three-hour sessions. Thus, the group worked on a set of textbook problems and discussed, within the group, the role that the use of the tool played in representing, exploring and solving each problem. During the sessions, one or two of the members of the group presented a task and possible ways to represent it through a dynamic geometry environment to the group in each meeting. During the presentation, the rest of the group got involved in open discussions that included asking for the clarification of issues, concept explanation or proposing other ways to approach the task. Later, the group discussion continued via online conferences. In this report, **the unit of analysis** is the group's work exhibited while the textbook problems were discussed. We do not intend to describe in detail the contribution of each group member to the solution; instead, we focus on what the group as a whole agreed and identified as important ideas associated with the problem solving process. In order to illustrate the common mathematical features that emerged during the solution process, we relied on a set of textbook tasks that appears at the end of the unit involving the study of perimeters and areas of triangles and finding loci. It is important to mention that an essential goal was to analyse the list of problems in terms of concepts involved and possible strategies needed to approach each task. The group discussion of the tasks was framed around two problem-solving principles:

- All tasks or problems are conceptualized as opportunities for learners to engage in mathematical explorations that go beyond reporting only a problem solution, i.e., teachers or learners should consistently look for connections and extensions of initial statements.
- Solving the tasks involves looking for different ways to represent, explore and solve the problems and contrasting mathematical qualities associated with the solution

process [10]. Specially, the construction and exploration of dynamic models associated with the tasks should be part of the tasks' solution process.

Throughout the discussion of the tasks, the group recognized the importance of identifying and connecting both the mathematical knowledge and processes involved in approaching the tasks and the didactical knowledge needed for teaching. "Mathematics teachers not only need to know mathematics and mathematical processes, but they also need to know mathematics in a way that is useful for helping someone else become proficient in mathematics" ([1], p. 981).

At the outset, it was found that the format and wording of the textbook problems, in general, asked to find a particular answer to each problem and in the problem statements, learners are not required or encouraged to think of multiple approaches or go beyond the asked solution. Here, the problems were regrouped and reworded to make explicit the goal of looking for different ways to represent and explore the tasks.

4 The Role of a Dynamic Geometry System (GeoGebra) in Solving the Task

An Initial Prompt. A textbook problem that involves finding areas, perimeters, and foci was chosen to illustrate what types of changes were introduced to transform the initial statement into a series of activities to foster mathematical inquiry.

The textbook statement: *Draw two triangles that share one side AB (base) and whose third vertex is located on a line L that is parallel to segment AB. Find the area of those triangles. Can you find more triangles with the same base and equal area?*

The Mathematical Foci. To identify and discuss mathematical contents and ways of reasoning involved in approaching the task, we followed a framework [8] to deal with routine problems. The framework distinguishes problem-solving episodes that value and promote both the use of computational technology and analytic approaches to represent, explore and solve the tasks. In this perspective, we identify and discuss relevant questions to understand the task, to think of different solution methods, to extend and connect the initial task with a series of concepts or mathematical situations, and to look back and reflect on what the solution process involved in terms of ways of reasoning and as a method to approach other problems.

A. Problem Solving Comprehension. Learners need to comprehend and make sense of what the problem statement is all about to get engaged into mathematical thinking [7]. This stage is crucial to start thinking of mathematical objects to represent and explore the problem statement [12]. This phase also includes the discussion of questions that extend or situate some elements of the problem in a wider context. For example, while examining the task, the team recognized the importance for students to focus on the role of the height and the parallel line in finding the area of the drawn triangles. Can we draw more than two triangles? How many could we draw? What happens to their areas? These types of questions intended to introduce the concept of infinity into the discussion by associating the third vertex (any point on line L) with the construction of the triangles (Fig. 1). What is the height of the triangles that are

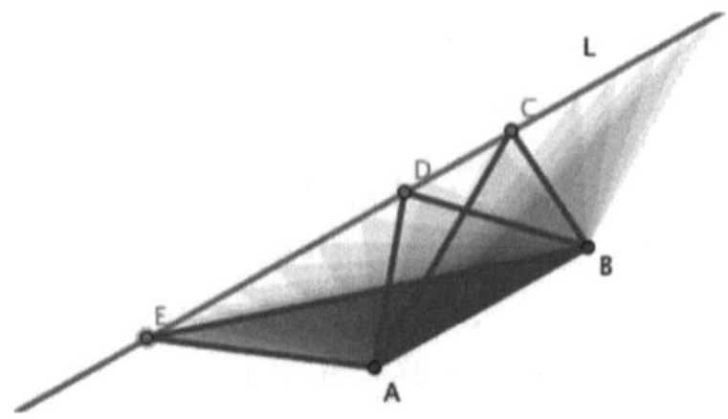

Fig. 1. How many triangles can be drawn when point E is moved along line L? What is the height of those triangles?

generated when point E (third vertex) is moved along line L? An algebraic approach involves recognizing that the height (h) of the family of triangles that are generated when the third vertex is moved along line L is constant and therefore their area becomes $\frac{d(A,B)h}{2}$.

The use of GeoGebra to represent the task demands that problem solvers rely on the tools' affordances to represent the task and to explore directly the behaviour of some attributes of the family of generated triangles, for instance, their areas or perimeters. The introduction of a particular notation becomes important to represent, explore, explain and communicate those behaviours.

B. A Dynamic Exploration. The use of the dynamic software allows to quantify particular parameters (side, area, perimeter, angles, etc.) embedded in the representation and observe their behaviours within the dynamic model. The team focused on graphing a relationship that involves the length AE (E moves on parallel L) and the perimeter of triangle with one side segment AB and third vertex point E. Thus, with the help of the software, it was possible to graph the variation of both perimeter and area as a relation of the length of side AE and the corresponding perimeter and area values as point E is moved along line L. That is, for each position of point E on line L, the corresponding length of AE is associated with values of the perimeter/area of the generated triangle ABE. It is important to mention that the graph of the perimeter variation was generated without making explicit the algebraic model associated with the perimeter behaviour. That is, the perimeter and area graphs were generated through finding the loci of points describing both behaviours. On the graph, point Q has the coordinates the length of side AE and the area of triangle ABE, i.e., the ordered pair (length of AE, area of triangle ABE). It could also be observed that the domain of the independent variable (side AE) is the interval [the height of the triangle ABE, ∞). The locus of point Q when point E is moved along line L is a ray as shown in the figure. That is, the function area is a constant. The locus of point P when point E is moved along line L represents the graph of perimeter behaviour. Likewise, one can see that the perimeter behaviour varies depending on the position of point E on line L. How does the perimeter graph behave or is there any particular type of triangle associated with, for example, a minimum perimeter value?

That Fig. 2 shows the graph of both perimeter (red curve) and area (black ray) behaviours:

In http://tinyurl.com/DynamicM1 is possible to explore directly the dynamic model by moving point E. The following conjecture emerged during the discussion of this

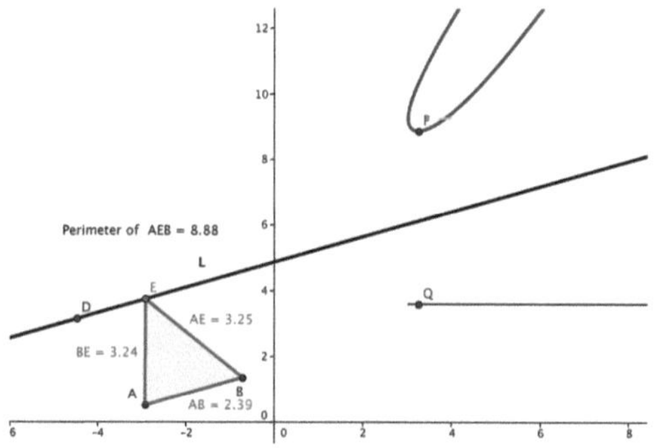

Fig. 2. The graph of the perimeter/area behaviour of the generated triangles. (Color figure online)

question.: *Of all the triangles formed by moving point E along line L, the one with minimum perimeter is the one obtained when point E is the intersection of line L and the perpendicular bisector of AB. That is, when triangle ABE is isosceles* (Fig. 3a).

Figure 3b shows the algebraic model of the perimeter of a family of triangles with fixed base and one vertex on line y = 4. The perimeter function is constructed by summing up $d(A, D) + d(D, B) + 4$. Point D has coordinates (*x*, 4). That is, $f(x) = \sqrt{(x+4)^2 + 16} + \sqrt{x^2 + 16} + 4$. It is observed that the perimeter minimum value is reached when the x value of point E is −2. That is, the conjecture is verified. With the use of the tool, it is easy to draw other objects within triangle ABE. For example, H1 and H2 are two heights of triangle ABE that get intersected at point C (Orthocentre). What is the locus of point C when point E is moved along line L? Figure 3c shows that the locus seems to be a parabola. Indeed, Fig. 3c shows some auxiliary construction to find the focus F and directrix D of the parabola.

To approach the general case, the team focused on finding the equations of two heights. That is, the equation of the lines r and s, $y = -[(t+m)(x-m)]/a$ and $y = -[(t-m)(x+m)]/a$ respectively. Then eliminating parameter t, the locus equation becomes $y = -x^2/a + m^2/a$. That is, it represents a parabola with vertex $D(0, m^2/a)$, focus $F(0, (4m^2 - a^2)/4a)$, and directrix $y = (4m^2 + a^2)/4a$.

C. An Extension. The first task also provided the context to address another question: Can you draw others triangles sharing the same base AB and the same perimeter? The team discussed possible ways to draw triangles holding the required conditions and proposed two methods that involved dynamic models of the problem. Figure 4 shows the construction of an ellipse based on determining the locus of point F that is the intersection of two circles with centres A and whose sum of their radii is a constant, the segment of length 12. Figure 5 shows another approach to the problem based on the construction of a perpendicular bisector.

In Fig. 4, segment AB is the common side and segment CD is the sum of the other two sides of the triangle. E is a point on segment CD. Two circles are drawn: One with its centre at point A and radius CE and the other with its centre at point B and radius ED.

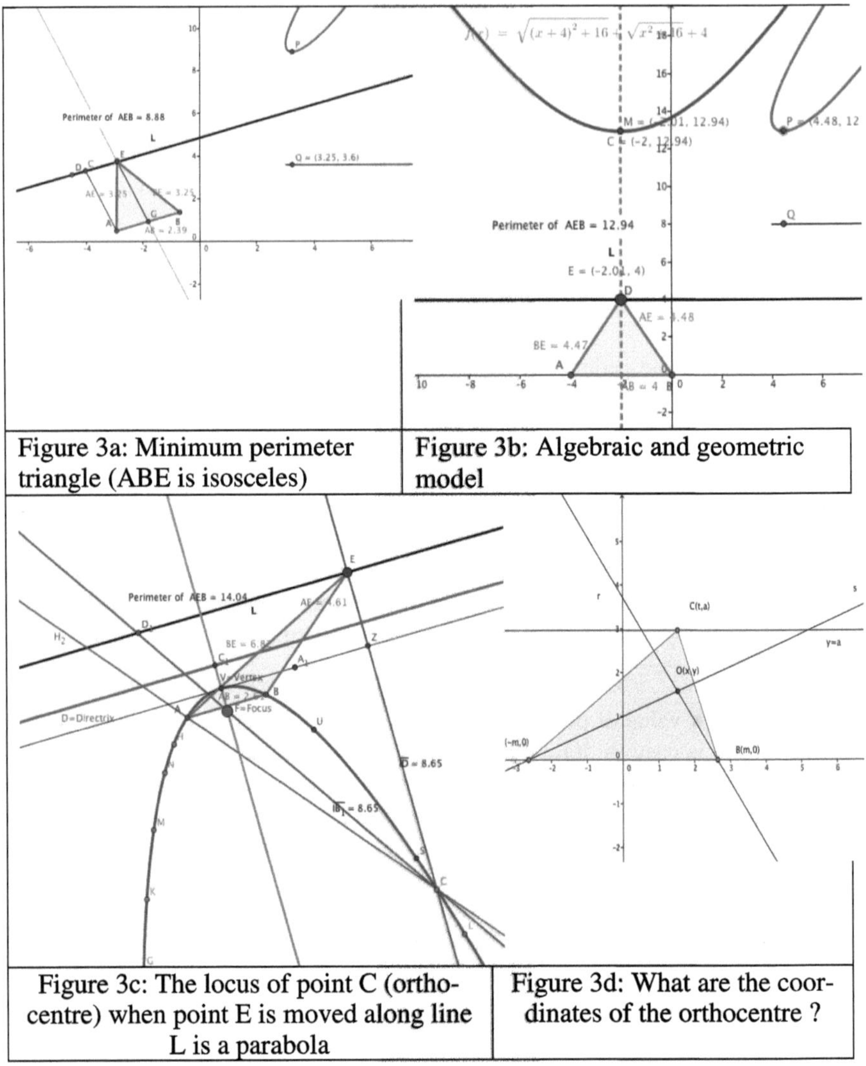

Fig. 3. (a) Minimum perimeter triangle (ABE is isosceles), (b) Algebraic and geometric model, (c) The locus of point C (orthocentre) when point E is moved along line L is a parabola, (d) What are the coordinates of the orthocentre?

These circles intersect each other at points F and I. The locus of point F when point E (and I) is moved along segment CD is an ellipse and each point on this locus could be the third vertex of triangle ABE with a fixed perimeter, the sum of lengths of sides AB, AF and BF cm. The triangle collapses when the third vertex is located on the intersection of the ellipse and line AB (Fig. 5a).

Another method of drawing triangles sharing the same base and a fixed perimeter involves the use of the concept of perpendicular bisector (Fig. 6).

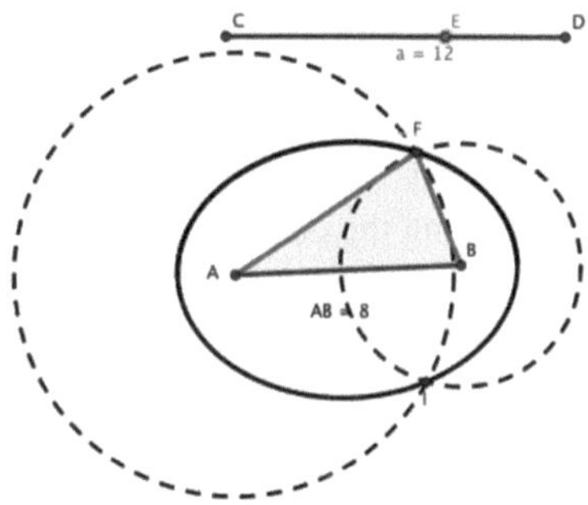

Fig. 4. What is the locus of point F or I when point E is moved along segment CD? (http://tinyurl.com/DynamicM2a)

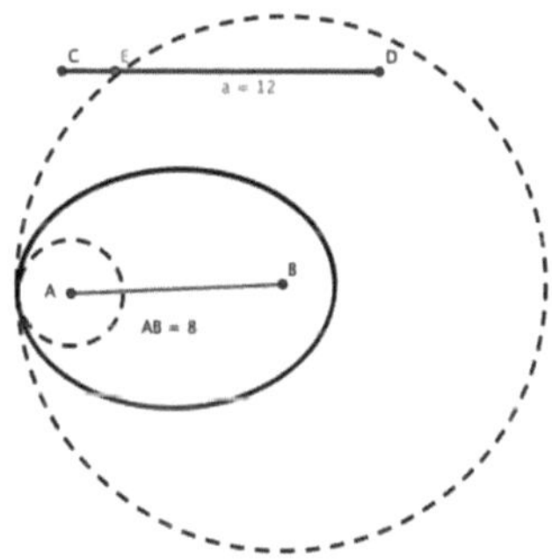

Fig. 5. What happens when the third vertex becomes the intersection between the ellipse and line AB?

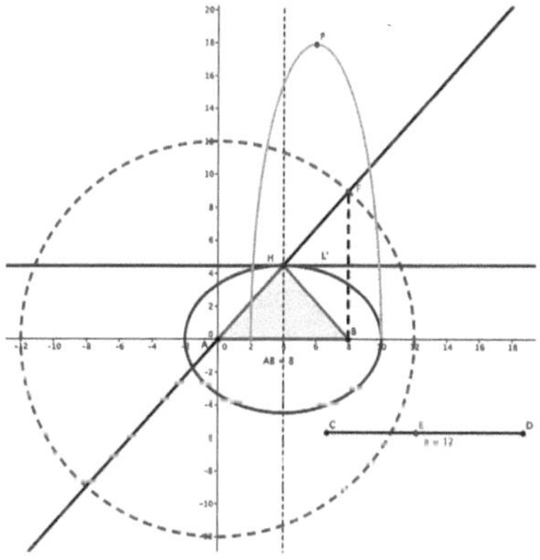

Fig. 6. Drawing triangles holding the conditions via the perpendicular bisector. In http://tinyurl.com/DynamicM2, move point F to generate the ellipse and to observe the area variation of the family of triangles.

In Fig. 5, segment AB represents the common triangle side and segment CD the sum of the other sides of the triangle. Point A is the centre of a circle with radius segment CD and AF is a line passing through F (F is any point on that circle). L' is the perpendicular bisector of segment BF which intersects line AF at point H. The locus of point H when point F is moved along the circle determines the set of points that are the candidates to locate the third vertex to form a family of triangles with a fixed perimeter. Furthermore, the locus is an ellipse since HB = HF (definition of perpendicular bisector) and AF is the radius of a circle (a constant). In addition, point P has coordinates the length of side AH (x-coordinate) and the corresponding area of triangle ABH (y-coordinate), then the locus of point P when point F moves along the circle represents the area variation of the triangles generated for different values of side AH. One can see that the maximum area of the generated triangles is reached when the triangle is isosceles. The issues addressed by the team while examining both dynamic models (Figs. 4 & 5) included:

- The relationship between the common side AB and the sum of the other sides (segment CD), and when can the triangle be drawn? (triangle's inequality).
- Definition and properties of the ellipse.
- The area variation of the family of generated triangles. The intersection point of the perpendicular bisector of segment AB and the perpendicular bisector of segment BF determines the third vertex where triangle ABH reaches its maximum area (Fig. 5).

It was observed in both cases, one involving finding the minimum perimeter of the family of triangles generated in the initial task (Fig. 2) and the former case of determining the maximum area of the family of triangles generated in the extension task (Fig. 5), that the solution involves an isosceles triangle.

5 Discussion and Final Reflections

In response to the research question posed, we argue about how important it is for researchers, prospective and in-service teachers to work on and discuss, within a group, what aspects the use of the tool enhances in terms of ways of representing, exploring, solving and extending routine mathematical tasks. As a result, typical tasks found in textbooks offer a starting point to construct dynamic models or tasks in which problem solvers can identify and explore not only different mathematical processes and ways of reasoning (contrasted with algebraic approaches) to solve them, but can also address possible extensions or connections of the task that bring new contents or concepts into the discussion. For example, the task extension, in this case, provides an opportunity to introduce the study of conic sections, in particular of the ellipse, and also to explore the behaviour of a family of triangles. Finally, we argue that high school teachers should discuss mathematical tasks and the use of digital tools within a group that includes mathematicians, educators, and practicing teachers. This type of interaction allows the group to discuss not only mathematical contents, problem solving strategies, and ways to support conjectures; but also possible didactic routes to implement problem solving approaches that enhance the use of computational tools. By reflecting on the main issues addressed in the initial research questions, we learned that:

(a) Many of the routine problems or exercises that appear in textbooks could be transformed, with the use of the tool, into a series of activities to engage learners in problem solving experiences.
(b) Prospective teachers can gain experience in the use of the tool by experimenting and discussing strategies that involve moving or dragging objects within the representations, finding loci of particular objects, quantifying attributes such as areas, lengths, perimeters, perpendicular bisectors, loci of points and by contrasting other learners' approaches to the problems.
(c) Working on the routine tasks with the use of the tools helped us design worksheets that can be used to guide teachers in the process of transforming the tasks into a platform to formulate conjectures and ways to explore and support them.
(d) The construction of a dynamic model of the tasks offered opportunities and conditions for the participants to explore in "real time" ways in which some parameters behave as a result of moving objects within the problem configuration. This process involves visualizing the parameters behaviours, quantifying attributes, and coordinating visual and numeric data to detect either invariance or change.
(e) The coordination and simultaneous use of visual, quantitative, and graphic approaches provided not only key information to identify conjectures or mathematical relations, but also ways to explain or support those conjectures. Thus, teachers need to structure and organize the information around the solution process in order to communicate and explain tasks solutions or results.

Acnowledgements. This report is part of wider project that deals with prospective and secondary school mathematics teachers' use of digital tools in extending both mathematics and didactic knowledge. Reference numbers: Conacyt-168543 (México), EDU2011-29328, EDU2015-65270-R, EDU2009-07298 and EDU2014-54526-R (National I + D+I Plan of MEC-Spain).

References

1. Conner, A., Wilson, P.S., Kim, H.J.: Building on mathematical events in the classroom. ZDM Math. Educ. **43**, 979–992 (2011)
2. Even, R.: The relevance of advanced mathematics studies to expertise in secondary school mathematics teaching: practitioners' views. ZDM Math. Educ. **43**, 941–950 (2011)
3. Hoyles, C., Lagrange, J.-B. (eds.): Mathematics Education and Technology-Rethinking the Terrain: The 17th ICMI Study. Springer, New York (2010)
4. Hoyles, C., Noss, R.: Next steps in implementing Kaput's research programme. Educ. Stud. Math. **68**, 85–97 (2008)
5. Kahneman, D.: ThinKing Fast and Slow. Penguin Group, New York (2011)
6. Leung, A.: An epistemic model of task design in dynamic geometry environment. ZDM Math. Educ. **43**, 325–336 (2011)
7. Polya, G.: How to Solve It. Princeton University Press, Princeton (1945)
8. Santos-Trigo, M., Camacho-Machín, M.: Towards the construction of a framework to deal with routine problems to foster mathematical inquiry. PRIMUS **19**(3), 260–279 (2009)

9. Santos-Trigo, M., Camacho-Machín, M.: Framing the use of computational technology in problem-solving instruction. Math. Enthusiast J. **10**(1&2), 279–302 (2013)
10. Santos-Trigo, M., Reyes-Rodriguez, A.: The use of digital technology in finding multiple paths to solve and extend an equilateral triangle task. Int. J. M. Educ. Sci. Technol. (2015)
11. Schoenfeld, A.H.: How We Think: A Theory of Goal-Oriented Decision Making and its Educational Application. Routledge, New York (2011)
12. Santos-Trigo, M., Camacho-Machín, M., Moreno-Moreno, M.: Using dynamic software to Foster prospective teachers' problema solving inquire. In: Ubuz, B., Haser, C., Mariotti, M.A. (eds.) Proceedings of the Eight Congress of the European Society for Research in Mathematics Education, pp. 2714–2723. Middle East Technical University, Ankara (Digital) (2013). ISBN: 978-975-429-315-9

The Knowledge Management into Technology Based Firms (Model Proposal)

Jorge Leonardo Puentes, Nancy Yurani Ortiz(✉), and José Ignacio Rodriguez

Universidad Distrital Francisco José de Caldas, Bogotá, Colombia
jorgelpmorantes@hotmail.es,
nyortizg@gmail.com, jirodriguezmolano@gmail.com

Abstract. This article works on how the knowledge management could helps a specific kind of companies (technology based firms) to increase and take advantage of the benefits that its implementation can carry out. It was made a research about the technology-based firms (TBF's) and its main characteristics, after it's described the main contributions of the most representative Knowledge Management model from which are obtained important pillars to finally presents and develops a proposal KM model for TBF's.

Keywords: Technology based firms · Knowledge management · Knowledge cicle · Stakeholders · Continuous improvement

1 Introduction

The technology based firms have been found themselves immersed into an environment where it has to adapt to a constantly changing. If it doesn't go well, it generates waste of time and money on constant and repetitive training in specific processes and specialized in the development of their missionary activities, as well as in the transmission of specific knowledge within all their areas.

For the Colombian TBF's, it is not the only issue it has to overcome, also the lack of good funding sources and stakeholders make harder the process of innovation and the development of its goals and mission. Keeping in mind this perception of the current business environment and their needs, it presents a Knowledge management model applicable to technology based firms (TBF's) with the structure and tools needed to implement it, besides this model could be used as guide for the future development of similar models applied to different kind of companies.

2 Main Contributions to the Knowledge Management

Around the Knowledge Management could be found a lot of information and data, all the authors try to explain according to their context what the KM is, and how it works into a real company. Below it is shown the main models contributions found in the research, according each one to its context (Table 1).

L. Uden et al. (Eds.): LTEC 2016, CCIS 620, pp. 15–24, 2016.
DOI: 10.1007/978-3-319-42147-6_2

Table 1. Relevant characteristics of the knowledge management main models. (Source: own development based on the different authors named)

Model	Main settings
NONAKA Y TAKEUCHI [1]	Tacit and explicit knowledge division. Implementation of organizational conditions (intention, autonomy, fluctuation, redundancy, and variety). And application of the knowledge cycle through Socialization, Externalization, combination and internalization
WIIG [2]	Application of Check - Conceptualize - Reflect -Act for the development of the KM cycle. Propose a Knowledge inventory and improvement actions.
CIBIT MODEL [1]	Organization Knowledge Management through three steps: Focus, organize, Perform.
GARCIA-TAPIAL [3]	Implementation of a more specific structure for the KM through the process of identification - Creation -Storing - Structuring - Distribution -Maintenance - Accounting.
	Establish the requirements for KM measurement indicators
KARAGABI MODEL [4]	Handle three main steps: An intervention methodology, a KM models library, and a knowledge base to save the experience gained through the model application.
	Specific Application Filtering and cataloging within the process of inventory of Knowledge. Dissemination of knowledge and information acquired.
DELGADO & MONTES [5]	Focus on companies which works on projects applying the model of Nonaka and Takeuchi and the integrated projects management.
	Systemic KM approach through the cycle: Identification - Acquisition and development of knowledge - knowledge retention - Knowledge distribution and sharing. Handling specific cataloging for the knowledge retention.
TRIANA, MEDINA & RODRIGUEZ [6]	Propose the application of a model of excellence (EFQM) in KM. Approaching to the use of information and communication technology. Management and interaction with Stakeholders. Assessment of the relevance of the KM in the company to continuous improvements.
FLOREZ GONZALES [7]	Using specific tools for defining KM strategies. Definition of knowledge gaps - organizational knowledge gaps. Using indicators for KM measuring.
GOMEZ [8]	Handling and proximity to Stakeholders. Applying learned lessons as an important source of organizational knowledge.

It was found some common characteristics that helps the implementation of the KM in TBF'S, but it was not found specific criteria based or applied for technology based firms, most of the models are generalists tools that superficially cover the structure and needs of the company. The common characteristics are as follows:

- The Common structure to implement the organizational KM is follow by the next steps: Analysis of the existing Knowledge within the company – New knowledge acquisition for the company – Knowledge structuring for the company use – Communication of the new knowledge to the collaborators and establishment of knowledge within the company.
- Measurement of knowledge gap: Maps and other tools to know the knowledge gap for the knowledge inventory within the company are very useful; the knowledge databases are powerful and necessary tools in Knowledge Management for traceability of knowledge, avoiding rework or loss of important knowledge; and the generation of knowledge measuring tools for continuous improvement in the company considering the knowledge management as a cyclical process.
- The Nonaka and Takeuchi model [9] strengthens the knowledge structure through knowledge flow explained in their model.

3 The Technology Based Firms

The TBF's born as a innovative project which get funding sources from tactical stakeholders to develop as an enterprise the new innovation. The main characteristic of those ones are presented below:

- TBF's are SMEs with intensive knowledge and immersed in high-tech sectors, based on the intensity grade of R&D+I [10].
- These companies produces innovator goods and services, compromised with its design, development and production, through the systematic application of technical and scientific knowledge [7, 11].
- This kind of companies works by projects.
- These companies have mostly an academic beginning as innovative business ideas, which are linked to collaborators such as business incubators, research centers, science parks, universities and others who from its birth have given support and infrastructure. It works by projects [12].

4 Model Proposal of Knowledge Management for Technology Based Firms

It is proposed a KM model for TBF's oriented to adapt and focus the resources and procedures of existing KM and the relational structure between the knowledge of the companies, employees and its mission to gain a competitive advantage. The KM model includes three main parts: the core, development and the periphery, as shown in Fig. 1.

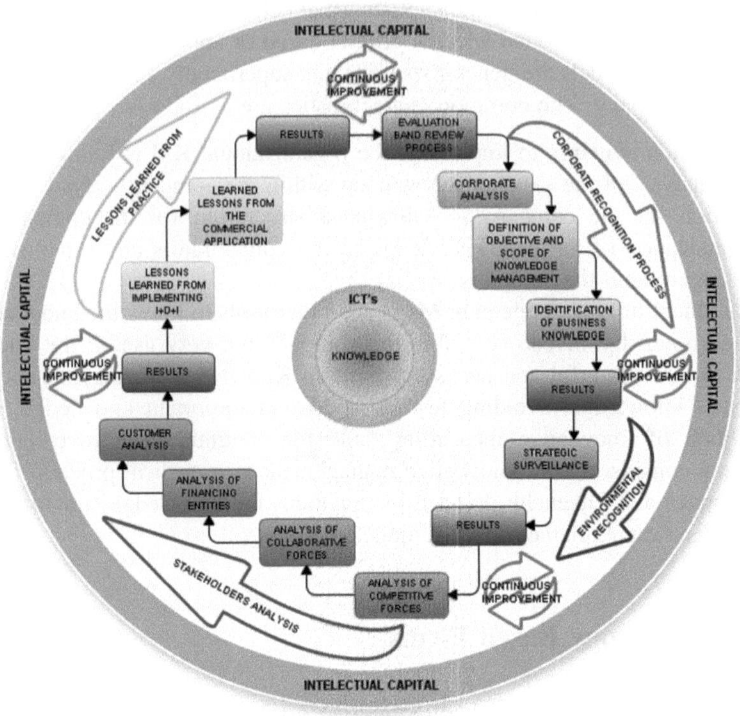

Fig. 1. Knowledge management model for technology based firms (TBF's). (Source: Own development (Authors))

The "core" refers to the factors which must have the TBF's to apply the KM model proposed. In this case, the TBF's must have some kind of relevant knowledge to the development of their missionary activities, and must have the interest and desire to manage and improve their activities and products/services. Also the TBF's should have a minimum infrastructure in information technology and communication as a base to store, share and disseminate the results of the different model [14].

"Development", refers to the main structure of the model. This section is divided into five (5) core processes which are shown and explained later: The Business Recognition, the environment recognition, the Stakeholder analysis, the Lessons Learned by Practice and the continuous Improvement.

These components are grouped into what are known as intellectual capital (periphery), which is composed by: Human Capital, Strategic capital, and Relational Capital [12]. Through this section the TBF'S could generate and manage an atmosphere of openness and welfare, making this an attribute of its context, could perceive greater initiative and participation of employees, which they will act consistent with its own objectives and own powers, and in line with the organization objectives [15]. The five (5) model processes are described below:

4.1 Corporate Recognition Process

The Corporate Recognition process aims to establish the current status of the TBF's facing Knowledge Management to define the strategies to follow and create a project with an orientation and planning according to the requirements, needs and problems identified by the SWOT analysis [7, 11]. Clarifying that the orientation of KM project in the company should first of all be focus on a determination, compilation and analysis of captured tacit knowledge and an update, if is required, about explicit knowledge registered by the company.

The process consists on different subprocesses that allow the company, once it has decided to enter the field of knowledge management, get a view of the current situation. The subprocesses related to get this goal are:

Corporate Analysis. This subprocess aims to recognize the current situation of the company with regard to knowledge management from identification, compilation and analysis of internal and external factors which affects it, in order to define the company needs in terms of knowledge and its management through the adaptation of strategic planning tools. According to the work done by David [16] and Macias Calvario [17] in terms of strategic planning, have raised the tools to analysis the TBF'S versus the KM. Regarding the strategic planning it was decided to work with these tools because they let to analyze the business situation and to develop strategies. The analytical model for strategy formulation admits three stages: Supplies Stage, adequacy and decision, for this development supplies stages were taken, specifically matrices assessment of external factors, the evaluation matrix of internal factors; and the adaptation stage where worked with the SWOT matrix and internal-external Matrix (IE). Using those tools it is pretend to get the criteria to begin the implementation of the Knowledge Management into the company.

Definition of Objective and Scope for Knowledge Management. At this stage determinants aspects should be defined to guide and limit the project to be done, such as the project title to work, start and end dates expected for the project; there are other important properties at this stage and are assigning responsible employees for the management and supervision activities where is essential to select the project manager and senior management auditor, respectively. Based on Triana et al. [11] it is identified the importance of having a stage looking for planning and project organization to be worked for achieving strategic decisions, these "are the starting point of all individual SMEs at time to introduce Knowledge Management and restore Knowledge Management again and again".

The proposed model is not limited only to be applied in the whole organization, according to the approach and the need expressed by the company can be applied to different areas within the same company, the whole company or a single area, this is allowed by the focus taken in the preliminary stages. After it is defined all characteristics of the sub-process, it should be disseminated to interested employees and the ones related in order to increase awareness and interest in the KM project and gain greater participation for the next stages, initially on identifying business knowledge.

Identification of Business Knowledge. This sub-process seeks to capture and collect the proper knowledge of the company and which does not currently own and must acquire to reduce or eliminate the "gap" of knowledge. The identification should be done with respect to the three levels of intellectual capital, seeking to assess each of the company skills and lackings in order to make a realistic approach to knowledge management.

Because of these maps are involved in processes that have a strong dependence on intellectual capital, it is necessary a specific structure that helps the link within the tool and further, facilitate the structuring of generated knowledge, it is recommended a general form for creating knowledge maps as the shown for Kazi et al. [18].

4.2 Environmental Recognition Process

This process consists on the Strategic Surveillance sub-process that allows the TBF's identifying relevant information for the project environment once it has defined the orientation of project, an internal idea to work or it has identified a call for external financing with possibility of participation.

Strategic Surveillance Subprocess. Its design was based on the GTC 186 oriented to the management of R&D+I and management surveillance system (v), seeking to establish tools and activities that keep the requirements of the Guide. Surveillance in the GTC 186 [19] is divided into three (3) stages: identification, search, treatment and validation.

These three stages helped to design an oriented tool which has five stages: planning, monitoring, Information search, monitoring report, and validation for the surveillance expert.

The process will define a strategic monitoring report covering four (4) pillars:

- Technology: Regarding the technical information relating to technique and science technology as substitutes, complementary, patents products, among others.
- Commercial: Identification of information by customers, suppliers and funding agencies, market information (7p's: Plaza, Product, Price, Promotion, People, Processes and Physical Evidence) among others.
- Competitive: Information related to current and potential competitors of surveillance topic (product/service/technology)
- Environment: Designed to identify information concerning regulations, policies, economy, environment and others.

At the end of the process, a management report presenting the significant results of the monitoring carried out will be obtained.

4.3 Stakeholders Analysis

This process was designed to collect, analyze, storage and select the most relevant Stakeholders information for the TBF'S according to the needs and scopes, this process contains elements from Krick et al. [20] and David [16]. Consisting on different types of sub-process, allowing the TBF's to identify, store and analyze information from each of the external parties involved in each of the activities of the company in order to identify and meet market participants and allied to the business. The sub-process are: Analysis of competitive forces, analysis of collaborative forces, analysis of financing entities and customer analysis.

Each of these sub-process is developed similarly, where through a cycle in the first stage of each sub-process are identified and collected data and knowledge about competitors, co-workers, financiers and customers to make a detailed analysis and define their strengths and weaknesses that will provide the critical factors for comparison between similar entities and the TBF's, at this stage we enter the creation of knowledge from gathered information from stakeholders. Finally at this stage is identified a contrast and create new possibilities for differentiating the company or products as needed. When the process is ended, an inform presents the strongest competitors, the best allies, the most relevant financing entity, and customer feedback will be obtained too.

4.4 Lessons Learned from Practice

It is the knowledge acquired during a project or task that shows how they should be addressed in the future events of the project or task, in order to improve future performance [21]. Learned lessons from practice consists of different types of sub-process that allows the technology-based company to collect and store learned lessons in a standardized way for two areas or fields for different purposes but with the same level of importance. The sub-process are:

Lessons Learned from Implementing R&D+i. It allows to collect, validate and store the generated lessons as part of the experience in the implementation of research technological developments and/or innovation in order to assess the learned lessons in the implementation of the three previous processes of the model within the company and additionally allows to follow the actions related to the improvement of activities or overcoming of issues on R&D+i.

Lessons Learned from the Commercial Application. It allows to collect, validate and store the generated lessons as part of the experience in carrying out project/product/service in order to assess what was learned during the development of these activities. Learned lessons from the commercial application are directed under the principle of PMI where learned lessons should be documented so those can be part of the historical database for both; the project and the performing organization. Historical information and learned lessons are transferred to the knowledge base of learned lessons for use in future projects or phases. This may include information about incidents and risks, as well as techniques that worked well and can be applied in the future [21].

4.5 Continuous Improvement Process

This process consists of different types of sub-process that allows the TBF's share, communicate and disseminate the results of each process, in addition to assessing compliance indicators. The sub-process are:

Diffusion and Communication of Results. In applying the model of knowledge management for TBF's it is necessary that the organization disseminates all relevant information resulting from each process and communicate to the employees that the process affects, in order to ensure the whole development process for the KM model within the company and avoid possible problems for disinformation or misinformation.

The Assessment and Review Processes. The assessment and review processes. Looking for ensure the excellence within the application and maintenance of knowledge management into the organization, it has taken for the evaluation and review process as a basis specific characteristics of the EFQM model (European Foundation for Quality Management) which defines the model quality and excellence as a route to self-evaluation and determination of continuous improvement processes, specially focused on the development of projects.

In order to assess the ability of compliance with each of the processes established in the proposed KM model that allows to the company measures its effectiveness and relevance, different types of indicators were generated about knowledge management. The indicators developed for this model were based on the article by Kazi et al. [18]; Castro & Roncallo [22]; European Committee for Standardization [23] and Moreno [24].

5 Model Validation

The validation was made by experts judgments oriented to the individual aggregation, which is, to obtain information from each expert without they have any kind of contact, link or relationship [25]. The expert judments are taken as three different points of view: The company (TBF's) view; The stakeholders view with the participation of technology development and research centers, and the transfer of research results office of Bogotá, and finally the academic view, with the participation of la teachers specialized in the theme from different universities from Bogotá.

First, the specific knowledge level for each expert was evaluated in the research topic. A survey to know the expert competence coefficient (K), where every experts obtained a K bigger than 0,8 points and less or equal than 1, indicating a high level of influence from all sources.

Each of the experts made a trial using the KM model executable, examined the model and the attached tools giving a different scores for each of the model steps, evaluating different topics for each phase. The conclusion for the validation results was favorable from the three perspectives, considering that the model is very relevant in terms of knowledge management for this kind of companies and as improvement they advise to improve the instructions to be easier to work with the executable.

6 Concluding Remarks and Future Work

It is important to point out and clarify that there must be elements at the core and the periphery, ie, business skills that wish to maintain and protect technological infrastructure in terms of information and communication the intellectual capital of the TBF's for the implementation of the model.

The model of Knowledge Management for Technology-Based firms was designed according to the identified TBF's process, which starts with an idea, contextualize, develops and applies it to the market. It also has a close relationship with the processes of creation, identification, collection, analysis, storage, dissemination and communication of knowledge of the TBF's.

The model of knowledge management for TBF's can be established as a first step towards innovation processes with the company to achieve the kind of innovation that aspire, given the applicability of the model and the possibility of orientation towards product innovation, process, marketing and/or organization, depending on the strategy of the TBF's.

The proposed model was validated by experts taking a different point of view for each one; The company view, the academic view and the research view. All of them agree about the relevance of the model on knowledge management, easy use, the fulfillment of its purpose and its coherence were right.

Along the research it was identified improvements, these ones could be the new start point for a wider KM model which works no just for Technology Based Firms.

The time for the implementation of the model within the company are directly dependent on the variables mentioned at the top, among them, the experience and expertise of those responsible for the implementation of the model and the prioritization the enterprise gives to knowledge management respect to other projects.

References

1. Agencia Nacional De Infrastructura: Guia Para La Gestión Del Conocimiento. http://ani.gov.co/sites/default/files/u233/8_guia_para_la_gestion_del_conocimiento_ani.pdf. Accessed 19 Apr 2015
2. Arís, E.P.: La gestión tecnológica del conocimiento. EDITUM (2007)
3. García-Tapial, J.: Gestión del conocimiento y empresa Una aproximación a la realidad española. EOI (2002)
4. Capote, J., Llanten, C.J., Pardo, C., Collazos, C.: Knowledge management in a software process improvement program in micro, small and medium-sized enterprises: KMSPI Model. Rev. Fac. Ing. Antioquia, 223–235 (2009)
5. Delgado, R., Montes de Oca, R.: Modelo de GesGtión del Conocimiento organizacional para Empresas que trabajan por Proyectos, vol. 5 (2011)
6. Triana, J., Medina, V., Rodriguez, J.I.: Modelo para fortalecer el rol de las PYMES en el emprendimiento de Bogotá D.C.. Rev. Científica Cienc. e Ing. la Univ. Dist., Bogotá, Colombia **17**, 131–147 (2012)
7. Flórez, S.V.. La Gestión Del Conocimiento Como Herramienta Para La Innovación En Una Empresa De Base Tecnológica. Instituto Politécnico Nacional De México (2011)

8. Gomez, J.: Modelo conceptual de Gestión del conocimiento, en un Sistema de Incubadoras de Empresas de Base Tecnológica (2011)
9. Nonaka, I., Takeuchi, H.: The Knowledge-Creating Company: How Japanese Companies Create the Dynamics of Innovation. Oxford University Press, New York (1995)
10. March, I., Mora, R.: Creación de empresas de base tecnológica: factores de éxito y fracaso. Revista de contabilidad y dirección, no. 5. Asociación Catalana de Contabilidad y Dirección, ACCID, pp. 97–120 (2007)
11. Briones, A.J., Garcia, J.C.: Estrategias para industrias con base tecnológica: aspectos significativos en la creación de empresas innovadoras de base tecnológica. FISEC-Estrategias - Fac. Ciencias Soc. la Univ. Nac. Lomas Zamor, vol. 20, pp. 131–148 (2008)
12. Merritt, H.: Las empresas mexicanas de base tecnológica y sus capacidades de innovación: una propuesta metodológica. Trayectorias **14**(33–34), 27–50 (2011)
13. Asociación Nacional de Centros Europeos de Innovación Españoles, La creación de empresas de base tecnológica: una experiencia práctica, Primera. KEN, Navarra (2003)
14. Fernández Marcial, V.: Gestión del conocimiento versus gestión de la información. Inv. Bibliotecológica **20**(41), 44–62 (2006)
15. Acosta Prado, J.C., Longo-Somoza, M., Fischer, A.L.: Capacidades dinámicas y gestión del conocimiento en nuevas empresas de base tecnológica. Cuad. Administración **26**(47), 35–62 (2013)
16. David, F.R.: Conceptos de Administración Estratégica. Pearson Educación, México (2013)
17. Macias, G.G.: Metodología para calcular el pronóstico de la demanda y una medición de su precisión, en una empresa de autopartes: Caso de estudio (2007)
18. Kazi, A., Wohlfart, L., Wolf, P.: Hands-On Knowledge Co-Creation and Sharing: Practical Methods and Sharing (2007)
19. Instituto Colombiano de Normas Tecnicas y Certificación (ICONTEC), GTC 186 -Gestión de la investigación, desarrollo e innovación (I+D+i). Gestión de la I+D+i: sistema de vigilancia (v), p. 21 (2009)
20. Krick, T., Forstater, M., Monaghan, P., Sillampää, M.: De las palabras a la acción. El compromiso con los stakeholders. Manual para la práctica de las relaciones con los grupos de interés. AccountAbility, p. 135 (2006)
21. Project Management Institute, Guía de los Fundamentos Para la Dirección de Proyectos (Guía del PMBOK®). Quinta Edi. Project Management Institute (2013)
22. Castro, J.P., Roncallo, M.: Diagnóstico de la gestión del conocimiento en una empresa grande de Barranquilla (Colombia). Doctor, pp. 70–103 (2004)
23. European Committee for Standardization: European Guide to good Practice in Knowledge Management-Part 4: Guidelines for Measuring KM. Knowl. Manag., p. 35 (2004)
24. Moreno, J.L.: Guía para la aplicación del Modelo EFQM de Excelencia (2007)

Informational Technology Skills and Media Literacy in Students: A Case Study

Jorge Chavez(✉), Claudia Jaramillo, and Dario Liberona

Centre for Teaching and Learning (UNIE),
University of Santiago, Santiago, Chile
jorge.chavez@usach.cl

Abstract. There is agreement on the contribution of technology to teaching and learning. Given its potential we can find a number of features that promote learning as the possibility of establishing a two-way communication, the potential of the interaction between teachers and students, the ability to organize, adapt and be flexible with information based on the needs and requirements of students. Notwithstanding, there's not much information on the effects of using technology in the teaching and learning process or the elements we should consider to analyze the use of technology in teaching and learning. In order to answer these questions, the work presented here aims to assess the current state of the research in the area of ICT skills and media literacy in Chilean students.

Keywords: Learning technologies · Media literacy · ICT skills · Educational research

1 The Use of Technology in Educational Settings

Educational institutions, since its inception, have used different technological resources to support their teaching and learning activities, taking into account the changes brought about by the introduction of new technologies in different human activities [27]. However, the use of these resources in education has been aimed primarily at transmission and unidirectional communication of information and used mainly to support traditional teaching formats, this statement has been widely share by existing researchers [37]. However, there is not much information on the effects of using technology in teaching and learning situations or the elements that need to be taken into consideration when to analyzing the use of technology in educational contexts.

In this section we will discuss some key concepts in CSCL, a multidisciplinary research perspective based on collaborative learning and information and communications technology. CSCL or Computer Supported Collaborative Learning (Collaborative Learning Computer) primarily focuses on the idea that the construction of knowledge and subsequently learning are processes that occur through the mediation of technology [10]. This research area states that technological tools or artifacts can be used in order to facilitate the learning process acting as a mediating device between teaching and learning when people work in groups [3, 7, 9, 10].

L. Uden et al. (Eds.): LTEC 2016, CCIS 620, pp. 25–38, 2016.
DOI: 10.1007/978-3-319-42147-6_3

This research area has developed significantly during recent decades due to the increase of the devices and the various uses generated by information and communications technologies - ICT [20, 36]. However, given the variety of uses of technology environments, there are increasing questions regarding the contribution of these tools to learning processes [7]. This research subject states that learning relates to three metaphors. The first metaphor considers that learning is the acquisition of knowledge in individual terms; the second, conceives learning in terms of increasing participation in communities of practice; and the third refers to the creation of knowledge, according to which both new knowledge and social practices are created through collaboration. These metaphors relate to the major psychological approaches to teaching learning and -Processing information, distributed and situated cognition constructivism and socio-cultural orientation, respectively.

The concepts arising from this subject perspective are related mostly to the use of technology in educational settings. When it comes to the use or application of technology to educational contexts, we're commonly referring to digital technologies in general, which can include software, television, interactive multimedia, smartphones and internet [14]. In short, all those technologies and digital resources used in order to communicate, create, disseminate, store and manage information in situations of teaching and learning.

In this sense, distance learning or e-learning, online learning or online education, is defined as all situations of teaching and learning where teachers and students do not share the same space and time [17], this implies that the communication sustained by the participants is asynchronous. This is also related to the concept of blended learning or b-learning which addresses the combination of both face to face and non presential contexts. Allen and Seaman [1] declare that b-learning (also known as hybrid learning) corresponds to instructional processes where much of the content (30 % to 80 %) is provided online.

Notwithstanding the above, and despite the variety of theoretical sources, there are certain aspects that belong to the basic domain of CSCL [22]. Among these we can mention, the conception of learning as something that is built on interaction with the environment, the use of interaction analysis as a mechanism for reaching an understanding of collaborative processes [11] and the assertion that learning takes place in specific contexts, so that both - learning and context- are interdependent and cannot be studied separately [5, 16, 23]. However, beyond the thematic diversity, for the purposes of the study, it is interesting to note that research in CSCL has focused mostly in the interaction between equals, and more specifically, in formal education scenarios and education, focusing on how teaching and learning processes are favored by technological artifacts when people collaborate in an educational situation.

In short, it becomes most relevant to understand the role of tools or technological devices in the practice of intellectual tasks, associated with collaboration between individuals, where certain tasks could not only be attributed to individual cognitions [32]. It is therefore necessary to have a conceptual framework to advance the understanding on how these tools are used in the classroom, paying special attention on how these devices are inserted in educational contexts and at the same time, the interactions that these can improve.

In this context, most of the work in this area has failed to explain the real impact of ICT in teaching and learning or have shown a low impact of ICT into the classroom, unable to account for the factors that affect these processes [2, 3, 4, 21]. Taking this into consideration, it is possible to point out that ICT has not yet managed to generate changes or the expected improvements in educational contexts using these technological tools as facilitators of learning [8, 26].

In consideration of the elements described here we explored the case of Chile, aiming to assess the current state of the research in the area of ICT skills and media literacy.

2 Methodology

The design of the revision corresponds to a critical analysis of the research. Critical analysis, unlike other reviews, correspond to an analysis that systematize in an organized manner the evidence around a theme or subject area through strict and rigorous use of a set of pre-defined criteria to make explicit and reproducible the search procedure, observing the rules of rigor present in empirical studies: objectivity, systematization and replicability of results [15, 28, 35]. The search and selection procedures were previously defined in order to identify, select and critically evaluate research related to the use of information and communication technology communication in educational settings in Chile. In relation to this, the development of the review is summarized in 2 large steps, described below.

2.1 Classification and Organization of the Research

An initial search resulted in 90 items that matched the criteria described above. This first approach considered books, dissertations, articles indexed in publications of various kinds, conference proceedings and working papers. To organize the papers found, we compiled the following information: author(s), year of publication, title, nature of the article (as theoretical/empirical distinction), research objectives, hypothesis and/or research questions, and finally, publication indexing. Considering the information gathered and the objective of this review, three thematic dimensions emerged from the data collected, as shown in Fig. 1: Systematization of educational use of ICT in higher and school education (28 %), theoretical perspectives on learning in virtual environments (10 %) and empirical studies on ICT and education (62 %).

After these only peer reviewed papers were selected, with the aim of safeguarding the quality of the review. This limited the number of items to 71. Subsequently, using as input the systematized information, categories and subcategories were identified from the three thematic dimensions, as shown in the summary (Table 1):

After this first categorizing the items were re-classified by research type (empirical/theoretical), giving rise to a second categorization. For this review we chose to consider only empirical work (Empirical studies on ICT and education in Chile), as indicated in the table above. This second and final categorization included 45 items, of which the vast majority focuses on research related to the use and development of ICT skills.

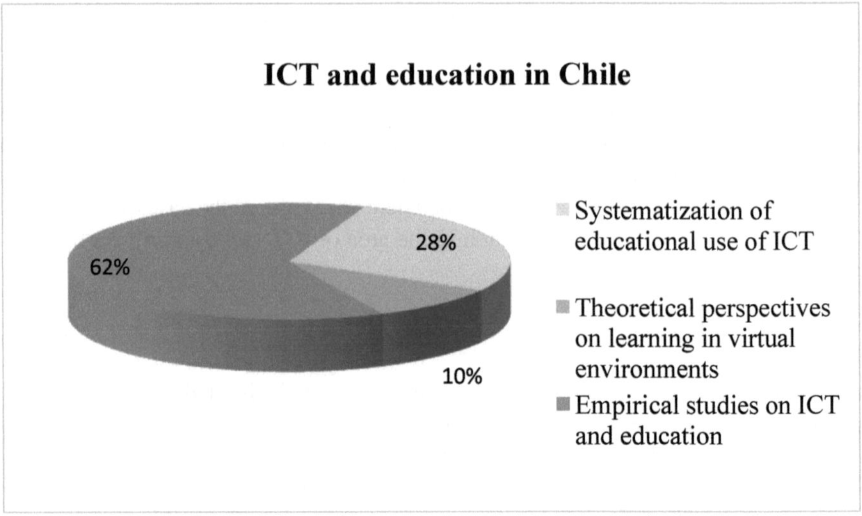

Fig. 1. Classification of articles by thematic dimension.

Table 1. Classification of peer-reviewed papers by thematic dimension, categories and subcategories

Thematic dimension	Categories	Subcategories
Systematization of educational use in ICT	Experiences in K-12	
	Experiences in higher education	
Theoretical perspectives on learning in virtual environments		
Empirical studies on ICT and education in Chile	ICT skills/media literacy in students	Cross-national studies
		Case studies
		(a) ICT skills/media literacy in k-12 and higher education; (b) Use and implementation of technology in k-12 and higher education
	ICT skills in teacher training	ICT skills in higher education in TT
		ICT skills in initial teacher training
	ICT tools (portable/mobile)	Digital learning games
		ICT devices (hardware/software)

2.2 Preparation of the Critical Analysis

The papers were selected, organized and orderly consigning the array information, including title, summary/objectives, keywords, methodology and results/conclusions. Each item was assessed considering methodological design, theoretical approach and results. The synthesis of this information allowed systematize all information collected and identify different approaches present in empirical research developed around technologies of information and communication applied to education. As shown in the figure above, most research in this area of study refers to empirical studies related to ICT and education, which in turn is related to the measurement or the development of skills and/or abilities in the use ICT teachers and (school and university) students and empirical study focused on the use of virtual technological support (software) or materials (portable or mobile devices). This study specifically addresses empirical research related to "ICT skills/media literacy in students" as shown in the table above (cross-national and case studies on the field of ICT skills/media literacy and use and implementation of technology in k-12 and higher education).

3 Findings

3.1 ICT Skills/Media Literacy in Students

Research in this subject addresses empirical research on the use of ICT in various educational institutions. Empirical research can be divided into two subcategories: comparative studies and case studies. Revised cross-national research are studies that contrast the skills and abilities of Chilean students in the use of ICT with students from other countries with similar development conditions. Case studies, meanwhile, relates to research but focused on university and school education in Chile.

3.1.1 Cross-National Studies

The studies referenced in this category consist of studies which based their analysis on the comparison between countries based on results of standardized instruments (skills in using ICT) applied on national and international contexts. Most of the research referenced herein is based on the comparison of results of SITES 2006 between Chile and other countries participating in this study. The SITES 2006 - Second Information Technology in Education Study [24] is an international study involving the participation of 22 countries and aimed to understand and measure the impact of ICT in teaching mathematics and science in a group of 18 countries. SITES addressed several issues: infrastructure, management skills, public policies and vision of teachers and school administrators in each of the countries where the study was conducted.

In the first three studies shown on Table 2 [18, 25, 34] the results of SITES 2006 measurement are analyzed and a comparison of learning outcomes achieved by students in different areas was done, considering key aspects of education systems in each country to understand the adoption and integration of ICT and other aspects related to infrastructure and management. Along with the analysis of these components the social and cultural context of each country was explored, relieving those factors that could be contributing or interfering with the integration of ICT in educational systems.

Among the most important findings it appears significant the active participation of schools especially teachers, taking into account that the introduction of ICT in the classroom depends on the view that teachers have regarding the use of technology and the strategic use of time and resources.

Table 2. Cross-national studies

Authors/years	Method/instrument	Purpose/central focus	Main results
Sánchez et al. 2011	Cross-national study, SITES 2006	Implementation of Information and Communication Technology (ICT) in education systems in Chile and South Korea	In both educational systems ICT are aimed at reducing existing inequality in both countries. In the example of South Korea the technology is linked to the development project of the country, ensuring its successful implementation
Howie 2010	Cross-national study, SITES 2006	Analysis and comparison of ICT implementation of public policies in school education in South Africa and Chile	This research conducted in South Africa revealed that Chile's strategy on development and implementation of its ICT in education seems to be very different in terms of design, organization, strategies adopted, resources used and, above all, in its approach to teacher development
Light 2010	Cross-national study, SITES 2006, interviews, focus groups and observation	Analysis of the contextual factors that could facilitate the ability of teachers to transfer a program of professional development about ICT strategies and innovative teaching to their classrooms, in India, Turkey and Chile	In all three countries, the educators interviewed felt that the course had helped to change their practice, but it was also found to be a combination of programs and policies, along with good leadership, that allowed schools to innovate with the on-line course
Fariña et al. 2015	Cross-national study, SITES 2006, PISA 2009	Relationship of computer use for academic reading among students of 15 years in Chile, Uruguay, Spain and Portugal	In the countries analyzed, the students that use computer at home and have a willingness to technology, use the computer to read more often. In Chile, Portugal and Spain boys use the computer to read more often than girls. In Chile and Uruguay computer use for academic reading is related to the socioeconomic and cultural level of students. As for the results of PISA 2009, there is no relationship between computer use and development of reading skills in students

In the same line of thinking the revised research concludes that implementing technology alone is not enough to improve learning, as shown in Sanchez et al. [34], where it's stated that in South Korea the adoption and integration of ICT in education has been higher than in Chile. The difference is that in South Korea has a long-term view on the development of ICT and education, placing them as the linchpin for the country's progress, i.e., creating the structural and social conditions necessary to achieve such development.

Moreover, the work of Fariña et al. [12], unlike the work mentioned above, focuses on more specific aspects of the integration of ICT in education systems. Specifically addresses the use of the computer and the relationship it has with the development of reading skills in 15 years old students in Chile and other countries in similar conditions of development, taking into account social, economic and cultural conditions of students for each country. The main findings of the study indicate that there is no significant relationship between computer use and results related to the development of reading skills of students.

3.1.2 Case Studies

The work reviewed in this section correspond to studies conducted in Chile in the field of skills and the use of ICT in students from different educational levels. Overall, the use of technologies for educational purposes is related to certain abilities called media literacy, consisting of those skills or competencies closer to higher order cognitive skills that are linked to content creation and construction of knowledge, which involves sharing and collaborating with others through the mediation of technological tools or devices [19].

The referenced research related to the use and development of skills in educational settings was organized into two subcategories: skills/media literacy in k-12 and higher education and use and implementation of technology in k-12 and higher education.

3.1.2.1 Skills/Media Literacy in K-12 and Higher Education

In the field of skills and abilities in the use of ICT (Table 3), most of the research was focused on assessing students' skills in the use of technology in k-12 and higher education [13, 30] through the application of national questionnaires and standardized tests. Most of these studies agree that most Chilean students have skills related to the use and management of information and very few have skills related to skills of a higher cognitive order (as it was mentioned above). Similarly, these studies suggest that effective implementation of ICT in education is related to the implementation of an educational model based on TEL (Technology Enhanced Learning), that is, pedagogical models that consider the technology and its use from a curricular integration.

3.1.2.2 Use and Implementation of Technology in K-12 and Higher Education

Most of the research developed in the subject of use and implementation of technology in k-12 and higher education (Table 4), relates to the evaluation of government programs or initiatives aimed at the implementation of ICT in local educational contexts [17, 29–31, 33], emphasizing the conditions of implementation of programs of public initiative (context of schools, indicators related to the implementation process, outcomes, assessment tools, etc.). These studies agree that there is an adequate infrastructure but there's need to improve critical dimensions that have a direct impact on

Table 3. ICT Skills/media literacy in k-12 and higher education

Authors/years	Method/instrument	Purpose/central focus	Main results
García et al. 2014	Quantitative case study, ICT skills test	Evaluate whether the use of ICT on students is related to working memory tasks. In addition, the study examined whether the use of ICT and performance in working memory tasks are related to socioeconomic status and gender of the students of the seventh year of basic school	Higher scores on the digit durability test are related to user´s profiles that combine the use of PC and video games, that is, those users identified as complete ones, both as PC users and as users of consoles. The study found no interaction effect of gender or socioeconomic status and ICT use
Rodríguez et al. 2010	Quantitative case study, questionnaire	Monitoring and evaluation (M&E) scheme for ICT4E program that supports teaching and learning processes with a mobile computer	No statistically significant differences were found between students whose teachers showed higher levels of adoption of online education program and those from the defined control groups. A monitoring and evaluation system supports the intervention process, providing real-time information for decision-making through the implementation of assessment tools according to a decision-monitoring plan
Claro et al. 2012	Quantitative case study, ICT skills test	Evaluate ICT skills in 15-years-old Chilean students	The majority of students are able to solve the tasks related to the use of information as consumers, that is, about three-quarters of the students are able to find information and half of them are able to organize and manage digital information. Very few students are able to succeed in the tasks related to the processing and creation of new content. Only a third of them are able to develop their own ideas in digital environment and less than a fifth - to refine digital information and create a representation in a digital environment

(*Continued*)

Table 3. (*Continued*)

Authors/years	Method/instrument	Purpose/central focus	Main results
Claro et al. 2015	Quantitative case study, SIMCE	Provide data that will help to understand a digital gap that exists in Chilean education, by analyzing the effects of economic, social and cultural situation of Chilean students (ESCS) on their digital skills in maths and language	The marginal effect of the ECOS as a whole on the digital skills of students is equal to the effect on mathematics and greater than the effect on language. The level of parental education is the most important factor out of all CES factors to explain the results of students in the digital test, rather than in mathematics and language
Jara et al. 2015	Mixed case study, SIMCE ICT, interview and questionnaire	Identify and characterize the factors that are associated with digital skills of 2nd year high school Chilean students (10th grade)	There is a relationship between high scores in a digital skills test and access to computer at home. It is also related to the socioeconomic status of the family, number of years that students use the technology, their language skills and their perception of their own digital skills

Table 4. Use and implementation of technology in k-12 and higher education

Authors/years	Method/instrument	Purpose/central focus	Main results
Ramírez-Correa et al. 2010	Quantitative study, online questionnaire (TAM)	Explore gender differences in the adoption of e-learning technology among university students in Chile	In a sample of a Chilean university students, the conduct of accepting the e-learning technology, firstly, coincides with the TAM model, and secondly, no statistically significant differences were found between female and male students
Ortiz 2013	Quantitative study, questionnaire	Describe an experience of the use of ICT particularly developed to support technical managers and teachers	The main conclusion out of the experience is that the most useful and well evaluated by teachers ICT applications are difficult to implement in schools in the absence of management conditions and appropriate incentives
Arancibia et al. 2010	Qualitative study, interview	Understand the use of ICT and its relationship with the concepts on teaching and learning of teachers of History	Theoretically constructed categories (Transmitter/Reproductive, Interactionist/Constructive and Open/Autonomous) allowed to adequately characterize the concepts

(*Continued*)

Table 4. (*Continued*)

Authors/years	Method/instrument	Purpose/central focus	Main results
			on educational use of ICT of History teachers
Hinostroza et al. 2011	Quantitative study, questionnaire	Compare the results of the survey on the availability and use of computers, in a group of preschool students, with the similar one in primary and secondary schools	Although preschoolers have little access to computers and their teachers have relatively low ICT skills, they have similar impacts and obstacles that the secondary school students. Preschool students use computers in the classroom more often than their peers in primary and secondary schools
Butter et al. 2014	Quantitative study, questionnaire	Evaluate whether teachers working in intercultural contexts develop ICT skills using virtual platforms	The participating teachers increased their ICT skills in different dimensions of the use of ICT: educational management, knowledge management, deepening of knowledge, social, ethical and legal dimensions, through the application of knowledge and talent management models
Hinostroza et al. 2013	Quantitative study, questionnaire	Evaluate the results of analysis of teaching and learning activities with ICT in state subsidized schools in Chile	Teachers and students tend to use ICT more frequently in specific activities, which represents an opportunity to promote the use of ICT in schools. In teaching and learning activities in primary and secondary schools the results show that despite the fact that the general educational activities are different, activities with ICT are very similar, which demonstrates the lack of differentiated strategies for the use of ICT
Sánchez and Salinas 2008	Qualitative study, documentary analysis and secondary data	Evaluate the Links program	Links has had a positive impact in terms of infrastructure, connectivity, ICT use and teacher training process in many schools, however, this impact is not clearly seen in the results of students learning. The data and the results are limited by the structural bottlenecks in educational and social systems

(*Continued*)

Table 4. (*Continued*)

Authors/years	Method/instrument	Purpose/central focus	Main results
Salinas and Sánchez 2009	Mixed study, questionnaire and interview	Analyze the contribution of a teacher in improving digital inclusion in rural schools in Chile using a multidimensional definition of a digital gap	Teachers do not explicitly show students how to use ICT, but when teachers have high expectations, capabilities and free access to ICT, the results are favorable
Rodríguez et al. 2012	Mixed case study, questionnaire and interview	Propose an evidence-based framework to determine the ability of a ICT4E model to improve constantly before evaluating its final results	The proposed framework makes it explicit the relationships between each of the activities and expected outcomes (in an intermediate and final levels) in each process of the ICT4E program. It also allows teachers to identify which elements (knowledge and practices, stakeholders, activities, resources) may be absent
Sánchez et al. 2011	Qualitative study, interview	Analyze the ideas related to the appearance of a new type of student, or native digital, through the discourses of Chilean teachers and students	Technologies have a significant presence in everyday experiences of students. There is no significant relationship between the frequency of use of ICT and the socioeconomic status of students. ICT use varies depending on gender and certain attributes of users

student learning (ICT skills of teachers, integration of ICT into the educational curriculum and integration and management of ICT in the classroom).

4 Conclusions

The findings of this review suggest that comparative research developed in the field of ICT and education in Chile provides valuable information to understand the context of the implementation of technology into the educational system as well as in other countries with similar development conditions. As noted in the research carried out in this subject, information on the context of each country reveals those aspects that facilitate or impede the introduction of technology, especially in the school system, emphasizing on cultural aspects (vision of states regarding the importance ICT for education), social (digital divide) and economic (access) that are reflected in public policies or initiatives implemented for this purpose. These aspects operating at a macro level do not provide information on those aspects associated with the use of technology in local teaching situations. Most of the research in this area relates to structural aspects of educational institutions such as infrastructure, management and resources.

This ‘macro’ view on the implementation of technology into the Chilean education system comes primarily from standardized instruments (PISA, SITES 2006 and other evidence of national and international application) which are intended to address these structural issues mentioned above and also identify some general trends in the introduction of technology at a ‘micro’ level (local educational contexts). These studies generally agree that the introduction of technology by itself does not produce improvements in student learning, but do not analyze the phenomenon in all its complexity.

There are also other comparative studies that account for micro aspects that relate to the use of technology in educational settings and the effects of such use on student learning, as the work of Fariña et al. [12] focusing on determining the relationship between the development of reading skills in adolescents and the use of computer.

Research related to the measurement of digital skills in students comes from the analysis of the results of standardized tests of national and international application such as SIMCE ICT, PISA and SITES 2006, instruments that fail to address in a deep manner how and what is the real use of technology in schools and higher education institutions and finally what are the effects and impacts of these uses on student learning. According to what was stated above, this has to do with the use of technology in the classroom, as it was stated in of the studies reviewed [6] that indicate that the use of technology for educational purposes is sporadic and is not properly integrated into curriculum.

References

1. Allen, I.E., Seaman, J.: Changing Course: Ten Years of Tracking Online Education in the United States. Sloan Consortium (NJ1) (2013). Recuperado a partir de http://eric.ed.gov/?id=ED541571
2. Blamire, R., Kefala, S.: The ICT impact report. A review of studies of ICT impact on schools in Europe, 11 (2006)
3. Bodemer, D., Dehler, J.: Group awareness in CSCL environments. Comput. Hum. Behav. **27**(3), 1043–1045 (2011)
4. Bransford, J.D., Zech, L., Schwartz, D., Barron, B., Vye, N.: The Cognition and Technology Group at Vanderbilt. In: Fostering mathematical thinking in middle school students: lessons from research. The nature of mathematical thinking, pp. 203–250 (1996)
5. Brown, J.S., Collins, A., Duguid, P.: Situated cognition and the culture of learning. Educ. Res. **18**(1), 32–42 (1989)
6. Claro, M.: Impacto de las TIC en los aprendizajes de los estudiantes: estado del arte (2010). Recuperado a partir de http://repositorio.cepal.org/handle/11362/3781
7. Coll, C., Monereo, C.: Educación y aprendizaje en el siglo XXI: Nuevas herramientas, nuevos escenarios, nuevas finalidades. In: Psicología de la educación virtual, pp. 19–53 (2008)
8. Conlon, T., Simpson, M.: Silicon Valley versus Silicon Glen: the impact of computers upon teaching and learning: a comparative study. Br. J. Educ. Technol. **34**(2), 137–150 (2003). http://doi.org/10.1111/1467-8535.00316

9. Dillenbourg, P.: What do you mean by collaborative learning? In: Collaborative-Learning: Cognitive and Computational Approaches, pp. 1–19 (1999)
10. Dillenbourg, P., Järvelä, S., Fischer, F.: The evolution of research on computer-supported collaborative learning. In: Balacheff, N., Ludvigsen, S., de Jong, T., Lazonder, A., Barnes, S. (eds.) Technology-Enhanced Learning: Principles and Products, pp. 3–19. Springer, Netherlands (2009)
11. Dillenbourg, P., Baker, M.J., Blaye, A., O'Malley, C.: The evolution of research on collaborative learning. In: Learning in Humans and Machine: Towards an Interdisciplinary Learning Science, pp. 189–211 (1995)
12. Fariña, P., San Martín, E., Preiss, D.D., Claro, M., Jara, I.: Measuring the relation between computer use and reading literacy in the presence of endogeneity. Comput. Educ. **80**, 176–186 (2015)
13. Garcia, L., Nussbaum, M., Preiss, D.D.: Is the use of information and communication technology related to performance in working memory tasks? Evidence from seventh-grade students. Comput. Educ. **57**(3), 2068–2076 (2014)
14. Gikandi, J.W., Morrow, D., Davis, N.E.: Online formative assessment in higher education: a review of the literature. Comput. Educ. **57**(4), 2333–2351 (2011)
15. Green, B.N., Johnson, C.D., Adams, A.: Writing narrative literature reviews for peer-reviewed journals: secrets of the trade. J. Chiropractic Med. **5**(3), 101–117 (2006)
16. Greeno, J.G.: The situativity of knowing, learning, and research. Am. Psychol. **53**(1), 5 (1998)
17. Hinostroza, J.E., Labbé, C., Matamala, C.: The use of computers in preschools in Chile: lessons for practitioners and policy designers. Comput. Educ. **68**, 96–104 (2013)
18. Howie, S.J.: ICT-supported pedagogical policies and practices in South Africa and Chile: emerging economies and realities. J. Comput. Assist. Learn. **26**(6), 507–522 (2010)
19. Jara, I., Claro, M., Hinostroza, J.E., San Martín, E., Rodríguez, P., Cabello, T., Ibieta, A., Labbé, C.: Understanding factors related to Chilean students' digital skills: a mixed methods analysis. Comput. Educ. **88**, 387–398 (2015). http://doi.org/10.1016/j.compedu.2015.07.016
20. Janssen, J., Erkens, G., Kanselaar, G., Jaspers, J.: Visualization of participation: does it contribute to successful computer-supported collaborative learning? Comput. Educ. **49**(4), 1037–1065 (2007)
21. Jonassen, D.H., Carr, C., Yueh, H.-P.: Computers as mindtools for engaging learners in critical thinking. TechTrends **43**(2), 24–32 (1998). http://doi.org/10.1007/BF02818172
22. Jonassen, D.H., Rohrer-Murphy, L.: Activity theory as a framework for designing constructivist learning environments. Educ. Technol. Res. Dev. **47**(1), 61–79 (1999)
23. Lave, J., Wenger, E.: Situated Learning: Legitimate Peripheral Participation. Cambridge University Press, Cambridge (1991)
24. Law, N., Pelgrum, W.J., Plomp, T. (eds.): Pedagogy and ICT Use in Schools Around the World: Findings from the IEA SITES 2006 Study. CERC Studies in Comparative Education, vol. 23. Springer, Netherlands (2008)
25. Light, D.: Multiple factors supporting the transition to ICT-rich learning environments: the Intel® teach essentials course and changing teacher practice in India, Turkey, and Chile. Int. J. Educ. Dev. ICT **6**(4), 39–51 (2010)
26. Littleton, K., Wood, C.P., Staarman, J.K.: International Handbook of Psychology in Education. Emerald Group Publishing, Bingley (2010)
27. Monsalve, J.C.: Importancia de la educación a distancia en la actualidad. Revista de Ingeniería "Lámpsakos" **6**, 20–22 (2011)
28. Perestelo-Pérez, L.: Standards on how to develop and report systematic reviews in psychology and health. Int. J. Clin. Health Psychol. **13**(1), 49–57 (2013)

29. Rodriguez, P., Nussbaum, M., Dombrovskaia, L.: ICT for education: a conceptual framework for the sustainable adoption of technology-enhanced learning environments in schools. Technol. Pedagogy Educ. **21**(3), 291–315 (2012)
30. Rodríguez, P., Nussbaum, M., López, X., Sepúlveda, M.: A monitoring and evaluation scheme for an ICT-supported education program in schools. J. Educ. Technol. Soc. **13**(2), 166–179 (2010)
31. Salinas, A., Sánchez, J.: Digital inclusion in Chile: internet in rural schools. Int. J. Educ. Dev. **29**(6), 573–582 (2009)
32. Salomon, G.: Cogniciones Distribuidas: Consideraciones psicológicas y educativas. Amorrortu, Buenos Aires (2001)
33. Sánchez, J., Salinas, A.: ICT & learning in Chilean schools: lessons learned. Comput. Educ. **51**(4), 1621–1633 (2008)
34. Sánchez, J., Salinas, Á., Harris, J.: Education with ICT in South Korea and Chile. Int. J. Educ. Dev. **31**(2), 126–148 (2011)
35. Sánchez-Meca, J., Botella, J.: Revisiones sistemáticas y meta-análisis: Herramientas para la práctica profesional. Papeles del Psicólogo **31**(1), 7–17 (2010)
36. Stahl, G., Koschmann, T., Suthers, D.: Computer-supported collaborative learning: an historical perspective. In: Cambridge Handbook of the Learning Sciences, pp. 409–426 (2006)
37. Stojanovic, L.: Las tecnologías de Información y Comunicación en la promoción de nuevas formas interactivas y de aprendizaje en la Educación a distancia. Revista de investigación **59**, 121–140 (2006)

A Case of Emotional Intelligence for Teachers' Professional Development: Emotions and Connections are Ubiquitous in Second Life

Ioanna Giannakou, Fotini Paraskeva(✉), Aikaterini Alexiou, and Hara Bouta

Department of Digital Systems, University of Piraeus, Karaoli and Dimitriou Street 80, 185 34 Piraeus, Greece
joanna-giannakou16@hotmail.com, {fparaske,xmpouta}@unipi.gr, katialex@webmail.unipi.gr

Abstract. Success in teaching requires teachers' strong social and emotional competences to effectively manage and develop students' emotional development in every day practice. Having identified the important role of these competencies in schools, virtual learning environments (VLEs) and specifically environments like Second Life (SL) could be selected in order to enhance teachers' and students' social and emotional intelligence. Teachers could reflect, practice and improve their use of social and emotional competences in the classrooms by using Teachers' Professional Development programs (TPD), thereby making further improvements to their teaching. These training programs could support teachers by using suitable frameworks aligned with social and emotional learning (SEL). In this paper, we highlight the significance of TPD programs by presenting a SEL workshop on SL in order to better understand and enhance Emotional Intelligent (EI) for teachers' competencies. This study reveals that after having received training in a Social and Emotional Learning (SEL) workshop on Second Life (SL), teachers 'effectiveness in recognizing the EI components is highly increased.

Keywords: Teacher Professional Development · Second Life · Apt2Emotional Intelligence World · Arigatou

1 Introduction

Education faces new socio-economical challenges and technological advances which highlight the need for teaching students to respect diversity and learn to live together in harmony. Furthermore, 21st century teachers should focus not only on the appropriate teaching methods but also on affective skills, such us emotional intelligence, collaboration, communication, creativity, critical thinking and problem solving. An effective teacher should be an emotional literate teacher. Emotional literacy refers to the ability to recognize, manage and appropriately express emotions. Consequently, effective are

L. Uden et al. (Eds.): LTEC 2016, CCIS 620, pp. 39–50, 2016.
DOI: 10.1007/978-3-319-42147-6_4

those schools that tend to recognize and encourage emotions [14]. Thus, every teacher should be able to help each student to develop emotional and social skills such as self-awareness, self-regulation, empathy, communication and collaboration. In order to assist students to acquire emotional skills, teachers need to get trained in Emotional Intelligence.

Towards this direction, there is a need for delivering teacher-focused social emotional programs. The term social and emotional program refers to activities aimed at enhancing students' social and emotional skills [2]. Consequently, teachers need to be trained to design such activities and to be more emotionally supportive of their students. This could be achieved by using virtual learning environments (VLEs) (such us Second Life, Active Worlds, etc.) as delivery platforms for Teachers' ongoing professional development. Furthermore VLEs support participants to be empathetic and to develop positive interpersonal relationships [15]. In this research, we selected Second Life (SL) which is a Web 2.0-based, three-dimensional virtual-reality world developed in 2003. The proposed 3D VLE consists of tools that may enhance self-awareness and self-regulation competencies when opportunities are given to the participants to reflect upon their actions and emotions. Taking all the above reasons in consideration, this research is aimed at designing, developing and implementing a Social and Emotional Learning Workshop in the context of Teachers Professional Development (TPD) in Second Life. This world is named "Apt2Emotional Intelligence World" after the Apt2 Lab (Applied Learning Psychology in Teaching and Technology).

2 Review of the Literature

2.1 Teachers' Professional Development (TPD) and 3D VLEs

Teachers, nowadays, need to be adaptive and lifelong learners by continuously developing their skills and knowledge [20, 29]. Teachers' professional development (TPD) can be achieved through training sessions with the aid of digital oriented environments [21, 25]. By means of this process, which can either stand on its own or be complementary, teachers can assess, update and expand their relation to the moral aims of teaching in order to become the reflectors of them at the school environment. That is the acquisition and development of the critical skills, knowledge and the emotional intelligence needed to become great professional thinkers and doers with children, young people and colleagues at each step of their teaching careers [12, 23].

There is a major need to seek new high level and easily accessible and online TPD implementations in the field of literature [13]. The question is how effective these types of programs are, as very poor research is held to look into their actual effectiveness, despite their popularity [8, 20, 28]. One could say that, nowadays (e.g. mobiles, wikis, 3D virtual worlds) and future technologies (e.g. gesture based, augmented reality, immersive worlds) enable teachers to set effective learning activities on pedagogical level [7] that promote experimental and experience based learning, bolstering and enhancing motivation and the involvement of each learner [4].

Recently, an exploration of potential of 3D virtual learning environments is taking place, where instruments, environments, and stakeholders can be duplicated as a virtual artifact, a result that can be quickly accomplished on a low budget [18]. Learners become the observers of a simulation of an event as if in a real life surroundings, such as a hospital, a classroom, or a factory [4]. Moreover, 3D virtual environments reinforce the sense of presence and profound engagement [23] along with the interactive manners of the learner [11]. Teacher's interaction is simultaneous and their engagement reaches higher levels. Due to this fact, such environments are highly suitable for teacher's professional development programs as they enhance teachers' work by new teaching methods. Furthermore, they bring about a deeper insight into students' different learning patterns and as a result teachers' professional skills and ethics are reinforced [19].

In conclusion, the great variety of applications and the fact that users can always adapt their targets, present us with an adjustable and powerful teaching environment that follows the teachers' needs as well as the demands of the learning practice [6]. So users are double benefited by attaining new practical abilities and skills, but mostly because they are presented with inventive ways to use new technology.

2.2 Emotional Intelligence (EI) and 3D VLEs

Goleman developed the Emotional Intelligence (EI) Theory based on Gardner's interpersonal and intrapersonal intelligence [16]. The popularized definition by Goleman states that emotional intelligence is "the ability to control one's desires and to delay the desires' satisfaction, to control others' mood, to isolate feelings and thoughts, to walk in one's shoes and to hope. Also, to have skills as self-control, persistence, eagerness and also the ability to stimulate others by providing motives". According to Gottman, the components of Emotional Intelligence are the following: self-awareness, self-regulation, motivation, empathy and social skills. A teacher should encourage his/her students to develop these skills, as long as he/she has utilized these skills, according to the Professional Teaching Standards [27] (Table 1).

The importance of being an emotionally literate teacher is increased due to the fact that children should be encouraged to develop emotional and social skills from an early age. When neglecting children's emotional and social development for entire generations, major social problems may arise.

Emotional Intelligence is a significant predictor of an individual's social life function. Therefore, it is evident that teachers' emotional competence is essential not only for their well-being and for their effectiveness and quality of teaching, but also for the children's social and emotional development [1, 25]. In addition to all these, emotional competence is an indicator for an individual's success at work. All kinds of professions require emotionally competent professionals and particularly those involved in social relations, such as teachers.

Successful teaching requires successful social interaction, which develops within different interpersonal relations. However, teachers have great responsibility for their students, since they can influence the children's emotional and social development significantly. As far as the school environment is concerned, a teacher needs to be socially and emotionally competent so as to be able to manage relationships with parents and other colleagues and most importantly to be able to cooperate with them for

Table 1. Components of emotional intelligence [16] and the professional teaching standards [27]

Components of Emotional Intelligence	Definition [16]	Professional Teaching Standards - Qualification(Q) [27]
Self-awareness	The ability to recognize and understand your moods, emotions, and drives, as well as their effects on others	[Q8] Have a creative and constructively critical approach towards innovation, being prepared to adapt their practice where benefits and improvements are identified
Self-regulation	The ability to control or redirect disruptive impulses and moods The propensity to suspend judgment – to think before acting	[Q2] Demonstrate the positive values, attitudes and behavior they expect from children and young people [Q9] Act upon advice and feedback and be open to coaching and mentoring
Motivation	The propensity to pursue goals with energy and persistence	
Empathy	The ability to understand the emotional makeup of other people The skill to treat people according to their emotional reaction	[Q4] Communicate effectively with children, young people, colleagues, parents and carers [Q5] Recognize and respect the contribution that colleagues, parents and carers can make to the development and well-being of children and young people, and to raising their levels of attainment [Q21b] Know how to identify and support children and young people whose progress, development or well-being is affected by changes or difficulties in their personal circumstances, and when to refer them to colleagues for specialist support
Social skills	The proficiency in managing relationships and building networks	[Q1] Have high expectations of children and young people including a commitment to ensuring that they can achieve their full educational potential and to establishing fair, respectful, trusting, supportive and constructive relationships with them [Q32] Work as a team member and identify opportunities for working with colleagues, sharing the development of effective practice with them

the children's best benefit. Various studies concerning EI are really encouraging. Boyatzis' [9] study proves that students can develop EI competencies. Singh [26] conducted a study which concluded that different professionals need different levels of EI to be successful. According to the results, teachers need to be highly emotionally intelligent in order to succeed.

Moreover, schools need to launch programs focused on EI so that students acquire all the basic qualities required for an individual to be successful in social adult life. It is, then, suggested that teachers need to be emotionally intelligent and also to participate in professional development training programs designed to meet that need. Also, this type of training programs is necessary in order to enable teachers to meet the challenges of an increasing diverse student population.

Second Life was selected to support a workshop about EI, since according to Donkor [12] VLEs can support EI, because:

- VLE resources such as forums, videos, feedback tools enable students to grow in confidence and self-esteem.
- Self-awareness and self-regulation competencies can be enhanced by VLEs. This happens because participants are given opportunities to reflect upon their actions and emotions (self-awareness & self-regulation).
- VLEs can help an individual to be empathetic (empathy).
- VLEs support positive interpersonal relationships (social skills).

2.3 Second Life as a 3D Virtual Learning Environment

Second Life (SL) is a Web 2.0-based, three-dimensional virtual-reality world developed in 2003by a San Francisco Company, named Linden Lab. Although SL presents the characteristics of a digital game, it is not one. Users create accounts and develop avatars that represent them in the virtual world. Avatars in SL can interact with each other as well as with objects and environments. Avatars can utilize the handy tools to build and program objects so as to configure the environment as one desires. Each avatar can walk, run, fly, teleport and get a new look. Users communicate with each other through voice or text chat. For all the transactions in SL the users handle virtual money, called Linden Dollars.

Educators examine teaching and learning in virtual worlds and utilize SL for distance learning. Numerous universities all over the world design lectures on SL. An education organization called “Teachers without borders” has an increasing progress in Second Life since 2009. Virtual worlds might be useful tools in online teaching due to their ability to engage students in interactions with the instructor and others in the class as well as with their environment. Interactions in a virtual world can help to build a sense of community in classes [4, 5]. This virtual world enables educators to collaborate, exchange ideas and understand the potentials of SL both in teaching and in their own professional development. To this end, this research aims to design, develop and implement the Apt2Emotional Intelligence World in SL so as to familiarize teachers with Emotional Intelligence dimensions.

3 Method

The aim of this research is the design, development and implementation of Apt2E motional Intelligence World, which delivers a Social and Emotional Learning (SEL) Workshop in the context of Teachers Professional Development (TPD) training program. An experimental research (as a case study) was, therefore, conducted within a Computer Science Department of a Greek University. A random sample of 12 in-service teachers (primary and secondary education) participated in the experimental procedure. They have teaching experience and an adequate technological background.

This study seeks to answer the following research question:

"To what extent does the proposed SEL workshop in the Apt2Emotional Intelligence World enhance teacher's Emotional Intelligence?" To be more specific, to what extent does the *Apt2Emotional Intelligence World* improve

RQ1.1 teacher's 'self-awareness'? RQ1.2 teacher's 'self-regulation'?
RQ1.3 teacher's 'empathy'? RQ1.4 teacher's 'social skills'?

In order to answer the RQs a questionnaire was distributed to the participants before and after the workshop. This questionnaire includes 30 ill-structured problems in which the participants are expected to recognize the EI skills needed to solve the problems. This questionnaire was evaluated by the Cronbach's alpha test, ranking the score of 0,749, thus verifying its reliability. An example of the questionnaire is presented in Table 2.

Table 2. Examples of the questionnaire's ill-Structured problem along with the Emotional Skills needed.

Ill-Structured problem	Emotional skills (Components of EI)
Shilu listens to her friends talking about their problems and understands them. Which skill/s of EI does she have?	Choose between self-awareness, self-regulation, empathy and social skills Correct answer: empathy
Phoebus is unable to remain calm when his classmates are mad at him. Which skill/s of EI does he need in order to deal with?	Choose between self-awareness, self-regulation, empathy and social skills Correct answer: self-awareness, self-regulation

The RQs examine whether the trained teachers will be able to recognize the emotional intelligence skills that compose EI in various ill-structured problems presented in multiple activities.

3.1 The "Apt2Emotional Intelligence World" Design

The SEL Workshop consists of numerous activities, which were designed based on the program "Learning to Live Together" (Arigatou Foundation) [3], the Emotion Coaching Model and the Anchored Instruction Model (Table 3).

Firstly, "Learning to Live Together" is an Intercultural and Interfaith Program for Ethics Education. This program aims to strengthen children's commitment to justice, to promote respect for human rights and to build strong harmonious relationships between individuals coming for different cultural environments. This program has been developed in close cooperation with UNICEF and UNESCO.

Table 3. Workshop design

Sessions	Anchored instruction	Emotion coaching model [16]	Arigatou activities [3]
Session 1	1st Anchor	Emotion-awareness	My Life Tree-Compare it
	2nd Anchor	Emotion-recognition	Unjust Situations-Bobby's Story
Session 2	3rd Anchor	Empathetic Listening of emotions	Meditate on myself – a silent journey-Personal experience sharing
Session 3	4th Anchor	Label emotions	Using Case Studies-Stories for the Soul
	5th Anchor	Problem solving	Dilemmas

Secondly, the SEL Workshop followed the principles of the Emotion Coaching Model [17] so as to support and train teachers to be Emotion Coaches. In detail, according to [17] there are four types of parents: the dismissive parent, the disapproving parent, the laissez-faire parent and the emotion coach. An Emotion Coach should follow some specific stages [17]: Stage 1: Emotion-awareness: Be aware of your child's emotion, Stage 2: Emotion-recognition: Seeing Expressions of Emotion as Opportunities for Teaching and Intimacy, Stage 3: Empathetic Listening of emotions: Treating a Child's Feelings with Empathetic Listening and Validation, Stage 4: Label emotions: Helping the Child to Find Words For Their Emotions, Stage 5: Problem solving: Helping the Child Problem Solve and Setting Limits.

Thirdly, the workshop is organized based on the Anchored Instruction Model. Anchored instruction was developed to compensate for learners' lack of experience and knowledge. Anchors consist of multimedia scenarios that are designed to improve learners' understanding of the problems to be solved [10]. The main anchor is the main problem; the communication problems and conflicts between students due to their differences. The main anchor is divided into five smaller anchors in each of which the participants experience a stage of the Emotion Coaching Model [17]. Moreover, in the fifth anchor the Six Thinking Hats Method is incorporated into the activities, so as to promote creative thinking (de Bono, 1999).

3.2 Experimental Design

The SEL workshop took place in the virtual learning environment of Second Life (Apt2Emotional Intelligence World). The participants visited SL for three sessions. Before the workshop starts taking place the participants are called to fill in a questionnaire about EI skills.

1st Session: The trainer coordinates the procedure. The participants are welcomed into the SEL Center in the Leucadia island in Second Life. They watch a presentation where they take information about the workshop. The 1st Session lasts 120 min. This session consists of the activities:

My Life Tree-Compare it: The participants visit the meeting corner where they get to know each other by posting notes on the life tree answering the questions posed on the trees frames. Then, they discuss about their differences and consequently realize that they are not the only ones differing from each other, but so are their students (Fig. 1).

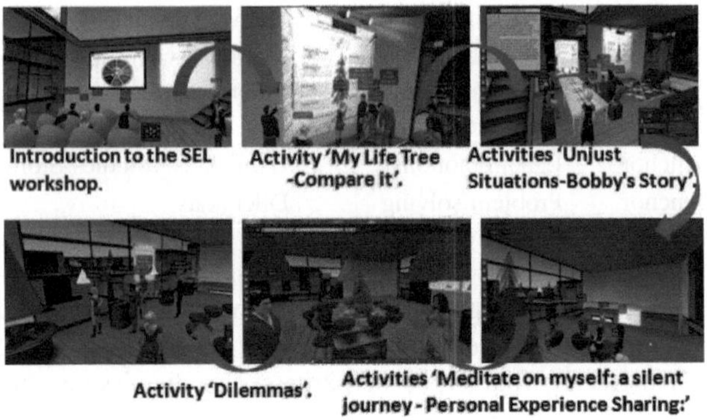

Fig. 1. The experimental design in Second Life

Unjust Situations-Bobby's Story: The participants visit the discussion corner where they receive a notecard by clicking on the table. This notecard describes the story of a child named 'Bobby'. Bobby is a child different from the others and has no friends. The participants recognize Bobby's feelings, their feelings about Bobby, other children's feelings and discuss about the way they would handle this situation if they were Bobby's teacher (Fig. 1).

2nd Session: The trainer coordinates the procedure. The 2nd Session lasts 90 min. This session consists of the activities: **Meditate on myself: a silent journey - Personal Experience Sharing:** The participants visit the second floor of the SEL Center and sit on the pillows around the Christmas tree. They are called to meditate on themselves about experiences concerning their students' fight or arguments. They share their experiences if they wish to and the others listen to them with empathy (Fig. 1).

3rd Session: The trainer coordinates the procedure. The 3rd Session lasts 90 min. This session consists of the activities:

Using Case Studies-Stories for the soul: The participants sit on the pillows and click a random ball on the tree. A notecard is shared. The notecard describes a story of a child which experiences an unpleasant feeling. Each ball contains a notecard with a different story. The participants are called to name the feeling of the child in their story, exactly as they would if they were speaking to the child (Fig. 1).

Dilemmas: The participants are divided into three groups. There are four participants in each group. They visit the cooperation corner. There they click on each hat and they are given a notecard with a dilemma and directions to solve the problem exposed. Each hat examines the dilemma by a different perspective. The group recognizes the feeling, discusses and finally ends up with a solution for the dilemma (Fig. 1).

After having completed the workshop the participants are requested to fill in the same questionnaire about EI skills that they filled in before the seminar took place.

4 Findings

The results presented are based on the data analysis carried out. The data analysis is quantitative, employing the statistical package SPSS. Four variables were created for the results to be manifested. Each variable represents a total score for every indicator concerning the EI components. The p-value used for significance level is 0,05 and the statistical criterion is Anova (Table 4).

Table 4. Descriptive analysis for the indicators "self-awareness", "self-regulation", "social skills"

(self-awareness): Descriptive analysis (ANOVA)

	Mean	Std. Deviation	N
pre-self-awareness	5,25	2,500	4
post-self-awareness	7,75	0,500	4
Sig.	0,141		

(self-regulation): Descriptive analysis (ANOVA)

	Mean	Std. Deviation	N
pre-self- regulation	8,00	1,732	11
post-self- regulation	14,55	0,522	11
Sig.	0,000		

(social skills): Descriptive analysis (ANOVA)

	Mean	Std. Deviation	N
pre- social skills	8,11	2,315	9
post- social skills	16,33	1,000	9
Sig.	0,000		

* The mean difference is significant at the 0,05 level.

RQ1.1: To what extent does the proposed SEL workshop in the Apt2Emotional Intelligence World familiarize participants with the indicator of self-awareness, as a component of EI? There is no statistically significant difference between the indicator of self-awareness before and after the experiment (p-value = 0,141). Therefore, the participants did not familiarize with the 'self-awareness' EI competence to a great extent. This result does comes as a surprise, since the participants already seemed familiar with the indicator of self-awareness in the first place.

RQ1.2: To what extent does the proposed SEL workshop in the Apt2Emotional Intelligence World familiarize participants with the indicator of self-regulation, as a component of EI? There is a statistically significant difference between the indicator of self-regulation before and after the experiment (p-value = 0,000). Therefore, the participants familiarized with the 'self-regulation'EI competence to a great extent. This result can be explained by the fact that the SL world was designed in a way that the participants were encouraged to move around, self-regulate and make decisions when dealing with ill-structured problems, such as dilemmas.

RQ1.4: To what extent does the proposed SEL workshop in the Apt2Emotional Intelligence World familiarize participants with the indicator of social skills, as a component of EI? There is a statistically significant difference between the indicator of self-regulation before and after the experiment (p-value = 0,000). Therefore, the participants became familiar with the 'social skills'competence; to a great extent. This result can be explained by the fact that the SL world was designed in a way that the participants were prompted to interact with one another. Also the activities were designed to promote collaboration among participants.

Table 5. Descriptive analysis for the indicator "empathy"

(empathy) (Test Statistics) (Wilcoxon)	
	post-empathy- pre-empathy
Z	−2,536
Asymp. Sig. (2-tailed)	0,011

RQ1.3: To what extent does the proposed SEL workshop in the Apt2Emotional Intelligence World familiarize the participants with the indicator of empathy, as a component of EI? The Wilcoxon test was used to measure the statistically significant difference between the indicator of empathy before and after the experiment, since the indicator of empathy does not follow normal distribution (Table 5). There is a statistically significant difference between the indicator of empathy before and after the experiment (p-value = 0,011). Therefore, the participants familiarized with the 'empathy'EI competence to a great extent. This can be attributed to the fact that the participants were encouraged to put themselves in others' shoes and recognize the emotions that the others may experience in multiple ill-structured problems.

5 Conclusions and Discussion

Social problems affect our everyday life and thus it has become crucial to work on emotions and encourage emotional growth of children in classroom. The precondition to achieve that is to infuse EI into TPD training programs. Teachers need to be trained in EI order to recognize and manage not only their own feelings but also others' feelings. Towards this direction, the present study pinpoints the design, development and implementation of a SEL workshop for TPD in SL (*Apt2Emotional Intelligence World*), to examine whether teachers familiarize with EI competencies. The results of the study reveal that the SEL workshop for TPD in *Apt2Emotional Intelligence World* familiarized the participants with all the indicators of EI, except for the self-awareness one. However, the participants seemed to already be familiar with that indicator. So, the statistical difference was not significant. These results are really important because the teachers seem to be able to recognize the EI indicators needed in problematic situations and are possibly prepared to design activities so as to promote their students' EI.

For future research, it would be really interesting to examine the configuration of Arigatou's activities in SL for students and measure students' EI skills. In addition to this, research should focus on comparing the learning outcomes of a TPD training program in SL and a TPD program in another VLE, such as OpenSim. Furthermore, a different topic workshop should be designed to take place at SL, in order to examine different affective and social indicators. Last but not least, it would be really important to train teachers in a traditional class and compare the results so as to examine whether SL provides more motives to learn and whether there are even better learning results.

Acknowledgements. This work has been partly supported by the Research Center of the University of Piraeus.

References

1. Adelman, H.S., Taylor, L.: Technical assistance sampler on protective factors/resilience. Canter for Mental Health in Schools at UCLA. Author, Los Angeles, CA (2008)
2. Anderson, L.: Increasing Teacher Effectiveness, 2nd edn. UNESCO International Institute for Educational Planning, Paris (2004). http://unesdoc.unesco.org/images/0013/001376/137629e.pdf. Accessed 26 July 2015
3. Arigatou Foundation: Learning to Live Together: An intercultural and interfaith programme for ethics education (2008). http://unesdoc.unesco.org/images/0016/001610/161059e.pdf
4. Bai, X., Lavin, J, Wright, R.: Virtual Learning in Health Education. In: International Conference on Future Computer and Information Technology (2013)
5. Baker, S., Wentz, R., Woods, M.: Using virtual worlds in education: Second Life® as an educational tool. Teach. Psychol. **36**, 59–64 (2009)
6. Bocconi, S., Kampylis, P., Punie, Y.: Innovating learning: key elements for developing creative classrooms in europe. In: European Commission -Joint Research Centre- Institute for Prospective Technological Studies, EUR 25446 EN, Seville. Publications Office of the European Union, Luxembourg (2012)
7. Bouta, H., Retalis, S., Paraskeva, P.: Utilising a collaborativemacro-script to enhance student engagement: a mixed method study in a 3D virtual environment. J. Comput. Educ. **58**(1), 501–517 (2012)
8. Bottino, R.M.: The evolution of ICT-based learning environments: which perspectives for the school of the future? Brit. J. Educ. Technol. **35**(5), 553–567 (2004)
9. Boyatzis, R.: A twenty year view of trying to develop emotional, social and cognitive intelligence competencies in graduate management education. J. Manag. Dev. **27**(1), 92–108 (2008)
10. Bransford, J.D., Sherwood, R.D., Hasselbring, T.S., Kinzer, C.K., Williams, S.M.: Anchored instruction: why we need it and how technology can help. In: Nix, D., Spiro, R.J. (eds.) Cognition, education, and multimedia: exploring ideas in high technology. L. Erlbaum, Hillsdale (1990)
11. Dalgarno, B., Lee, M.: What are the learning affordances of 3-D virtual environ-ments? Brit. J. Educ. Technol. **41**(1), 10–32 (2010)

12. Day, C.: Developing Teachers: The Challenges of Lifelong Learning. Falmer Press, London (1999)
13. Dede, C., Ketelhut, D., Whitehouse, P., Breit, L., McCloskey, E.: A research agenda for online teacher professional development. J. Teach. Educ. **60**(1), 8–19 (2009)
14. DfES: Every child matters: change for children (2004). http://cw.routledge.com/textbooks/9780415478724/downloads/every-child-matters.pdf. Accessed 26 July 2015
15. Donkor, F.: The emotionally intelligent virtual learning environment (VLE): how it may be constructed from the perspective of secondary education. (Unipublished Doctoral thesis), Brunnel University, London, England (2013)
16. Goleman, D.: What Makes a Leader? Harvard Bus. Rev. **82**(1), 82–91 (1998)
17. Gottman, J.: The Heart of Parenting: Raising an Emotionally Intelligent Child. Simon & Schuster, New York (1998)
18. Hew, K.F., Cheung, W.S.: Attracting student participation in asynchronous online discussions: A case study of peer facilitation. Comput. Educ. **51**(3), 1111–1124 (2008)
19. Leu, E., Ginsburg, M.: In-service Teacher Professional Development. EQUIP1 First Principles Compendium. American Institutes for Research, Washington, DC (2011)
20. Ostashewski, N., Moisey, S., Reid, D.: Constructionist principles in online teacher professional development: Robotics and hands-on activities in the Classroom. In: Proceedings of ASCILITE - Australian Society for Computers in Learning in Tertiary Education Annual Conference 2010, pp. 721–729. Australasian Society for Computers in Learning in Tertiary Education (2010)
21. Pellas, N., Boumpa, A.: Blending the CoI model with Jigsaw technique for pre-service foreign language teachers' continuing professional development using Open Sim and Sloodle. J. Educ. Inf. Technol. 1–26 (2016)
22. Rose, J., Reynolds, D.: Teachers' continuing professional development: a new approach. In: Paper presented at 20th Annual World International Congress for Effectiveness and Improvement (2006)
23. Schmeil, A., Eppler, M.J.: Knowledge sharing and collaborative learning in second life: a classification of virtual 3d group interaction scripts. J. Univ. Comput. Sci. **15**(3), 665–677 (2008)
24. Seezink, A., Poell, R.: Continuing professional development needs of teachers in schools for competence-based vocational education. J. Eur. Ind. Training **34**(5), 455–474 (2010)
25. Sutton, R., Wheatley, K.: Teachers' emotions and teaching: a review of the literature and directions for future research. Educ. Psychol. Rev. **15**(4), 327–358 (2003)
26. Singh, D.: Emotional Intelligence at Work: A Professional Guide. Sage Publications, New Delhi (2003)
27. TDA (Training and Development Agency): Professional standards for teachers (2007). https://www.rbkc.gov.uk/pdf/qts-professional-standards-2008.pdf. Accessed 26 July 2015
28. Whitehouse, P., Breit, L., McCloskey, E., Ketelhut, D.J., Dede, C.: An overview of current findings from empirical research on online teacher professional development. In: Dede, C. (ed.) Online Professional Development for Teachers: Emerging Models and Methods, pp. 13–30. Harvard Education Press, Cambridge (2006)
29. Whitehouse, P., Reynolds, R., Caperton, I.: Globaloria pilot year one: new directions for 21st century teacher professional development. In: Gibson, I., et al. (eds.) Proceedings of Society for Information Technology & Teacher Education International Conference 2009, pp. 1590–1597. AACE, Chesapeake (2009)

Using Games to Improve Learning Skills in Students with Cognitive Disabilities Through Kinect Technology

Dacarth Sarmiento[1], Yesid Díaz[1], and Roberto Ferro[2(✉)]

[1] Axon Research Group, CUN University Bogotá, Bogotá, Colombia
{Dacarth_sarmiento, Yesid_diaz}@cun.edu.co
[2] Axon-Lider Research Group,
Universidad Distrital Francisco José de Caldas, Bogotá, Colombia
rferro@udistrital.edu.co

Abstract. The purpose of this paper is to present the use of ICT tools to improve the performance of students with some cognitive disabilities in Colombia, the use of tools and software based on .Net and Java can build interesting alternatives that can be evaluated and applied learning different fields, such as mathematics, physics and others, through interactive games that make learning how to be more successful students.

1 Introduction

Today, innovation has become a key aspect for humanity, becoming increasingly common technological inventions we use in our daily lives. Today, technological developments combine areas such as electronics, mechanics and systems, which together manage to solve human needs of different kinds. The development of such innovation is a crucial aspect of the entity to be overcome by having researchers from a country with cutting edge technological development; the above thanks to the premises of the theory of education that allows these developments bring and share our country. Thanks to this it is possible to learn, design and transfer this technological knowledge to researchers at the institution who replicate these actions to teachers and students achieving a comprehensive training and enabling the development of women cornerstone of our society and being in sync with the mission and vision of the institution. After reaching a high level of knowledge transfer it is to make based on innovation to solve problems that transform the population with some degree of disability either genetic or because of the armed conflict that our country has suffered applications. According to statistics published by the institute 6 people out of every 100 Colombians suffer from some type of cognitive impairment due to this a close to 840.000 of people with some form of cognitive impairment due to this reason population here. The group Axon in CUN University estimated it has been doing software development to help improve the way these people can learn much faster and with a bigger motivation and therefore future inclusion in working life [1].

L. Uden et al. (Eds.): LTEC 2016, CCIS 620, pp. 51–60, 2016.
DOI: 10.1007/978-3-319-42147-6_5

1.1 Colombia Disability Legal Framework

In Colombia the Foundation for Research in Special Education (Fides) and the University Health Sciences Foundation (Fucs) they conducted a cooperation agreement for research on population issues in special condition [2], according to the data provided in Colombia disability is a public health problem that requires a joint effort between the State work, private organizations, social organizations, universities and civil society, in order to transform the determinants of disability, to prevent its occurrence and promote the development of the potential of people, self-fulfillment and the free participation of all members of society in their work dynamic [3].

The legal framework to include people with mental disabilities in Colombia initiated from the political constitution of the country, since 1991 when it is established, in Article 13 where it enshrines “the State especially protect those people whose economic, physical or mental condition, are in obviously vulnerable circumstances and punish any abuse or ill-treatment perpetrated against them”; Article 68 stipulates that “the eradication of illiteracy and education of persons with physical or mental limitations or with exceptional capabilities are special obligations of the State”; Article 47 also makes a specific reference to cognitive disabilities stating that “the State will promote a policy of planning, rehabilitation and social integration of physical, sensory and mentally handicapped, who require specialized care will be provided” [3].

In 1981 the government issued Decree 2358, which rules on vocational rehabilitation and employment of disabled persons, Decree 2177 of 1989 and the Juvenile Code, Decree Law 2737 created 1989. As for the history of formulating plans for “Policy Prevention and disability”, whose main objectives were to improve the quality of life of the population in general and the achievement of their social and economic integration: the issue of disability, in 1995 the CONPES 2761 was issued; in 1997 the government published the Law 361 of 1997, “by which mechanisms of social integration of people with limitations established”. There mechanisms for prevention, education, rehabilitation, employment integration, social welfare and accessibility. In terms sport issues Law 181 of 1995 this law, which dictates rules for the promotion of sport associated with people with cognitive disabilities guiding measures for their rehabilitation and social integration was issued. The government also established the “National Plan of Care for People with Disabilities for the years 1999–2002” and “Basis for Developing a Public Disability Policy 2003–2006” which is presented to the Presidential Council for Social Policy as the organization responsible for coordinating the activities of interaction between the different national institutions involved. Now reviewing the state of the art in legal matters you can see that there is a broad range of articles and laws on the subject but “the real situation for these people is unfavorable and the marginalization in cultural, educational and work spaces is evident [3]. This without discrimination in political and social processes.

1.2 Treaties and Conventions About People with Disabilities

In this section we will review the state of the art on international issues of persons with disabilities and which have been ratified and approved by the government of Colombia.

The United Nations, have enacted different texts and declarations, conventions, plans and Recommendations container containing some Proposals Concerning the rights of persons with Disabilities. There Duties of States and of society towards them are Identified and action guidelines are drawn to Prevent disability, providing care and creating conditions for social integration and overcoming any form of discrimination [3]:

- American Convention on Human Rights. Deals with measures to protect minors and equality before the law.
- Convention 159 on vocational rehabilitation and employment of disabled persons.
- Additional to the American Convention on Human Rights Protocol on Economic, Social and Cultural Rights - Protocol of San Salvador. States Parties undertake to adopt, in accordance with their constitutional procedures, legislative or other measures as may be necessary to give effect to these rights without discrimination for different prone to some kind of violation populations.
- Children's rights convention. It is established that a mentally or physically disabled child should enjoy a full and decent life, in conditions which ensure dignity, reach self-reliance and facilitate their active participation in the community.
- American Convention on the Elimination of All Forms of Discrimination against persons with disabilities.
- Declaration of the Rights of Mentally Retarded.
- Global Programme of Action for people with disabilities.
- Vienna Declaration and Programme of Action. Situation of disabled people in the Americas.
- Panama Commitment to Persons with Disabilities in the Americas OEA.
- UN Standard Rules on the Equalization of Opportunities for Persons with Disabilities.
- Human Rights of Persons with Disabilities.

2 Learning Disabilities by Areas

The frase "Specific learning disability" means a disorder in one or more basic psychological processes involved in understanding or in using language, spoken or written, that may manifest itself in an imperfect ability to listen, speak, read, write, spell, or to do mathematical calculations. The term includes such conditions as perceptual disabilities, brain injury, minimal brain dysfunction, dyslexia, and developmental aphasia. The term does not apply to children who have learning problems that are primarily the result of visual, hearing, or motor disabilities, of mental retardation, of emotional disturbance, or of environmental, cultural, or economic disadvantage [4].

According to publication form Reid the Learning disability is a general category of special education composed of disabilities in any of seven specific areas [5]:

- Receptive language (listening)
- Expressive language (speaking),
- Basic reading skills

- Reading comprehension
- Written expression
- Mathematics calculation
- Mathematical reasoning.

These separate types of learning disabilities frequently co-occur with one another and also with certain social skill deficits and emotional or behavioral disorders such as attention deficit disorder. Learning disability is not synonymous with reading disability or dyslexia although it is frequently misinterpreted as such.

However, most of the available information concerning learning disabilities relates to reading disabilities, and the majority of children with Learning disability have their primary deficits in reading. Now according to the above definitions and statistical publication made by the DANE [6] in Colombia for people in disability status, it is possible to distinguish several related to the classification criteria proposed by DANE, in Table 1 the data collected in a survey is presented and census people for the city of Bogotá to be a very important population sample in our country.

Table 1. Data on disability status people living in Bogota Colombia DANE source [6].

Corporal function	Total		
	Total	Men	Women
Total	476,991	186,973	290,018
Nervous system	76,153	33,483	42,670
Eyes	73,063	27,932	45,131
Ears	28,784	12,619	16,165
Smell, touch, taste	5,568	2,448	3,120
Voice, talking	24,029	12,545	11,484
Cardio respiratory system and defenses	84,560	29,343	55,217
Digestion, metabolism, hormones	47,430	15,971	31,459
The genital and reproductive system	19,466	8,245	11,221
The movement of the body, hands, arms, legs	99,650	37,187	62,463
Skin	9,417	3,713	5,704
Other	8,871	3,487	5,384

The result of Table 1 can be graphed in Fig. 1, here you can make the first analysis related to people in disability status for men and women and their total in the Bogotá city taken as a representative sample in Colombia. By correlating the data, it can be seen that in Bogotá most people on disability status is of female origin, while for men the number is much lower. The largest number of people with disability status are those with problems the movement of the body, hands, arms, legs, then suffering problems of the nervous system, respiratory condition, eyes, ears, speech and then the rest. Once we collect and analyze the raw data we can think about creating software applications that

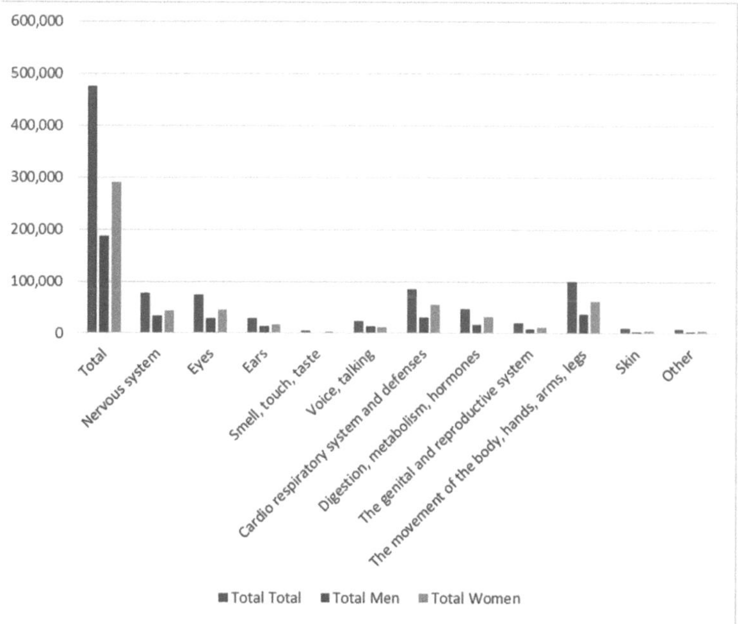

Fig. 1. This figure shows the relationship of people in a state of disability in Bogotá in Colombia as a representative sample, the data are taken from DANE [6]. (Color figure online)

allow these people to improve their learning, to achieve this we investigate new technologies and applications of Kinect and began to study it can be developed to achieve present innovative and practical designs in our country.

3 Development Project for People with Cognitive Disabilities Based on Kinect

The main objective of this project is to develop comprehensive solutions consisting of Kinect technology [7] and ICT application software that allows people with disabilities who can improve their daily lives, these problems can be of any kind and to start serious power identify obstacles to the center, left or right of them, through differentiating sounds (whistles, vocals or indications) for each of the obstacles that in the case of blind and application development to improve learning for people with cognitive disabilities, also it formulated the possible development of other applications for disability type engine can generate new alternatives to create rehabilitation therapies, linking people with disabilities quadriplegic type for work or other insertion. The results from this research will tend by creating real Kinect-based applications and software.

The creation and generation of research projects contributes to the mission and institutional factors CUN to give compliance with the specific issues that affect the renewal of qualified registration and future with high quality accreditation that finally allows high cohesion between the missional aspects, teachers, and students, social and educational institution. This project generates new knowledge products that allow positioning the AXON group and its allies in the School of Engineering at the national research system. Products generated contribute to the social work of the institution and social responsibility in our country and the world. The results will position the institution as an entity capable of creating new developments and technology at national and international level. The Kinect project facilitates the exchange of researchers and teachers between countries like Japan, Spain and Colombia.

3.1 Identification Technology

In this stage, a review of the current state of it was made; finding a differentiation in the Kinect devices that have been developed by Microsoft.

On the one hand is the first version that was released with the XBOX 360 in 2010; this device while fully recognizes the movements and allows interaction with sound and voice commands; It requires ample space to identify movements and elements, with limited compatibility to software development. On the other hand is the latest version of Kinect to hit the market in late 2014 with the Xbox One console, which besides being much smaller and portable, has a higher degree of accuracy and speed of movements and does not require such a large space as the previous version. In addition to the above, the SDK developed by Microsoft for building software applications, is fully compatible with the device, and has tools that facilitate maximizing the services offered by the Kinect.

3.2 Working with SDK API

Within this stage, it has been identified that the Kinect for Windows SDK in its version 1.8 includes some key features such as:

Background Removal: An API that is downloaded and installed, eliminates the background behind the active user, so that it can be replaced with an artificial background designed by the user. This "green-selection" effect was one of the first requests from users who made the first developments. This service is especially useful for advertising, augmented reality games, training and simulation, and other immersive experiences that put the user in a different virtual environment [8]. Capture realistic color with Kinect Fusion: Another API, the "Kinect Fusion" scans the color of the scene along with the depth information so you can capture the color of the object along with its three-dimensional (3D) model (Fig. 2).

Improved tracking robustness Kinect Fusion: This algorithm makes it easier to scan a scene. With this update, Kinect Fusion is able to maintain its lock on the scene as the camera moves, producing a more reliable and consistent scanning. Shows the interaction HTML: This service allows the implementation of buttons Kinect enabled

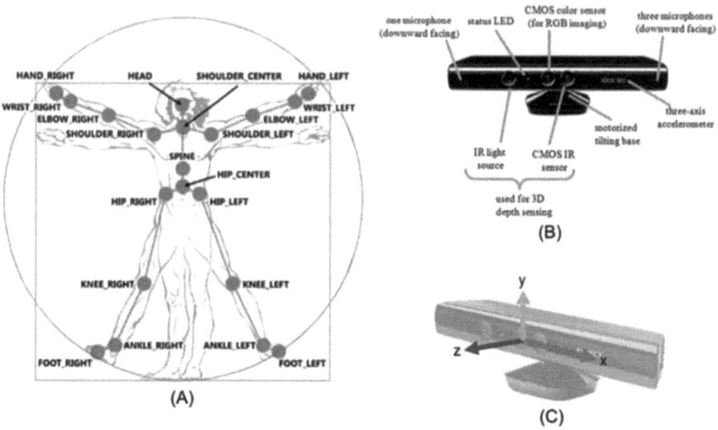

Fig. 2. Kinect description, uses infra-red light and a video camera to 3D map the area in front and a randomized decision tree forest algorithm [7]. (Color figure online)

through a simple user interface, and use of a flow background removal in HTML5. This allows developers to use HTML5 and JavaScript to implement user interfaces compatible with Kinect, which was not previously possible.

Multi-sensor Kinect Fusion: This service allows developers to simultaneously use two sensors to scan a person or object from both sides for a possible construction of a 3D model without having to move the sensor or object.

4 First Software Development Game

According to research conducted in this section we made the first developments are presented and created using Kinect aspects and applications proposals under the Windows operating system [10, 11].

4.1 Example Kinect Sensor Code Testing Game

To start programming the sensor Kinect was necessary to investigate the Microsoft Web page as you must initialize the same for initial testing and commissioning of the project to achieve this is to run the following code provided by Microsoft [10]:

```
namespace
Microsoft.Samples.Kinect.SkeletonBasics
   //namespace Microsoft.esqueleto
   {
       using System.IO;
       using System.Windows;
       using System.Windows.Media;
       using Microsoft.Kinect;

       /// interactua con MainWindow.xaml

       public partial class MainWindow :
Window
       {
           /// redibuja la salida
           private const float RenderWidth =
640.0f;

           /// Height of our output drawing
           private const float RenderHeight =
480.0f;

           /// Thickness of drawn joint lines
           private const double
JointThickness = 3;

           /// Thickness of body center
ellipse
           private const double
BodyCenterThickness = 10;

           /// Thickness of clip edge
rectangles
           private const double
ClipBoundsThickness = 10;

           /// Brush used to draw skeleton
center point
           // 1. private readonly Brush
centerPointBrush = Brushes.Green;
           private readonly Brush
centerPointBrush = Brushes.Black;

                   /// Brush used for drawing
joints that are currently inferred
           // 3. private readonly Brush
inferredJointBrush = Brushes.Yellow;
           private readonly Brush
inferredJointBrush = Brushes.Red;

           /// Pen used for drawing bones
that are currently tracked
          // 2. private readonly Pen
trackedBonePen = new Pen(Brushes.Green, 6);
           private readonly Pen
trackedBonePen = new Pen(Brushes.Black, 6);
                   /// Pen used for drawing
bones that are currently inferred

           private readonly Pen
inferredBonePen = new Pen(Brushes.Gray, 1);
```

```
             /// Active Kinect sensor
             private KinectSensor sensor;
           /// Drawing group for skeleton
rendering output

           private DrawingGroup drawingGroup;
           /// Drawing image that we will display

           private DrawingImage imageSource;
           /// Initializes a new instance of the
MainWindow class.

           public MainWindow()
           {
               InitializeComponent();
           }

           /// Draws indicators to show which
edges are clipping skeleton data
           /// <param name="skeleton">skeleton to
draw clipping information for</param>
           ///                              <param
name="drawingContext">drawing context to draw
to</param>
           private static void
RenderClippedEdges(Skeleton skeleton,
DrawingContext drawingContext)
           {
               if
(skeleton.ClippedEdges.HasFlag(FrameEdges.Bottom)
)
               {
                   drawingContext.DrawRectangle(
                       Brushes.Red,
                       null,
                       new Rect(0, RenderHeight -
ClipBoundsThickness,             RenderWidth,
ClipBoundsThickness));
               }

               if
(skeleton.ClippedEdges.HasFlag(FrameEdges.Top))
               {
                   drawingContext.DrawRectangle(
                       Brushes.Red,
                       null,
                       new Rect(0, 0,
RenderWidth, ClipBoundsThickness));
               }

               if
(skeleton.ClippedEdges.HasFlag(FrameEdges.Right))
               {
                   drawingContext.DrawRectangle(
                       Brushes.Red,
                       null,
                       new Rect(RenderWidth -
ClipBoundsThickness, 0, ClipBoundsThickness,
RenderHeight));
               }
           }
```

The image on the right in Figure Kinect medium body, the sensor detects the points of the head, neck, shoulders, elbows, wrists and hands. With that information we will work to tell the game and sensed data from the Kinect sensor. This forms a ball game which is inserted into the top box and so it is introduced to use a joystick is implemented (Fig. 3).

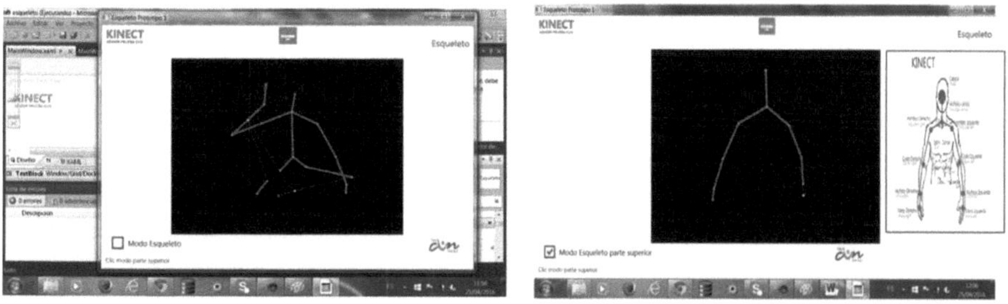

Fig. 3. Game Kinect testing process in laboratory Engineer Systems University. (Color figure online)

4.2 Methodology Desing Game with Kinect

Once the population studied in disability status game design is done based on Kinect, for this the following laboratory tests, based on e-learning are made, we must design a game practice-based learning nicely and motivation that meets the following characteristics:

(a) The teaching-learning skills
(b) Autonomy of the individual disability status
(c) Inductive reasoning
(d) Creativity
(e) Knowledge of basic disciplines.
(f) Requirement Specification (input-output)
(g) Type of game (strategy, memory, clustering agreement)

The methodology used for the design of a game is based on the publication by Luca Galli [12], the author establishes a series of steps to achieve design a game for a development team consisting of programmers, graphic designers and other technical managers of each of the stages [13] (Fig. 4).

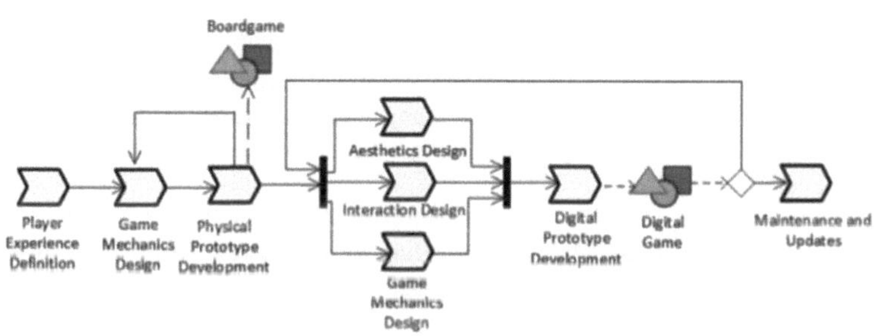

Fig. 4. Game development process, from modeling the guidelines and best practices Fullerton and Galli [12].

5 Conclusion and Future Works

The population status of disability in Colombia is a compelling factor to which is necessary for the government, research institutes, the univerisdades and research groups actively involved with the sole purpose of helping these people to develop as citizens with full use of their rights and enabling a more comprehensive development to make decent work according to their status, to achieve this purpose the use of ingenious developments with the Kinect device which allows you to create custom applications and achieve developments quite useful in pro cognitive development and reintegration at all levels.

References

1. DANE: Información estadística de discapacidad, pp. 1–16, Bogotá, Colombia (2004). http://www.dane.gov.co/files/investigaciones/discapacidad/inform_estad.pdf
2. Vanguardia: 6 de cada 100 colombianos sufren discapacidad física o cognitive. http://www.vanguardia.com/actualidad/colombia/258099-6-de-cada-100-colombianos-sufren-discapacidad-fisica-o-cognitiva
3. Forero, A.: Estudio de antecedentes sobre el tema de discapacidad cognitiva y su legislación, pp. 1–16. Cámara de Representantes (2004). ftp://ftp.camara.gov.co/UATL/eal/028%20Discapacidad%20Cognitiva.pdf
4. Code of Federal Regulations, Title 34, Subtitle B, Chapter III, Section 300. Cornell University (2006). https://www.law.cornell.edu/cfr/text/34/part-300
5. Reid, G.: Learning Disabilities. In: The Future of Children. Spring (1996). https://www.princeton.edu/futureofchildren/publications/docs/06_01_03.pdf
6. DANE, Departamento Administrativo Nacional de Estadística: Localization and characterization of people with disabilities. Bogotá, Colombia. http://www.dane.gov.co/index.php/esp/component/content/article/119-demograficas/discapacidad/2850-discapacidad-por-localidades-bogota
7. McCutcheon, J., Hwang, S., Ying, C., Koontz, A.: The Feasibility Of using kinect for transfer assessment. In: Resna Annual Conference, pp. 1–5 (2014). https://www.resna.org/sites/default/files/conference/2014/Wheelchair%20Seating/Student%20Scientific/McCutcheon.html
8. Clark, R.A., Pua, Y., Fortin, K., Ritchie, C., Webster, K.E.: Validity of the microsoft kinect for assessment of postural control. Gait Posture **36**, 372–377 (2012)
9. Clark, R.A., Pua, Y., Bryant, A.L., Hunt, M.A.: Validity of the microsoft kinect for providing lateral trunk lean feedback during gait retraining. Gait Posture **38**(4), 1064–1066 (2013)
10. Microsoft. Kinect for Windows 1.8, Human interface guidelines v.1.8 (2015). http://go.microsoft.com/fwlink/?LinkID=247735
11. C# Frequently Asked Questions, Start Coding for the Kinect (2012). https://blogs.msdn.microsoft.com/csharpfaq/2012/02/06/start-coding-for-the-kinect/
12. Galli, L.: Matching game mechanics and human computation tasks in games with a purpose. In: Presentation held at ACM Workshop on Serious Games at ACM Multimedia 2014 to Introduce Techniques, Berlin, Heidelberg, New York, pp. 1–50 (2014). http://www.slideshare.net/Leyart1/matching-game-mechanics-and-human-computation-tasks-in-games-with-a-purpose
13. Oksanen, K., Hamalainen, R.: Game mechanics in the design of a collaborative 3D serious game. Simul. Gaming **45**, 255 (2014)

Web Framework for Developing Real Time Applications for Education

Werner Creixell and Cristóbal Ganter(✉)

Universidad Técnica Federico Santa María,
Mercedes 461, Dept. 807, Valparaiso, Chile
cganterh@gmail.com

Abstract. SCALE-UP classrooms are designed to provide an environment for active and collaborative learning. These teaching techniques rely heavily on the collaboration between students, and implementing them in courses with a high number of students is a challenge. Therefore the use of technology is needed.

In this work we have developed a modular education-oriented Web framework that provides: a real time communication infrastructure; a simple access mechanism; a user interface; and positioning and identification of students in the classroom. The framework is primarily (but not exclusively) intended to be used with the mobile devices that the students already have. The whole code is publicly available on the Internet under the GNU Affero General Public License.

On top of this framework, we are developing a set of modules to be used in SCALE-UP classrooms. This whole platform will provide a working environment for the classroom activities and, by monitoring the responses of students, the platform will make possible to identify students with different answers, encouraging discussion and collaboration among them.

Keywords: Active learning · Collaborative learning · Learning catalytics · Open source · Real time interaction · SCALE-UP · Web framework

1 Introduction

The concept "Active Learning" refers in general to all teaching methods in which the students take an active role in their education. "Active learning" has received considerable attention from the research community in education, as there exist evidence that it can produce good results in the student's learning [1,7].

Among the teaching methods that can be classified as "Active Learning" the ones that stand out are: "Interactive learning with real-time response" [8], "Collaborative learning" [5] and "Problem-based learning" [7]. "Interactive learning with real-time response" refers to teaching methods using interactive technology in which students can interact with each other and with the teacher, in real time. "Collaborative learning" corresponds to all teaching methods where

L. Uden et al. (Eds.): LTEC 2016, CCIS 620, pp. 61–74, 2016.
DOI: 10.1007/978-3-319-42147-6_6

students work together with a common goal. Finally, the methods grouped as "Problem-based learning" are those that present a problem at the beginning of each session in order to encourage the active development of the class. The works [1,2,6,8,9] indicate that the use of teaching methods such as "Active Learning" greatly improves participation and student learning. However, this does not mean that traditional teaching methods are not useful.

Sometimes, active learning methods can be difficult to implement, whether because of the high number of students or due to the distribution of furniture in conventional classrooms. These are designed for the current scheme of "presenter" and "public" but are not very useful in a paradigm of active and collaborative learning. An alternative to solve this problem is the use of SCALE-UP classrooms. SCALE-UP is the acronym for "Student-Centered Active Learning Environment With Upside-down Pedagogies" [12]. The SCALE-UP classrooms are environments created to facilitate the use of active learning methods in a workshop-type environment.

Commonly these classrooms have round tables in which students work collaboratively. They seat at each table forming groups, which become learning communities [1]. The Fig. 1 shows a photo of students in a SCALE-UP classroom. The activities that can be performed in such classrooms are: small practical assignments, exercise solving, laboratory activities or problem solving. The teacher is not the center of the class, he/she is dedicated to timely give advice to the students, compare responses of different groups, identify the advanced groups that can help others, etc. In other words, the teacher must constantly interact with students, guiding them, receiving feedback of the progress of the groups and organizing interactions between students.

The emergence of various teaching methods classified as active learning and the development of SCALE-UP classrooms, correspond to a global trend called scientific teaching. This is a pedagogical approach through which teaching and learning are addressed with the same rigor as science itself. This approach formalizes the study of different teaching strategies, which allows real progress in this area. Today scientific teaching uses active learning strategies, and teaching methods that have been tested systematically and have proven effective in various types of student [4].

The situation described above opens the opportunity to develop a framework that could enhance the use of SCALE-UP classrooms by using the newly available real time web technologies. Emphasizing on the use of the smartphones that the majority of the students now owns.

There is a lot of software that aims to support education. Some projects simply try to illustrate concepts on a specific subject. Others focus only on a discipline such as physics, chemistry or language. On the other hand, there exist education management systems. These can cover a variety of needs, such as course management, content management, course enrollment or student evaluation. There's even experimental software that tries new ways of teaching, such as ludification software [3].

Fig. 1. Students in a SCALE-UP classroom at UTFSM [1]

Among the most popular education management systems, the vast majority of them meet the needs of organizing courses and content distribution. These solutions are very similar to the Moodle platform, which in addition to being one of the most popular solutions in this area, stands out for being an open source application.

We have found two applications that aim to support the collaboration within the classrooms (which is the category in which this work is classified).

The first, with less similarity to what is described in this work, is called Plickers. This is a simple tool that allows teachers to collect assessment data in real time, without the need for students to have any device [11]. Plickers allows the students to answer alternatives questions, raising cards printed with codes. The teacher then uses the mobile application to read the codes through the phone's camera and get the answers quickly.

The other, called Learning Catalytics, aims to support the collaboration within the classroom in a broader sense. In general terms, this application has the following functions:

- Communication between students and teacher, during and after class.
- Positioning of students in the classroom.
- Sending activities to the students.
- Students can answer activities directly on their phones.

- It has a “don’t understand” button to indicate that the student does not understand.
- It presents performance statistics from the students.
- Gives the possibility to share the activities written by the teacher with the Learning Catalytics teacher community.
- Create groups of students based on different criteria.

The Learning Catalytics functions are similar to what we want to achieve in this work. However Learning Catalytics is designed for conventional classrooms, is a proprietary solution (not open source), it’s a fixed solution (we want to develop a web framework that can be used to generate real time education applications for a varied range of needs) and, to use it, one must pay a yearly subscription from at least 20 USD per student [10]. Under these conditions, the possibility to modify Learning Catalytics to achieve the objective raised in this paper is discarded.

[1] describes the different factors that were considered when implementing active learning methods at UTFSM, to improve the student’s learning. The relation between these factors is described in Fig. 2. In this paper we added a new factor: real-time mobile Web technology. Our hypothesis is that the addition of this new factor can have a positive influence on the basic abilities developed by the students, the active learning methods used by the professors and the attitude of the students. All of which should improve the student’s learning. The research question we want to address is: how does the mobile Web technology for real-time interaction enhance collaboration and student learning?

In order to explore this question, we first have to develop a flexible and stable tool, that will allow us to implement new real-time Web mobile applications, which then can be tested on real classrooms. Concretely, we have designed a modular Web framework that provides a real time communication infrastructure, an extremely simple access mechanism and a fast and clutter free user interface. On top of our framework we are now developing a set of modules, designed for our University’s SCALE-UP classrooms, which can show the potential of our Web framework. While the design and testing of our solution will be focused in this kind of classrooms, our solution is general enough to be used and adapted to a wide range of uses. This paper, which is part of a bigger work, will focus on the description of our solution. In the upcoming months we plan to test the application, and gather data about the student’s response to this new tool. This upcoming work should be published in further papers.

This is an open source project, which means that the code is openly available to the community, without any copy or modification restrictions. This is usually beneficial for such projects because it increases the likelihood of a community forming around the project, which can maintain and improve it. For this project we have chosen the Affero General Public License. This is a derivative of the GNU General Public License. Both licenses allow commercial use, distribution and modification of the software and require the derivative works to be distributed with the same license as the original work. Any copy, distributed under these licenses, must include the source code of the software.

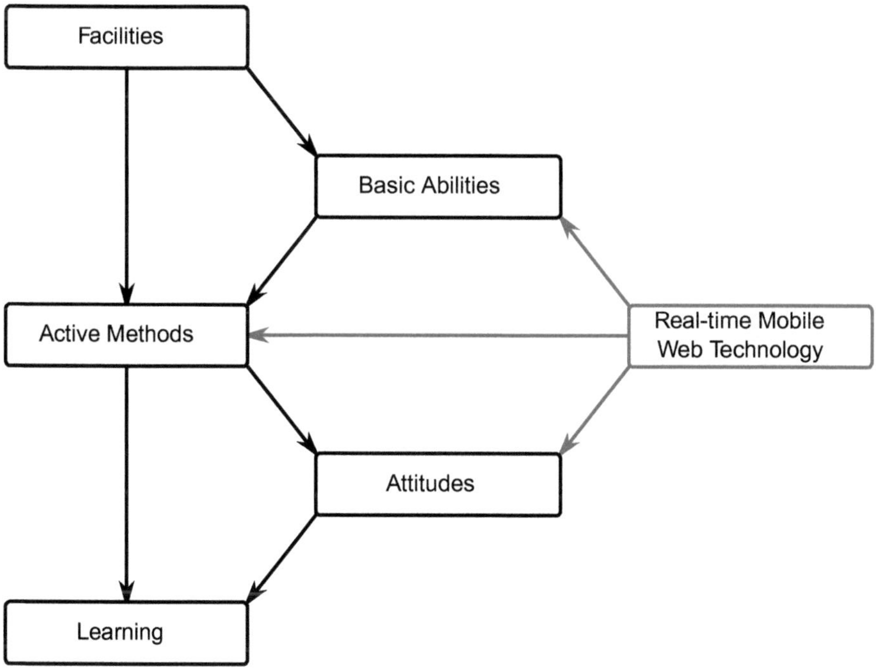

Fig. 2. Relation between factors that were considered when implementing active learning methods at UTFSM [1], the "Real-time Mobile Web Technology" factor was added in this paper

In Sect. 2 we will discuss the context in which our project will be used. To do so, we elaborated a small survey. Next, the architecture of our proposal will be explained. This will be made from different perspectives, ranging from how the internals of the framework are designed, to explaining the access and module architecture. Finally, in "Conclusion and future work", we discuss the actual state of the project and what remains to be done.

2 Context

The first part of this work was to elaborate a survey in order to gather the necessary requirements to start the software development process. We made two types of questions: about preferences regarding the classes and about the use of different technologies. Some questions targeting specifically teachers or students, were added too. The audience that the survey was oriented to, were users of the SCALE-UP classrooms in our University. Therefore it was decided to survey all students and teachers who used this type of classrooms in a period of one week. At the end of the week the number of survey respondents was 609.

Also, a visit to an active learning physics class was made, with the goal of having an approach to the activities that take place in these classrooms.

From the analysis of the survey and the visit to the active learning class, we got the following conclusions:

- The framework must be able to show slideshows and videos.
- Teachers should be able to send assignments to students.
- The agility of the system is a very important attribute, it should be developed with this in mind.
- It is good to allow the anonymity of the students.
- The framework must enable the teachers to better utilize their time in the classroom.
- The framework must be very stable, even if it is necessary to sacrifice some functionality.
- The application should use standards that guarantee correct operation in the modern browsers and future compatibility in the less modern ones.
- The system must be robust to losses of Internet connection.

Finally, a minimum set of modules, that meet the current needs of SCALE-UP classrooms, was designed. These modules will be described in detail in the "Module architecture" section.

3 Proposed System

3.1 Framework Access

The framework was designed in a way that simplifies the access of the users. The goal is being able to enter the application as quick as possible without having to remember a web address. This system consists of QR and/or NFC codes stuck to the tables in the classrooms, one code in front of each seat. When the students scan the code corresponding to their seat with their smartphones, the application starts automatically. In addition, there is a code on the door of the classroom, which should be used by the teacher to open the application and start the class. In the particular case of the NFC codes, opening the application implies the simple gesture of putting the smartphone on the table.

The Fig. 3 shows a diagram of the access system described in the preceding paragraph. The square on the left represents a SCALE-UP classroom, with tables (circles), the QR and/or NFC codes, the smartphones and its door. Each smartphone is connected wirelessly over the network to the server.

The codes store a web address that allows the application to start, knowing the code from which it has been launched. To accomplish this, the web address contained in each code has a unique identifier that consists of five alphanumeric characters. From now on the word "code" will be used to refer to the unique identifier, unless otherwise stated.

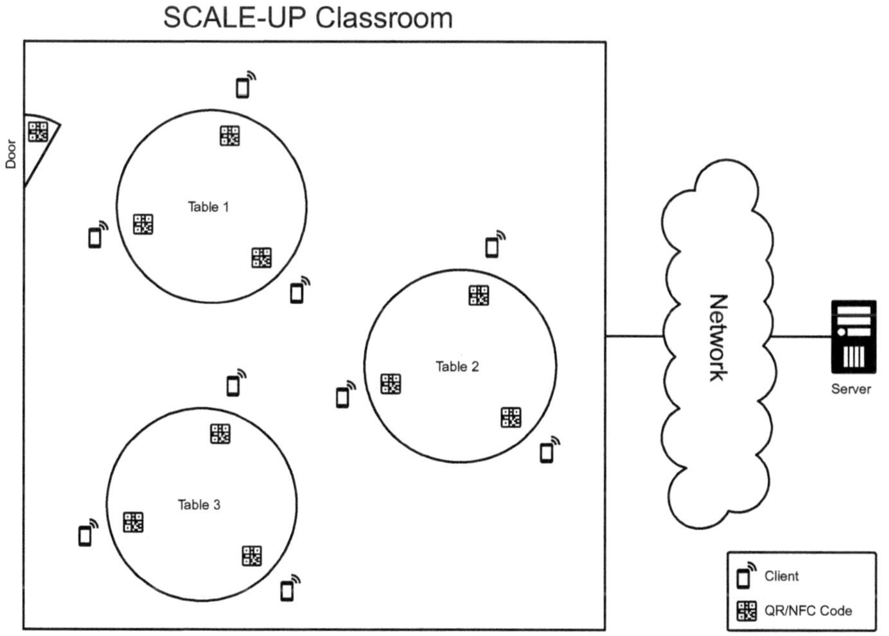

Fig. 3. System access diagram

3.2 General Architecture

The framework architecture is composed of a set of classes and modules that serve different HTTP requests made by the clients. The Fig. 4 shows the general architecture of the framework. The upper block, labeled *Client*, represents the browser used by the users. The cloud, labeled *Internet*, represents the network used to communicate the client with the server, as well as third-party services that may be on that network. All components that are below the *Internet* cloud are part of the server.

The framework works using modules. Each module is a group of classes, having one or more of them. There are three main types of classes that can be part of a module:

`WSClass`. Depicted with the green *COM* labels in the Fig. 4, is a class designed to implement the logic and communication of a module. Each object of this class has access to three communication channels:

- Local Channel. Is a channel that communicates messages between procedures of the server. For each client there is one independent and isolated local channel. This channel is mainly used to communicate the different modules assigned to a client; and to route, filter, and process messages.
- WebSocket Channel. It is a channel used to exchange messages between a client and the server. As with local channels, there is a WebSocket channel for each client, and they are independent and isolated from each other.

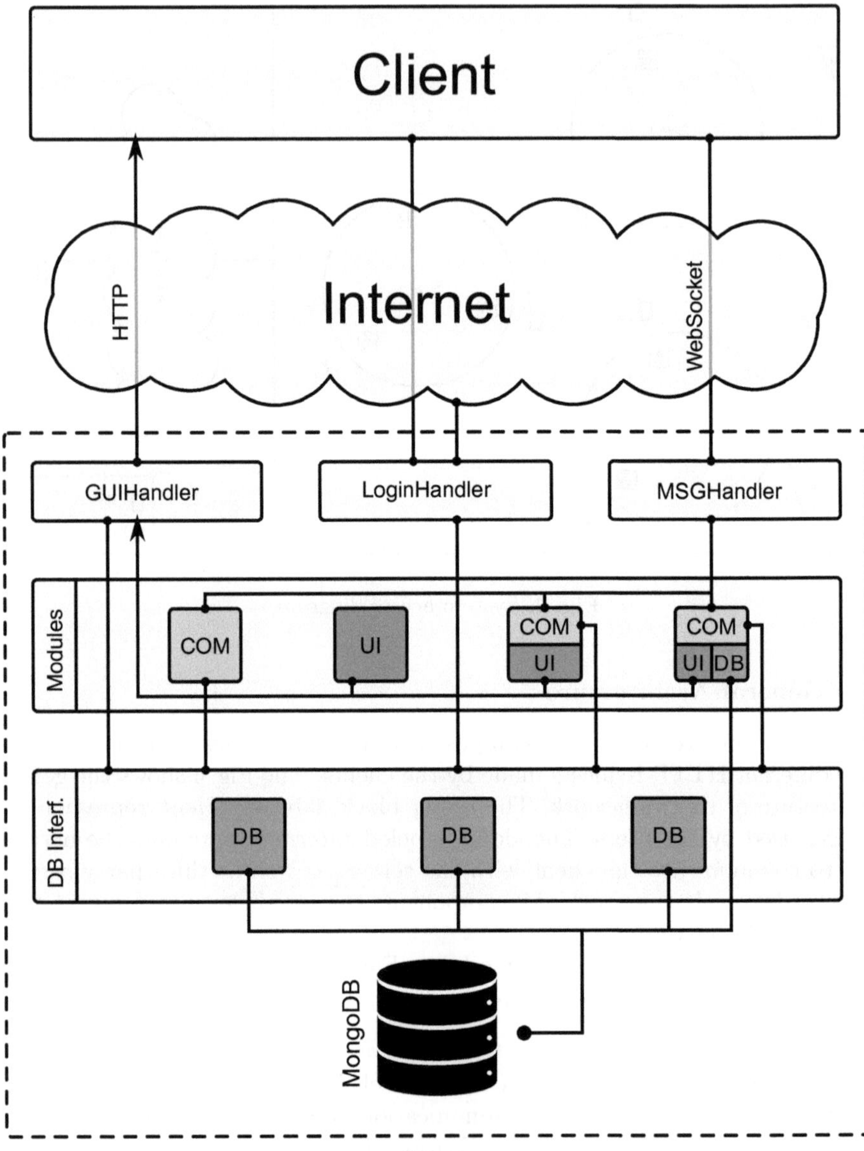

Fig. 4. General framework architecture. The colored squares (*COM*, *UI* and *DB*) are not real modules of the system; they only exemplify various class combinations. (Color figure online)

Database Channel. It is a single channel in which multiple instances of one application can exchange messages. It is possible to run multiple instances of one application in order to horizontally scale the system. In order to coordinate all the instances, so it appears that there is only one of them, it is not only necessary to share the same database, the messages should be shared too. This is achieved using a special collection of the database as a message transmission channel.

Each of these channels can be accessed through an adapter, the `PubSub` class, which standardizes the access to the channel. These adapters exchange messages, created using Python dictionaries, analogously to the JSON objects exchanged in a web application through HTTP. The minimum requirement to send a dictionary through a `PubSub` adapter is that it has to contain the `'type'` key. The object associated to the `'type'` key, usually a text string, aims to identify the format of the other keys in the dictionary. When an object knows the format associated with a message type, it can subscribe its methods to these messages in the `PubSub` adapter and/or send messages with that format through the adapter. Once the adapter receives a message, all methods subscribed to that message type are executed.

The name of this class, `WSClass`, has been kept from the beginning of the project, when these objects only had access to the WebSocket channel. In future versions of the application, this name should be changed to something more descriptive.

`BoilerUIModule`. Depicted with the blue *UI* labels in the Fig. 4. The purpose of this class is to define a graphical component (HTML, CSS and JavaScript) to be inserted into the HTML document that will be sent to a user. This class also facilitates the inclusion of CSS and JavaScript files, to be sent with the HTML document, allowing to store this files independently of the rest of the application. In practice, when a `BoilerUIModule` is used in a module, it is common to implement the module as a package. This way you can store the CSS and JavaScript files within the same directory.

`DBObject`. Depicted with the orange *DB* labels in the Fig. 4, it is a class that allows the access to the documents stored in MongoDB as if they were a Python object. The classes that inherit from `DBObject` have to define the class attribute `coll`. This way it is possible to define the collection in which the documents, associated with this class, should be stored. In addition, instances of this class, work as a cache, keeping data from a document in memory while the instance is being used.

A client can make different kinds of HTTP requests to the framework: empty requests (`/`), code requests (`/7f13x`), authentication requests (`/singin`) or WebSocket connection requests (`/ws`). Depending on the type of request, the client is served by an instance of `GUIHandler`, `LoginHandler` or `MSGHandler`. These three classes, which will be explained in the following paragraphs, are represented in the Fig. 4 right under the *Internet* cloud. And they are the interface through which the server communicates with the client. Thus, empty requests and code requests (`/` and `/11bs8`) are served by instances of `GUIHandler`; authentication requests (`/singin`) are served by instances of `LoginHandler`; and WebSocket connection requests (`/ws`) are served by instances of `MSGHandler`.

The purpose of `GUIHandler` is to send the front-end to the client. There are three ways in which you can load the front-end in the client: as a teacher, as a student or "none" (meaning that the user does not participate in any class and does not take a role of student or teacher). The way the front-end is loaded depends on the request:

- If the request is a code request and the code is associated with a classroom, the teacher's front-end is loaded.
- If the request is a code request and the code is associated with a seat, the student's front-end is loaded.
- If the request is an empty request, the "none" front-end is loaded.

To send the front-end, it is first necessary to build it using the `BoilerUIModule` classes defined in the application modules. The classes that are used depend on how you want to load the front-end and this in turn depends on the type of request and the code used. The process is represented in the Fig. 4 with the arrows that enter and leave the `GUIHandler` block. These connections are the only ones with arrows, indicating the direction in which information flows from the modules through `GUIHandler` and to the client.

The front-end of the framework is mainly composed of panels and indicators. Panels can load graphic components in the main section of the framework. While indicators can only load graphic components on the right side of the header.

Once the front-end is loaded, it is verified whether there is a session identifier in that client. If the session identifier does not exist, the `HomeLockingPanel` is shown. This panel contains the title of the application and a welcome message. It also provides a button to authenticate the user using a Google account. The result of authentication is a session identifier.

When the user presses the Google authentication button, an authentication request is sent (`/signin`) to `LoginHandler`. Using the data sent with the request, `LoginHandler` redirects the client to a Google authentication page. After the authentication, the client sends a code generated by Google to `LoginHandler`. With this code, `LoginHandler` can access the user's data, create a new session identifier, sign the session identifier with the secret assigned to the user and send it to the client. Once the new session identifier is stored in the client, the client makes a new request to `GUIHandler`. This time, the front-end will find the session identifier, and instead of showing the `HomeLockingPanel`, a loading panel is displayed and the process of creating a new WebSocket connection is started.

When the front-end is loaded in the client, and there is already a session identifier, the front-end sends a WebSocket connection request. This request is served by an instance of `MSGHandler`. When a `MSGHandler` instance is created, this also creates an instance of the `WSClass` of each module of the application. In this way, the graphic component of each module in the front-end, can communicate with its counterpart in the server through the new WebSocket channel.

The first message that is exchanged through the WebSocket channel is of type `'session.start'`, and contains the session identifier and the code used to load the application. In this way, the user, his/her role (student teacher or none) and the user's location, are associated with that instance of `MSGHandler`. If all data sent with the `'session.start'` message is correct, and the session identifier has not expired, the message is answered with a message of type `'session.start.ok'`. Otherwise, it is answered with the message type `'logout'`, which forces the front-end to remove the session identifier from the client and to close the WebSocket connection.

The instances of `GUIHandler`, `LoginHandler` and `WSClass` use several objects of the database interface layer (block with the *DB Interf* label in the Fig. 4). Some of these objects, to give an example, belong to the `Course`, `User` and `Room` classes. All of them are subclasses of `DBObject`. In addition, as already mentioned, the application modules can define their own `DBObject` sub-classes, in order to define new collections in the database. The new sub-classes of `DBObject` can be registered at the database interface layer, so they can be used from other modules. They can also stay privately within the module, depending on the desired implementation.

3.3 Module Architecture

The architecture that is described in the previous section, allows the design of module groups and their relationships in an abstract way. The set of modules shown in Fig. 5 was designed using the previously obtained requirements. There are two service modules: *Presentation* and *Remote Control*. Both modules provide a service to other modules.

The *Presentation* module is a panel that can display content in full screen. One can display any HTML element on it, whether it is text, images, videos, simulations or games.

The *Remote Control* module allows other modules to display buttons. Its aim is to provide a panel from which you can access the most important functions of the application.

The *Slideshows* module can load slides in different formats into the system. It uses the *Presentation* module to display a slideshow file. It also uses the *Remote Control* module to instantiate buttons that can be used to control the presentation. The *Slideshows* module will be loaded in the client only when the user is a teacher. It is also possible to display a slideshow on a computer while the smartphone is used as a remote control.

Finally, by using the services provided by the *Alternatives* module, the *Slideshows* module allows to send questions to the students. In addition, it is possible to display the results of the questions in the *Presentation* module, using a button instantiated in the *Remote Control* module.

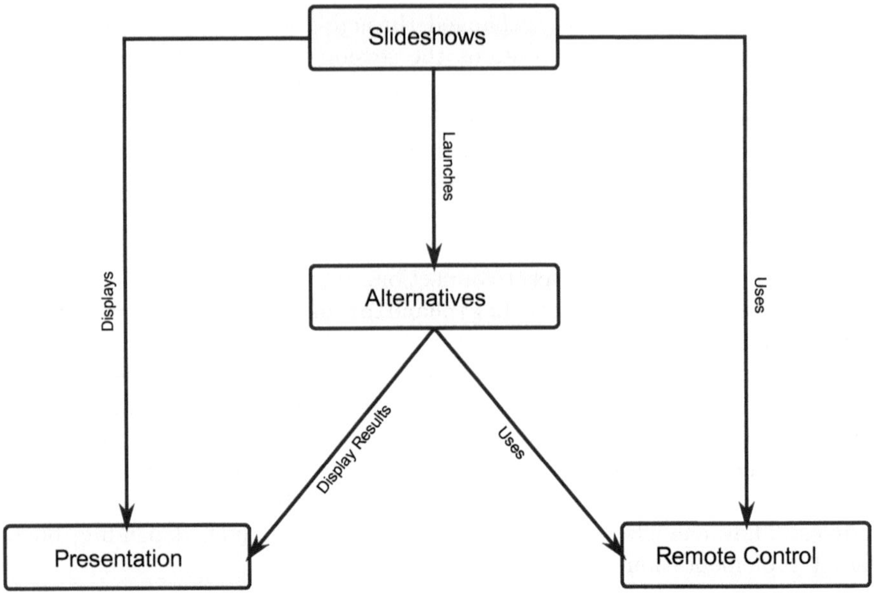

Fig. 5. Module architecture diagram. The arrows show how the different modules relate to each other.

There is a set of system modules that has not been mentioned and does not appear in the Fig. 5. These are:

- Courses
- Router
- Critical
- Home
- Lesson Setup
- Loading
- Student Setup
- Connection Indicator
- Don't Understand
- User

These modules provide system functions and part of the user interface, but they are not of major importance in regard to what the application can do.

4 Conclusion and Future Work

During development of this work the project has grown to become a robust framework, dedicated to the development of tools for collaboration within the classroom and in real time. The actual value is not only in the user modules, but also in the ability to provide an open environment where new modules can be developed depending on the needs of the community.

A considerable amount of time has been invested on the scalability and robustness of the core architecture. Which is reliable, easy to use and has few barriers to adoption among users.

Because of the self-contained nature of the modules, the development of new ones is a simple task. It also helps the automatic documentation system and the CLI, both included with the framework. In the framework's CLI one can execute common commands and inject code while the application is running, making the debugging process easier.

Today the application has the necessary modules to create and use courses and presentations. However much remains to be done:

- New modules should be developed to complement existing ones. Such as the questions module, students communication modules or modules that can integrate the framework with other services.
- Currently the *Slideshows* module supports a single presentation format. However, this module is extensible, being able to easily write new parsers for different file types. It would be good to add a few more parsers to this module.
- The ratio of documentation lines to code lines is currently 0.24. Which is still very low, being desirable a ratio of more than 1.
- New question types should be added in order to take advantage of the mobile devices. The types of questions that could be implemented are: drawing, selecting areas in images, numerical questions, etc.
- Details should be adjusted in some existing modules, such as: add buttons to remove presentations and courses, and automatically update the list of courses in the student view.

References

1. Aizman, A., Alarcón, H.: Modelo Integrador para una Docencia que Promueve el Aprendizaje Activo en Primer Año de Ingeniería en la UTFSM. Viña de Mar, Chile (2013)
2. Deslauriers, L., Schelew, E., Wieman, C.: Improved learning in a large-enrollment physics class. Science **332**, 862–864 (2011). doi:10.1126/science.1201783
3. Hamari, J., Koivisto, J., Sarsa, H.: Does gamification work? - A literature review of empirical studies on gamification. In: 2014 47th Hawaii International Conference on System Sciences, pp. 3025–3034. IEEE (2014)
4. Handelsman, J.: EDUCATION: scientific teaching. Science **304**, 521–522 (2004). doi:10.1126/science.1096022
5. Johnson, D.W., Johnson, R.T., Smith, K.A.: Cooperative learning returns to college what evidence is there that it works? Change Mag. Higher Learn. **30**, 26–35 (1998). doi:10.1080/00091389809602629
6. Pejcinovic, B.: Application of active learning in microwave circuit design courses. Atlanta, USA (2013)
7. Prince, M.: Does active learning work? A review of the research. J. Eng. Educ. **93**, 223–231 (2004). doi:10.1002/j.2168-9830.2004.tb00809.x

8. Tsai, F.S., Natarajan, K., Ahipasaoglu, S.D., et al.: From Boxes to bees: active learning in freshmen calculus. In: 2013 IEEE Global Engineering Education Conference (EDUCON), pp. 59–68. IEEE, Berlin (2013)
9. Tsai, F.S., Yuen, C., Cheung, N.-M.: Interactive learning in pre-university mathematics. In: 2012 IEEE International Conference on Teaching, Assessment and Learning for Engineering (TALE), pp. T2D-8–T2D-13. IEEE (2012)
10. Learning Catalytics. https://learningcatalytics.com/pages/pricing. Accessed 22 Mar 2016a
11. Plickers. https://plickers.com/. Accessed 22 Mar 2016b
12. SCALE-UP Site. http://scaleup.ncsu.edu/. Accessed 22 Mar 2016c

Learning Tools and Environment

Proposal of a Standard Architecture of IoT for Smart Cities

July Katherine Díaz Barriga(✉), Christian David Gómez Romero, and José Ignacio Rodríguez Molano

Universidad Distrital Francisco José de Caldas, Bogotá, Colombia
julykdiazb@gmail.com, dagoro06@gmail.com,
jirodriguez@udistrital.edu.co

Abstract. The Internet of Things (IoT) makes reference to the interconnection between different devices and internet; in the last years has been studied its development, impact and improvement, to answer to common needs of society, its requirements and to the kind of applications that demands to be developed. That contributes largely to the technology development and hence also to the growth of the cities. Nevertheless, so far applications just reply to particular necessities, so it is important to know how its structure can be developed to attend to the general requirements of cities to become those into Smart Cities, without affecting their correct performance. This paper aims to show a proposal of a standard IoT architecture for Smart Cities done from author's research, review and analysis of available data, especially of generic and implemented structures in some Smart Cities around the world.

Keywords: Internet of Things (IoT) · Smart City · Architecture · Applications · Cloud Computing

1 Introduction

Nowadays, the Internet of Things is a term increasingly related to our daily life and that is positioning as one of the leading technologies, thanks to that it has the potential for significantly influencing in everything we do and in how we interact with all around us. In this way IoT aims to transform traditional cities into Smart Cities focusing on the management's manners the diverse areas that compose it [1].

Internet of Everything's original idea was to design a network that gives to each physical object a label or sensor (e.g. Radio Frequency Identification - RFID label or Near Field Communication - NFC sensor) which serves as identifier of the object in a global network, allowing to be connected in any moment and to interact with other devices [2–5]. In this way, it is possible monitoring any kind of relation that users suggest like health care and energy waste, among others. The Internet of Things is not use just to make reference to the global network of smart devices, but it also includes the set of need technologies as well as the group of applications and services that take advantage of this kind of technologies [6].

It is worth mentioning that IoT's applications not just aim to be directed to an individual final user but those look for guarantee the vital lines of the Smart Cities, it

L. Uden et al. (Eds.): LTEC 2016, CCIS 620, pp. 77–89, 2016.
DOI: 10.1007/978-3-319-42147-6_7

means the assurance of the normal operation of the vital systems of the city [7] like the water and energy supply, fire alarms, the correct functioning of specialized processing and production companies, among others [8]. In this way, there have been developed many applications making use of technologies, for example sensors incorporated in cars and integrated in smartphones to lead drivers to the nearest parking place and the smart publicity which integrates RFID labels, as can be seen across United States [9].

Currently, business models have been adapted gradually with the Internet of Thing's technologies in the Smart Cities environments due to the high scope that is offered by the different domains since in logistics, security, public lighting, traffic control, health care [10] and smart buildings as in China, Korea and Japan [1]. In order to create value and improve its financial benefits draw front its production development [3], automated monitoring of devices and task management [11], including information flow and data interchange.

There are each time more research efforts to resolve the challenges impose by the Internet of things in terms of security, privacy, storage and confidence towards the devices and to the information management, that is why in this paper is going to be explore the future challenges that IoT technologies pretend to solve in the Smart Cities. It should be made clear that some problems of users' adaptation are being treated in an integral focus like the implemented by the UPECSI (User-driven Privacy Enforcement for Cloud-based Services in the Internet of Things) [12] or the storage problems that are trying to solve through the study of integration paradigms between the IoT and the Cloud Computing, that receive the name of Cloud IoT paradigms [7].

2 Methodology

According to the research objective, available data (findings from research) have been studied to give the next order to the investigation. First of all, the paper presents a short introduction to know the importance of Internet of Things. After that, there is a conceptualization about IoT meaning and the development of its architectures, making emphasis in which are the vital components of it and following the done proposals by some authors, correctly cited in this document. The next sections show a proposal of a standard architecture done from the review of different authors' prototypes in order to solve problems of integration of technologies and of information for the development of applications, which are its possible problems and challenges, then authors' proposals and the concluding remarks are defined.

3 Conceptualization

3.1 Internet of Things (IoT)

This term refers to the identifiable physical objects connected to internet [13], as new technologies like Information Technologies (IT), the IoT has many paradigms that envisions near future [14] in which with a global infrastructure can be offered many services by interconnecting virtual and physical things (from life things to sophisticated devices [15]) based on the interoperability of Information and Communication Technologies (ICT) [16]. The IoT's concept was coined by Kevin Ashton in 1999 [17–19], when the viewpoint of a broader device to device communication became a reality [2]. It can be defined too as a self-organizing system of unfettered devices providing converged systems that pretend to improve the efficiency [20] of the information management.

3.2 IoT Objectives

The applications of IoT are built to solve problems and necessities by the integration of some pairs of elements that guarantee the following basis (Fig. 1):

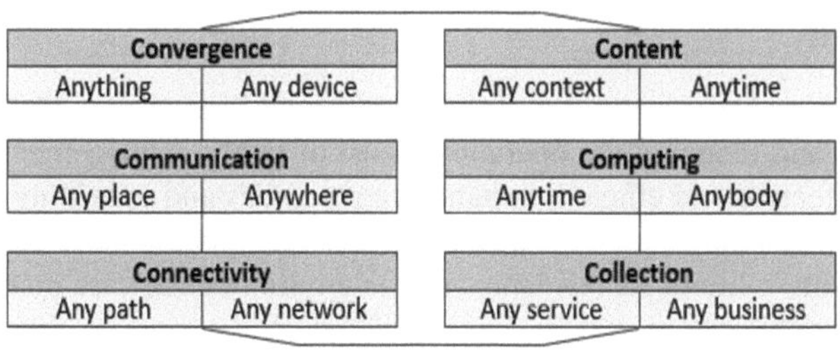

Fig. 1. .Internet of Things objectives. [21, 22]

As expressed in the figure above, there are seven main objectives which are dependable of two characteristics (each one) that look for coverage in all available way to get a correct management of the information. In this manner, it is possible to get IoT structures that allow to solve from common to specialized problems, as can be appreciated in Europe [23], UK and Canada [24], among others [25].

3.3 IoT General Framework

As mentioned before the Internet of Things main idea is to interconnect devices to internet, according to that authors established the next basis for the framework:

Users. They are the reason why informatics systems are needed, given that they provide the information and in the IoT framework directly or indirectly they are the final link when they receive processed (new and classified) data [15].

Devices. Through incorporated technologies those are the physical medium to give and get information, thanks to devices it is possible not just to live connected but also communicated.

Technologies. There are many ways to read the information and get real data, some of those are the sensors used to monitoring the environment [26], labels like RFID and some smart systems such as PLC (Programmable logic controller) and MES (Manufacturing Execution System) [22].

Storage. Given by the cloud, because of its directly relation with the Internet of Things, it receives the name of "IoT Cloud" or "Internet Computing". Defining Cloud Computing as unlimited storage, compute and network capabilities to provide elastic runtime infrastructure for IoT systems [27], its power settle down in that allows to users to drive the information wherever and in any time [28].

Processing and Classification. Big Data is the way to manage the information, this term refers to a large scale of complex data originated from different sources that exceed the capabilities of traditional data processing technologies [29]. Its principal objective is to look for the exploration of data in almost real time and the efficient extraction of useful data for practical uses [28] as is required by IoT implementation for the Smart Cities.

3.4 Smart City

It is the city that makes a better use of public resources, increasing the services quality for the citizens and reducing the operational cost of public management [14]. Its main goal is to be effective and efficient at handling resources and providing services to the citizens [30]. Thus a Smart City is a place that seeks to integrate necessary technologies to improve quality's life of its residents and the environmental care making the correct use of different resources.

3.5 IoT Development in Smart Cities

There are not exactly dates about when was implanted the Internet of Everything in a Smart City, the available data do not allow to determine how was given that. Nevertheless, both concepts aim to the same general objective that is continuous evolution. The IoT as mentioned before was named and started to work in 1999 and the Smart City's concept began is development around the 1990's [30], so it means that one goes hand in hand with the other. The IoT platforms for Smart Cities has been developed round about public services like energy, water, air quality and transportation (traffic) among others [30, 31]. The IoT vision for Smart Cities is to improve the 'liv-ability', given by six principals that are transportation choices, expand location and energy efficient, improve economic competitiveness of neighborhoods, target federal funding, align federal polices and funding and enhance exclusive characteristics of the communities through investment [16].

3.6 IoT Applications in Smart Cities

Some authors and entities like Pike [32], Gathner [33] and Forbes [34], deem that for 2020 there are going to be more than 50 billion of devices with IoT technology and that the Smart City sector is going to reach several hundred of billion dollars, which means that this area is going to have an important growth and technological development that provide information from multiple heterogeneous systems [2], allowing the generation of new services and aiming to get a synergistic connection with the industry and the environment. Different kind of applications developed for the Smart Cities include in their programming the use of Information and Communication Technologies (ICT) [17] such as the integration of IoT with Cloud Computing (CC) [12] in their development. As shown in Table 1, there is a classification given by the nature of the apps and the trends on emerging technologies.

Table 1. Classification of applications for Smart Cities

Application classification	
Smart lighting	Noise monitoring
Automation and salubrity of public buildings	Waste management
Smart parking	Structural health of buildings
City energy consumption	Surveillance cameras
Traffic control	Centralized and integrated system control

According with Table 1, adapted of [26, 14], some of the applications with high impact and influence on the Smart Cities are going to be explained bellow:

Smart Lighting. It rises up from the need of reaching the optimal and efficient usage of the public lighting resources available in the city [14], through the use of sensors that point during the day, illumination requirements given by the traffic and citizen transit [35], just as intelligent solutions like the adaptable street lighting [36].

Noise Monitoring. An urban IoT application that offers tracking service and data analysis of different sources of noise. The measurements generate adaptive maps that represent the affected areas by this kind of contamination in real time [14], it also detects the principal sources and the negative effects in local areas [37].

Surveillance Cameras. It has become in a need for company and manufacture buildings as well as any private or public place that demand this kind of security's monitoring, in order to track any questionable activity. Nowadays, it is one of the applications with more problems in its development due to users refuse about the violation of their privacy [6].

4 IoT Architecture for Smart Cities

4.1 IoT Architecture Development for Smart Cities

According to the architectures studied, there can be said that platforms look for solving specific problems and aim to pay more attention on connectivity and livelihood services [38]. Then, the architecture development can't be define in a clear way, but there can be stated that it started when the IoT applications focused on resolve public problems and in to do an efficient usage of the Information and Communication Technologies.

4.2 Development Sectors of Architecture

Below development sectors are described according to developed applications in some Smart Cities, the next categories were given by authors of the present paper aiming to establish an integral proposal that allow to cover the general needs of cities in process to become in Smart Cities:

E-Government. The IoT platform should encompass all relevant areas that are possible, it requires of information relevance to stave of 'information island' effect and ensure network and data security [22]. E-government strategies try to attend city's necessities giving security about all applicable data for government systems as well as transactions available for citizens and employees.

Public Services. Urban IoT implementation for Smart Cities looks for the optimization of traditional public services [14], which cover a wide variety of citizens' needs, however the applications cover three important services: Energy supply and demand [23], with the monitoring of the whole city to know the requirements for public lighting, traffic, control cameras among others [14]. Water supply as mentioned in [25, 31, 39] through smart waste management [23], studying the variation of data in real time for traffic flow [24, 31] and Natural gas [40] supply systems [41].

Public Safety. Systems in this area propose to support real-time monitoring and respond to disaster events [38] or accidents [42], in order to improve life quality [13].

Health Services. It represents the most outstanding application field, whereby IoT adoption has been harnessed to create mechanism for ensuring privacy of personal and sensitive information [6]. There have been developed multiple applications like Tele-HealthCare [3] and e-Health services (fall detection, medical fridges, sportsmen care, patients surveillance, ultraviolet radiation [16] and Healthcare for elders [13]). Some potential applications are triage, patient and personnel monitoring, disease spread modeling and containment real-time status and predicted information to assist practitioners in the field, policy decisions [17], among others.

Business Implementation of ICT. Different applications are developed in this area, responding to business demand from private and public sector, the IoT applications on this area seek to integrate Information and Communication Technologies to companies and enterprises for reducing costs, focusing on three areas among which are telecommunications, internet and industry business models [43]. Applications are developed around companies and enterprises as shown in Fig. 2.

Traffic Mobility. With applications like Smart Parking (to reduce air pollution and the time of drivers to find a parking place) [44] and Smart Traffic (to enable citizens and visitors to get access to urban mobility and transportation resources) [42]. The purpose of a traffic condition quantifier and this kind of applications is to quantify roads' status [45] to know about traffic jams and accidents [46], also to know about the best routes to get into a specific place [24], new public transport routes [47], environ-mental conditions and some other areas of interest for citizens and visitors.

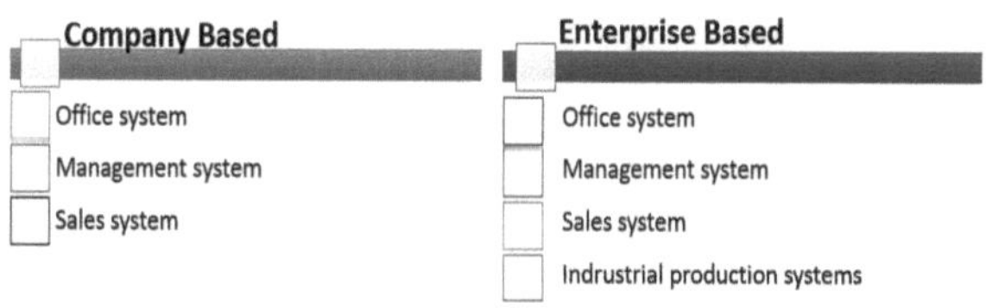

Fig. 2. IoT platforms for business. Adaptation from [22]

Smart Building and Areas. This is one of the most well-known IoT applications and many innovative ideas are being developed in order to guarantee buildings security, in this way buildings may be insulated against noise [37], excess lighting and other important factors. The Smart Home or Buildings focus on automation (e.g. Building access by e-cards [1]), using sensors built into building infrastructure to control different building subsystems like smart lighting, smart thermostats and number of occupants [41] and to guide first responses in emergencies and disaster scenarios [17].

Another important application to name are the Intelligent Building Management Systems which as Public buildings look for monitoring energy usage behavior [21, 25] with the objective to minimize the consumption and carry out its rational use [47].

4.3 Architecture Characteristics

After doing a strict review of the studied architectures, there are some really important elements that authors consider decisive in the IoT architecture's work to get a real growth in the Smart Cities:

Sensing. An IoT architecture based on sensing improves the energy efficiency and allows the dynamic utilization of sensors based on the context [48], if sensors do good readings and if those are in programmed time intervals, the information flow is not going to be interrupted.

Communication. IoT pretends to interconnect users with devices, devices with devices and users with users that is why authentication process and network formatting occur simultaneously to ensure a secure IoT communication [49].

Connectivity. The systems' design should be characterized by complex and unpredictable interactions between highly heterogeneous resources, which provide programing abstractions that allow developers to balance the consistency and flexibility of connectivity [50] allowing safe and efficient solutions to get secure access to information.

Information Flow. The correct use of technologies aim to achieve a flexible resource matching and an efficient flow control [51], given the quantity of data IoT solutions should ensure right flow of the different kind of information.

Privacy and Security. The architecture has a great impact with the involved stakeholders, because of the information management requires the protection of personal and private information [52].

5 IoT Architecture for Smart Cities

Following the analysis, in Fig. 3; there has been identified the general characteristics of different IoT's architectures proposed for the Smart Cities, which allowed to establish a general framework (as shown in Sect. 3) that collected the most relevant information in links which are going to compound the proposal architecture, as well as to determine the different intermediary actors (users, enterprises, governments, etc.), that are going to make possible the design of applications or services in the areas mentioned above (in Sect. 4). The information flow goes from user to the interested sectors as shown in the proposal architecture, being users - the main source of data, devices - the collecting media, technologies - the transfer media, storage - the keeping media, information management - the way to manage, classify and organize data and applications sector's - the final destination of the platform to generate new applications under a scheme that allow to integrate data for the sustainable development of Smart Cities. The proposal architecture establishes the necessary links to develop an app with a standard that can allow future integrations of software and erase or reduce the gap of compatibility, given that if applications follow a similar structure, studies of integration in the different processes of information management could be developed easier than with the current independent architectures.

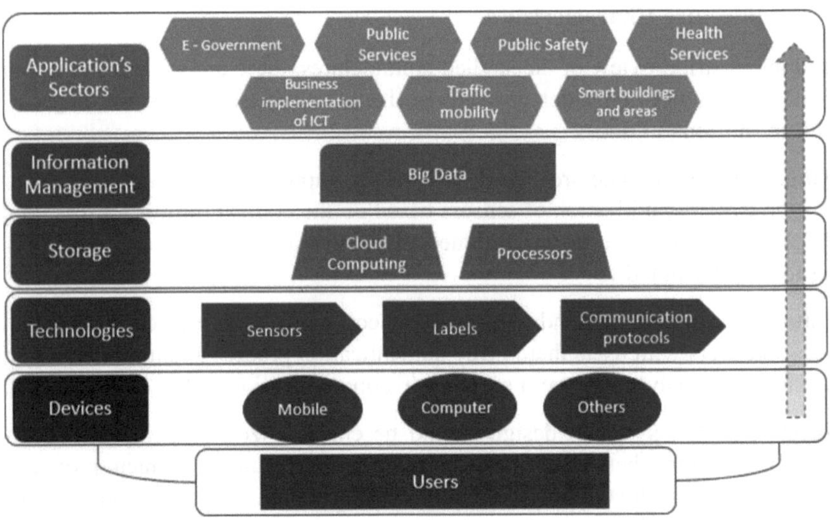

Fig. 3. IoT proposal architecture for Smart Cities

6 Architecture Developments

It is clear that technologies developed increasingly have a greater impact in the world, wherein problems require of emergent technologies like IT and IoT to solve issues that involve interconnections between humans and machines. Currently the Internet of

Things is generating different initiatives on the part of research organizations, industries and even the government to face the challenge of strengthening and improve the scope of their business environment to a global market [1, 10], being an important stimulus facilitator for the modern economy, through investments and the strategic development of industry [22]. The major challenges which have to be faced by the development of the Smart City are in the field of human condition such as development factor and some technologic implementation aspects named by other authors [26]. In accordance with the above, this section discuss the main present and future challenges that the Smart City aims to solve in technical and management terms:

Principal Worries. How to store, manage and process the data? Who will do it and what is the cost? With which mediums and value will be added to the information? These and many others are the questions that come up due to high growth in data generation and who is going to manage it. The development of IoT in partnership with the Cloud Computing open the discussion about the data handling, due to there is going to arise diverse services and new business opportunities. Currently the Smart City has its main problems in processing, storage and property (privacy) of data, and in the general framework of its architectures, on which its applications will be designed allowing the autonomous adaptability of raw data [53].

Standardization. From a perspective of regulation, users demand an internal control of organizations in order to keep a limited access to the collected information to third parties and to establish higher levels of security for private data that can be delivered or misused in purposes that were not foreseen and previously unauthorized [12, 54]. The lack of standards is considered a big trouble of the CloudIoT inasmuch as currently most of the devices are connected to the cloud using internet based interfaces [7], but there is not a general standard shared in its architecture.

It is easy to understand that companies recognize in data an added value for marketing strategies and the development of other departments like design, communications and sales among others, and that is why users stand for the protection their information to avoid the violation of their privacy and human rights.

Privacy. Society generally shares basic information such as dates of birth, income, comments on social networks, addresses of residence, but this sharing experience changes when information is generalized and a wide range of organizations can gain access to the data that users considers private and that could be irrelevant for the development of company studies, as an example there are the monitoring of eating habits, travel itinerary, health care expenses and debts. Consequently, people in their daily lives will be immersed in an Internet network without perceiving it, since direct or indirect interactions with Smart Objects will generate valuable data. From this perspective arise several questions that must be studied in the future, like until when society is going to allow to be controlled by devices? [54]. Does the society need to be monitored to ensure its vital line? And should data be available to all citizens for their respective monitoring? While the development of Smart Cities is gaining impulse through its intelligent systems, necessarily the trust and the acceptance of IoT by users is going to depend on the privacy's protection [5].

Security. It is known that Smart Cities' development improve the prospective and the productivity of companies and the living standard of people [5], but at the same time increase the risk to get attacked by hackers and/or cybercrimimals; in this regards security should guarantee that users have a private access to their sensitive data [12], to avoid thefts or improper manipulation, reason why investigations aim to study multiple goal scenarios, software and informatics platforms with maintenance's services or control of platforms [7], delivering reliability to users [12].

Technology. In this field, IoT pretends to overcome the limited energy efficiency of devices [55], such as reduce the heterogeneity of the architectures in development. Technology represents a challenge given that, with its proper use can improve the information flow, the monitoring for devices with low battery, the management of data in real-time (cloud, big data and data mining) and the compatibility among the developed architectures which is nor a reality today [7].

7 Concluding Remarks

The Internet of Things has obtained a great impact worldwide since the concept of globalization gave way to the integration as a vital factor for the development and evolution of societies. In search to that integration, the IoT has studied the different relations between devices and users to understand how to do the management of information, the problem on this area do not arise exactly from the challenges or complications presented in developed platforms, those come too from the lack of unification in the links of architectures and in their programming.

Following the study, the authors evaluated many architectures as presented before to generate a patron platform for the IoT in the Smart Cities, aiming to get an optimal design to give answer to cities general needs. Essential links were identified for the general framework such as their components and the order of the structure was given, according to the proposal architectures of other authors and to the information flow of systems, being the users the source of information and receiver of the resulting applications, and possible challenges were determined in order to show that the proposal architecture of the present paper seeks to be a model of standardization from the developed frameworks in pro of a thinkable integration of software and programming to generate compatibility in systems for the development of applications the IoT in future Smart Cities.

References

1. Borgia, E.: The internet of things vision: key features, applications and open issues. Comput. Commun. **54**, 1–31 (2014)
2. Efremov, S., Pilipenko, N., Voskov, L.: An integrated approach to common problems in the Internet of Things. Procedia Eng. **100**, 1215–1223 (2015)
3. Dijkman, R.M., Sprenkels, B., Peeters, T., Janssen, A.: Business models for the Internet of Things. Int. J. Inf. Manage. **35**(6), 672–678 (2015)

4. Nguyen, K.T., Laurent, M., Oualha, N., Weinberg, B.D., Milne, G.R., Andonova, Y.G., Hajjat, F.M.: Survey on secure communication protocols for the Internet of Things. Bus. Horiz. **58**(6), 17–31 (2015)
5. Lee, I., Lee, K.: The Internet of Things (IoT): applications, investments, and challenges for enterprises. Bus. Horiz. **58**(4), 431–440 (2015)
6. Miorandi, D., Sicari, S., De Pellegrini, F., Chlamtac, I.: Internet of things: vision, applications and research challenges. Ad Hoc Netw. **10**(7), 1497–1516 (2012)
7. Botta, A., de Donato, W., Persico, V., Pescapé, A.: Integration of cloud computing and Internet of Things: a survey. Futur. Gener. Comput. Syst. **56**, 684–700 (2015)
8. Tran, T., Ha, Q.P.: Dependable control systems with Internet of Things. ISA Trans. **59**, 303–313 (2015)
9. Erguler, I.: A potential weakness in RFID-based Internet-of-things systems. Pervasive Mob. Comput. **20**, 115–126 (2015)
10. Glova, J., Sabol, T., Vajda, V.: Business models for the Internet of Things environment. Procedia Econ. Financ. **15**(14), 1122–1129 (2014)
11. Alvi, S.A., Afzal, B., Shah, G.A., Atzori, L., Mahmood, W.: Internet of multimedia things: vision and challenges. Ad Hoc Netw. **33**, 87–111 (2015)
12. Henze, M., Hermerschmidt, L., Kerpen, D., Häußling, R., Rumpe, B., Wehrle, K.: A comprehensive approach to privacy in the cloud-based Internet of Things. Futur. Gener. Comput. Syst. **56**, 701–718 (2015)
13. Ma, J.: IoT: Technology Evolution and Challenges. IEEE Conf. Publitations (2014)
14. Zanella, A., Bui, N., Castellani, A., Vangelista, L., Zorzi, M.: Internet of Things for smart cities. IEEE Internet Things J. **1**(1), 22–32 (2014)
15. Benazzouz, Y., Munilla, C.: Sharing user IoT devices in the cloud. In: 2014 IEEE World Forum Internet Things, 6–8 March 2014, pp. 373–374 (2014)
16. Jara, A.J., Sun, Y., Song, H., Bie, R., Genooud, D., Bocchi, Y.: Internet of Things for cultural heritage of smart cities and smart regions. 2015 IEEE 29th International Conference on Advanced Information Networking and Applications Workshops, pp. 668–675 (2015)
17. Gubbi, J., Buyya, R., Marusic, S., Palaniswami, M.: Internet of Things (IoT): a vision, architectural elements, and future directions. Futur. Gener. Comput. Syst. **29**(7), 1645–1660 (2013)
18. Montenegro, C., Rodríguez, J.: Redes de Ingeniería Redes de Ingeniería Redes de Ingeniería, pp. 37–44 (2015)
19. Weber, R.H.: Internet of things – need for a new legal environment? Comput. Law Secur. Rev. **25**(6), 522–527 (2009)
20. Basu, S.S., Tripathy, S., Chowdhury, A.R.: Design challenges and security issues in the Internet of Things. In: 2015 IEEE Region 10 Symposium, pp. 90–93 (2015)
21. Burange, A.W., Misalkar, H.D.: Review of Internet of Things in Development of Smart Cities with Data Management & Privacy (2015)
22. Ganchev, I., O'Droma, M.: A generic IoT architecture for smart cities. In: 25th IET Irish Signals and System Conference 2014 and 2014 China-Ireland International Conference on Information Communities Technologies (ISSC 2014/CIICT 2014), pp. 196–199 (2014)
23. Bonino, D., Alizo, M.T.D., Alapetite, A., Gilbert, T., Axling, M., Udsen, H., Soto, J.A.C., Spirito, M.: ALMANAC: Internet of Things for smart cities. In: 2015 3rd International Conference Future Internet Things Cloud, pp. 309–316 (2015)
24. Lea, R., Blackstock, M.: City hub: a cloud-based IoT platform for smart cities. In: 2014 IEEE 6th International Conference on Cloud Computing Technologies Science, pp. 799–804 (2014)
25. Skarmeta, A., Moreno, M.V., Garda, D.: SMARTIE project : secure IoT data management for smart cities, no. 609062, pp. 7–9 (2015)

26. Weinberg, B.D., Milne, G.R., Andonova, Y.G., Hajjat, F.M.: Internet of Things: convenience vs. privacy and secrecy. Bus. Horiz. **58**(6), 615–624 (2015)
27. Nastic, S., Sehic, S., Le, D.-H., Truong, H.-L., Dustdar, S.: Provisioning software-defined IoT cloud systems. In: 2014 International Conference on Future Internet Things Cloud, pp. 288–295 (2014)
28. Candía, R., Díaz, J., Cruz, C.: Public management of IT : Comparative case study between a developing and a developed. In: IEEE Conference Publitations, pp. 1–8 (2015)
29. Amato, A., Di Martino, B., Venticinque, S.: Big data processing for pervasive environment in cloud computing. In: 2014 Internation Conference on Intelligent Networking and Collaborative Systems, pp. 598–603 (2014)
30. Hofer, S.: Smart Cities and the Internet of Things, pp. 485–494 (2014)
31. Lea, R., Blackstock, M.: Smart cities. In: Proceedings of the 2014 International Workshop of Web Intelligence Smart Sensing Systems, IWWISS 2014, pp. 1–2 (2014)
32. Smart Technologies and Infrastructure for Energy, Water, Transportation, Buildings, and Government: Business Drivers, City and Supplier Profiles, Market Analysis, and Fore-casts, Navigant *(*2016). http://www.navigantresearch.com/research/smart-cities
33. Gartner: Gartner Says 4.9 Billion Connected 'Things' Will Be in Use in 2015 (2014)
34. Internet of Things by the number: Market estimated and forecast, Forbes (2015). http://www.forbes.com/sites/gilpress/2014/08/22/internet-of-things-by-the-numbers-market-estimatesand-forecasts/
35. Kumar, N.: Smart and intelligent energy efficient public illumination system with ubiquitous communication for smart city. In: 2013 IEEE International Conference on Smart Structures and Systems, ICSSS 2013, pp. 152–157 (2013)
36. Vakali, A., Anthopoulos, L., Krco, S.: Smart cities data streams integration: experimenting with Internet of Things and social data flows. In: 4th International Conference, pp. 1–5 (2014)
37. Singh, N., Davar, S.: Noise pollution-sources, effects and control. J. Hum. Ecol **16**(3), 181–187 (2004)
38. Tao, C., Ling, X., Guofeng, S., Hongyong, Y., Quanyi, H.: Architecture for monitoring urban infrastructure and analysis method for a smart-safe city. In: 2014 International Conference on Measurement Technology Mechatronics Automation, pp. 151–154 (2014)
39. Silva, R., Silva, J.S., Boavida, F.: A symbiotic resources sharing IoT platform in the smart cities context, pp. 7–9, April 2015
40. Suciu, G., Halunga, S., Vulpe, A., Suciu, V.: Generic platform for IoT and cloud computing interoperability study. In: International Symposium on Signals, Circuit*s* and Systems, ISSCS2013, pp. 1–4 (2013)
41. Chuah, J.W.: The Internet of Things: an overview and new perspectives in systems design. In: 2014 International Symposium on Integrated Circuits, pp. 216–219 (2014)
42. Formisano, C., Pavia, D., Gurgen, L., Yonezawa, T., Galache, J.A., Doguchi, K., Matranga, I.: The advantages of IoT and cloud applied to smart cities. In: 2015 3rd International Conference on Future Internet of Things and Cloud, pp. 325–332 (2015)
43. Jia, X., Wang, J., He, Q.: IoT business models and extended technical require-ments. In: IET International Conference on Communication Technology and Application *(ICCTA 2011)*, vol. 1, pp. 622–625 (2011)
44. Mainetti, L., Patrono, L., Stefanizzi, M.L., Vergallo, R.: A smart parking system based on IoT protocols and emerging enabling technologies (2015)
45. Yee, B., Li, S., Yeung, L.F., Tsang, K.F.: Analysing traffic condition based on IoT technique pp. 0–3 (2014)
46. Yan, Z., Zeadally, S., Park, Y.: A novel vehicular information network architecture based on named data networking (NDN). IEEE Internet Things J. **1**(6), 525–532 (2014)

47. Moreno, M.V., Skarmeta, A.F., Jarat, A.J.: How to intelligently make sense of real data of smart cities, pp. 7–9, April 2015
48. Hassanalieragh, M., Page, A., Soyata, T., Sharma, G., Aktas, M., Mateos, G., Kantarci, B., Andreescu, S.: Health monitoring and management using Internet-of-Things (IoT) sensing with cloud-based processing: opportunities and challenges. In: Proceedings - 2015 IEEE International Conference on Services Computing, SCC 2015, pp. 285–292 (2015)
49. Chze, P.L.R., Leong, K.S.: A secure multi-hop routing for IoT communication. In: 2014 IEEE World Forum Internet Things (WF-IoT), no. 3, pp. 428–432 (2014)
50. Sicari, S.: Security, privacy and trust management in the internet of things era - SePriT. Ad Hoc Netw. **11**(8), 2623–2624 (2013)
51. Qin, Z., Denker, G., Giannelli, C., Bellavista, P., Venkatasubramanian, N.: A software defined networking architecture for the internet-of-things. In: IEEE/IFIP NOMS 2014 - IEEE/IFIP Network Operations and Management Symposium Management in a Software-Defined World (2014)
52. Weber, R.H.: Internet of Things – New security and privacy challenges. Comput. Law Secur. Rev. **26**(1), 23–30 (2010)
53. Kyriazis, D., Varvarigou, T.: Smart, autonomous and reliable Internet of Things. Procedia Comput. Sci. **21**, 442–448 (2013)
54. Weber, R.H.: Internet of things: Privacy issues revisited. Comput. Law Secur. Rev. **31**(5), 618–627 (2015)
55. Yan, Z., Zhang, P., Vasilakos, A.V.: A survey on trust management for Internet of Things. J. Netw. Comput. Appl. **42**, 120–134 (2014)

Investigating the Experience of Moodle Adoption Through Expert Voices

Jane Sinclair(✉) and Anne-Maria Aho

School of Business and Culture,
Seinäjoki University of Applied Sciences, Seinäjoki, Finland
j.e.sinclair@warwick.ac.uk, Anne-Maria.aho@seamk.fi

Abstract. Virtual learning environments (VLEs) such as Moodle are now widely used in universities and other organisations. One crucial factor in the successful employment of such platforms is the ability and commitment of teaching staff to adopt the system. Despite the importance of this role, there has been little work to examine the experience of using VLEs in practice. This paper presents initial, qualitative research aimed at understanding how Moodle is being used and the different experiences and perspectives of the staff involved. To generate themes and areas of interest for future investigation this paper uses interview data from two "expert witnesses" who have a deep understanding of how the platform is used. Emergent themes include: divergence between confident and basic users; the spread of usage within an academic community; lack of progression to innovative teaching methods.

Keywords: Virtual learning environment · Moodle · Technology adoption

1 Introduction

Many institutions use a virtual learning environment (VLE) to present learning resources and manage course delivery. In recent years, the open-source, extensible Moodle environment has become the most popular free platform in higher education [1]. Reasons for its widespread adoption include its free availability and open source nature, extensibility, wide range of functionality and social constructionist ethos [2]. Current research on the use of Moodle tends to focus largely on two main issues: practice reports giving details and evaluations of how courses were implemented (such as [3]); and user acceptance investigations. Such analysis provides basic insight into how Moodle is being used but it is often limited to a narrow, quantitative view given by a small number of basic descriptive data items. Questions exploring richer, more qualitative areas, such as how (different) users experience a platform such as Moodle, how practice develops and what pedagogical approaches are adopted, have received little attention. Such an understanding is needed to identify the ways in which the system is used, directions in which it could be utilised for more effective teaching and learning, and the barriers to moving towards more innovative use of the platform.

As a first step towards better understanding the various users' experience of Moodle, this study seeks to gain a general perspective on the ways in which Moodle is used and to generate themes and areas of interest for future investigation. The approach

L. Uden et al. (Eds.): LTEC 2016, CCIS 620, pp. 90–102, 2016.
DOI: 10.1007/978-3-319-42147-6_8

taken in this paper is to use qualitative interview data from two "expert witnesses" both of whom have considerable experience in providing Moodle technical and pedagogical support for University teachers. Using qualitative data analysis, the responses allow themes to be identified and topics of interest and concern to emerge.

The following two sections introduce background work and describe the methodology used in this paper. Results are then reported, noting emerging themes and differences developed from and supported by categorisation applied to the words of the expert witnesses. The findings and their implications are discussed.

2 Background Work

Since its release under the General Public Licence Agreement in 2001, Moodle has rapidly increased in popularity as VLE of choice in schools, universities and businesses around the world [2]. In detailing reasons for the growth of Moodle, Costello [2] cites cost, fear of lock-in with proprietary vendors, its "ethos" as a vibrant, growing open-source platform, its flexibility and its pedagogic reputation as a learning-centred (rather than tool-focused) VLE. Different stakeholders will have different reasons for adopting Moodle. A number of studies of Moodle (and indeed on the acceptance of technology by teachers in general) have been based on the widely used Technology Acceptance Model (TAM) and results report a range of findings, for example, that students' perception of ease of use of Moodle is directly influenced by the availability of technical support [4] and that perceived usefulness is the main factor influencing students' intention to use the system [5]. However, the findings of such studies often appear to be contradictory and lacking in generality. Further, there is a lack of richer understanding about why participants answer as they do or how to interpret the results effectively.

There is far less published work investigating staff motivations for using Moodle. In some cases, institutional adoption has made its use compulsory. MacKeogh and Fox [6] find that motivating factors for staff include the potential to reach new students and to explore new technology whereas demotivating factors are generally more pragmatic, such as concerns over technical support or time needed. Walker et al. [7] note the pivotal role of teaching staff in the user experience of Moodle since they are responsible for creating content. They observe that there is often a big difference between the student perspective (frequent use, enthusiasm) and the staff view (infrequent use, reluctance) and that patchy staff use of the platform leads to a very variable learning experience for students. Staff training is often noted to be an important factor in the introduction of Moodle with "Moodle champions" or local experts frequently seen as the best way to spread enthusiasm and disseminate the necessary training [8].

Practice reports of using Moodle include accounts of how a course has been developed, how it is delivered and results of evaluation, often at the level of student satisfaction survey [3, 9]. A further way to gain information about system usage is by analysis of the large amount of log data gathered by the platform. A number of papers report results from Moodle learning analytics. For example, Agudo-Peregrina et al. [10] discover a relationship between engagement in types of learning activity and academic performance. Drăgulescu et al. [11] provide one of a number of accounts of adding analytics functionality to Moodle.

A number of authors make the claim that Moodle is more learner-centred than other VLEs [12]. However, there seems to be little exploration within the literature of how Moodle is really used and few papers address the use of innovative pedagogy within Moodle (or indeed any VLE). Bromham and Oprandi [13] note the need to incorporate active learning strategies rather than simply providing a repository of materials. However, Alves et al. [14] note that even where varied, dynamic resources are offered, they may be accessed and attempted by only a minority of students. Such studies underline the fact that, as with any VLE, the platform provides a wide range of functionality and how it is used by both staff and students can vary greatly. There is a need for further work to investigate how Moodle's affordances are being exploited in practice in order to determine directions for future development.

3 Methodology

To elicit themes relating to users' experience with Moodle which can inform the direction of more detailed future work, this research applies a qualitative analysis to data derived from semi-structured interviews with Moodle experts who have extensive experience of driving the introduction of Moodle and supporting teaching staff at two different European universities. In qualitative research, the number of data sources used varies depending on the methodological and epistemological perspective of the work undertaken. Rather than trying to cover a representative sample of users, an ethnographic approach seeks to generate a rich, subjective portrayal of a phenomenon as experienced by authentic users [15]. In the current research, the intention is to identify emergent issues in an area where little is currently known. For this purpose, two European universities were selected, each of which supports but does not mandate the use of Moodle. Key Moodle support staff were identified as experts who had overview of Moodle adoption across the whole institution. Detailed, in-depth interviews were chosen as the means to collect data to inform a deep exploration of how the system is experienced in two different contexts that have a similar Moodle adoption policy [16].

3.1 Data Collection

Semi-structured interviews were held with the two expert witnesses, each session lasting roughly one hour. The questions covered the following general areas: how and why Moodle is used in their institution; support provided for teachers and technology issues; the student perspective; how use of Moodle has developed since the time of its introduction; challenges to the use of Moodle; plans and ideas for future development.

Both interviews were recorded and later transcribed. The themes listed above were used as the categories for a high-level coding exercise in which content analysis was performed on the transcribed data by the two authors independently. Differences were discussed and agreement reached on the analysis output. Relevant key areas within the categories were noted and the data grouped and analysed accordingly to identify emergent themes, similarities and differences. Possible explanations for observed phenomena and areas for further investigation are then noted.

In this paper we report the first part of the analysis conducted on this data which relates to adoption of Moodle within an institution, staff attitudes and perspectives and the observed spread of use of the platform. The work brings together data relating to the themes stated and draws together issues of adoption and progression which create relationships between themes.

3.2 Institutional Settings

One interview was conducted with a Moodle support officer in a University of Applied Sciences in Finland (referred to as expert F). The other was held with an educational technologist responsible for Moodle development and support in a research university in the UK (expert E). The Finnish university has been using Moodle for ten years, and prior to that the institution had some experience with using WebCT. The UK institution has been using Moodle for three years, prior to which there had been no VLE, with material hosted in a basic web format. At both institutions, the use of Moodle is now the VLE of choice, with central support and training provided by the university. However, in neither case is the use of Moodle mandated, and each department is left to decide on its own approach. Hence, for some staff, Moodle use may in effect be compulsory due to departmental policy. Others are free to make a personal choice and may either find that they are lone adopters in their area or that they are part of a self-selecting local group.

The UK university has an undergraduate population of around 13,000 and a post-graduate body numbering nearly 10,000. The majority of undergraduates come straight from school, are resident at the university and pursue a full-time degree. Postgraduates are a mixture of MSc students (largely on taught courses) and PhD by research. This institution does not have a history of distance learning or e-learning, with most courses being taught face-to-face, on campus.

The Finnish university is a multidisciplinary institution of higher education. The number of full-time students is 5000 and academic and other staff members 380. Seinäjoki UAS has 19 Bachelor and 7 Master degree programmes. This institution has ten year´s history of Moodle usage, however Moodle is not totally accepted among the whole university.

4 How Moodle Is Used

In both institutions, members of staff are not required to make use of Moodle (or indeed any VLE). However, both experts noted that in many cases, departmental decisions haves been made, causing Moodle to be effectively mandated within individual departments.

4.1 Patterns of Adoption

As noted by expert E, *"some departments use it for absolutely everything and there's just no exception, everything's in there. And then other departments you just get a small handful of modules."* A patchwork of use as described here is perhaps inevitable where adoption is not compulsory. The institution supported by E has been using a VLE for only a short amount of time (three years) and it might be supposed that after a longer period a spread of use might occur to the extent where adoption is practically universal. However, as observed by expert F, *"we still have teachers here in our school who aren't using Moodle even though we have had it for 10 years".*

In terms of the proportion of staff using Moodle, E estimates that this was around 50 %, noting that "*there's been a dramatic increase in the number of people using it".* After a decade of use, F puts the usage figure at around 80 %, indicating that adoption rates slow down and that some staff still do not intend to use the platform at all. Participation rates are a little difficult to estimate as teachers may be involved with a course that uses Moodle but not directly using it themselves. Or, as raised by F, someone may have asked for their resources to be put on Moodle so *"you might have a course there but you're not actually utilizing it in any way".* With use not controlled by the institution, a number of issues arise, from knowing the extent and nature of usage within the platform, to the appearance from the students' perspective.

4.2 Consistency

When resources are provided in different ways there is a danger that students will become confused. E describes a course managed between four different departments: *"some of whom use Moodle, some of whom still have their materials on the normal web pages, and then in the Business School where they have their own customised VLE. So there's a huge disparity in terms of the way that resources are provided, how you access them. So many different places to go and look for resources or where to submit assignments. It must be horribly confusing for those students. And they'd be rightly very unhappy about it."*

E describes the consistency issue as one of the major challenges posed by allowing gradual platform adoption. There are dangers that students may be affected, not just by irritation and inconvenience of different formats, but by issues which may materially affect their studies such as failure to find resources or even mistaking the way to hand in an assignment. E further describes the reaction to patchy provision as one of disbelief from many students. *"Students will phone up IT services and say: 'My friend next door to me in my hall of residence can see all their modules in Moodle but I can't see anything. There must be something wrong– can you fix it for me?'*

While a free choice of VLE adoption may have many advantages and may be preferred by many staff, it can appear to students as an irrational source of discrimination between them and their friends on different courses.

Different policies on whether to make resources available in Moodle or by some other means is one source of inconsistency. Even within Moodle itself, courses can be presented in many different ways causing similar issues. F comments: *"My opinion is we should maybe require some things, some basic things like the description of the course, timeline or how this course can be done, teachers information and things like that. But then I would leave the rest for the teacher because otherwise everything will look the same. It's very boring."*

The question of interesting materials and individual choice is important to both experts. Each is keen to promote the use of Moodle as a platform for innovative teaching, and the teachers' own experimentation and creative design are crucial to new pedagogic discovery and progressive development. E discusses the need to provide consistency while maintaining choice and allowing diversity. In relation to the use of templates he says: *"That was something that didn't happen originally, that everybody just had a blank Moodle course where they would put their own material into it for whatever they were teaching. And it would be related to their module but there was not really the consistency. One of the big things that I think has emerged from the use of Moodle here is that, perhaps the rise of the consistency argument and that's not a conformity argument, not "You must do it this way" but just from a student experience point of view, from an ease of use for both staff and students that there is some visual and logical consistency to the way that things work. So many departments now have a template. And that's not to say that people don't deviate from that template. But you deviate from that template for a good pedagogical reason."*

The increasing recognition of student experience as an important driver in good teaching and learning points to a need to ensure that VLEs contribute to a positive experience for the learner. There appears to be a balance necessary here between, on the one hand, allowing enough flexibility for good, innovative teaching to develop and, on the other, providing some level of consistency for the learners. The previous quote also raises the issue of consistency for the benefit of staff, suggesting that many course developers may benefit from a more structured approach but acknowledging that this should not be something that constrains or restricts them.

Although appearance may seem a minor issue compared to underlying pedagogy, problems inconsistency and poor basic design can be off-putting to the learner. This is one of the more common problems noted by E. *"There are some examples that we've got where you look at the course and it is just visually a total mess. There are lots of different fonts. There are images which are scaled in weird ways so the aspect ratio is wrong and font sizes are all over the place and things aren't aligned properly and visually it is quite jarring to look at. However, the material that's there and the structure can be quite good."*

From the staff perspective, it can be a very time-consuming endeavour to make a course look visually appealing and ensure consistency across all aspects. The effort of moving materials to Moodle at all may take up a good deal of time and staff may be unwilling to pursue more detailed fine tuning of visual appearance. There may also be an issue of technical knowledge if resources from different sources need to be adjusted in various ways. F suggests that lack of technical confidence and skill is a major barrier to many of the staff she sees, indicating an area that may affect both willingness to use the VLE at all and a barrier to developing good courses. *"They're scared of technology and that's their threshold. That's why they can't get over – it's too big and it's getting bigger every day. Because we get new things every day and maybe they didn't bother to learn– or maybe we didn't teach them when they were studying to be a teacher they didn't have any education for using computers to help in teaching. So they don't know how to utilise it."*

This raises a number of issues which underlie important themes not just of Moodle adoption, but also of moving to more effective and innovative use of the system, of staff training and development and of the increasing complexity of the system itself. It indicates that a further area of inconsistency is in the knowledge and skill levels of staff, with some very adept at using the system and others not having started. Understanding the complexity of Moodle options and creating effectively-structured courses can be a demanding task and with each subsequent upgrade of the system some staff may be left further behind.

4.3 Mandating Use

Despite issues caused by inconsistency of use and patchy adoption, both experts believe that their institution is taking the correct approach in allowing staff the choice of whether to adopt Moodle or not. E expresses his perspective on the approach to adoption in the following way. *"The thing I wouldn't do, but people have suggested in the past, is saying that everybody should be mandated to use Moodle. I think that would actually be the wrong thing because I think that allowing for adoption at a pace that suits individual modules and courses and academic is a much better approach from an educational point of view - and it helps the institution unpack what it wants to do in this space. Rather than just force everybody to use a technology it means that people think about 'how am I delivering what I'm doing, what other ways could I deliver this' and it gives them room to think that through".*

This response is an interesting combination of what is best for teaching staff and their courses, but also brings in consideration of the institution's own development and its positioning within a growing global e-learning market. Imposing a system on staff may cause resentment and, while mandated use can ensure that resources are placed in a VLE, it does not guarantee effective or committed use of the platform.

F's perspective also supports the idea of gradual evolution and of supporting and encouraging staff to move forward as and when they are ready. *"Every time somebody asks me something I try to add something – have you noticed that we also have this and we also have this? To make them a little bit interested so that next time maybe it will stay somewhere there in their mind and then they come back and say hmm once you mentioned – maybe we should try it now."*

This may be effective in encouraging use of different features of the platform and in involving teaching staff in the pace of their own development with respect to its use. It allows innovation to be needs-led as teachers relate their current teaching requirements to aspects of the system they have heard about but not yet tried out.

5 Use of the Platform

Given freedom in deciding whether to use a system and in what way, further questions arise of how staff approach the task and what Moodle features they employ.

5.1 Initial Use of Moodle

Both experts agree that for the majority of staff, initial use of Moodle consists mainly of putting existing resources on to the platform. As described by E: "we'll look at a module if there's some problem and it's not much more than a list of files for slides or things to read". However, he continues to talk about noticing a development of practice over time. *"When Moodle started ... most people were treating it as a place to put resources. Now it's been running for a few years we've got a lot more examples of people who've been using it for some kind of innovative teaching practice."*

The kinds of activities used initially generally mirror and support an existing face to face course. Teachers may be using the platform as an online repository to made slides and reading material available on the web. F discusses the typical usage of Moodle features. *"I would say most of the teachers put their material – use the assignment, that their students return the assignment in there. They can use discussion board and some use exams. And that's not even half of the potential Moodle has."*

Here, F makes the point that the features used by most staff are fairly limited and tend to be those that are similar to the traditional methods of delivery. This is perhaps hardly surprising and, following on from E's observation regarding development, it might be supposed that a pattern of evolution would be evident. However, the restricted use is noted not just in new users but in the majority of long-term users as well. F states: *"So I would think most of the teachers are using it very lightly. Even though they think they are heavy users because they might have 10 courses in there with lots of material in there. But they aren't using the whole palette of things."*

Even though a teacher has made Moodle versions of many courses, they may still only be using the system in a very limited way. This is a pattern observed by F in the majority of Moodle users: *"most of the people they only put their material in Moodle and then they think, ok that's it, I can stop here."*

This indicates a possible divergence between what teachers think is effective use of the system and the unexploited potential that could be used to create novel and creative learning opportunities which exploit the affordances of the platform.

E expresses similar views and suggests reasons for the lack of progression. Again, he stresses that in some cases there may be legitimate motivations for a limited Moodle provision, but in general sees the failure to exploit more features of the system as a missed opportunity. *"I'm sure there are many cases where it is simply that there are lots of potential opportunities that could be exploited. It's a limitation of imagination, of interest, of time. It's their relative importance."*

While many teaching staff may point to a lack of time to create inventive online courses, others find the necessary time. As F puts it *"I don't know how some of the teachers have time (but others do not)"*. For some, the importance of investing effort in developing a creative Moodle course comes low on the list of priorities. Again, F refers to this, saying: *"They're not interested in computers and digitalization and doing things online or whatever. They want to teach the subject they came here to teach and they're not interested in how to add a picture somewhere"*. This suggests that the lack of interest is not simply in being unwilling to invest time in learning about the system, but that it is a manifestation of an absence of curiosity, a failure to experiment with technology in general: *"A lot of teachers want to use things that are told them are easy things. I use this and I am not even looking at anything else. So that's the problem. I would like them to be open minded. You get this new thing and I want them to be interested in if I push this button what happens."*

Teachers' views on and facility with technology in general inevitably have an effect on their willingness to explore and experiment in a digital environment. A better understanding of this and of its relationship to usage of a VLE could point to practical ways of providing better support.

5.2 Super Users

While many users fail to progress or develop their Moodle courses, a minority are keen adopters of the platform and display an eagerness to improve their teaching by using online functionality to develop and enhance the overall experience offered by their teaching. F says: *"Some teachers take it on by themselves and they don't even need any help. ...We tell them where you find Moodle and how to log in and they start doing things on their own."* She describes the users a filling a triangle where the base is formed of the majority of users who view the system as nothing more than a repository. The middle of the triangle contains those who consider use of features which might lead towards an enhanced online course experience, such as the introduction of an online discussion. The apex of the triangle represents the "super users". *"So the ones up there on top – they don't ask questions. They know how to find things on their own. But then it's the big mass of people and they don't."*

F refers to *"a grass-roots, a bottom-up approach where individual members have tried things, have experimented"*. These staff may act as motivators within their departments, push forward the use of Moodle, experiment and think of inventive ways to use features and develop teaching. F describes them as *"staff who in effectively act as the proxy for many members of staff"*. Both E and F estimate that this type of user accounts for less than 10 % of staff. They each view this minority of staff as being crucial to the introduction and development of Moodle and they describe how this has occurred in their institution. E sees the super users as a source of inspiration and motivation for others in the institution. Thus, *"there's people who benefit from people at the cutting edge who won't go first but when they see people make the first step they follow behind"*. These users act as progressive forces: *"they are in effect corralling academic staff to put things in to Moodle"*. The super users set an example, showing colleagues what can be achieved and reassuring them that the technology is robust enough to be trusted: *"Both on a technological level that the technology didn't just break every five minutes. But also at an educational level that it worked in some way for somebody's module, somebody's delivery of a course. So I think it gives other people confidence to see yes it could be done and you could do it too."*

However, F's experience has been that the super users act more as loners and that the grass-roots, inspirational effect is not being observed. She describes them in the following way: *"They're loners doing the job on their own because nobody – everybody else is so behind they can't get any help from them."* Asked if there is transmission of knowledge and skill to others she says: *"That doesn't happen ... sharing is not happening."* As a future activity, F intends to look into ways and means for promoting better sharing of good Moodle practice within the university.

Although attitude to technology has been raised as a barrier to effective use, it does not appear to be the "techie" teachers who generally emerge as super users. The following list of characteristics associated with these users is compiled from the words of both experts: lack of fear of technology; not a techie expert but willing to explore; good basic online skills; interest in pedagogy; concern for development of good teaching practice; willingness to adopt new pedagogy; lack of fear of failure; interest in new ways of supporting students; general attitude of being open to experimenting; self-awareness about their own levels of skills; awareness of what they are and are not doing well; a willingness to ask for help. The most effective users are not necessarily early adopters but are keen experimenters. E introduces the analogy of Moodle as a door. It provides the means to access a wide range of other technologies and possibilities. By going through the door, teachers take the first step towards unlocking that potential.

6 Discussion

Although we have looked at Moodle, the findings are on the whole generic and it might be reasonable to suppose that similar issues relating to adoption, staff attitudes, ongoing pattern of uptake and so on would be observed in the use of other VLEs. The findings also have implications for attempted moves to more inventive use of diverse new technologies in education in general and the way that this might be best approached. There was generally an agreement between the two expert witnesses on both fact and perspective.

Models such as the Technology Acceptance Model (TAM) [17] and its variants have developed in the field of information systems in an attempt to explain what influences people to accept and use a technology. Such models are highly relevant to the use of a VLE such as Moodle in the case where adoption is not mandatory. However, even in the finer models, their limited capacity to explore richer data and explain observed phenomena means that that they are limited in providing deeper understanding.

Where use of a learning platform by staff is not made compulsory, it appears that adoption may initially rise rapidly but does not necessarily continue to spread. The question of why users adopt Moodle initially is certainly of interest, however, the ways that staff use the system differ. It is not simply a question of whether a teacher has materials on Moodle or not, but how they are using it, why some stay with a basic set-up and others move on, how and why use develops over time and what pedagogy is developing that can promote enhanced learning and inspire staff. Further, the research raises questions about the way in which use of the system does or does not spread within an institution. Again, this is not just about numbers, but, as indicated by our expert witnesses, involves a more subtle narrative involving staff development, institutional positioning and even the evolution of a concept of teaching which can encompass new and disruptive approaches and which may be alarming to some staff.

There is a danger that many staff may already be left behind by the technology and that the gulf between the adopters and the non-adopters is growing. However, the issue goes deeper than confidence in using technology, exposing a gulf in pedagogical approaches. At one extreme there are those who embrace the disruptive potential of a rich online experience and are keen to work with students in exploiting the possibilities. At the other are the staff who see changes in terms of negative effects, such as lowering student attendance, for whom acceptance involves a paradigm shift in their whole approach to education. Understanding the experience and perspective of users, whether staff, students, educational technology support or management, is vital in uncovering and tackling the challenges and barriers to use.

On the question of whether adoption should be gradual and by choice or whether it should be an institutional decision, both experts were clear that the model of recommending but not forcing staff to adopt Moodle is best. They would not like to see it made compulsory. They support their view by pointing to the benefits of allowing a situation to evolve. For staff, forced usage may well be bad usage. They also mention the benefits to the institution of being able to find its way in the e-learning space and working out the policy that best suits its objectives. To maximise the benefits of adoption and to allow both concerns and creativity to emerge, a better understanding of different user experiences and perspectives is needed.

F introduced the metaphor of Moodle as *"a door"*. By entering that door, teachers have the potential to harness new technology and develop novel pedagogy. The first step is in unlocking that door. Beyond that, there is further work to do in translating the potential into actuality using the subject knowledge and creative skills which the teachers themselves bring. The suggestion from these interviews is that for the majority of users this progression is not happening.

7 Conclusions and Future Work

This study has generated themes relevant to the exploration of Moodle usage and users' experience which are likely to provide fruitful areas for further investigation. "Use" of a VLE such as Moodle may mean many different things. Uptake in terms of having a course presence in Moodle does not indicate how the platform is being used. Teachers may regard themselves as "expert" Moodle users because they use it as a platform for all their resources but in practice they may be exploiting very few of its features. There is no natural progression to a "higher" level of use for most users.

Super users are noted by both experts as being instrumental in furthering the introduction of Moodle, but there is a difference in their described role. In one case, the super users were seen as instrumental in spreading good practice and in motivating colleagues to adopt Moodle and try new approaches. However, in the other they were seen as loners and little evidence of sharing good practice was observed. This raises the question of whether good practice does spread in this way and, if it does happen in some institutions but not in others, what are the factors that promote sharing and dissemination of good practice between colleagues? This is an area for future work. In addition, we wish to investigate both teaching staff and students' perspectives and experiences of VLE usage. The overview provided by our expert witnesses and the themes that are emerging provide the basis for investigation with these further classes of user. In addition, our findings begin to suggest ways in which existing adoption models may be extended and point to barriers to usage which can be addressed.

Compulsory use of a VLE has consistency advantages, but may hide genuine concerns and barriers and these will hinder progress even if adoption is mandatory. A balance is needed between allowing enough flexibility for good, innovative teaching to develop on the one hand and providing some consistency for the learners on the other. Initial work and training has often concentrated on getting staff started with Moodle. The lack of progression and development by the majority of users seems to indicate that attention needs to be paid to how teachers can be encouraged to explore the affordances of the platform (and related technologies) further.

Acknowledgement. We are immensely grateful to our expert witnesses who generously gave their time and shared their deep knowledge and insights relating to Moodle adoption and use.

References

1. Green, K.C.: New technology and higher education overview. J. Collect. Bargaining Acad. **8**, 9 (2013)
2. Costello, E.: Opening up to open source: looking at how Moodle was adopted in higher education. Open Learn. J. Open Distance e-Learn. **28**(3), 187–200 (2013)
3. Martín-Blas, T., Serrano-Fernández, A.: The role of new technologies in the learning process: Moodle as a teaching tool in Physics. Comput. Educ. **52**(1), 35–44 (2009)
4. Sánchez, R.A., Hueros, A.D.: Motivational factors that influence the acceptance of Moodle using TAM. Comput. Hum. Behav. **26**(6), 1632–1640 (2010)
5. Escobar-Rodriguez, T., Monge-Lozano, P.: The acceptance of Moodle technology by business administration students. Comput. Educ. **58**(4), 1085–1093 (2012)
6. MacKeogh, K., Fox, S.: Opening access to higher education to all? What motivates academic staff in traditional universities to adopt elearning? In: European Distance & eLearning Network 5th Research Conference (2008)
7. Walker, S., Prytherch, D., Turner, J.: The pivotal role of staff user experiences in Moodle and the potential impact on student learning. In: Second International Conference on e-Learning and e-Technologies in Education (ICEEE), pp. 192–197. IEEE, September 2013
8. Gramp, J.: Beyond the baseline: working with e-learning champions to transform e-learning at a research-led university. In: Second Moodle Research Conference, pp. 24–32, October 2013
9. Seluakumaran, K., Jusof, F.F., Ismail, R., Husain, R.: Integrating an open-source course management system (Moodle) into the teaching of a first-year medical physiology course: a case study. Adv. Physiol. Educ. **35**(4), 369–377 (2011)
10. Agudo-Peregrina, Á.F., Iglesias-Pradas, S., Conde-González, M.Á., Hernández García, Á.: Can we predict success from log data in VLEs? Classification of interactions for learning analytics and their relation with performance in VLE-supported F2F and online learning. Comput. Hum. Behav. **31**, 542–550 (2014)
11. Drăgulescu, B., Bucos, M., Vasiu, R.: CVLA: integrating multiple analytics techniques in a custom moodle report. In: Dregvaite, G., Damasevicius, R. (eds.) ICIST 2015. CCIS, vol. 538, pp. 115–126. Springer, Heidelberg (2015)

12. Cole, J., Foster, H.: Using Moodle: Teaching with the Popular Open Source Course Management System. O'Reilly, Sebastopol (2007)
13. Bromham, L., Oprandi, P.: Evolution online: using a virtual learning environment to develop active learning in undergraduates. J. Biol. Educ. **41**(1), 21–25 (2006)
14. Alves, G.R., Viegas, M.C., Marques, M.A., Silva, A., Costa-Lobo, M.C., Formanski, F., Silva, J.B.D.: Student performance analysis under different Moodle course designs. In: 15th International Conference on Interactive Collaborative Learning (ICL), pp. 1–5. IEEE, September 2012
15. Cohen, L., Manion, L., Morrison, K.: Research Methods in Education, 7th edn. Routledge, Abingdon (2011)
16. Baker, S.E., Edwards, R., Doidge, M.: How many qualitative interviews is enough?: Expert voices and early career reflections on sampling and cases in qualitative research. National Centre for Research Methods Review Paper (2012). http://eprints.brighton.ac.uk/11632/. Accessed 12 Oct 2015
17. Davis, F.D.: Perceived usefulness, perceived ease of use, and user acceptance of information technology. MIS Q. **13**(3), 319–340 (1989)

Learning Strategies and Interpersonal Relationships of Students Learning Cooperatively Online

Jonathan Kaplan(✉)

Institute of Sciences and Practices of Education and Training (ISPEF), Lumière University Lyon 2, 86 Rue Pasteur, 69365 Lyon, France
kaplan@kaplan-consultants.org

Abstract. Adult learners studying cooperatively are thought to have an innate predisposition to help each other in the process of learning, but cooperation among learners online who do not necessary know each other may not occur spontaneously. It has often been suggested that learning online requires being autonomous and able to effectively regulate one's learning. Research using two scales, one to measure Self- and Co-Regulation (SCoR) of learning, the other to measure interpersonal relationships, was carried out with first-year Master's in education students (N = 38) taking an online course in quantitative research methodology. The course was designed using a cooperative learning method enabling to study SCoR strategies in relation to the quality of interpersonal relationships, as well as achievement in this setting. The research is presented. Conclusions point to the role of individual anticipation strategies and to the quality of peer relationships in relation to higher achievement.

Keywords: Self-regulation · Co-regulation · Interpersonal relationships · Cooperative learning · e-Learning

1 Introduction

Directions for research have been suggested in pursuit of bettering online learning on the basis of principles that can apply to learning with social media [10]. Among the proposed directions, areas that relate to peer interactions included dialogue and empathy. Questions such as the eventual need to learn how to be dialogic when learning online, learning to be attentive and accepting of others' opinions were raised. Empathy, which entails feelings, cannot be taught. Can online learners feel empathy towards peers and provide them with support in environments where knowing others is often knowledge at a distance? The research presented here ventured to study strategies that learners use to manage

Education, Cultures & Policies (EA 4571) research unit. CHArt-UPON (EA 4004) research unit.

L. Uden et al. (Eds.): LTEC 2016, CCIS 620, pp. 103–111, 2016.
DOI: 10.1007/978-3-319-42147-6_9

their learning process in conjunction with the quality of interpersonal relationships. Thirty-Eight distance education students in a first year Master's programme using Blackboard Learn[1] to interact, responded to two scales: ERICA [11], an instrument that was developed in order to study Self- and Co-Regulation (SCoR) strategy use when learning; and EQRI [15], an instrument designed to measure interpersonal relationships. ERICA was developed to measure strategies that adult learners deploy when studying in any environment such as when learning online, and to address the absence of an instrument designed to measure co-regulation.

2 Learner Action Oriented Strategy Use in Regulating Learning

The conceptual model of regulation phases that served the development of ERICA is a goal oriented model which builds on Zimmerman's [18] three phases of self-regulation but in which monitoring is separated from Zimmerman's Performance or Volitional Control phase. The conceptual model further adds a decision making phase drawing from Heckhausen's Rubicon model of action phases [1,2,7]. Kaplan's conceptual model [9] thus comprises of four regulation phases conceptually preceding, taking place during and following the core cognitive activity (action of learning). These are: Anticipation, Monitoring, Assessment, and Decision making. Macro-level strategies that can be observed with ERICA relate to these four phases. They are: Individual Anticipation of materials and References (IAR), Individual Environmental Control (IEC), Individual Tracking and Monitoring (ITM), Collective Evaluation of Content (CEC), Individual Evaluation of Method (IEM), and Collective Decisions for Method change (CDM). The measures of levels of use of these strategies are scored 0–4 on a Likert-type scale.

3 Interpersonal Relations

Studying interpersonal relationships can shed light on regulations carried out with others. CEC and CDM are such regulations. Sénecal et al. [15] validated a scale to measure the quality of interpersonal relationships. The scale was chosen for the purpose of studying the hypothesis of a relation between the quality of interpersonal relationships and co-regulation. The scale measures five spheres of relationships: relationships with family members, love relationships, relationships with friends, relationships with peer learners, and relationships with people in general. Each of these spheres of relationships is expressed with four attributes that respondents score on a Likert-type scale graded 0–4.

---

[1] Blackboard Learn is a trademark of Blackboard Inc. and an e-learning platform the company commercialises.

4 Research Hypothesis and Method

The research aimed at studying SCoR strategy use by students in a given educational situation; relations that may exist between these SCoR strategies and the quality of interpersonal relationships; and, relations SCoR strategy use and interpersonal relationships may have with academic achievement. The exploration of strategy use may be valuable for future research in order to identify patterns that may exist in the way students regulate their learning in specific learning environments and contexts. The primary interest regarding this research was to shed light on regulation strategies when using an instructional design that deploys a Cooperative Learning (CL) method [16] in the realm of e-learning. The hypothesis was that a positive relation would exist between more frequent use of co-regulation strategies and the quality of interpersonal relationships. Cooperation among adult learners [8,9] could rely on empathy between learners. In the situation studied in the research presented here, cooperation was externally motivated through teacher instructions and by providing criteria for grading that rely on cooperation. Even though the use of incentives may compensate personal propensity for social relationships, it was assumed that personal characteristics could play a role in group performance, reflected in course grades. Course grades served as an indicator of the quality of performance since the grading was based on the outcome of assignments to be carried out collectively.

4.1 Course Description and Design

Respondents (N = 38) were graduate students in their first year of an Education Master's that is run online. The digital campus for education sciences[2] is run conjointly by two French universities and the French national centre for distance education. Respondents were taking a course on quantitative research methodology that used a CL design. The course took place during the second semester of the 2014–15 academic year. It began by convening the learners on campus during which a face-to-face session with the course instructor took place. The purpose of the class was to engage students in the process, explain the course design and tasks to be carried out, answer students' questions, form CL groups, and generally offer a friendlier opportunity to get to know the instructor and peers. This was the only opportunity during this course for students to meet with their instructor who from that point onward interacted with students online only. Eight groups were formed by the students, each with four to seven participants. On the Web-based e-learning application, each group had private group services including a forum with file exchange means. Groups could not access other groups' online services, but could conduct online conversations in other areas such as the general first-year Master's forum. Students were instructed to use their group's forum for all matters related to their learning in the course and hand in work for the instructor to monitor and assist with in their private

[2] Formation et Ressources en Sciences de l'Éducation (FORSE) http://www.sciencedu.org.

group space. Students were advised to help each other in the process of understanding the educational materials of the course and generally cooperate during their learning. The main assignment given each group was to come up with a research question, devise a small survey to study the question and submit it to all the other students taking the course, to statistically analyse the results and to hand in a report including their findings. The report had to also include a personal account, annexed by each participant, of the student's contribution to the group's work and had to have the account signed by the other group members as a mark of approval. Group members were all given the same score for their collective production. The final grade for the course, given to each student, was based on the group's score for 70 % of it. The remaining 30 % was made up of a score given on the basis of the personal account annexed to the collective report of the student's participation in the group's effort. All students also learned during this process from the other groups when they responded to other groups' questionnaires. Questionnaires had to include instructions for respondents, comply and inform about ethical considerations such as confidentiality and privacy matters.

Participants received an e-mail with an invitation to take part in the research survey at the end of the 12-week course. The e-mail contained the Web address of the survey questionnaire. Participants were asked to provide their student numbers in order to enable to later associate their responses with their course grades. In the e-mail and in the instructions on the first page of the online questionnaire, a commitment to confidentiality and to preserving anonymity was stated. All data manipulations were ensured to be carried out using software in such a way as to not reveal personal identity.

5 Research Results

Analyses were carried out using R, version 3.2.2 [13]. Respondents were 38 students (34 female and 4 male). Their ages ranged 22–55 years (M = 34.76, SD = 8.84). Descriptive statistics and internal consistency reliability using Cronbach's alpha [3] are provided for each dimension of ERICA in Table 1. Values higher than .70 are considered to be adequate [12]. The value for IAR is acceptable and is good for the remaining dimensions. The gamut of the scale gradation is 0–4, where 0 represents the response: 'I never thought of doing this', referring to the regulation strategy, and 4 representing the response: 'I do this systematically'.

Descriptive statistics and internal consistency reliability, tested using Cronbach's alpha, are provided for each sub-scale of EQRI in Table 2. The values for relationships in general (General in Table 2) is good and excellent for the remaining sub-scales. EQRI scores are calculated by adding item scores for a type of relationship. Responses to each item can range 0–4. Added together the score for each type can therefore range 0–16.

Grades can span 0–20. In this course the min. grade was 8.3 and the max. was 16 (M = 12.86, SD = 2.68).

Table 1. Internal Consistency and Descriptive Statistics for SCoR Dimensions

Dimension	α	Min	Max	M	SD
IAR	0.74	0.8	4.0	2.74	0.68
IEC	0.87	0.6	4.0	2.76	0.94
ITM	0.81	0.0	4.0	1.63	1.06
CEC	0.84	0.0	3.6	1.75	0.80
IEM	0.88	0.6	3.0	2.04	0.72
CDM	0.83	0.0	2.4	1.21	0.74

Table 2. Internal Consistency and Descriptive Statistics for EQRI Sub-Scales

Sub-Scale	α	Min	Max	M	SD
Family	0.96	0	16	13.00	3.77
Love	0.92	3	16	13.91	3.35
Friends	0.92	6	16	13.44	2.79
Peers	0.90	4	16	10.15	3.32
General	0.85	6	16	11.35	2.57

6 Analysis of Correlations

Intercorrelations for each scale and correlations between ERICA and EQRI dimensions as well as with age and course grades were sought (see Table 3). Intercorrelations between ERICA dimension are significant for IAR with IEC (r = .364, p = .027) and for IAR with ITM (r = .442, p = .007). These moderate correlations demonstrate that students who individually anticipated materials and references for their learning also controlled their environment and deployed tracking and monitoring strategies more. Students who tracked and monitored their learning also controlled their environment (r = .379, p = .021), evaluated methods they used (IEM) (r = .366, p = .026) and made decisions collectively (CDM) (r = .417, p = .014). This points to the central role of tracking and monitoring for self-regulation of learning, as noted by Steffens [17], in the service of adjusting environmental parameters, evaluating methods and making choices through discussion with others. In accordance with the conceptual model [9], assessing the adequacy of methods deployed and making decisions about strategies rely on metacognitive input made available through tracking and monitoring. Collective decision making is not only positively linked to individual tracking and monitoring but also to individual evaluation of method (r = .462, p = .005). Collective evaluation of content (CEC) however, is not significantly correlated with the use of other SCoR strategies in this study.

Intercorrelations among EQRI dimensions point to only one significant link, between the quality of relationships with friends and relationships in general

(r = .588, p = .000). This may point to respondents confounding these two types of relationships.

Correlations between SCoR strategies and the quality of relationships reveal that there is a positive relation between individual anticipation of resources (materials and references) and the quality of intimate love relationships ($r = .380$, $p = .029$) and that there is a positive relation between individual environmental control and the quality of relationships in general ($r = .369$, $p = .025$). These findings indicate that affective dimensions are related to preparing for cognitive processes to come, a future oriented perspective demonstrated when the quality of the love relationship is stronger. Furthermore, the quality of relationships in general is positively linked to providing oneself with suitable surroundings and befitting environmental conditions for learning.

Interestingly, individual anticipation of resources is carried out more by older students (r = .406, p = .013). These older students might have developed through experience, strategies that are more advantageous to the learning process. As these self-regulation strategies are also positively linked to student grades ($r = .407$, $p = .017$) it is reasonable to infer that longer experience in educational settings led to developing more effective strategies, reflected in higher grades as an indicator of achievement. Last but not least is the positive relation between the quality of relationships with peers and grades (r = .493, p = .006). This positive relation can probably be imputed to the instructional design of the course which used a CL method.

Table 3. Intercorrelations, Correlations Between ERICA Dimensions, EQRI Dimensions, Age and Student Grades

	IAR	IEC	ITM	CEC	IEM	CDM	Fam	Love	Frien	Peers	Gen	Age
IAR	1											
IEC	.364[a]	1										
ITM	.442[b]	.379[a]	1									
CEC	.215	.085	.238	1								
IEM	.294	.153	.366[a]	.288	1							
CDM	.296	.032	.417[a]	.252	.462[b]	1						
Family	.043	.033	.057	−.141	−.253	−.183	1					
Love	.380[a]	.243	.206	−.001	.195	.290	.156	1				
Friends	.010	−.096	.129	−.276	−.048	.038	.301	.281	1			
Peers	.160	.049	−.101	.071	−.180	−.211	.179	.151	.271	1		
General	.199	.369[a]	.186	.006	−.016	.159	.264	.283	.558[c]	.273	1	
Age	.406[a]	.318	.043	−.071	.067	−.108	.255	.104	−.264	.003	−.144	1
Grade	.407[a]	−.023	.265	.281	.023	−.088	.039	.058	−.073	.493[b]	−.080	.159

Note. [a] $p < .05$; [b] $p < .01$; [c] $p < .001$

7 Conclusions

Analyses provide indications on the use of strategies at the macro-level [6], deployed by learners in their first year of an online Master's in education programme. The data collected at the end of a course on quantitative research methodology which was designed using CL elements, provides a basis for future studies of SCoR strategy use in conjunction with other constructs related to cognition, metacognition, motivation, volition and affect. Studies of these constructs that involve environments using different instructional designs could enable comparisons to further elucidate which cognitive and metacognitive salient strategies students use in relation to course design and environmental features. Students may not use strategies to the same extent in different learning environments. Studying differences in strategy use would help develop awareness of the play between environmental factors and student learning regulation strategies, including their ability to self- and co-regulate autonomously [4,5,14].

One of the questions that was introduced at the beginning of this paper was the proclivity for collective regulation strategies when using an instructional design that deploys a CL method. In future research, a quasi-experimental research design with a group of students using a CL method and a control group backed by an individualistic instructional design could shed light on the hypothesis of different types of regulation strategies deployed in courses using different instructional designs.

The analysis of the data gathered in this research did not support the hypothesis that a relation exists between more use of co-regulation strategies when stronger interpersonal relationships were reported, apart for relationships with peer students. None of the types of interpersonal relationships correlates significantly with either collective evaluation of content (CEC) nor with collective decision making for change of method (CDM). Perhaps the CL design of the course had a stronger effect on the co-regulation strategies that learners used, overshadowing any relation that may exist to the quality of interpersonal relationships other than relationships with peers. On the other hand, relationships with peers are positively linked to group performance, reflected in higher course grades. This suggests that the cooperative climate of the group, the capacity of its members to work together towards goals and achieve the expected learning outcomes, is not primarily a matter of their co-regulation as much as the mix of personal characteristics that come into play in the way the group forms a productive and effective community of peer learners. It is noteworthy that groups who did function well in terms of forming a learning community supporting each other's learning cooperatively, were higher achievers. Studying various other variables that may play a role in forming a favourable climate for cooperation among learners would be useful. Another variable that is linked to achievement is more use of individual anticipation of materials and resources (IAR) for learning. Though IAR is positively correlated to student age, older students are not better achievers ($r = .159$, ns).

Further investigation of SCoR strategies in CL situations in conjunction with affective dimensions such as empathy and the quality of dialogue should enable better understanding of environmental conditions that promote them. Supporting empathy and dialogue would enable reducing incentives and instructional prompts to cooperate. Learning cooperatively can then rely on autonomous motivation and ensuing autonomous regulation of learning. Autonomous motivation and regulation are important to autonomous learning which is characteristic of adult learners and is particularly appropriate to learning online. Studying learner well-being in conjunction with autonomy is another direction that could shed light on conditions that predispose learners to cooperate. Conditions for gaining confidence in peers' contributions to the collective effort is still another direction for future research.

References

1. Achtziger, A., Gollwitzer, P.M.: Motivation and volition in the course of action. In: Heckhausen, J., Heckhausen, H. (eds.) Motivation and Action, pp. 272–295. Cambridge University Press, Cambridge (2008)
2. Achtziger, A., Gollwitzer, P.M.: Motivation and volition in the course of action. In: Heckhausen, J., Heckhausen, H. (eds.) Motivation and Action, pp. 275–299. Cambridge University Press, Cambridge (2010)
3. Cronbach, L.J.: Coefficient alpha and the internal structure of tests. Psychometrika **16**(3), 297–334 (1951)
4. Deci, E.L., Ryan, R.M.: Intrinsic Motivation and Self-Determination in Human Behavior. Perspectives in Social Psychology. Plenum, New York (1985)
5. Deci, E.L., Ryan, R.M. (eds.): Handbook of Self-Determination Research. University of Rochester Press, Rochester (2002)
6. Greene, J.A., Azevedo, R.: A macro-level analysis of SRL processes and their relations to the acquisition of a sophisticated mental model of a complex system. Contemp. Educ. Psychol. **34**(1), 18–29 (2009)
7. Heckhausen, H., Gollwitzer, P.M.: Thought contents and cognitive functioning in motivational versus volitional states of mind. Motiv. Emot. **11**(2), 101–120 (1987)
8. Kaplan, J.: From self-direction to co-direction in adult cooperative learning. In: Brigham, S.M., Plumb, D. (eds.) Connected Understanding: Linkages Between Theory and Practice in Adult Education, pp. 176–180. Adult Education - Congresses, Montreal (2010)
9. Kaplan, J.: L'autodirection dans les apprentissages coopératifs: Le cas des Cercles d'Étude. Éditions Universitaires Européennes, Sarrebruck (2010)
10. Kaplan, J.: Applying adult cooperative learning underpinning principles to learning with social media - an overview and implications for research. In: Uden, L., Liberona, D., Welzer, T. (eds.) LTEC 2015. CCIS, vol. 533, pp. 93–103. Springer, Heidelberg (2015)
11. Kaplan, J., de Montalembert, M., Laurent, P., Fenouillet, F.: ERICA - an instrument to measure individual and collective regulation of learning [ERICA - un outil pour mesurer la régulation individuelle et collective de l'apprentissage] (submitted)
12. Nunnally, J.C.: Psychometric Theory. McGraw-Hill, New York (1978)
13. R Core Team: R: A language and environment for statistical computing. R Foundation for Statistical Computing (2015). https://www.R-project.org/
14. Ryan, R.M., Deci, E.L.: Self-determination theory and the facilitation of intrinsic motivation, social development, and well-being. Am. Psychol. **55**(1), 68–78 (2000)

15. Senécal, C.B., Vallerand, R.J., Vallières, E.F.: Construction et validation de l'échelle de la qualité des relations interpersonnelles (EQRI). Revue européenne de psychologie appliquée **42**, 315–322 (1992)
16. Slavin, R.E.: Cooperative Learning: Theory, Research and Practice. Allyn & Bacon, Needham Heights (1995)
17. Steffens, K.: Self-regulated leaning in technology-enhanced learning environments: lessons of a european peer review. Eur. J. Educ. Res. Dev. Pol. **41**(3–4), 352–379 (2006)
18. Zimmerman, B.J.: Attaining self-regulation: a social cognitive perspective. In: Boekaerts, M., Pintrich, P.R., Zeidner, M. (eds.) Handbook of Self-Regulation, pp. 14–39. Academic Press, San Diego (2000)

Teaching Students to Learn IDEA: The Impact of Learner Attitudes

D'Arcy Becker(✉), Dawna Drum, and Aimee Pernsteiner

University of Wisconsin – Whitewater, Whitewater, USA
beckerda@uww.edu

Abstract. Technology is pervasive every profession. Successful professionals must be able to learn new technologies throughout their careers. Students who learn new technologies as part of a college curriculum are more equipped to meet this challenge; this effect is enhanced if the technologies learned in college are used in the student's future profession. However, some students learn course-specific technologies more easily than others. Our study investigates accounting students who learn the auditing software IDEA. While prior research has shown that technology acceptance and aptitude for learning technology both are relevant to technology adoption decisions of organizations, prior research has not applied these models to teaching and learning professional-level technology. We found that technology acceptance and self-perceptions of the ability to learn had significant impacts on students' achievement with the new technology. When students believed their aptitude for learning technology was higher, they showed higher achievement in using IDEA.

Keywords: Teaching technology · Learner aptitude · Technology acceptance · IDEA software

1 Introduction

In 2005, the American Institute of Certified Public Accountants (AICPA) sets standards for the public accounting profession in the United States. The AICPA model curriculum framework addresses technology as one of the functional competencies necessary for accounting undergraduates (AICPA 2005). The framework states that people entering the accounting profession must acquire the necessary skills to use technology tools effectively and efficiently throughout their careers.

In 2014, the Fourth Annual IT Audit Benchmarking Survey completed by the Information Systems Audit and Control Association (ISACA) reported that companies faced significant IT audit staffing concerns in filling positions. ISACA surveyed over 1300 IT professionals at medium and large-sized companies and accounting firms. Results showed that a shortage of skilled entry level accounting and auditing staff was the second-highest technology concern for companies, behind concerns over cybersecurity (ISACA 2014). Technology training and skill development for entry level accountants remains a major concern.

Computer aided audit techniques (CAATs) are an accounting technology that is used commonly in financial statement auditing. CAATs provide data analytics, support

L. Uden et al. (Eds.): LTEC 2016, CCIS 620, pp. 112–121, 2016.
DOI: 10.1007/978-3-319-42147-6_10

for sampling, statistical analysis, among other types of support for audits. The effectiveness of CAATs in the conduct of audits has been recognized by both regulatory bodies and accounting practitioners, as shown in a variety of accounting research settings (e.g. Weidenmier and Ramamoorti 2006; Brennan 2008; Baker 2009).

CAATs are appropriate for students to learn in college accounting programs because they usually require little or no computer programming skill. Teaching CAATs is an appropriate way to improve the technology learning experience of accounting students (Kuruppu 2012).

Prior research regarding CAATs such as IDEA and ACL has tended to provide descriptions of assignments without linking the assignments to auditing course content. Further, the assignments have tended to promote skill development but stop short of introducing students to the decision making elements of using the software (for example, how to choose among the software options when following an audit program).

Failure to successfully learn the technology component of an auditing course has negative implications for the student's future ability to learn new technologies throughout their careers. College instruction most likely provides more guidance and practice than would be provided in a professional training course. In addition, there are more important consequences to mis-using CAATs in auditing practice.

This study investigates the impact of technology acceptance on success in learning IDEA. Computer User Learning Aptitude (CULA) a concept developed by Warner et al. (2014), is discussed below. Prior research has shown that technology acceptance impacts CULA. It has also shown that CULA impacts student achievement in learning a new technology. If a student perceives a technology is useful, it is easy to use, and they intend to use it in the future, the student may perceive that they have higher learner aptitude for learning the technology. The result may be higher CULA, and consequently higher learning achievement.

Therefore, technology acceptance may play an important role in student achievement in learning a new technology. We propose that applying the concepts of the technology acceptance model (Davis 1989) can explain some of the variability in students' ability to learn IDEA auditing software.

2 Prior Literature

Fifteen years ago, accounting educators were challenged by Russell et al. (2000) to examine the accounting curriculum thoroughly and take the necessary steps to enhance the curriculum so as to ensure its relevance and effectiveness. Part of staying relevant included equipping students with the skills and experiences necessary to become professionals (Dickins and Reisch 2009). To become successful auditors, students needed to understand audit theory, the relationship between theory and audit practice, and current audit techniques (Weidenmier and Herron 2004).

CAATs have become central to the manner in which audits (both external and internal) are conducted, and therefore students should obtain some level of skill in using them while in college. These technology-related skills enhance students' ability to contribute to their new employers. Clune and Gramling (2012) stated that one of the most important characteristics sought by firms hiring for internal audit positions directly from universities was the student's ability to be productive immediately upon hire, including the ability to use auditing software.

Baker (2009) reported results of a survey of IT audit professionals which found that the most commonly used IT audit tool is data analysis software. Three-quarters of respondents used some form of software to perform analysis, and IDEA was one of the most commonly named. Training on this software would improve student readiness for external and internal auditing positions.

Learning about CAATs such as IDEA can improve students' technical software skills as it helps them understand how auditing concepts are implemented in practice (e.g. Weidenmier and Herron 2004). Prior research related to CAATS has provided a variety of IDEA (and competitor software product ACL) assignments to use in auditing courses. These papers provide software instructions and information about effective ways to introduce students to the software (e.g. Gelinas et al. 2001; Arel et al. 2003; Weidenmier and Herron 2004; Murthy 2010; Kuruppu 2012).

Despite these resources, this technology training has the same challenges as all other technology training: overcoming student differences in their abilities to learn technology. Among the factors that may impact a student's technology ability are: work experiences, technology in different courses, tolerance for ambiguity, and problem solving ability, among others. CULA (Warner et al. 2014) was developed as an extension of the Technology Acceptance Model (Davis 1989) to address learner differences that are specific to technology.

Teo and van Schaik (2012) called for research that investigates mediating or additional variables that impact the intention to use technology in educational contexts, including previous experience or usage, and other user characteristics. We believe CULA is one of those variables. CULA may be important to the success of technology training because higher CULA means the user finds it easier to learn the technology. Warner et al. (2014) showed that when there are substantive costs in terms of effort required to learn a new technology, CULA plays a role in determining training success. The overall model we tested is shown in Fig. 1.

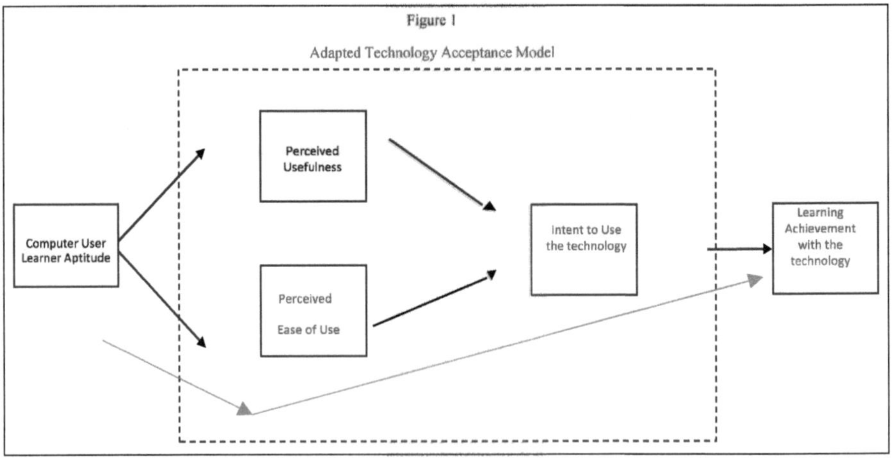

Fig. 1. Adapted technology acceptance model

Technology acceptance refers to a user's willingness to employ information technology for the tasks it is designed to support (Teo and van Schaik 2012). In an educational setting, technology acceptance is the student's willingness to employ a technology to learn topics required by a course. The technology acceptance model (TAM) includes user intent to implement a new technology, the technology's perceived usefulness, and its perceived ease of use (Davis 1989).

CULA, based on the same premise found in Bandura's (1986) concept of self-efficacy, may be important to the success of technology training. People who believe they have ability for a task tend to perform better on the task.

As CULA is impacted by students' perceptions of a technology's usefulness and ease of use, it may also impact their learning achievement. Holden and Rada (2011) showed that user psychological characteristics such as self-efficacy (which is similar to learner aptitude) can be important in technology acceptance. Ahmed (2010) showed that student achievement in technology learning was impacted by student acceptance of the technology. We test this premise in our study.

3 Study Overview and Hypotheses

Our goal was to find out more about student success in learning to use IDEA. That is, would achievement be higher when the drivers of technology acceptance were higher? Would student achievement be higher when aptitude for learning technology was higher?

We implemented a 3-stage IDEA curriculum, and measured student achievement at the end of the module; students took a quiz that required them to analyze data files using IDEA software. We measured students' perceptions of their aptitude for learning new technology and their technology acceptance at the end of the learning module.

We hypothesize that the relationship between technology acceptance model elements and CULA that have been shown in professional settings also exist in the classroom setting.

Hypothesis 1: A student's level of Computer User Learning Aptitude affects their technology acceptance (ease of use, usefulness). Students who perceive their aptitude for learning technology to be strong will report finding technology is easier to use, and it seems more useful to them. These questions are asked in general terms to allow us to relate students' overall impressions of their learning aptitude for technology to their general impression of ease of use, and of usefulness rather than their specific impressions of their aptitude for the specific software used in this study. This was done to ensure our measures were as valid and reliable as those used in prior research.

H1a: The impact of CULA on perceived ease of use of a technology is significant.
H1b: The impact of CULA on perceived usefulness of a technology is significant.

We further hypothesize that students who have higher CULA will learn to use IDEA software with greater proficiency (as assessed by quiz scores). The quiz was taken just before the students completed the survey questions measuring their aptitude and attitudes toward learning technology. Students did not yet know their performance on the quiz. We believe students who report a higher aptitude for computer learning will have scored better on the quiz; they will have a achieved a higher level of success in learning the new technology.

H2: CULA will have a significant impact on student achievement measured by quiz score.

H3: Finally, we hypothesize that self-reported ease of use and perceived usefulness will impact student learning achievement. In keeping with TAM, students who generally find a new technology relatively easy to learn will demonstrate a higher level of proficiency with the new technology. In addition, students who perceive technology to be useful will demonstrate a higher level of proficiency with the new technology.

H3a: The impact of perceived ease of use of a technology on student achievement as measured by quiz score is significant.
H3b: The impact of CULA on perceived usefulness of a technology on student achievement as measured by quiz score is significant.

4 Measures

We adapted the questions used to measure CULA from Teo and van Schaik (2012) and Warner et al. (2014). The survey also included measures of perceived usefulness, perceived ease of use, and intent to use IDEA software once the student begins their professional career. These measures have been validated in prior studies and are considered reliable (Erasmus et al. 2015). We acknowledge that these questions have inherent measurement issues. They are matters of opinion. We believe this set of measures is suitable for purposes of this study because prior research has demonstrated that a learner's opinion of their ability, how easily they learn a new technology or how easy the technology is to use all affect whether the learner will be successful with the new technology. We relate students' opinions of their aptitude with their actual achievement as a means of evaluating their opinions.

5 Integrating IDEA with Auditing Concepts

Participants in the study were 83 fourth year accounting majors enrolled in a required first course in auditing. Using a lecture and class discussion style, students spent one week just before the IDEA section of the course learning concepts related to auditing revenue. IDEA software training was related to software capabilities normally used to audit revenue.

IDEA training included the three phases below. Each phase lasted one week, or two 75-minute class sessions, and the phases were conducted in back to back weeks.

1. Introductory level in-class instruction on basic IDEA skills which walked students through various functions.

2. Intermediate in-class instruction where students were led through basic audit program steps related to auditing revenue and accounts receivable.
3. Advanced in-class instruction where students tried to fulfill audit program steps by choosing the IDEA functions and client data to use.

Students took the quiz at the end of IDEA training. The quiz required students to use IDEA to fulfill audit program requirements. Sample audit programs students used in training phases 2 and 3 are shown in Appendices 1 and 2.

6 Results

Participants in the study were 83 fourth year accounting majors enrolled in a required first course in auditing. All were fourth year accounting majors and none were pursuing a double major in a technology area such as Information Systems or Computer Science.

Student responses to the questions included in each factor were summed to create the student's score for ease of use (maximum score 20), usefulness (maximum score 20), and intent to use IDEA (maximum score of 15). The maximum score for CULA was 20. Student scores on the quiz were determined based on a scale of 0–100 %.

Table 1 shows the average ratings for each of the measures. All items were rated on a 5-point Likert scale from strongly disagree (1) to strongly agree (5).

Table 1. ANOVA results for student computer user learning aptitude on perceived ease of use of technology

	Sum of squares	df	Mean square	F	Sig.
Between groups	132.826	11	12.075	4.95	.000
Within groups	170.735	70	2.439		
Total	303.561	81			

H1: A student's Computer User Learning Aptitude impacts their level of technology acceptance (ease and usefulness).

Results for H1a: A student's perceptions of their CULA had a significant impact on perceptions of their ease of use of technology. The ANOVA table, Table 1, shows the significance level is <.01. Hypothesis H1a is supported. Students with higher perceptions of their aptitude for learning technology reported higher ease of use of technology.

Results for H1b: A student's perceptions of their CULA had an insignificant impact on perceptions of the usefulness of technology The ANOVA table, Table 2, shows the significance level is <.01. Hypothesis H1b is not supported. No relationship was found between this aptitude measure and student ratings of perceived usefulness.

H2: CULA will have a significant impact on student achievement measured by quiz scores.

Table 2. ANOVA results for student computer user learning aptitude on perceived usefulness of technology

	Sum of squares	df	Mean square	F	Sig.
Between groups	78.461	11	7.133	1,496	.153
Within groups	333.844	70	4.769		
Total	412.305	81			

Results for H2: ANOVA on the impact of ending CULA on student quiz scores showed a significant impact (p = .025) as shown in the ANOVA table, Table 3. H2 is supported. Further, student quiz scores showed that the IDEA training was successful in leading students to a high level of achievement in IDEA use. Students were asked to perform sophisticated tasks using the software, and (on average) scored quite well. The average quiz score was 87 %; the range of scores was 60 % to 100 %.

Table 3. ANOVA results for the impact of student computer user learning aptitude on student learning achievement (quiz score)

	Sum of squares	df	Mean square	F	Sig.
Between groups	3944.140	11	358.558	2.185	.025
Within groups	11487.872	70	164.112		
Total	15421.012	81			

H3: Perceived ease of use and perceived usefulness will affect student achievement as measured by quiz score.

Results for H3a: The impact of perceived ease of use of a technology on student achievement measured by quiz score is insignificant as shown in the ANOVA table, Table 4. The p-value is .317; students who reported higher ease in learning new technology did not out-perform students who reported more difficulty in learning new technology.

Table 4. ANOVA results for the impact of ease of use of technology on student learning achievement (quiz score)

	Sum of squares	df	Mean square	F	Sig.
Between groups	1777.673	8	222.209	1.189	.317
Within groups	13824.134	74	186.813		
Total	15601.807	82			

Results for H3b: The impact of CULA on perceived usefulness of a technology on student achievement measured by quiz score is significant as shown in the ANOVA table, Table 5. The p-value is .018; students who reported higher perceptions of technology usefulness performed better on the IDEA quiz.

Table 5. ANOVA results for the impact of perceived usefulness on student learning achievement (quiz score)

	Sum of squares	df	Mean square	F	Sig.
Between groups	3328.181	8	416.023	2.508	.018
Within groups	12273.626	74	165.860		
Total	15601.807	82			

Students who perceive learning new technology to be easier were not more successful in learning the technology than students who find learning new technology to be more difficult. However, students who find technology to be more useful did show they had learned to use IDEA at a more proficient level.

This may be partially due to the important nature of the technology used in this study. Students were made aware that they will most likely use IDEA (or a very similar competitor software) in their careers as accountants. The software's analytical abilities transcend the audit profession, making it useful to accountants in a variety of different professional positions. When students know technology will be a part of their future careers, they appear to learn the new technology better. Students who do not perceive IDEA to be useful may not intend to work in accounting once they graduate, and therefore learning CAATs is unimportant to them. They don't think it will be useful, and they don't learn to use the software at a proficient level.

7 Conclusions and Limitations

Auditing students need to learn the concepts and practices they are likely to encounter at the start of their careers. CAATs are among the most likely technologies students will use, and implementing them in auditing classes should become more commonplace. Students benefit from both learning the CAAT software and from understanding how it is implemented as part of an audit.

We implemented IDEA in an auditing class with a goal of leading students to understand the basic functions of the software as well as some of the decisions auditors face when using IDEA. However, we only addressed the types of audit program steps used in a basic audit program for revenue and accounts receivable. Students became familiar with a wide variety of IDEA functions and in future iterations of this study, students could apply their new skill set to an entirely new type of accounting data. This would be a more pure measure of student achievement than the one used in this study. The ability to carry analytic skills to new settings would require a higher level of knowledge than was needed to score 100 % on the quiz used in this study.

Detailed software instruction is needed to ensure students are able to use CAATs, and that they understand the capabilities these programs can provide to accountants. Student knowledge of IDEA itself was measured using quiz grades; these graded results showed that students did learn to use the software at a level above basic button-pushing. Future research may include the more expansive UTAUT model parameters, especially if a wider and larger sample of respondents could be organised from several cohorts over two or three years.

We acknowledge that we only taught students IDEA, not a variety of CAATs. Other auditing software programs are available for use in college accounting classes, most prominently software called ACL. Weidenmier and Herron (2004) showed that ACL and IDEA may be taught in very similar manners; the programs are similar in many ways. Teaching technology in functional settings such as an auditing class helps students understand that all areas of accounting involve technology. There is no reason to believe that our results are specific to IDEA alone.

The next logical stage of this research is to try to design ways of teaching technology that impact students' computer user learning aptitude and its drivers. As a starting point, collecting data about CULA before and after the training is necessary. If we can influence a student's CULA, then there may be general implications for teaching and learning of all new technologies. We do not usually consider the student's attitude toward learning a subject when designing our lessons. However, this paper demonstrates that there may be benefits to student learning if this is considered.

References

Ahmed, H.S.: Hybrid E-Learning Acceptance Model: Learner Perceptions. Dec. Sci. J. Innovative Educ. **8**(2), 313–346 (2010)

American Institute of Certified Public Accountants (AICPA). Core Competency Framework & Educational Competency Assessment (2005). http://www.aicpa.org/interestareas/accounting education/resources/pages/corecompetency.aspx

Arel, B., Pany, K., Zhang, J.: Integrating Generalized Audit Software into the Auditing Curriculum. American Accounting Association annual meeting (2003). http://aaahq.org/Audit/midyear/04midyear/papers/Arel%20Pany%20and%20Zhang%20ACL.doc

Baker, N.: Software Trend Spotting. Internal Auditor (2009). http://www.theiia.org/intAuditor/free-feature/2009/august/software-trend-spotting/

Clune, R.R., Gramling, A.A.: Hiring recent university graduates into internal audit positions: insights from practicing internal auditors. Curr. Issues Auditing **6**(2), A1–A14 (2012)

Davis, F.D.: Perceived usefulness, perceived ease of use, and user acceptance of information technology. MIS Q. **13**(3), 319–340 (1989)

Dickins, D., Reisch, J.T.: Ready to work. Intern. Auditor **66**(6), 42–46 (2009)

Gelinas Jr., U.J., Levy, E.S., Thibodeau, J.C.: Norwood office supplies inc.: a teaching case to integrate computer-assisted auditing techniques into the auditing course. Issues Accounting Educ. **16**(4), 603–636 (2001)

Holden, H., Rada, R.: The influence of perceived usability and technology self-efficacy on teachers' technology acceptance. J. Res. Technol. Educ. **43**(4), 343–367 (2011)

ISACA. 2014. Fourth Annual IT Audit Benchmarking Survey: A Global Look at Best Audit Practices. http://www.protiviti.com/en-US/Documents/Surveys/4th-Annual-IT-Audit-Benchmarking-Survey-ISACA-Protiviti.pdf

Kuruppu, N.: A structured pedagogy for integrating generalized audit software into the auditing curriculum. Bus. Educ. Accred. **4**(1), 113–121 (2012)

Murthy, U.S.: Tampa electronics: an instructional case in computer-assisted fraud examination. Issues Accounting Educ. **25**(3), 547–552 (2010)

Russell, K., Kulesza, C., Albrecht, W., Sack, R.: Charting the course through a perilous future. Manage. Accounting Q. **2**(1), 4–11 (2000)

Teo, T., van Schaik, P.: Understanding the intention to use technology by preservice teachers: an empirical test of competing theoretical models. Int. J. Hum. Comput. Interact. **28**(3), 178–188 (2012)

Ulrich, T.A., Michenzi, A.R., Blouch, W.E.: An importance – effectiveness analysis of the contemporary auditing course. Acad. Educ. Leadersh. J. **13**(4), 1–17 (2009)

Warner, J.A., Koufteros, X., Verghese, A.: Learning computerese: the role of second language learning aptitude in technology acceptance. Educ. Psychol. Meas. **74**(6), 991–1017 (2014)

Weidenmier, M.L., Herron, T.L.: Selecting an audit software package for classroom use. J. Inf. Syst. **18**(1), 95–110 (2004)

Emotion Determination in eLearning Environments Based on Facial Landmarks

Tobias Augustin(✉)

Fernuniversität in Hagen, Hagen, Germany
tobias.augustin@fernuni-hagen.de

Abstract. Massive Open Online Courses (MOOCs) are a new kind of e-Learning environment, which enables us to address untold numbers of students. MOOCs allow students all over the world to participate in lectures independent of place and time. The sessions that are in some cases joined by more than 100,000 students are based on small units of teaching material containing videos or texts.

However today's MOOCs are static environments, which do not take into account the diversity of the students and their situational context. Current MOOCs can be seen as mass processing but not as an individual treatment of individual students. Thus MOOCs need to be personalized in addition to massive.

In order to personalize an e-Learning environment it is first of all necessary to collect data, or personal factors, about the student, his or her current environment and his or her situational context. This data should later be processed and used as input for adaptive functions. Basically there are many input factors imaginable, such as cognitive style, preknowledge, currently used device or personal goals. The input factors can be grouped into technical, personal and situational factors. Especially situational factors may help to support students in different learning situations.

This paper describes an approach to detect the student's current mood as a situational input factor. The mood of a student in a learning situation might be an interesting feature that can be used as an instant feedback for the currently used teaching materials. The proposed approach is based on widespread availability of built-in cameras in devices that are used by students, such as smart-phones, tablets or laptop computers. The captured frames from these devices are processed by a Java-based server component that detects selected facial landmarks. Based on the relative position of these landmarks the potential shown emotion is determined.

The output of the system may be used to adjust the difficulty level of tests or to determine the preferred media type.

1 Introduction

Adaptive systems are generally characterized by the capability of gathering personal or situational user data and the capability to adjust the system behavior regarding the user needs. In order to first get an accurate picture of the user, it is necessary to determine and detect the different factors influencing a user.

L. Uden et al. (Eds.): LTEC 2016, CCIS 620, pp. 122–136, 2016.
DOI: 10.1007/978-3-319-42147-6_11

This work focuses on the detection of the user's emotion in specific learning situations as one influencing factor. The aim of the proposed approach is to identify the current emotion of a student in camera images based on particular facial landmarks. Most of the used fundamental techniques, such as face and landmark detection, are known approaches. We show how these approaches can be integrated in modern web-based learning environments and how they can be used to determine an emotion in such an environment. The required cameras are nowadays available in most devices such as smart-phones, tablets or laptop computers.

The generated data can be used to adjust the behavior of the eLearning environment. Typically the success of learning situations depends on many personal and situational factors of the individual user. But the success of a learning session does not only depend on the current situation of the student, but also on the presented learning materials. A good teacher is always able to interact with a group of students. For example, it is possible to get attention from a group of tired students by using lively or funny examples. Static learning environments that usually follow a linear storyline are not able to interact with the students due to limited alternatives in terms of learning materials and missing knowledge in terms of the learner's current situation. Therefore John Hennessy, President of Stanford University, said we cannot expect MOOCs to be the base of academic education in the 21st century. He expects that we will have intelligent and automatic tutoring systems that create individual learning materials based on individual strength and weaknesses [23]. It needs to be pointed out that detecting the learner's current mood is not the single, big solution, but one piece of the puzzle. There is more research needed to identify further personal, situational and technical input factors that have influence on a learning session. Furthermore courses need to be developed that do not follow one static storyline but have alternatives for each piece of information in difficulty level, used media and educational approach. The discussion towards standardized Open Educational Repositories (OER) might be a useful approach.

Figure 1 gives a general overview of the proposed system and its process flow. For the emotion identification we need to make a distinction between two major tasks. The first task is the facial landmark detection, which is used to find the important landmarks and their position in the picture. The facial landmark detection process is described in Sect. 4. The second major task, described in Sect. 5, is the emotion analysis, which is used to classify the shown emotion.

Besides the two major tasks, several additional tasks need to be performed. First a homogeneous and platform independent way for transporting the captured data from the client's device to the server side needs to be found as described in the second section. This is essential to support most devices available on the market regardless of their platform and operating system. Additionally the client should not need to install additional software components as most current eLearning systems are web based.

After that a preprocessing at the server side is needed to normalize the transferred images regarding resolution, dimensions and color space. The details of applied preprocessing techniques are described in the third and subsequent sections.

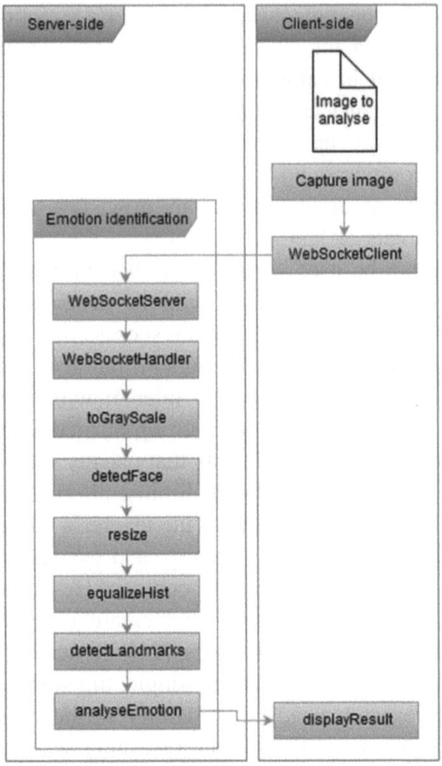

Fig. 1. General process overview

2 Transport

This section describes the image capturing on the client side and the following transport mechanism to the server component for further processing.

As user acceptance for components working "out of the box" is increasing, we searched for a way to capture images at the client side and transport them to the processing server component without the need to install additional software or plugins on the client's side. Furthermore we searched for a native, platform and operating system independent access to the device without the need to cover different camera models.

Since HTML5 was released in October 2014 it is possible to access the user's video and audio devices without the use of third party plug-ins. Now it is possible to access the user's camera device directly through a powerful JavaScript-API [1]. Most widely distributed web browsers, such as Microsoft Internet Explorer, Mozilla Firefox, Google Chrome and Apple Safari support HTML5 and it's new features. So it is very easy to implement a piece of JavaScript code that can be integrated in most web based eLearning environments and allows us to access the users video device. However, the device will ask the user for permission to start the camera, based on the security settings.

WebSocket is a web technology providing full-duplex communications channels over a single TCP connection [2]. WebSocket is designed to be implemented in web browsers and web servers, but it can be used by any client or server application. In this example we will use a Java server and a JavaScript client.

Figure 2 shows a minimal example that checks if `UserMedia` is available, creates an instance of a WebSocket server connection to the server's IP-address on port 9999. Once the connection is established it sends an image from the camera to the server every second.

```
var video;
function start(){
    video = $("#live").get()[0];
    var canvas = $("#canvas");
    var ctx = canvas.get()[0].getContext('2d');

    navigator.getUserMedia= ( navigator.getUserMedia
                             ||navigator.webkitGetUserMedia
                             ||navigator.mozGetUserMedia
                             ||navigator.msGetUserMedia
                           );

    if (navigator.getUserMedia) {
      navigator.getUserMedia ({video: true,audio: false},
        function(localMediaStream) {
          var video = document.querySelector('video');
          video.src = window.URL.createObjectURL(localMediaStream);
             timer = setInterval(
            function () {
                ctx.drawImage(video, 0, 0, 320, 240);
                var data = canvas.get()[0].toDataURL('image/jpeg', 1.0);
                newblob = dataURItoBlob(data);
                ws.send(newblob);
            }, 1000);
            ws = new WebSocket("ws://132.176.66.179:9999/8711");
        },
        function(err) {
          console.log("The following error occured: " + err);
        }
      );
    } else {
      console.log("getUserMedia not supported");
    }
}
```

Fig. 2. Client-side JavaScript Code for camera access and connection to WebSocket Server

On the server-side we use the Java based webserver Jetty which provides a Web server and javax.servlet container, plus support for HTTP/2, WebSocket, OSGi, JMX, JNDI, JAAS and many other integrations [3]. The server-side implementation is also quite simple. The Java class WebsocketServer shown in Fig. 3 opens a TCP port and registers a handler class that processes all incoming messages.

The WebSockerHandler class shown in Fig. 4 shows some functions with annotations that are called for different events. Once the connection is established and the client sends frames from the camera device to the server, the function `onFrame (byte[], int, int)` is called for every incoming frame. The implementation of the function converts the `byte`-Buffer to an `IplImage` which is shown in a canvas Frame on the server. IPL stands for Intel Processing Library, as the openCV Library was first maintained by Intel.

```java
package workingSet;
import org.eclipse.jetty.server.Server;

public class WebsocketServer{
    public static void startWSS() throws Exception {
        Server server = new Server(9999);
            WebSocketHandler wsHandler = new WebSocketHandler() {
                @Override
                public void configure(WebSocketServletFactory factory) {
                    factory.register(DemoWebSocketHandler.class);
                }
            };
            server.setHandler(wsHandler);
            server.start();
            server.join();
    }
}
```

Fig. 3. Server-side Java implementation of the WebsocketServer class

```java
package workingSet;
import static org.bytedeco.javacpp.opencv_core.CV_8UC1;

@WebSocket(maxBinaryMessageSize = 500 * 500)
public class DemoWebSocketHandler {
    private Session session;
    CanvasFrame canvasFrame = new CanvasFrame("Class WSS Handler");

    @OnWebSocketClose
    public void onClose(int statusCode, String reason) {
        System.out.println("Close: statusCode=" + statusCode +
                ", reason=" + reason);
    }

    @OnWebSocketError
    public void onError(Throwable t) {
        System.out.println("Error: " + t.getMessage());
    }

    @OnWebSocketConnect
    public void onConnect(Session session) {
        this.session = session;
        System.out.println("Hostname: "+
                this.session.getRemoteAddress().getHostName());
    }

    @OnWebSocketMessage
    public void onMessage(String message) {
        System.out.println("Message: " + message);
    }

    @OnWebSocketMessage
    public void onFrame(byte buf[], int offset, int length){
        ByteArrayOutputStream bOut = new ByteArrayOutputStream();
        bOut.write(buf, offset, length);
        IplImage originalImage = cvDecodeImage(cvMat(1,
                bOut.toByteArray().length,CV_8UC1,
                new BytePointer(bOut.toByteArray())));
        canvasFrame.showImage(originalImage);
    }
}
```

Fig. 4. WebSocketHandler class

This compact example shows how the captured image data can be transferred from the client to the server with the use of HTML5 and WebSockets. To use this mechanism in a multi-user environment it is also necessary to make a distinction between individual users. This can easily be achieved by appending a unique user ID to the WebSocket endpoint URL on the client and extracting it on the server side as shown in Fig. 5.

```
String url = this.session.getUpgradeRequest().getRequestURI().toString();
int uid = Integer.parseInt(url.substring(url.lastIndexOf("/")+1, url.length()));
```

Fig. 5. Server-side UID extraction

3 Image Preprocessing

Now that the images for further analysis are available in the server-side Java stack this section describes how the image data is preprocessed for the following face detection. Usually the resolution and color space of captured images depend on the used camera device. Besides that the lighting conditions and the field of view depend on the camera position and environment.

Further processing techniques, especially face classification algorithms are extremely sensitive regarding lighting conditions, used color space and image dimensions. The preprocessing is necessary to normalize incoming frames regarding resolution, dimensions and color space. Additionally histogram equalization is applied to each frame. Some of these techniques need to be applied initially to incoming frames; more over some of them need to be applied after the following processing steps.

3.1 Color Space Transformation

The techniques used for face extraction and face classification work on the basis of differences in light intensity, so they require grayscale images. Transforming a color image to a grey scale image can be done by using the openCV function `imread` [14] with a specified color model for initial loading operations as shown in the following example.

```
Mat testImage = imread(
        "S059_002_00121509.png",
        CV_LOAD_IMAGE_GRAYSCALE
        );
```

To transform incoming captured frames the function cvCvtColor [15] can be applied as shown in the following example.

```
cvCvtColor(originalImage, grayImage, CV_BGR2GRAY);
```

3.2 Resizing

To achieve good results from algorithms for face classification it is necessary to provide pictures with the same resolution for training images and those which are analyzed. In this scenario we use images with a size of 200 × 200 pixels. This size is used for all training images and all images that are analyzed. As the face classification does not work on the complete images as provided the resizing is applied after the face extraction for the area that contains the face. OpenCV provides a function [16] that resizes a given image to a given size.

```
resize(originalImage, resizedImage, new Size(200, 200));
```

3.3 Histogram Equalization

Histogram equalization is a very simple method of automatically standardizing the brightness and contrast of images. This method usually increases the global contrast of images, especially when the usable data of the image is represented by close contrast values. Equalization means mapping the given distribution to a wider and more uniform distribution of intensity values, so the intensity values are spread over the whole range. Through this adjustment, the intensities can be better distributed on the histogram. This allows to gain a higher contrast for areas of low local contrast (Figs. 6, 7, 8 and 9).

OpenCV provides the function `equalizeHist` [17] to apply histogram equalization.

```
equalizeHist(imageToAnalyse, imageToAnalyse);
```

Fig. 6. An unequalized image

Fig. 7. The same image after histogram equalization

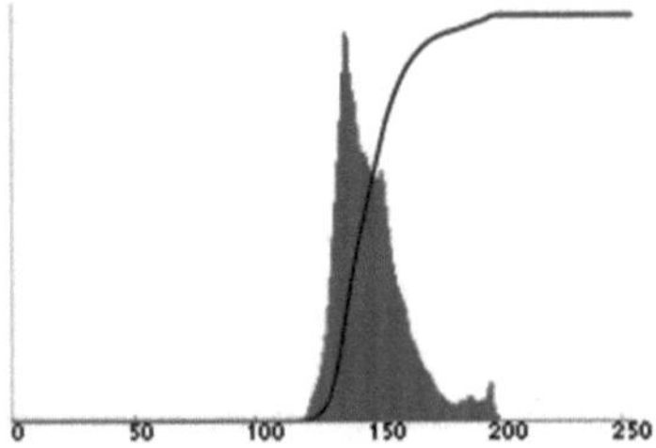

Fig. 8. Corresponding histogram (red) and cumulative histogram (black) (Color figure online)

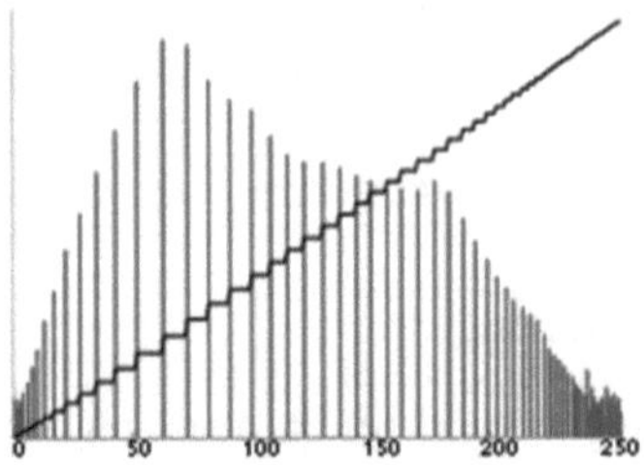

Fig. 9. Corresponding histogram (red) and cumulative histogram (black) (Color figure online)

3.4 Face Extraction

This section describes the face extraction which consists of face detection in the first stage followed by a segmentation to provide a sub image that contains the detected face.

There are several approaches to detect faces in images such as using the Hausdorff Distance [4] or Edge-Orientation Matching [5]. The breakthrough in face detection happened with Viola and Jones [6]. Using a cascade of "weak-classifiers", using simple Haar features, can – after excessive training – yield impressive results. This approach has proved to be very effective and reliable. The method, published in 2001, made it possible to implement face detection on gray scale images in real-time.

The approach is based on so called "Haar features" that represent features that are tried to match regions in the analyzed image. To find objects, features based on difference in light intensity are tested on different regions of the analyzed image. For example the eye area is usually darker than the cheeks and the eyes are darker than the bridge of the nose (see Fig. 10).

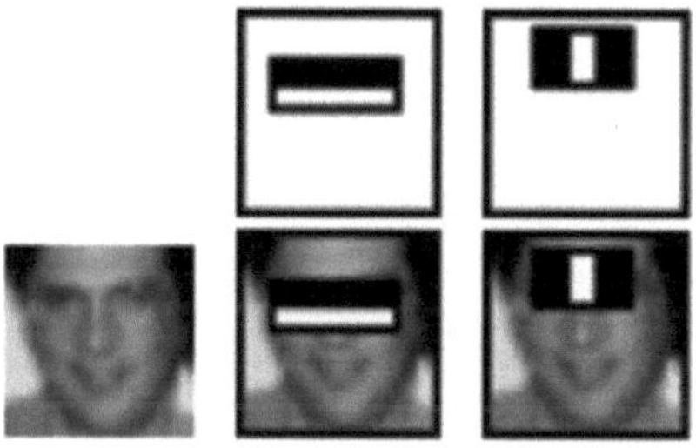

Fig. 10. Two features shown in the top row and then overlayed on a training image in the bottom row. The first feature measures the difference in intensity between the region of the eyes and a region across the upper cheeks. The second feature compares the intensities in the eye regions to the intensity across the bridge of the nose [6].

Figure 11 shows the set of features used by Viola and Jones. The features can be used in any scale and position to match a region in the original image. Therefore a huge amount of attempts needs to be performed. However the method uses two techniques to achieve fast and efficient processing, cascading and the so called integral image.

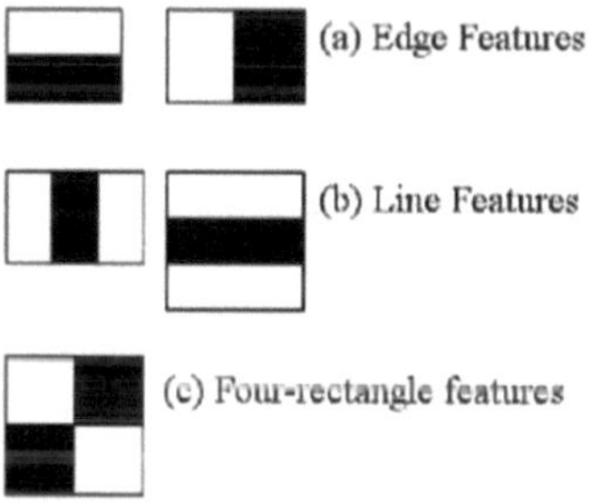

Fig. 11. Features used by Viola and Jones [6]

In 2002 Lienhart et al. extended the method by Viola and Jones with a set of 14 features and were able to improve the processing time again [7, 8]. Therefore the features shown in Fig. 11 are deployed. The original approach by Viloa and Jones only takes into account the features 1a, 1b, 2a, 2c and 4a (Fig. 12).

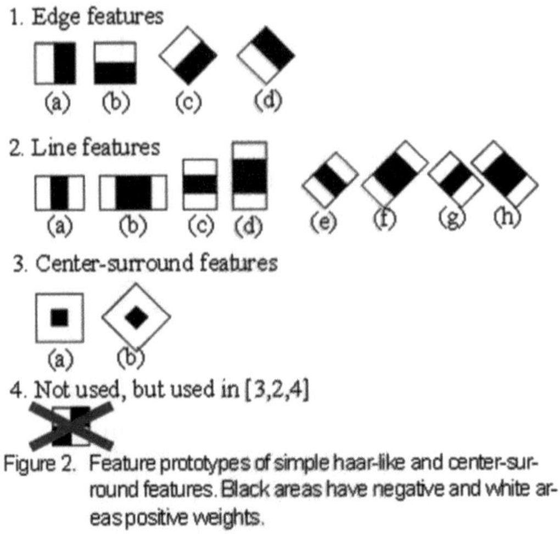

Fig. 12. Extended features used by Lienhart et al. [8]

Cascade. In most cases an image contains large regions that can easily be identified as background and only a few regions with potential faces. Only the regions containing a potential face are further analyzed. As a face can only be detected reliably by the use of many features, a mechanism is needed to discard background regions in a first step and to perform further detailed analysis on potential faces. Therefore, Viola and Jones used a decision tree based on the work of Amit and Geman [9] called cascade. Each node of this cascade has a binary classifier that determines whether or not the analyzed region can be treated as background (Fig. 13).

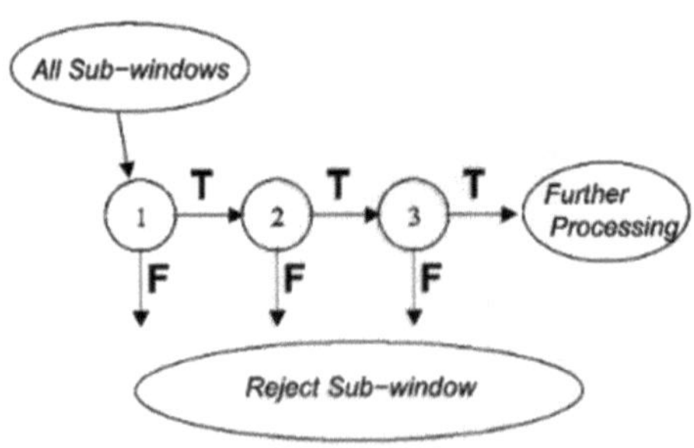

Fig. 13. Cascade used by Viola and Jones. A series of classifiers is applied to every region of the image. The initial stage eliminates a large number of negative examples with very little processing time. Subsequent stages work on a radically reduced amount of regions and eliminate additional negatives but require more processing time [6].

If a region is classified as background, the cascade is stopped and no further analysis is performed on this region. If the region is classified as potential face the region is processed by the next node of the cascade. Each region that passes all nodes is accepted as face. The essential advantage of the cascade structure is that early nodes contain less complex and fast classifiers while further classifiers become more complex and time consuming. In concrete terms the first node contains a classifier with two features and recognizes 60 % of the regions containing no face as background and almost 100 % of the regions containing a face as positive for further processing. The second node contains a classifier with five features and analyses all positive regions from the first classifier. This classifier is already able to detect 80 % of the regions as background that do not contain a face. In further steps three classifiers with 20 features, two classifiers with 50 features, five classifiers with 100 features and 20 classifiers with 200 features are used [6].

The complete cascade for face detection in XML representation is available as part of the Open Computer Vision Library [10].

Integral Image. The second technique to achieve fast processing is based on an alternative way of image representation called integral image. With the use of this technique rectangular features, from which Haar-features are made of, can be calculated in a very efficient way. An integral image contains the cumulated values of the pixels. As the method is based on difference in light intensity, only gray scale images can be processed. Usually 8-bit gray scale images are used, so that a distinction between 256 different brightness values is done. The value of the integral image at a specific point results from the sum of all pixel values above and left of the specific point.

$$ii(x,y) \quad \sum_{x' \leqq x, y' \leqq y} i(x',y'),$$

Where $ii(x,y)$ is the integral image and $i(x',y')$ is the original image. The value of the integral image in point (x,y) in Fig. 14 is the sum of all pixel values inside the gray area.

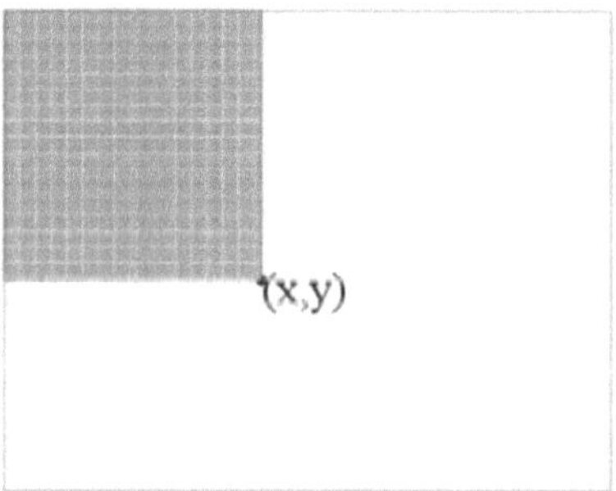

Fig. 14. Demonstration of an integral image

The integral image itself can be calculated in one pass with the following formulas, where s is the cumulative row matrix and ii is the integral image:

$$s(x,y) = s(x,y-1) + i(x,y)$$

$$ii(x,y) = ii(x-1,y) + s(x,y)$$

The coherence can easily be seen with a simple example of a 3 × 3 binary image, where i is the original binary image, s is the cumulative row matrix and ii is the resulting integral image.

$$i = \begin{Bmatrix} 1 & 0 & 1 \\ 1 & 1 & 1 \\ 0 & 0 & 1 \end{Bmatrix} \quad s = \begin{Bmatrix} 1 & 1 & 2 \\ 1 & 2 & 3 \\ 0 & 0 & 1 \end{Bmatrix} \quad ii = \begin{Bmatrix} 1 & 1 & 2 \\ 2 & 3 & 5 \\ 2 & 3 & 6 \end{Bmatrix}$$

The advantage of this method is that after the initial integral image has been calculated the sum of all pixel values of a square from the point of origin to the specific point can be looked up with only one access. Once the integral image has been calculated, it is possible to retrieve the sum of pixel values of any rectangular area of the image.

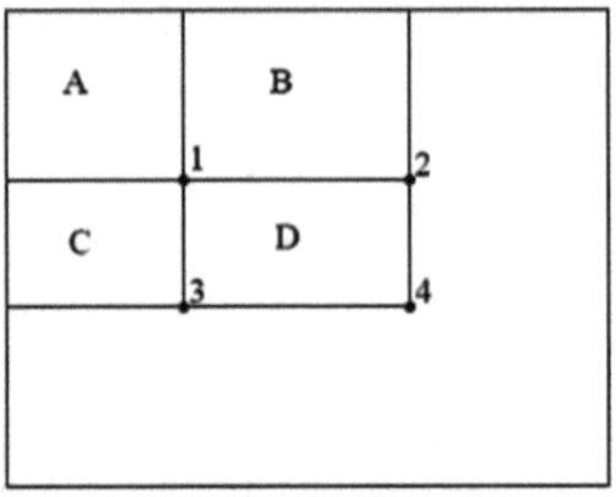

The value of the integral image at point 1 is the sum of all pixel values of square A. The value of the integral image at point 2 is the sum of the squares A + B, at point 3 A + C and at point 4 A + B + C + D. Thus the sum of all pixel values in square D can be calculated as follows:

$$D = ii(x_4,y_4) + ii(x_1,y_1) - (ii(x_2,y_2) + ii(x_3,y_3))$$

4 Landmark Detection

For the emotion identification we use selected facial landmarks. The following method is applied to a normalized image that only contains the face portion of the original image. The next chapter describes how the shown emotion is determined based on the relative position of these landmarks.

Once the facial area is detected, the key points can be detected. This is a very crucial step in the processing chain, as the facial key points need to be detected quickly enough to allow for a real-time video application, but also need to be accurate enough to be used for expression recognition. Our facial landmark detection is based on flandmark [13], due to its performance and speed. Flandmark is an open source library implementing a facial landmark detector for static images containing a face. The flandmark libarary detects eight facial landmarks (two for corners of each eye, one for tip of nose, two for corners of mouth, and one for center of face) by using Deformable Part Models (DPM) [20] that has been trained by Stuctured Output Support Vector Machines (SO-SVM) [13]. The general approach is similar to the Viola & Jones approach and also similar to that of edge orientation histograms. This detector uses a sliding window approach, where a filter is applied at all positions and scales of an image. The filter is based on the Histogram of Oriented Gradient (HOG) [21].

The classifier determines whether or not there is an instance of the target category at the given position and scale. Potential matches are marked for further analysis. The first stage captures coarse gradients histogrammed over fairly large areas of the input image while further features capture finer gradients histogrammed over small areas.

With this approach the part filters represent finer resolution edges that are localized to greater accuracy when compared to the edges represented in the root filter.

The flandmark libaray provides the function `flandmark_detect` that returns an array containing all landmark positions for a given face area within a given image. The face area within the image is provided from the face detection approach as described in Sect. 3.4.

Fig. 15. Input image with an overlayed red rectangle for the facial area and green circles for the detected landmarks. (Color figure online)

5 Emotion Analysis

The flandmark library returns an array that contains the position information for every detected landmark. This information can be used to display the detected landmarks with basic geometric forms as seen in Fig. 15. Here we use this information to analyze the face regarding the shown emotion and have chosen a very simple approach. Therefore we determine the relative distance of particular landmarks.

A brief example is the distance between the left and right corners of the mouth. Therefore the distance in pixels is determined and has to be set to the correct ratio with respect to the facial area dimensions.

$$distance = \frac{\sqrt{image_{width}^2 + image_{height}^2}}{\sqrt{(x_2 - x_1)^2 + (y_2 - y_1)^2}}$$

The distance between particular landmarks is interpretable as basic emotion. For example the distance of the mouth corners is usually closer for smiling faces than for surprised faces. With our basic approach we can achieve good results under controlled conditions by analyzing the distance of the corners of the mouth and mouth corners to outer eye corners. The current performance is 6 frames per second on a standard workstation (Dualcore @3 GHz, 8 GB Ram) which is sufficient for the proposed use case. It turned out that the limiting factor regarding reliability depends on the accurate detection of the position of the each landmark. The used library is very reliable in terms of identifying the landmarks but unfortunately it is not very reliable in terms of determining the exact position of the landmarks.

Currently the development team of the flandmark library prepares a further stage called CLandmark [22] that provides improvements in terms of quality and performance. Currently the developer's report of 68 detected landmarks at 100 frames per second with an improved confidence.

6 Discussion

The proposed approach shows that it is possible to implement a reliable emotion identification component based on various proven techniques. Some of the underlying techniques such as the face detection by Viola and Jones are state of the art. Some others such as standardized HTML5 mechanisms or WebSocket communication are emerging techniques and help to make the shown process as simple as described here. One new aspect is the use of facial landmarks and their relative positions to determine emotions in images of faces. Another new aspect is the integration of individual traits in static learning environments such as MOOCs. Due to the use of advanced preprocessing by analyzing only the facial region of an image that is normalized the approach is relatively robust concerning changing environmental conditions. However the accurate detection of facial landmarks is the weakest module concerning reliability of the detected emotion.

An alternative to landmark detection as discussed here, are holistic approaches, such as the fisherfaces or eigenfaces method [11, 12]. These approaches work on a database of known faces and try to match a given face to a class of faces from the database. Currently, the major case of application for these approaches is to identify persons, e.g. in access control solutions. When building classes of emotions from the database these approaches might also be useful for emotion identification. One of the main advantages is a higher reliability that can be expected when using large databases such as [18, 19]. But it needs to be pointed out that a large scale database is required and a time consuming initial training of the classifier needs to be performed.

In summary, it can be stated that the shown landmark-based approach is quite easy to implement and can be used ad-hoc in various environments without a training process. Compared to holistic approaches disadvantages can be expected in terms of reliability but also benefits through lower development costs and immediate operational readiness.

Currently we work on the development and evaluation of an emotion detection system based on a holistic approach. We also plan some research activity on the landmark based approach when a stable release of the CLandmak library is available.

In general it needs to be considered that detecting a mood is only one of many possible input factors to an eLearning situation. Mood detection can help to improve an eLearning session but it is only one of many factors on the way to real adaptive learning scenarios.

In addition to that it needs to be considered that the detection of situational or personal factors is only one first step in the development of adaptive eLearning scenarios as it is furthermore necessary to develop strategies how to react on particular input factors and interactions of multiple factors. Once the technology to detect situational or personal factors is available, strategies for the inclusion in the learning process need to be developed. Presumably these strategies will require different pieces of learning material for individual students, thus a MOOC might not have sufficient learning resources. Therefore another challenge on the way to adaptive learning scenarios is the search for modular learning resources.

References

1. Burnett, D.C., Narayanan, A.: Media Capture and Streams. W3C Editor's Draft, 25 June 2012. http://dev.w3.org/2011/webrtc/editor/getusermedia.html. Reffered on 8 Jan 2016
2. https://html.spec.whatwg.org/multipage/comms.html#network
3. https://eclipse.org/jetty/
4. Jesorsky, O., Kirchberg, K.J., Frischholz, R.W.: Robust face detection using the hausdorff distance. In: Bigun, J., Smeraldi, F. (eds.) AVBPA 2001. LNCS, vol. 2091, pp. 90–95. Springer, Heidelberg (2001). ISBN 3-540-42216-1, https://facedetection.com/wp-content/uploads/AVBPA01BioID.pdf

5. Fröba, B., Külbeck, C.: Real-time face detection using edge-orientation matching. In: Bigun, J., Smeraldi, F. (eds.) AVBPA 2001. LNCS, vol. 2091, pp. 78–83. Springer, Heidelberg (2001). ISBN 3-540-42216-1. http://link.springer.com/chapter/10.1007%2F3-540-45344-X_12
6. Viola, P., Jones, M.: Robust real-time object detection. Int. J. Comput. Vis. **4**, 34–47 (2001)
7. Lienhart, R., Kuranov, A., Pisarevsky, V.: Empirical analysis of detection cascades of boosted classifiers for rapid object detection. In: Michaelis, B., Krell, G. (eds.) DAGM 2003. LNCS, vol. 2781, pp. 297–304. Springer, Heidelberg (2003)
8. Lienhart, R., Maydt, J.: An extended set of haar-like features for rapid object detection. In: Proceedings of 2002 International Conference on Image Processing, vol. 1, pp. I–900. IEEE (2002)
9. Amit, Y., Geman, D., Wilder, K.: Joint induction of shape features and tree classifiers. IEEE Trans. Pattern Anal. Mach. Intell. **19**(11), 1300–1305 (1997)
10. http://docs.opencv.org/2.4/modules/objdetect/doc/cascade_classification.html
11. Turk, M., Pentland, A.: Eigenfaces for recognition. J. Cogn. Neurosci. **3**(1), 71–86 (1991a)
12. Turk, M.A., Pentland, A.P.: Face recognition using eigenfaces. In: Computer Vision and Pattern Recognition, Proceedings CVPR 1991, IEEE Computer Society Conference, pp. 586–591. IEEE (1991b)
13. Uricar, M., Franc, V., Hlavac, V.: Detector of facial landmarks learned by the structured output SVM. In: VISAPP 2012: Proceedings of the 7th International Conference on Computer Vision Theory and Applications (2012)
14. http://docs.opencv.org/2.4/modules/highgui/doc/reading_and_writing_images_and_video.html?highlight=imread#imread
15. http://docs.opencv.org/2.4/modules/imgproc/doc/miscellaneous_transformations.html
16. http://docs.opencv.org/2.4/modules/imgproc/doc/geometric_transformations.html#resize
17. http://docs.opencv.org/2.4/doc/tutorials/imgproc/histograms/histogram_equalization/histogram_equalization.html
18. Kanade, T., Cohn, J.F., Tian, Y.: Comprehensive database for facial expression analysis. In: Proceedings of the Fourth IEEE International Conference on Automatic Face and Gesture Recognition (FG 2000), Grenoble, France, pp. 46–53 (2000)
19. Lucey, P., Cohn, J.F., Kanade, T., Saragih, J., Ambadar, Z., Matthews, I.: The Extended Cohn-Kanade Dataset (CK+): a complete expression dataset for action unit and emotion-specified expression. In: Proceedings of the Third International Workshop on CVPR for Human Communicative Behavior Analysis (CVPR4HB 2010), San Francisco, USA, pp. 94–101 (2010)
20. Felzenszwalb, P.F., Girshick, R.B., McAllester, D., Ramanan, D.: Object detection with discriminatively trained part-based models. IEEE Trans. Pattern Anal. Mach. Intell. **32**(9), 1627–1645 (2010)
21. Dalal, N., Triggs, B.: Histograms of oriented gradients for human detection. In: CVPR, pp. I:886–I:893 (2005)
22. Uřičář, M.: CLandmark Open Source Landmarking Library (2016). http://cmp.felk.cvut.cz/~uricamic/clandmark/
23. Wiarda, J.: Rankings sind was für Angeber, Interview with John Hennessy, Die Zeit, Nr. 14, 23.003.2016

MOOC for Learning

A Practical Experience on the Use of Gamification in MOOC Courses as a Strategy to Increase Motivation

Miguel Morales[1], Hector R. Amado-Salvatierra[1(✉)], Rocael Hernández[1,2], Johanna Pirker[2], and Christian Gütl[2,3]

[1] GES Department, Galileo University, Guatemala, Guatemala
{amorales, hr_amado, roc}@galileo.edu
[2] IICM, Graz University of Technology, Graz, Austria
jpirker@iicm.tu-graz.ac.at,
christian.guetl@iicm.tugraz.at
[3] SIS, Curtin University, Perth, WA, Australia

Abstract. The rapid and constant pace of change in technology and the increasing involvement of educational institutions in the massive online open courses (MOOC) movement elicit a large myriad of opportunities and challenges. One of the main issues is the reported high dropout rate. In this sense, gamification strategies have been proposed as a complement to existing learning approaches providing a powerful and motivational learning experience to students. Examples of gamification strategies for MOOC environments include rewards for learning activities, applying levels and leader-boards to encourage progress and competition, and badges for participation in forums. The aim of this study is to contribute to the analysis of motivational factors to provide improved learning experiences for cloud-based learning services. This paper presents lessons learned from the MOOC course "Authoring tools for e-learning courses". 1678 participants experienced a mix of gamification strategies: Badges – Leaderboard forums; Students Classifier League and Reward strategy. Findings revealed the reward strategy as the most effective one, and indicated increased motivation to complete the assigned learning activities.

Keywords: Gamification · Learning strategies · MOOCs · Motivation · Learning engagement

1 Introduction

Massive open online courses (MOOCs) have raised the attention of educational communities, in particular in higher education and vocational training [1]. The MOOC movement was praised as a new way to provide better accessibility to education in remote areas and developing countries. Thus providing an opportunity to study with the high ranked instructors from leading universities, promoting the democratization of education, encouraging the development of specific skills through lifelong learning and providing learning communities for people with less access to education. However, different studies evaluating MOOCs have shown that learners who enroll and

L. Uden et al. (Eds.): LTEC 2016, CCIS 620, pp. 139–149, 2016.
DOI: 10.1007/978-3-319-42147-6_12

participate in the courses are actually students with a degree or are studying a degree in a university. This observation provides evidence that in a certain level, the MOOC movement does not really promotes the democratization of education. Reported problems may indicate that education has not improved as praised. In this sense there is much room to improve these learning experiences by providing improved learning activities to increase student's motivation [2]. There is also potential to research and use cloud-based services and learning activities [3] to foster participation in MOOC courses.

The Class Central Report [4] presents a summary of the rapid expansion of MOOCs over the past years. It states that 400 universities offered MOOCs in 2014, with 2,400 courses implemented and an average of 18 million enrolled students. Today, there are MOOCs offered in many different languages and participants from over the world. The wide interest in the MOOC movement, started in the United States, was extended over different regions. As an example in Europe, in the UK, the Open University set up a national MOOC platform called FutureLearn, as a European alternative to the well-known Coursera, EDx and Khan-Academy platforms. Also Spain offers its own platform MiriadaX, a cooperation between the Spanish company Telefonica and Universia, launched January 2013. From January to September 2015, there were implemented 792 MOOCs all over Europe [5]. In Latin America the MOOC movement has started to be expanded through the Telescope MOOC platform [10] and with the recently started MOOC-Maker initiative [11] which aims to provide guidelines to education institution on how to create MOOC courses based on best practices and successful experiences. In terms of courses design and pedagogical approach, MOOCs are usually based on traditional instructional design components, such as video-content, reading content, quizzes, videoconferences and activities.

Despite the hype of MOOCs over the last years there have been reported a variety of issues. One of the most criticized aspects is a high dropout rate [6]. Research has revealed different motivations for starting but not finishing a MOOC, which is called healthy attrition. This may include learners just interested in the learning content, or following the activities and just selectively participating. A bigger attention requires learners belonging to the group of unhealthy attrition who are aiming for completing but struggling of various reasons. Such reasons may include learning style, contexts, cultures, pre-knowledge and metacognitive abilities. Also, it is imperative to consider that there are students that could not be able to self-organize themselves for the learning sessions and the time needed to complete a course. Usually this is a fact for people without universities' studies that in some extend are used to organize their time to study, but otherwise, for students without a strong learning experience, they should be motivated and guided in order to have an acceptable performance in a course. All these factors can contribute to the increase of the attrition rate [7, 8].

With this context in mind, it seems important to research, develop and experiment improved or new approaches to better address student engagement in MOOCs. In this sense, promising results in other learning settings on gamification [9] have provided a motivation to transform different research results into innovative MOOC settings.

The remainder of this paper is organized as follows: Sect. 2 presents the identification of related work on Gamification in learning environments. Section 3 presents the experience description complemented with three gamified learning strategies.

Then Sect. 4 describes the course structure and initial findings. Finally, in Sect. 5 the identified results and conclusions are presented with a lookout for future work.

2 Related Work on Gamification

Taking into account the main dropout issues for MOOCs [7], gamification strategies were identified as a promising way to improve the engagement and completion rate of MOOCs. The term gamification is defined as "the use of game design elements in non-game contexts" [12], the majority of applications of gamification in the context of comparable e-learning approaches include rewards on the completion for some activity [13], e.g. using levels and leader-boards to encourage progress and competition, and badges for participation in forums, among others. Lately, gamification strategies have been used in educational models to engage students through their intrinsic motivation, typically making use of the competition instinct possessed by most people to motivate productive behaviors, is particularly suited to active learners. Even though many studies show the positive effect of gamification strategies, these effects strongly depend on the design, the context, and the users of such gamification strategies [24].

One approach to design games and also gamification strategy is to think of how to engage different types of users: in game design, different design strategies are engaging different type of gamers. Bartle [19], introduced a basic scheme to separate the different gamer types by their in game behavior interaction with other avatars and other players. He differs four different player types in multi-player game environments: (1) Achievers, who want to achieve as much as possible in the game (levels, collecting, points, or rankings), (2) Explorers, who are engaged by exploring and enjoying the environments (quest, story, environments), (3) Socializers, who want to interact with others, and (4) Killers, who are engaged by challenging and competing others.

In relation to the different gamer types defined by Bartle [19], Pirker et al. [20], mapped these player types to different learning types. In the blended learning approach MAL [20], they introduced different game design elements in an in-class environment and added game-based strategies inspired by these player types: (1) For learners, engaged by achieving as much as possible, badges and additional achievements were introduced. (2) For learners, who enjoy exploring, the possibility to solve lots of bonus assignments was introduced. (3) The possibility to solve many tasks in groups or with peers was introduced to engage Socializers. (4) For learners who are engaged by competing with others, they introduced point-based anonymized rankings.

An often-applied strategy to introduce gamification strategies in digital environments is the implementation of game elements such as rewards, levels, rankings, badges, or points. These elements can be usually integrated in a learning environment as visible user feedback based on user statistics and behavioral features without the need of redesigning the entire environment. Werbach and Hunter [14] describe this design strategy as "PBL-Triad", referring to points, badges, and leaderboards. Points give users feedback on their progression and can either motivate collectors to keep scoring or competitors to get more points than others. Badges are a visual representation of specific user achievements and are used to engage users to reach specific goals. They can be also used as status symbols for competitive users. Leaderboards and rankings give users a sense of their progression in comparison to other users. Designing meaningful and positive leaderboards, however, is a challenging task and needs a balancing between motivating and frustrating users. In terms of the sense of competition in MOOCs, according to Werback and Hunter [14], participants often want to know where they stand relative to their teammates providing a positive motivation. On the other hand, there is a chance to demotivate students in a MOOC course if they do not have too much time to follow the course or if they plan their time to complete the learning activities at the end of the week, when they finally manage the time to visit the course it is usual that they find themselves far behind the top participants. This is particularly true for massive courses with thousands of students.

Different successful online learning tools have used gamification strategies and the introduction of design elements inspired by games [21]. Khan Academy [22] is a good example of the usage of gamification strategies. It has been using gamification strategies more or less since its release. The learners collect point when they complete lessons or challenges, have added merit badges and energy points to the flow of instructional videos or assessments and provide statistics and analytics about their progress and improvement. Another successful implementation of gamification strategies for online learning was introduced by the language learning platform Duolingo [25]. They have used skill points and bonuses to engage users to learn on their platform regularly and constantly.

Also it is worth to mention that in MOOCs the use of game-design elements have been shown as a tool to achieve engagement goals. Anderson et al. have investigated in a large-scale experiment the impact of badges as incentive in MOOC forums. They show that well designed badges can be powerful motivators to engage users [23].

3 Gamification-Based MOOC Experience in the Telescope Project

The learning setting is based on previous MOOC experiences of the Telescope project, a MOOC platform in Latin America [10]. For this experience, a course titled: "Authoring tools for e-learning courses" was designed. The aim of the course was to provide an overview of the most used authoring tools to create learning content for e-learning courses. Teachers from higher education sector were the main target group of this course. For this course the xMOOC format was selected, which follows a more traditional approach of virtual learning. The focus was mainly on the transmission of information and implementation of smaller tasks through a series of lessons, mostly in the format of short videos, supported by additional readings with blunt assessments, allowing students acquire new knowledge.

The designed course has four innovative aspects compared with other traditional xMOOC courses: (1) an orientation unit (one week duration), which is the first activity within the course. It is intended for participants with the purpose to get involved and acquainted with the learning environment, communication tools and evaluation methods, as well as with assignments delivery process that will be used in the course. (2) The second innovative aspect is related to the types of learning activities used. In this approach, the learning activities were created using different cloud based tools (Web 2.0 tools). The aim is to reach the instructional objectives by fostering conceptual demonstration and structured knowledge representation. (3) Active learning, which stresses the importance of learning by doing. Therefore, the third aspect is related to the learning and evaluation strategies used in the learning experience. The course was implemented with a series of inter-related activities, with the aim of developing a final project, where the learning outcomes should provide evidence through the creation of artifacts (videos, presentations, applications, mind maps, etc.) demonstrating knowledge and skills about main topics of the course. (4) Finally, the last distinguished aspect is based on the use of social networks as a communication tool to create the sense of being part of a community of learning.

The course was designed in four learning units. For each unit the activities include 4 to 6 short videos, learning content presentation accompanied by interactive tasks and assessment associated with each topic. A peer review system was integrated into the platform to enable students to evaluate peers in an anonymous and random manner. For each activity a rubric evaluation was presented, which creates more objectivity for the assessment tasks. The system was set up so that all students were peer reviewed at least once, whereas averaging grades when more than one peer reviewed a given student assignment.

In order to mitigate issues related to task activities and motivation identified in precious MOOC experiences, gamification strategies have been applied to tackle three challenges. The first challenge, presented in Sect. 3.1, addresses the difficulty to obtain high participation of students in different topics for discussion forums. The second strategy, presented in Sect. 3.2, focused on the quality improvement of submitted assignments and performed peer assessments. The third strategy, presented in Sect. 3.3, addresses the increase of motivation related to task completion.

3.1 Enhanced Discussion Forum: Badges and Leaderboard

The aim was to encourage learners to actively participate in the discussion forum, share information and experience a widespread form of online collaboration. The Open Source Questions and Answers System (OSQA) [15], which also provides a leaderboard, has been integrated into the MOOC environment (see Fig. 1). By means of the gamification elements "competition" and "reward a positive effect on the motivation level and the development of a learning community is expected.

Throughout the course, participants could propose topics for discussion, answer questions posted by peers, comment, vote, and exchange views and information with the other participants. OSQA allows to offer different badges as electronic rewards for students. In addition. the system provides a leaderboard highlighting the most participative students. The badges awards are based on the contributions of participants and recognizes the most participative learners within the course learning community. As an example, for this course three badges were offered: 'leader', 'collaborator' and 'curious student'. The 'leader' badge was awarded for the first response to an open question with a positive vote. The 'collaborator' badge is assigned to any student providing a contribution in a discussion obtaining a positive vote. Finally, the 'curious student' badge is assigned to any participant asking a question related to the course topics with a

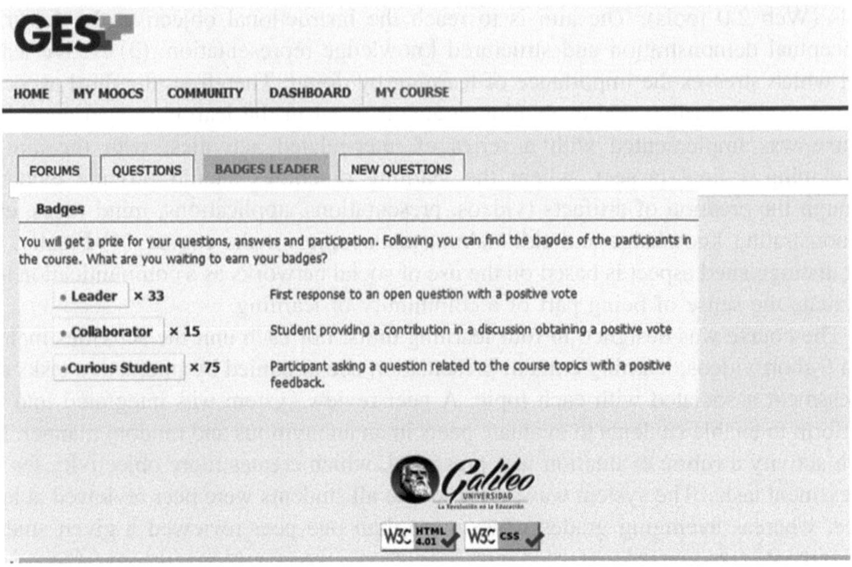

Fig. 1. Screenshot with the view of the leaderboard forums based on OSQA

positive feedback. It is worth to mention that further badges were defined within the course duration, and students were eager to get awarded these new badges.

3.2 Adapted General Leaderboard – Students Classifier League

The purpose of introducing leagues was to overcome negative effects of leaderboards. Thus, a plugin was developed to present an online leaderboard in the course portal. It enables the students to observe their relative rank and progress over time, but in their own league. The aim is to encourage students to work and upload their weekly assignments within a comparable group of students. The learning environment automatically classifies students into leagues according to their accumulated points, number of logins and number of posts in the discussion forums. Students are internally categorized in three levels according to the extent and quality of shared knowledge within the learning activities: Self-taught (expert), Curious (intermediate) and Passive (beginner). The group of 'Self-taught' are students that reached a good knowledge level without receiving direct support. 'Curious' group are students who need guidance and support, and finally, the 'Passive' group of students who do not actively participate and contribute into the course. The different levels are transparent to the students for reflection. Within the different levels, students can perform in a motivated manner in order to improve with their teammates without losing the sense of competency. With the creation of small leagues based on different aspects as country of origin, age or number of visits could hinder the idea of being part of a massive group without being recognized for the own contribution. The goal also was to establish working groups for the elaboration of projects as part of the learning activities according to their learning level and commitment.

3.3 Reward for Completed Activities

During activities in weeks 3 and 4, a reward strategy was implemented with the aim to increase students' participation. In these learning units, the students were informed using the different communication channels (e.g. news boards, emailing system, social networks) that the students that finished the weekly assignments and completed the online assessments for the unit on time, will get a complementary learning resources as a reward. It is worth to mention that the course aim was to help participants to identify authoring tools for the preparation of e-learning courses. In this phase, the students who submitted the learning activities' assignments and completed the online assessments received as a reward a template for a specific authoring tool (as an example there were pre-defined templates based on the exe-learning content authoring tool [16], including a set of useful images and a defined structure to help students to prepare e-learning content). The template was offered as a reward, thus keeping a certain degree of expectation on the students and a motivation to complete the assigned activities.

4 Course Experiences and Initial Findings

4.1 Study Setup

The instruments used for this study were a pre-test questionnaire comprising three sections. The first section focused on demographic data such as gender, age, country, academic level and occupation. The second section addressed aspects such as motivation to attend the course as well as the level of commitment to finalize it. Finally, the third section asked participants to evaluate the usefulness of tools for communicating with teachers. To complement the research, a complementary questionnaire (post-test) was prepared to explore on the participant's satisfaction with the course. Both instruments were prepared using the online survey system LimeSurvey [17] and data were statistically recorded and analyzed with the SPSS program [18].

4.2 Results and Findings

A total of 1,678 students were enrolled in the course "Authoring tools for e-learning courses". The pre-test questionnaire was presented to the students before the start of the learning experience. A total of 643 students answered to the pre-test questionnaire, this represent 40 % of the enrolled participants. Students enrolled mostly from Latin America: Guatemala (17 %), Spain (17 %), Mexico (11 %), Peru (10 %) and Argentina (7 %). In terms of course demographics, 58 % of learners were male and 42 % female. The average age was 42 years ($M = 42$, $\sigma = 11$).

In terms of academic level of the participants 32 % holds a graduate degree, 26 % have a postgraduate degree, 9 % were pre-university students, the rest of participants preferred not to include the academic level.

Regarding the occupation, 51.94 % of participants are employed full-time, 20.06 % are part-time employees, 7.93 % are students, 10.89 % have their own business and the rest of the participants preferred not to answer the question. The 56 % of participants have previously participated in other MOOC courses, the most popular platforms are: Miriadax (33.28 %), Coursera (28.30 %), Telescope (22.55 %) and Edx (8.40 %), among others.

In order to analyze the behavior of students over the duration of the course, an analytics report related to the access to the MOOC course was created. The report provided information related to the number of views for the videos in each unit and the amount of assignments uploaded. In terms of participation, a total of 789 participants logged in at least once (47 % of enrolled participants), compared to 40 % of the participants filled in the pre-test questionnaire. At the end of the course 100 students finished the course, which is a 12.67 % completion rate based on the amount of participants that logged in at least once in the MOOC platform.

The results of the post-test questionnaire presented an overall satisfaction related to the three gamified strategies used in the course; in the post-test a set of questions using a 5-point Likert motivational scale, from totally unmotivated (1) to totally motivated (5) were presented to the students that finished the course. A total of 58 participants completed the post-test questionnaire, representing a 58 % of the participants that finished the course.

The first strategy, related to the enhanced discussion forum including badges and leaderboard presented in Sect. 3.1 is for the three strategies the worst evaluated with an acceptable average of 3.71 with a maximum grade of 5.

Regarding the Adapted General Leaderboard – Students Classifier League strategy, presented in Sect. 3.2, 78 % of the students indicated that they were aware to their location in the leaderboard and they were monitoring their progress. They also commented that these gamification strategies increased their motivation to participate and perform well in the learning task.

Finally, it is worth to mention that 60 % of the students that completed the post-test questionnaire indicated that the templates provided as a reward (Sect. 3.3) are seen as very useful for creating their own resources or generating ideas for future work and this condition encouraged participation of students. Based on this, it is worth to mention that the preferred strategy was the Reward for Completed Activities, presented in Sect. 3.3.

Table 1 presents the results of three questions related to the strategies presented in Sects. 3.1, 3.2 and 3.3. It is important to notice that the students expressed that the reward strategy presented in Sect. 3.3, provided an increase in their motivation to deliver the tasks assigned in the course.

Table 1. Summary of the motivation scale for the three gamified strategies presented to the students.

Satisfaction questions	M	SD
Q1. The obtaining badges and recognition in the leaderboard forums, improved your motivation?	3.71	1.12
Q2. Do you think that the use of leagues classifier students motivates your participation and tasks delivery in the course?	3.98	0.99
Q3. Do you think that using a reward strategy as template-authoring tool motivates your tasks delivery in the course?	4.07	0.99

5 Conclusions and Future Work

This work presents a practical experience using three gamification strategies for a MOOC course titled "Authoring tools for e-learning courses" to overcome motivational issues and to increase the active participation in the MOOC. The three strategies prepared for the learning activities in the course were: (1) Badges – Leaderboard forums; (2) Students Classifier League and (3) Reward strategy. The idea behind the experimentation to increase student's motivation with the proposed strategies was to complement and adapt to a MOOC scenario the three game design elements that are most commonly used for gamification: points, badges and leaderboards [14].

Overall, based on the analysis of the responses from the learners that successfully completed the course and filled the post-test questionnaires, 80 % of the responding participants expressed that they were highly motivated to get the template reward by doing their learning tasks. In this sense, from the three gamification strategies, the Rewards Strategy presented in Sect. 3.3 was the most interesting activity according to the participants. In general, these gamification strategies had a good acceptance among enrolled students and provided motivation to complete and deliver the different assignments and specially generated great expectation for the rewards announced. Based on these initial findings, new experiences will be performed to continue exploring on the motivation based on gamified strategies, specifically related to the Rewards strategy in different context and topic courses.

Regarding the challenge to improve students communication in the implementation of a MOOC, the preliminary findings shows that earning badges in the gamified forums was neither important nor attractive to many students, in many cases, participants reported they did not understand the dynamics on how to earn badges or the utility, they stated that it was very confusing to have a conversation between a great amount of messages.

As a future step, it is planned for the next MOOC experiences to implement the reward strategy in all activities. In terms of gamification, the experience will improve the learning environment to start the course with live points as a player following real virtual games strategies, for this instead of giving points by completing assignments, the system will subtract and remove live points from the students, this in order to reflect that they are losing something (e.g. new knowledge, opportunities, their time), while they do not complete their assignments and therefore making a MOOC more competitive. It is important to mention that cloud based activities will play a special role in this type of gamified experiences, in this sense, this kind of activities will foster participation given the native nature of social games in actual virtual game environments.

Acknowledgments. This work was Co-funded by the Erasmus + Programme of the European Union MOOC-Maker (561533-EPP-1-2015-1-ES-EPPKA2-CBHE-JP). We are also gratefully acknowledge the financial support of the Institute of Information Systems and Computer Media, Graz University of Technology, as an in-kind contribution in the project for participating in the conference and presenting the results.

References

1. Yuan, L., Powell, S.: MOOCs and open education: implications for higher education. In: JISC CETIS. Centre for Educational Technology, Interoperability and Standards (2013). http://publications.cetis.org.uk/2013/667
2. Hernández, R., Gütl, C., Chang, V.: Must we be concerned with the Massive Drop-outs in MOOC? - an attrition analysis of open courses. In: International Conference on Interactive Collaborative Learning, ICL (2014)
3. Hernández, R., Gütl, C., Amado-Salvatierra, H.R.: Cloud learning activities orchestration for MOOC environments. In: Uden, L., Sinclair, J., Tao, Y.-H., Liberona, D. (eds.) LTEC 2014. CCIS, vol. 446, pp. 25–36. Springer, Heidelberg (2014)
4. Class-Central Report: MOOCs stats and trends (2014). https://www.classcentral.com/report/moocs-stats-and-trends-2014/
5. Open Education Europa: Open Education Scoreboard (2015). http://www.openeducationeuropa.eu/es/open_education_scoreboard
6. Morales, M., Hernández Rizzardini, R., Guetl, C.: Telescope, a MOOCs initiative in latin america: infrastructure, best practices, completion and dropout analysis. In: IEEE FIE 2014 Conference Proceedings, Madrid, October 2014 (2014)
7. Gütl, C., Rizzardini, R.H., Chang, V., Morales, M.: Attrition in MOOC: lessons learned from drop-out students. In: Uden, L., Sinclair, J., Tao, Y.-H., Liberona, D. (eds.) LTEC 2014. CCIS, vol. 446, pp. 37–48. Springer, Heidelberg (2014)
8. Jordan, K.: MOOC Completion Rates: The Data (2013). http://www.katyjordan.com/MOOCproject.html
9. Pirker, J., Riffnaller, M., Guetl, C.: Motivational active learning – engaging university students in computer science education. In: Proceedings of the 19th Annual Conference on Innovation and Technology in Computer Science Education, ITiCSE 2014, 23–25 June, Uppsala, Sweden 2014, pp. 297–302 (2014)
10. Hernández Rizzardini, R., Gütl, C., Chang, V., Morales, M.: MOOC in latin america: implementation and lessons learned. In: Uden, L., Tao, Y.H., Yang, H.C., Ting, I.H. (eds.) The 2nd International Workshop on Learning Technology for Education in Cloud. Springer Proceedings in Complexity, pp. 147–158. Springer, Heidelberg (2013)
11. MOOC-Maker initiative: constructing management capacities to build MOOCs in Latin America (2016). http://www.moocmaker.org
12. Deterding, S., Khaled, R.: Gamification: toward a definition. In: CHI 2011 Gamification Workshop. ACM (2011)
13. Deterding, S., Sicart, M., Nacke, L., O'Hara, K., Dixon, D.: Gamification: using game-design elements in nongaming contexts. In: CHI 2011 Extended Abstracts on Human Factors in Computing Systems, CHI EA 2011, pp. 2425–2428. ACM, New York, USA (2011)
14. Werback, K., Hunter, D.: For the Win: How Game Thinking Can Revolutionize Your Business, 1st edn. Wharton Digital Press, Philadelphia (2012)
15. Open Source Questions and Answers System. http://www.osqa.net
16. eXe Learning content authoring Tool. http://exelearning.org/
17. LimeSurvey FOSS survey tool. http://www.limesurvey.org
18. IBM SPSS Software Analytics. http://www.ibm.com/analytics/us/en/technology/spss/
19. Bartle, R.: Hearts, clubs, diamonds, spades: players who suit MUDs. J. MUD Res. **1**(1), 19 (1996)
20. Pirker, J., Riffnaller-Schiefer, M., Tomes, L.M., Gütl, C.: Motivational active learning in blended and virtual learning scenarios: engaging students in digital learning. In: Handbook of Research on Engaging Digital Natives in Higher Education Settings, p. 416 (2016)

21. Chou, Y.: Top 10 Education Gamification Examples that will Change our Future (2013). http://www.yukaichou.com/gamification-examples/top-10-education-gamification-examples
22. Khan Academy Website (2013). https://www.khanacademy.org
23. Anderson, A., Huttenlocher, D., Kleinberg, J., Leskovec, J.: Engaging with massive online courses. In: Proceedings of the 23rd International Conference on World Wide Web, pp. 687–698. ACM (2014)
24. Hamari, J., Koivisto, J., Sarsa, H.: Does gamification work?–a literature review of empirical studies on gamification. In: 47th Hawaii International Conference on System Sciences, HICSS 2014, pp. 3025–3034. IEEE (2014)
25. Duolingo Website (2010). http://www.duolingo.com/info

From MOOC to GOAL

Ubiquitous Networked Learning in Higher Education

Sabine Siemsen(✉)

Kassel, Germany
sabine.siemsen@studium.fernuni-hagen.de
http://www.core2zero.net/

Abstract. Higher Education tries to meet the call for openness and internationalization, moving (parts of) its learning-environments from brick and mortar universities to virtual learning environments. This implies a different and higher heterogeneity and requires an awareness and consideration of underlying and often unconscious cultural differences in understandings of learning and knowledge. "Throughputs" (like interaction, communication and interrelations) become more important than inputs (expert-knowledge) and outputs (skills and competences) and require theories, approaches, and concepts that go beyond mere technological solutions to make throughputs visible and to enable enhanced processes of learning.

Keywords: Learning-Process · Knowledge-Generation · New Learning-Culture · Competence · Heterogeneity · Online- and e-Learning · Academic learning · Networked learning · Ubiquitous learning · GOAL

1 Introduction

"Remember, if you educate one, you can change a life. If you educate many, you can change the world!" [14]

A rising amount of universities tries to meet the challenges that digitalization and technology bring about. They start to open their courses towards internationalization of content and participants/students. This brings about different processes and levels of changes. Therefore questions to be asked are: What has changed or is (about) to be changed, where do these changes take place, what is the "difference which makes a difference" [1], how can all participating elements be enabled to adequate competences, and how can these become visible?

Cope and Kalantzis [2] describe changes in education that are (at least in parts) enabled through digital media as "ubiquitous learning". However they infer that using such tools does not necessarily lead to a change of education paradigms. Digital media could make a change easier but they could also be used to "*learn old things in old ways [...] in our contemporary world to do old-fashioned didactic teaching*" [2].

Hence a plethora of recent approaches remain in relatively narrow frameworks of national education systems and range between an inclusion of elements of eLearning into traditional concepts of teaching, and an openness for innovative theories, concepts,

L. Uden et al. (Eds.): LTEC 2016, CCIS 620, pp. 150–161, 2016.
DOI: 10.1007/978-3-319-42147-6_13

and models. Many of them are connected with the illusion to be able to control and measure learning through a mere didactical redesign of learning-environments. Consequently they lack to consider differences in underlying understandings and definitions of learning and knowledge and learning-objectives. Most of them focus predominantly on »inputs« (knowledge) and »outputs« (competences) and tend to neglect or ignore the importance of »throughputs« (processes: interactions, interrelations, communication). However, these are the processes that decide on the difference between disruptive innovation and sustaining amendment.

Talking about necessary preconditions to participate in courses, tends to give the impression of apparently homogeneous learning-communities. Of course these do not exist, neither within western societies nor (even less) will they be found in global online courses. Nevertheless, such global online courses have started to unsettle institutions of higher education latest in 2012, the so called "year of the MOOCs". Meanwhile a good deal of MOOC literature presents overviews and arguments on recent forms of MOOCs and their attempt and success or failure to influence and change higher education (e.g. Donaldson et al. [3], Nanfito [8] or Paolucci [9]). They also show that the name MOOC (Massive Open Online Course) does not stand for a clearly definable educational concept, as meanwhile a panoply of variations with totally different theoretical and didactical concepts exist (e.g. xMOOCs which try to transfer traditional lectures into virtual learning environments and follow a behaviouristic learning theory; cMOOCs which follow connectivistic theories, POOCs which set the focus on individual learning, and many more). Therefore the term **GOAL** was created, standing for **G**lobal **O**nline **A**cademic **L**earning and will be used to discuss Ubiquitous Networked Learning in Higher Education in this paper.

To answer the above questions Sect. 2 will describe areas and levels of changes that result from challenges like digitalization, technology and the claim for openness and internationalization in the field of Higher Education. Section 3 will present the theoretical framework for the discussion of changed learning-processes and learning-cultures. A new definition of competence as well as a tool and method to enable the development of such a competence and to make it visible are described in Sect. 4, leading over the conclusion and desideratum.

2 From Brick and Mortar Universities to a Global Online University

"Ecology is an environment that fosters and supports the creation of communities. [...] learning ecology is an environment that is consistent with - and not antagonistic to - how learners learn." [4] Ehlers use of the metaphor of ecology is a perfect »missing link« between Gregory Bateson's understanding of the process of learning (Sect. 3 will go deeper into this), and recent discourses on the question how the process of learning changes due to technology and digitalisation. To come back to the first initial question of this paper (What has changed or is about to be changed, where do these changes take place) it is exactly »the environment« of where learning-processes take place that find themselves in a constant process of change. And environment includes the literally

locations (including facilities like learning-material, tools, etc.), where learning takes place, but also the composition of learning-communities, the heterogeneity of the groups.

2.1 Learning-Places

For many decades Higher Education was a rather elitist event and took place in brick and mortar universities. Due to educational reforms, a bulge in the birthrates and the impact of digitalization and globalization this started to change (at least in western societies). Universities were in the need to find solutions to deal with a rapidly raising number of students. First attempts to include elements of eLearning, respectively online learning, but also the first models of distance-education resulted hereof. Within the last years they transmuted more and more from supplement and compensation towards autonomous and equivalent concepts for higher education. Taylor [11] proposed five generations of distance education: correspondence education; integrated use of multiple, one-way media such as print, broadcasting or recorded media such as video-cassettes; two-way, synchronous tele-learning using audio or video-conferencing; flexible learning based on asynchronous online learning combined with online interactive multimedia; intelligent flexible learning, which adds a high degree of automation and student control to asynchronous online learning and interactive multimedia.

All of these models and institutions, nevertheless, cope with education within specific national frames of objectives, curricula and definitions. With the raise of MOOCs and OER these frames do not fit any longer as not only courses from different universities all over the world became open and available, but also participants from totally different learning-cultures were "huddled together" in the same courses.

What is lacking, is an explanation of how to use existing pieces of a puzzle (OER, digital tools, social networks, new roles, altered learning-processes), to enable all those learners to become self-organized, to adjust their individual (conscious) and social-cultural (often unconscious) learning goals and prior »knowledge«, respectively experiences, with those of the others (other learners, providers, teachers; possibly or probably being different).

2.2 Heterogeneity

All the changes in learning-places and »equipment« described above bring about a change of the formation of students gathered together in courses, a change in the definition of heterogeneity. Operationalizing heterogeneity as heterogeneity in learning-backgrounds, -cultures, -experiences and »foreknowledge« the first elitist brick and mortar universities were attended by a relatively homogeneous group of learners. This changed due to the above mentioned educational reforms. Highschool-students became heterogeneous in regard to their social backgrounds, their learning-experiences (school) and »foreknowledge« (in dependence from schools visited before). Correspondence Education and later Online-Courses and Distance Courses widened this heterogeneity again. Now students differed not only in social aspects and foreknowledge, but also in age and »private« contexts (like fulltime vs part-time studies, work-experience, family-status etc.). Nevertheless at least the "national frame" remained the same for (predominately) all of them. Former curricula had at least been similar, as well as criteria of certificates and learning-objectives.

In a concept of GOAL, with all its potentials regarding heterogeneity, a changed learning-culture, and the need for critical and conscious rethinking and generating knowledge, this common frame does no longer exist. Bringing together not only learners, but also teacher, experts, designers of learning-environments and technological standards from different learning-cultures brings about such a crucial change in heterogeneity that it will not be possible to cope with it through mere didactically or technologically enlarged concepts or platforms.

Numerous educational discourses already tend to speak of a new culture of learning. Nevertheless, they predominately remain within traditional frames of apparently homogeneous groups of learners, or at least of the illusion that differences could be »bridged« or »compensated«. Langer [6] listed as typical elements of this culture of learning peer-to-peer-learning, changed roles (tutor, facilitator), the attribute »open« (to share and participate) and situated learning.

However, all the described fast paced innovations lead to changes in what is called the process of learning. New criteria will have to go beyond the aspects, listed by Langer above, and will require an enhanced and enlarged understanding of learning processes and culture. They connect three levels, those of Educational Science (Research, Discourses), Educational Praxis (Conception, Implementation, and Evaluation of academic online courses) and Educational Policy and Politics (societies, institutions). Not a re-design but a re-thinking is needed.

Such a change in the way of thinking implies consciousness about relations between terminology and the herewith transported underlying definitions (Compare [12]). Ubiquitous and networked learning in global online-courses **implies** a high heterogeneity of its participants, and therefore a high risk to fail in communication by using terms that do not have the same meaning and definition for all of the participants. Communication in global online courses takes part using a language that is the native language for a part of the learners, and a foreign language for the other part. But even being able to communicate fluently in a »common« language (which still remains the mother language for one part and a second language, respectively a foreign language for all the others) does not automatically imply to have a common understanding of definitions and interpretations of the used terminology, so one will have to *"define something in terms of its relationships using contrast and context instead of isolating it with a name."* [1]

Questioning traditional models and rethinking learning – which is what (at least the core-idea of) MOOCs have in common - provokes fear and offence, and meets with criticism in traditional settings and long-established institutions. Its success will depend mainly on the question if MOOCs will be able to resist becoming just a new name for a concept that will be nothing else than a technological description of a variation in eLearning/Online-Learning (described above as being a rather technological addition to various processes of learning); and to succeed in becoming a really innovative approach for Learning Online as Global-Online-Academic-Learning **(GOAL)** with all its potentials regarding heterogeneity, a changed learning-culture, and the need for critical and conscious rethinking and generating knowledge through enhancement-competence (which will be discussed in Sect. 4).

3 Learning-Processes in and for GOAL

3.1 Theoretical Frame

Gregory Bateson was a scientist who already took nearly all of the above aspects into account, and his systemic approach seems to be a perfect background to reflect learning processes (including research and science as being learning processes!) for ubiquitous and networked learning. He always emphasized multidisciplinary research, and tried to fuse findings from natural science, especially mathematics and logic, with research in humanities. He separated between digital processes and analogue processes and already used terms like feed-back and self-organization (compare [7]), all of them of crucial importance and highly topical in today's educational science and practice.

Important parts of his work took part as a member of the School of Palo Alto which used primarily a systemic (cybernetic) approach and tried to transfer this onto human and social relationships. A systemic approach was not regarded as new science or discipline, but rather as a new kind to perceive reality, a method to analyze complex phenomena. The theory of communication developed in Palo Alto emphasized that communication is a process that always includes interactive and relational processes, and therefore one would not have to analyze the elements (individuals communicating), but the relations between those. They aimed to come to a synthesis by regarding elements of communication (and learning) as pieces of a puzzle that is assembled in a new structural and holistic way (compare [10]). He discussed the impact and influence of meta-communication on learning-processes and knowledge, which Marc and Picard [7] describe as a "*methodology of change*".

Another crucial idea within Bateson's theoretical framework is those of the importance of "context-markers". To give examples, le listed symbols that represent more complex sets of meaning, and lead to specific kinds of actions, or behavior (for example the observance of etiquette). As language is also a set of symbols, terminology can be used as "*digital context marker*" [1]. So in traditional settings »professor« may imply that a professor's statements are not be questioned, and resulting from this, »Knowledge« (depending on former and often unconscious experiences and resentments) becomes a context marker for content that is not to be questioned and is defined as being static, general and unchangeable.

Marc and Picard [7] give another good explanation for what can be understood as »context markers« . Bateson and Jackson (with whom Bateson worked together at Palo Alto) picked up the expression "*punctuation of patterns of patents*" from the Linguist Benjamin Lee Whorft[1], to describe aspects of communication by analyzing the way participants use to subdivide communication into several segments of »actions causing reactions« . A common cause for failures in communication is that the structure and classification is set differently. So different participants make different

[1] https://en.wikipedia.org/wiki/Benjamin_Lee_Whorf.

punctuations of cause and effect and therefore feel like victims of the other ones, and are unable to influence the relation within the interaction. And it does not matter if a punctuation is right or wrong (if this category exists at all) – but what matters is that this organizes behavior and therefore is part of every relation and interaction [7]. This can also be described using the term context-marker instead of punctuation. And as long as context markers remain unconscious, it will be impossible to change behavior.

Marc and Picard [7] therefore reason that the phenomenon of punctuation (or in other words: The setting and existence of context markers) shows the importance of meta-communication which functions as regulation, by bringing the existence of those context-markers into consciousness. This enables to eliminate misinterpretations, and to set new – common – context markers; which is what represents learning-processes in the sense of the described new learning culture. And it is crucial to emphasize that not only »students« are participants of these learning-processes, but also »teacher«, scientists and their respective contexts, including society and institutions.

3.2 Bateson's Learning Levels

Figure 1 summarizes Bateson's levels of learning and depicts their interrelationship with context, sets of context and context markers that are always interconnected with learning-processes. Bateson points out that "*the hierarchy of orders of learning is presented to the reader from bottom upward, from level zero to level III [...] but within the model it is assumed that higher levels are explanatory of lower levels and vice versa. It is also assumed that a similar reflexive relation - both inductive and deductive - obtains among ideas and items of learning*" [1].

For the focus of this paper, it is sufficient to describe and discuss the Learning Levels II and III more detailed, as the difference between those is exactly the "difference which makes a difference" [1] to describe what has changed (or will have to change) in learning-processes for ubiquitous and networked learning on the level of GOAL.

"*What is learned in Learning II is a way of punctuating events. [...] In fact, the propositions which govern punctuation have the general characteristic of being self-validating. [...] It follows that Learning II acquired in infancy is likely to persist through life*". [1] Learning II means remaining in an "*economy of thought processes*" [1] but only if, or as long as, learning on the level III is not reached. According to Marc/Picard [7] Bateson says that most of these learning-processes were unconscious, as one seldom can explain how they came into being. A human being on the level of Learning II, as a part of a »system« [2], has no direct access to contexts of fundamental processes of learning.

This is what learning processes of the level of Learning III change, they "*throw these unexamined premises open to question and change [... and are likely ...] to be difficult and rare even in human beings. Expectably, it will also be difficult for scientists, who are only human, to imagine or describe this process.*" [1]

[2] Each learning-process is integrated in interaction and therefore learning-processes are regarded as communication-systems.

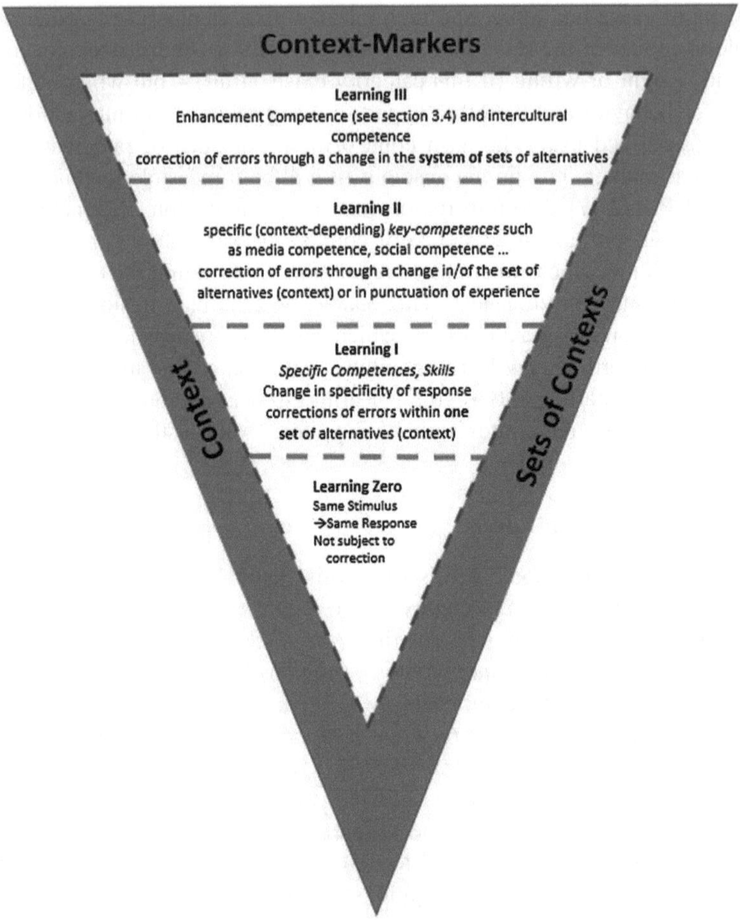

Fig. 1. Learning Levels and Contexts (Source: Authors' own compilation) basing on Bateson's [1] logical categories of learning

On this level assumptions and patterns that rule and control Learning II become conscious and this way can be modified. One learns how one had learned to learn, gets confronted with one's own premises, and learns to find reasons for one's own premises, patterns, and resentments. Learning on Level III can modify, or fasten, or alter processes of Learning II. In order to act basing on reflection, a learner has to be able, to realize that and in which ways contexts (alternatives) differ; then his responses, respectively reaction on the same stimulus, will be different in reliance to the respective context. Reaching this level of learning, he will be free from automatism and able to change routines and – if necessary – to develop new automatisms adequate to the new context.

Learning processes of the level III are a kind of synthesis, or fusion, of roles and patterns one has learned to »play« in communication processes and sequences of interaction. *"But if Learning III be [sic!] concerned with the contexts of these instances, then the categories of Learning II will be burst open"* [1].

And this is what is needed to transfer of Learning III from a theoretical model into educational praxis. The importance of context, sets of context, and context markers (compare Fig. 1) is crucial for each learning-process, as "*contexts are configurations of relations and interactions, basing on communication*" [11]. Each learning-process is a process of interaction and bases on communication, and interaction cannot be described in a linear way. This implies that is just not possible to predict that a specific didactic or technological approach or model can control a certain learning-outcome. Rather should the focus shift from analyzing inputs and outputs to analyzing throughputs: Communication, interaction and relations.

Learning on this level does not aim to recite given content but to generate knowledge. And knowledge-based learning in GOAL will have to avoid the risk of affecting one another in an unintended and hindering way what is likely to happen as long as different understandings and definitions of what learning and knowledge is, remain unconscious. To bring these into consciousness needs **Meta-Communication** and will lead to **Enhancement-Competence**: ***"Meta-Communication in Online-Courses*** *is highly heterogeneous learner-communities cooperatively re-defining and putting in question definitions of »Learning« and »Knowledge«, in front of and while participating online-courses; with the purpose to set new commonly found context-markers to create value by generating knowledge while efficiently and consciously developing* ***Enhancement-Competence*** *in and for learning networks including individual, social-cultural and digital-technological network."* [12]

Enhancement-Competence is rather a process than a discrete set of skills. Enhancement Competence includes, respectively implies, recent key competences like intercultural competence (as a heterogeneity of all cultures represents the utmost width of contexts that is possible) and media competence (as they are constituted on networking, using and questioning and regenerating all kind of information). Enhancement-Competence as a new terms fuses the terms learning (each learning-process leads to, respectively is, enhancement), knowledge (enhancement is change, and change implies a re-thinking of and re-generating of hitherto existing knowledge), and competence.

4 Enhancement-Competence and Meta-Communication in GOAL

Taking into account the change of roles (each participants teaches and learns; students as well as professors, designers and everybody else being part of a learning- system), learning III implies to change the punctuation and sequences of learning processes. This is what will happen in GOAL as soon as meta-communication is used as »tool« , enabling such learning processes.

Traditional (online-) courses follow a scheme of conception (technological and didactical design), implementation (learning and teaching content, exams), and formative and assumptive evaluation. The consequent implementation of meta-communication would change punctuation and sequences, as it already would have to take place in forefront of each segment:

- Before designing a course, designers and teacher would meta-communicate on expectations, contexts and preconditions (own and others; respectively of all involved participants).
- Before starting a course and dealing with content, learners would have (a coached and assisted) meta-communication about learning-contexts, experiences, expectations, which in turn will be basis for further evaluations.

This way the participants are enabled to re-think patterns and reframe context-markers. A formative and assumptive evaluation will have to concentrate on interactions, patterns of communication, relations instead of focusing individual »success« or traditional outcomes. Like this, all processes of interaction would be changed in regard to punctuation and sequences, and so become a landscape for learning on the level III and for enhancement-competence.

Such a change requires a transcending and holistic view on competence and to step back from specific contexts (in which specific interaction originate) to be able to see the meta-context and to reinterpret a situation (compare [12]).

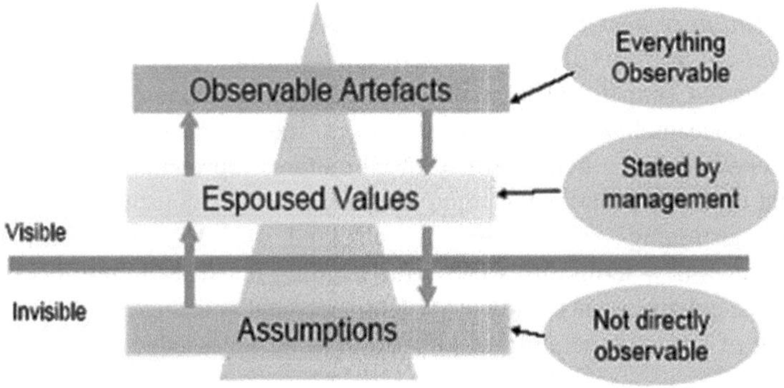

Fig. 2. Edgar Schein's Model of Culture [13] Source: http://www.tc.gc.ca/eng/civilaviation/standards/sms-info-oct2005-1367813-2484.htm

Figure 2 shows Edgar Schein's Model of Culture [4, 13] which was developed to describe and analyze organizational culture, and as Fig. 2 shows, it fits as well to educational institutions as to learning cultures itself.

Observable artefacts, which Schein ([2] (cited in [4]) also called "observable Behavior and Artefacts" describe measurable outcomes (e.g. numbers of participants completing a course, success in form of exams, certificates, or active participation analyzed by the number of posts). Espoused values comes up to what was described as learning-objectives, and competence grids (that what can clearly be communicated and manifested in rule books like curricula, syllabi and examination regulations).

Assumptions, which Schein also specifies as “Underlying Assumptions”, finally represent what was described as patterns, values and context markers that derive from multiple sets of context (see Fig. 1) and neither are “directly observable” nor recognizable to the individual itself. They are “unconscious and/or taken-for-granted beliefs” [2] (cited in [4]). And, as depicted in Fig. 2, these assumptions represent the biggest part of what defines a (learning) culture, comparable with the metaphor of an iceberg from which only the tip is visible. Whereas Schein came to the conclusion that underlying assumptions cannot be corrected, this paper hypothesizes that they could be called into question: through Meta-Communication and Enhancement Competence.

The competence grid in Table 1 (below) is an approach to conceptualize a tool to make a rise of Enhancement-Competence through Meta-Communication visible. Level I to IV raises the consciousness of contexts, sets of contexts, and context markers, using respective processes of meta-communication (column two). These are exemplary and can be altered and enlarged. What is important about them is that they have to activate learning processes on the level of learning III. Following Führung’s [5] “*approach through irritation*” which fosters “*an intensive awareness of ‘strange experiences’* and cultural self-reflection”, this can be reached through any question provoking to rethink patterns and to unveil cultural blind spots[3].

It is important to emphasize that using meta-communication does not per se have to take place as a discussion or discourse. It describes a level of »communicating about communication« which includes individual examination with aspects, like through writing research-diaries, weblogs, essays – in short: thinking by writing. The third column gives such examples of how to find evidence for the respective levels.

Table 1. Competence Grid (author’s own compilation)

Enhancemant Competence	**Meta-Communication enabled through**	**Evidence through**
Level I Recognizing dimensions and interrelations of »Learning-Culture« (according to Figure 3 of this thesis)	Tasks like research on different theories on and definitions of learning, knowledge, learning culture.	Thinking by writing: Weblogs, ePortfolio, essays ...
Level II Value-free identifying of other’s experiences, expectations, and thereof resulting definitions (context-markers)	Anonymized texts from the weblogs, eportfolios, and essays developed on level I.	Writing Peer-Feedback to weblogs, eportfolios, and essays developed on level I.
Level III Value-free identifying of own experiences, expectations, and thereof resulting definitions (context-markers)	Questions: What is your definition of learning, knowledge, competence? How did your definitions come into being, what do they base on? What are your expectations towards learning and being support in this course? ...	Thinking by writing: Weblogs, ePortfolio, essays ...
Level IV Finding relationships, alikeness and intersections	Questions: Are there aspects within definitions, theories (Task level I) these have in common? What could be a common interest leading to participating in this course? ...	First: Thinking by writing: Weblogs, ePortfolio, essays ... Then: Moderated and supported synchronous Meta-Communication like Virtual Classrooms, Hangouts, Skype ...
Level V Reframing, setting new context markers	Could the feedback to your reflections in level I and III change your initial definitions? Which kind of definition could you imagine that would focus on shared expectations? ...	First: Moderated and supported synchronous Meta-Communication like Virtual Classrooms, Hangouts, Skype ... Then: Thinking by writing: Weblogs, ePortfolio, essays ...
Level VI Permanent process of reflextion, enhancing consciousness, reframing and re-thinking	Starting a spiral process of levels I to V basing on material created in level V	

[3] Nora Bateson: https://www.facebook.com/norabateson.

As Enhancement Competence implies a permanent reflection and reframing of patterns (setting of new context markers) the fifth level starts a spiral process with a permanent recourse to individual and social knowledge generated through the previous four levels.

5 Conclusion and Desideratum

Places, procedures and preconditions for academic learning have changed tremendously and will continue to change permanently. This and a hence resulting widening of heterogeneity constitute the "difference which makes a difference" [1] between learning processes within national frames and learning-processes in a Global Online University. This requires an awareness of different contexts due to different learning-cultures, and of their impact and influence on learning-processes. In »Knowledge Societies« (that claim to be open, to be globally available, and to foster democracy in learning-chances) it should therefore become a crucial precondition for developing criteria to conceptualize, change, or evaluate learning-processes. Approaches and concepts for ubiquitous networked learning require »tools« that enable and foster meta-communication about different definitions and expectation on learning and knowledge, and to integrate these processes of meta-communication before, beside and after dealing with course-contents and into the whole process of conceptualizing, designing and evaluating learning environments.

The competence-grid in Sect. 4 is a first attempt to develop such a tool and will have to be tested and evaluated in praxis contexts. A plethora of universities from different learning-cultures and systems (for instance Finland, Estonia, Suisse, France, Great Britain, Malaysia, Chile, and Mexico) are recently discussing or planning changes in teaching and learning through different approaches towards network, openness and digitalization. Collecting data through a review of studies and questionnaires and interviews on the recent state of the use and integration of networking-tools, online-learning, digitalization and role-allocations would be basis for the conception of a MOOC (respectively GOAL) fostering Enhancement-Competence through the adoption of the competence grid. Combining this GOAL with recent courses from the different universities (using one sample participating both and another one participating only in the traditional course) will enable formative and summative evaluation of the differences within the learning-processes.

References

1. Bateson, G.: Steps to An Ecology of Mind;: Collected Essays in Anthropology, Psychiatry, Evolution, and Epistemology. Chandler Pub. Co., San Francisco (1972)
2. Cope, B., Kalantzis, M.: Ubiquitous Learning. University of Illinois Press, Urbana (2009)
3. Donaldson, J.: Massively open: how massive open online courses changed the world (2013)
4. Ehlers, U.-D.: Open Learning Cultures. Springer-Verlag Berlin and Heidelberg GmbH & Co. KG, Berlin (2013)

5. Führing, G.: *Begegnung als Irritation: Ein erfahrungsgeleiteter Ansatz in der entwicklungs bezogenen Didaktik* (Schriften der Arbeitsstelle "Eine Welt, Dritte-Welt-Initiativen" / am Institut für Didaktik der Geographie der Westfälischen Wilhelms-Universität Münster, Bd. 3). Waxmann, Münster, New York (1996)
6. Langer, V.: Social Learning: Internet-gestütztes soziales Lernen als neuer Trend: Auswirkungen auf die Zukunft des Lernens (2013)
7. Marc, E., Picard, D., Holl, H.G.: Bateson, Watzlawick und die Schule von Palo Alto (Athenäums Programm). Hain, Frankfurt am Main (1991)
8. Nanfito, M.: MOOCs: Opportunities, impacts, and challenges : massive open online courses in colleges and universities
9. Paolucci, R. (ed.): Learning With MOOCs: Massive Open Online Courses. Interlearning Company LLC., East Norriton Pennsylvania (2013)
10. Reinmann, G., Sesink, W.: Entwicklungsorientierte Bildungsforschung: Diskussionspapier. Universität Leipzig (2011)
11. Ruesch, J., Bateson, G.: Kommunikation: Die soziale Matrix der Psychiatrie, 1st edn. Carl-Auer-Systeme Verl. und Verl.-Buchh, Heidelberg (1995)
12. Siemsen, S.: Learning, knowledge and competence in global online-universities: how terminology shapes thinking. In: Uden, L., Liberona, D., Welzer, T. (eds.) LTEC 2015. CCIS, vol. 533, pp. 28–42. Springer, Heidelberg (2015)
13. TC Canada: Safety Management Systems - Information Session - Presentations - Day 1 (2010). http://www.tc.gc.ca/eng/civilaviation/standards/sms-info-oct2005-1367813-2484.htm
14. University Of The People: University of the People -Tuition-Free Online University: The First Three Years (2012)

Case Study on Using MOOC Materials in a Small Private Online Course

Whai-En Chen(✉)

National Ilan University,
No. 1, Sec. 1, Shennong Rd.,
Yilan City, Yilan County 26047, Taiwan, ROC
wechen@niu.edu.tw

Abstract. In National Ilan University, we utilize *Massive Open Online Courses* (MOOCs) as the courseware in a *Small Private Online Course* (SPOC). In this paper, we share the experience that how we manage and operate the SPOC course for the students in a part-time master program. We identify that the MOOCs can provide good learning materials. In addition, the teacher and TA pay lots of efforts on the courses such as answering the student's questions and online discussion. The students in the SPOC obtain better achievements than the students who complete the MOOCs.

Keywords: E-learning · Online test · MOOC · SPOC

1 Introduction

In *National Ilan University* (NIU), we offer a *Small Private Online Course* (SPOC) named "**Next Generation Internet Protocol and Technology**" for the master-degree and senior students. In the SPOC class, all students are *part-time* students in the *E-learning* master program and most of them do not have computer network background. In this course, we adopt an 8-week course "**Computer Network**" from MOOCs as a part (44 %) of the teaching materials to improve the students' background. Specifically, the course "**Computer Network**" is made by professor Nen-Fu Huang and his team from *National Tsing Hua University* (NTHU). We cooperate with Prof. Huang and his team to obtain the NIU students' scores from the MOOCs platform (ShareCourse [2]). In this case study, the materials are retrieved from the class in 2015 fall. The outline of the SPOC is listed in Table 1.

The teaching materials of weeks 2–5 and 7–10 from MOOCs include 8 chapters of computer network technologies. The teaching materials of weeks 6, 11 and 12–18 are provided by the NIU's teacher. In weeks 6 and 11, the online discussions are synchronized which means all members attend the online classroom at the same timeslot and have real-time interactions. During the discussion, the teacher, TA and the students meet online and discuss the problems that the students addressed. After the online discussion, the students solve their question and can take the online test. There are homework assignments in weeks 13, 15 and 17. The students should finish the homework and upload the documents to the e-learning platform in NIU [1].

L. Uden et al. (Eds.): LTEC 2016, CCIS 620, pp. 162–167, 2016.
DOI: 10.1007/978-3-319-42147-6_14

Table 1. Outline of "Next Generation Internet Protocol and Technology" course.

Week	Title	Note
1	Introduction to course	Face-to-face
2	OSI 7-layer model	Online (MOOCs)
3	Ethernet	Online (MOOCs)
4	Wireless LAN	Online (MOOCs)
5	Spanning tree algorithm	Online (MOOCs)
6	Online discussion and test	Online Test
7	Virtual LAN	Online (MOOCs)
8	Reliable transmission technology	Online (MOOCs)
9	Routers and interworking technology	Online (MOOCs)
10	Congestion control, AIMD and slow Start	Online (MOOCs)
11	Online discussion and test	Online Test
12	Introduction to IPv6	Online
13	ICMPv6 and neighbor discovery	Online, Homework
14	IPv6 transition- dual stack and tunneling	Online
15	IPv6 transition- IPv4/IPv6 translation	Online, Homework
16	Mobility management for IPv6	Online
17	IPv6 socket programming	Online, Homework
18	Final exam and discussion	Face-to-face

In the first week, the students should register to the MOOCs platform (i.e., Share-Course [2]). To retrieve the students' examination results from the MOOCs platform, we ask the students to fill the "nickname" by using the specific form **NIU_xxx** (e.g., NIU_R1234567, see Fig. 1).

Fig. 1. Registration form on sharecourse

In this class, there are 9 part-time master students. Two students have computer-related background and the others do not have computer-related background.

2 Course Activities

The course materials in each week include several 10–15 min video clips and exercises. The students are expected to spend 3 h or more on the online course. If the students have questions about the content in the video clips or the answers in the exercises, they can propose the question through multiple ways. The NIU's e-learning platform [1] provides a discussion board. The teacher, TA and students can subscribe the discussion board [see Fig. 2(a)]. If anyone post a message (e.g., an issue or an answer), the discussion board will send notification to the subscribers.

Fig. 2. The discussion board.

In addition, we organize a **LINE** group for real-time communication. This LINE group helps us to receive the status of the students. The students send many kinds of messages include their questions about the content and answers, the related links/topics and even their moods (see Fig. 3). However, the LINE system does not keep the message and figures after several days. In order to keep the discussion content, the TA posts the content from the LINE group to the discussion board [see Fig. 2(b)]. The students can join and follow the discussion [see Fig. 2(c)].

The third way is that we have *online* **office hour** in this course. Every Thursday evening (say 7 pm), the teacher or TA will wait in the online classroom. The students

Fig. 3. The LINE communication group.

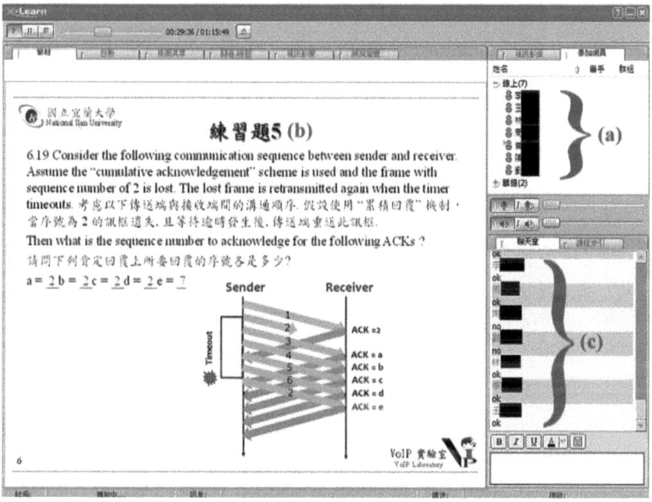

Fig. 4. The online office hour/discussion example.

can report their status and discuss with the teacher or TA in the office hours. Figure 4 demonstrates an example of the online office hour or discussion. We can see the online and offline students in (a) and the students' response in (c). The teacher and TA use (b) for discussion.

3 Discussion and Conclusion

In this course, the online tests are utilized to assess the students' learning results. The article [3] points out that online assessment is critical. In the current environments, the students may have multiple screens, multiple computers, and powerful searching engines. In the online tests, the system dynamically selects the questions from the question bank. The questions include multiple-choice questions, multi-select questions, and short-answer questions. To achieve the fairness, the system randomly changes the order of the choices of the questions and the teacher manually adjusts the parameters in some questions. With the above operations, the answers are changed. However, these methods cannot prevent the case where student A replaces student B to perform the online tests. The new technologies should be added into the online test system. For example, the system randomly take the photos during the test.

The online test results are listed in Table 2. The students with IDs 5 and 7 are approved temporary suspension of schooling. The other students complete the MOOCs and obtains the certificates (completion rate is 78 %). There are 6 students (67 %) obtain the average score more than 90, and the can receive the recommendation letters.

Table 2. The online test results.

ID	1st Online test	2nd Online test	Note
1	94.8	90.4	Average = 92.6
2	100	99.2	Average = 99.6
3	100	99.2	Average = 99.6
4	92.5	91.2	Average = 91.9
5	0	0	Temporary suspension
6	100	99.2	Average = 99.6
7	0	0	Temporary suspension
8	88.7	88.6	Average = 88.7
9	100	99.2	Average = 99.6

Based on the results, we can see the completion rate of the *Small Private Online Course* (SPOC) is higher than the general *Massive Open Online Courses* (MOOCs). With online activities, the students can quickly obtain the answers. The rules and instructions of the course also drive the students follow the progress of the course. The test results of the students in this SPOC are better than the students who complete the course in the MOOCs. Although the teacher and TA pay lots of efforts in answering the students' questions and perform the course activities, the students achieve good learning results. In this case study, we find that MOOCs is useful as the course material, and SPOC is good way for e-learning.

References

1. The NIU E-learning website. http://eschool.niu.edu.tw/mooc/index.php
2. The ShareCourse website. http://www.sharecourse.net/sharecourse/
3. Brown, B.: Online Testing, Is It Fair? http://elearnmag.acm.org/archive.cfm?aid=2893355

Open Education – A Challenge for E-training

Viktorija Florjančič(✉)

Faculty of Management, University of Primorska,
Cankarjeva 5, 6000 Koper, Slovenia
viktorija.florjancic@fm-kp.si

Abstract. Information and communication technology is dramatically changing the world we live in. Over recent years, open resources and open education have been part of different initiatives and projects. Nowadays, information can be easily reached from different sources and knowledge can be acquired outside of the traditional bricks-and-mortar institutions. Massive open online courses (MOOCs) are challenging higher education, however the experts and researchers are yet to reach a consensus on whether MOOCs will change the nature of higher education. This paper analyses the issues of whether MOOCs pose a threat to higher education institutions, if they are a feasible replacement for payable study programs or whether they support people willing to learn in their lifelong learning process. These questions are analyzed from a business perspective rather than from the point of formal (higher) education. We are asking if the MOOCs present the opportunity for in-house company training.

Keywords: Open education · E-training · Informal learning

1 Introduction

Information and communication technology (ICT), especially Internet penetration, is a prerequisite for a business operating in the digital age. In 2015, 93 % of enterprises from EU28, with at least 10 persons employed, had fixed broadband access to the Internet [11]. Enterprises in Finland, Denmark and the Netherlands represent the most developed countries in EU28 with 99 %, followed by Slovenia and the Czech Republic with 98 %. Bulgarian (71 %) and Romanian (83 %) enterprises are at the lower end of this scale. In 2011, 44 % of EU28 enterprises were giving portable devices that enable a mobile connection to the Internet to their employees. Employees in Swedish enterprises where 91 % of them were offered portable devices to access the Internet have an advantage over the average EU28 employee. Austrian enterprises were in second place with 65 % and France with 53 % in third place. In Slovenia, every second enterprise gave their employees portable devices. The ICT and Internet services, like the Web, offer enterprises a lot of opportunities for business all around the world. The Web not only increases revenue but also saves on costs and impacts on enterprises success [3, 25]. E-business is becoming a synonym for the global business [15, 21, 25]. The widespread implementation of e-business in EU enterprises is evident from Eurostat statistics [11]. In 2012, 44 %[1] of EU28 enterprises were sharing information on sales or

[1] Enterprises without financial sector with more than 10 persons employed.

L. Uden et al. (Eds.): LTEC 2016, CCIS 620, pp. 168–180, 2016.
DOI: 10.1007/978-3-319-42147-6_15

on purchases with the software used for any internal function, electronically. The leading EU country in this field was Austria with 64 %, followed by Portugal with 57 % of enterprises. In 2015, the processes of 17 % of EU28 enterprises were automatically linked to suppliers and/or customers' business processes. The most connected business processes were in Denmark (30 %), the least in Latvia (8 %), Hungary (9 %) and Romania (10 %). Also in 2015 one fifth (21 %) of EU28 enterprises were using Customer Relationship Management (CRM) systems to analyze clients' information for marketing purposes. Dutch enterprises were on top of CRM statistics with 30 % whilst Hungarian enterprises were at the bottom with 9 %. Only 17 % of Slovenian enterprises are using CRM systems. The development of e-business may be also be seen through Internet interactions between enterprises and public authorities, so called B2G (Business-to-Government) transactions. The data collected by Eurostat shows that 75 % of EU28 enterprises interacted with public authorities in 2010. In Finland 96 % of enterprises were registered to interact with public authorities, in Lithuania and in the Netherlands 95 %. More than 90 % of enterprises were registered in Denmark (92 %) and 90 % in Sweden and Luxembourg. 88 % of Slovenian enterprises interacted with public authorities in 2010.

E-business has changed how business is done today and how we live in everyday life. Knowledge gained in schools is becoming outdated and redundant. We all need new skills and new knowledge that may be required formally, non-formally or informally. Once an individual is employed, they no longer have time to go back to school and spend the whole day attending lectures and seminars. Employees have to be at work, they have families and other obligations. In-house training is becoming imperative for enterprises that want to have a competitive advantage on the global market. Well-tailored in-house training (seminars and courses) requires time and money. We have to take into account production and delivery costs, as well as employee costs (travel costs, training leave). The education revolution we have been observing in recent years, mostly in higher education, has given in-house training organizers the challenge of using open resources as flexible and freely accessible training content. Fee [13] exposes that digital technology has to be implemented in all business processes, including learning. Companies who fail to do so will not succeed.

In the paper below, MOOCs are presented as a possibility for everyone willing to acquire knowledge and skills. Based on data comparison we try to find out the differences between EU28 countries in the field of learning and training. Secondary data collected by Eurostat were used and analyzed using Excel and SPSS program. Data is presented in tables and figures.

2 Acquired Knowledge – from Closed to Open Content

2.1 Education and Training

As according to Jarvis [19] education has never been exclusively a childhood phenomenon, even though nowadays it is still mostly connected to schools and schooling age. Education that is institutionalized, intentional and planned is defined as formal education [1]. *Formal education* is hierarchically structured [31], institutionally organized and standardized. At the end of formal education a student is awarded by a certificate, diploma or degree that confirms a certain level of education gained in formal education.

Non-formal education is institutionalized and planned by education providers and mostly leads to qualifications that are not recognized as those that have been taken through formal education [1]. ISCED statistics makes no distinction between formal and non-formal education when they are collecting data for statistical purposes. The main difference between formal and non-formal education is in the final document (certificate, diploma or degree) that is widely accepted as a demonstration of attainment of certain level of education.

Informal education is intentional but not institutionalized, therefore less structural than formal and non-formal education [1]. Persons can acquire knowledge in any other form that is not organized and is not intentional. Like incidental or random learning (ibidem).

In the past, educationalists explained that education is more cognitive while training is more skills based learning [19] that occurs in a work environment. Fee [13] sees this difference as a result of an inappropriate learning delivery method. Training is a process of learning that is not to be delivered in dull ways as was the practice in the past (ibidem). ISCED [1] defines *training* as education to achieve learning objectives, mostly in vocational education.

Knowledge and skills may be acquired and developed through formal, non-formal or informal education. Nowadays, we do not distinguish between cognitive and skills learning. The main point is that learning is an activity of a learner [13, 22]. A teacher organizes a learning process, helps, motivates and guides a learner through the whole process.

We can learn using different sources – paper based or digital, to being in communication with other people, listening to the radio or watching TV etc. We are learning by doing everyday activities too, in our private life or work life [17].

Acquiring knowledge and skills from the youngest age to death is known as lifelong learning, which was accepted as a concept by the European Commission in the 1990s [19].

2.2 Massive Open Online Education

Internet users are using the network for e-business activities and to gain all kinds of data and information that help them build up-to-date knowledge and development skills. There are many resources freely available and accessible on the web, thus knowledge can be easily acquired out of the bricks-and-mortar classrooms and outside of formal education. Over the past years, the new massive open online courses – MOOCs phenomenon has arisen. We have been following MOOCs since 2012 even though the first MOOC was published in 2008. The first MOOCs providers are still playing an important role on the MOOCs market today – Udacity,[2] Coursera[3] in edX[4] [2, 29]. Coursera is still the leading provider on the MOOCs market (35.6 %), followed by edX (18.1 %) and Canvas.net (6.9 %), although its share on the MOOC market has slightly decreased (Table 1).

Table 1. MOOCs market (in %)

Providers	2013	2014	2015
Coursera	47.0	36.0	35.6
Canvas Networks	8.5	8.4	6.9
edX	8.3	16.0	18.1
MariadaX	6.8	5.3	3.7
Udacity	2.8	2.4	3.0
FutureLearn	2.8	4.7	5.7

Source: Shah 2013, Shah 2014, Shah 2015.

In the last two years, both edX (from 8.3 % in 2013 to 18.1 % in 2015) and FutureLearn[5] (from 2.8 to 5.7 %) have improved their market position, thus Coursera, Canvas networks and MiariadaX have lost their positions (Table 1). FutureLearn, owned by The Open University [30], the pioneer of distance education, may become the most important MOOC provider in the future.

Udacity, one of the first MOOC providers, covered subjects mostly from computer science and engineering, thus its market position has remained almost the same as in previous years (Table 1). The technical oriented courses are still the domain of Udacity, a platform developed by Stanford University, in 2011. Today, Udacity is providing several computer and programming courses covered by the name "Nanodegree"[6]. Computer and programming skills are the most sought-after skills on the market, so the Udacity initiative is a response to industrial demand.

The leading MOOCs provider Coursera was also developed by Stanford University. The open and freely available content from one of the highest-ranking universities in the world is more than welcome for the future of humanity. It is expected that the highest portion of participants in Coursera's MOOCs come from the USA (38.5 %), with 4 to 6 % of participants coming from Brazil, India, China, Canada and the UK [7]. The MOOC community is becoming really big and multicultural.

Today Coursera, with 140 partners, from 28 countries all around the globe, offers 1,818 courses[7]. Courses are grouped into ten different categories – from arts and humanities, business, computer, data and life science, to math and logic, personal

[2] https://www.udacity.com/.

[3] https://www.coursera.org/.

[4] https://www.edx.org/.

[5] https://www.futurelearn.com/.

[6] https://www.udacity.com/nanodegree.

[7] https://www.coursera.org/about/partners.

development, physical science and engineering to social science and language learning. The first MOOCs in 2011 and 2012 were mostly focused around computer science and programming, but in 2013 the MOOCs on humanities topics reached one fifth of the MOOC market (Table 2). And there are more and more business and management courses that are coming on the MOOC market.

Table 2. MOOCs subjects (in %)

Subjects	2013	2014	2015
Computer science & programming	16	16	9.7
Humanities	20	17	9.4
Business & management	15	14	16.8
Health & medicine	11	10	8.3
Education & teaching	8.6	9.5	9.4
Science	11	12	11.3

Source: Shah 2013, Shah 2014, Shah 2015.

MOOCs on Business and Management are the most frequented on Class Central portal[8] too (17.8 %).

The first MOOCs came from American universities, therefore they were taught in English. English still dominates the MOOC market, although its amount was reduced to 75 % in 2015 [30]. MiriadaX[9] provides MOOCs from 64 Latin-American universities in Spanish and Portuguese[10]. MOOC courses are available in French (France Université Numérique)[11], Arabic[12], Chinese[13] and many other languages[14]. MOOCs are presented in small countries like Slovenia[15] as well. There are two MOOCs providers in Slovenia. The Academic and Research Network of Slovenia (ARNES)[16] provide a MOOC about how to use the internet and appliance safety. The participants in this MOOC are mostly from the education field, but the MOOC is open to all those who are interested. The other Slovenian provider is the Institute of Information Science Maribor (IZUM)[17] who provides online training[18] for bibliographical database usage (COBISS/OPAC, ProQuest, EBSCOhost, Web of Science and Scopus). Courses are

8 https://www.class-central.com/subjects.

9 https://www.miriadax.net/es/cursos.

10 https://miriadax.net/web/guest/nuestros-numeros.

11 http://www.france-universite-numerique.fr/.

12 http://www.rwaq.org/.

13 https://www.xuetangx.com/.

14 https://www.mooc-list.com/languages.

15 Slovenia got 2 mio of citizens.

16 http://www.arnes.si/about-arnes/.

17 http://home.izum.si/izum/o_IZUMu/about_IZUM.asp.

18 http://izobrazevanje.izum.si/EntryFormDesktopDefault.aspx?tabid=22&type=web.

available to all those interested. All courses provided by ARNES and IZUM are in Slovenian and they are provided through the Moodle platform.

Moodle[19] is only one of the platforms used for providing MOOCs. Other known MOOCs providers offer MOOCs on their own platforms – the most known are edX, CourseSites by Blackboard, Udemy etc. Each platform has its advantages and disadvantages. Universities that use one of the learning management system (LMS) to support their own on-campus learning will probably use the same platform when it moves on to the MOOCs market.

ICT opens new business opportunities. Providing MOOCs platforms is one of them. The other can be noticed through companies that provide services to prepare online courses. Curricu.me[20] is one of them, willing to help organizations and enterprises build professional online courses on different platforms.

2.3 MOOCs as a Resource for Acquiring Knowledge

MOOCs came from well-known and recognized universities that also offer their own traditional bricks-and-mortar courses. Students from all over the world, even from less developed countries, are able to gain knowledge produced at high ranked universities. In 2015, there were 35 million students enrolled in MOOCs [30]. MOOC participants have different employment status – only 17.4 % of them are students, thus 50 % of them are employed full-time [5]. It is interesting that MOOCs are interesting for retired individuals as well (6.8 %).

MOOCs have a bad reputation, mainly due to lower completion rates. Less than 10 % of students (participants) successfully finish their MOOC. Devlin [8] rebuts the dropout rate as being a question of the methodology used to measure MOOC successfulness. It is recognized that half of participants only enrolled in the MOOC because of curiosity and have no intention of finishing the course [5]. Only 13.2 % of participants enroll to get a degree (ibidem)[21]. Normally a MOOC lasts a few weeks, like traditional courses with detailed structured weekly activities. Research shows that [20] the MOOC completion rate may be predicted. Based on data, 45 % of participants who successfully complete the first assignment will conclude the MOOC and 70 % of those who paid for the certificate. Participants leave MOOCs mainly due to lack of study time [16].

MOOC advocates expose the flexibility of MOOCs that traditional education is hardly able to provide. Participants are able to study at their own pace – to stop and rewind video and audio recordings, to watch video lectures as many times as they like and need to, test their knowledge more times etc. The main power of the MOOCs is the community that is formed in each course. The MOOC learning communities supported by facilitators or tutors support each participant willing to be supported. The peer-to-peer support and multicultural community is the most valuable characteristic of MOOCs. Being part of such a community is really worthwhile.

[19] https://learn.moodle.net/.

[20] http://curricu.me/.

[21] The respondents could pick more than one answer.

In several MOOCs the course content is available even after the conclusion of the course that allows students to revise the subject. We exposed the advantage of MOOCs for participants who are not able to keep pace with an average student, however there are other advantages. Students may skip topics they are already familiar with and focus solely on topics unknown to them. This enables them to complete the course faster, which is impossible on a traditional course.

Thrun [32] sees the MOOC as a support mechanism for lifelong learning (LLL), since they provide contemporary content that was not able, or even not present and known, at the time of an individual's formal school age. It is common to find MOOC participants with diplomas and degrees who are looking to update their knowledge or maybe they would like carrier career change. These groups of participants have no intention of finishing the course but are rather moving through the course looking only for those topics they are interested in. All these facts clearly support a question about the methodology used to measure MOOCs dropout rates.

The openness of course materials is obviously the main advantage of online learning, even if not all MOOCs are really open. Some of them are payable. "Open" has different meanings [4, 19]. Openness has a dimension of accessibility, flexibility and learner control over content and structure [19].

Openness is frequently connected to low quality education and therefore criticized a lot. There are some doubts that MOOCs are threatening to traditional universities where study is payable; students will substitute traditional bricks-and-mortar university courses with MOOCs – Stanford University for Udacity and/or Coursera. Thrun [32] is convinced that this will not happen, as cinema never replaced theatre and TV did not replace radio. Horn [18] sees freely accessible courseware in MOOCs but not good pedagogy. MOOCs can help students, especially more gifted students, to have access to additional digital materials and an international community. On the other side, MOOC providers, like edX, prepared a several courses to help students prepare for college or university study. From this point of view the MOOCs are a good supplement to higher education and not a potential replacement of it.

MOOCs present a real revolution in education, which is also recognized by the European Commission (EC). The EC launched the "Opening up education" initiative in 2013. The main goal of this initiative was to stimulate the development of high-quality innovative ways of learning, based on ICT and digital content [12].

3 Acquired Knowledge in Figures

3.1 Learning in Eurostat Data

In this chapter some of the data collected by Eurostat is presented. Some of them were collected for 2015, but others are similar old (from 2010 or 2011).

In 2015 [10], one tenth of EU28 citizens participated in education and training over the 4 weeks before data collection. In Denmark almost one third of the population (31.4 %) aged between 25 and 64 acquired knowledge, regardless of their employment status – employed (32.0 %), unemployed (29.0 %) or inactive[22] (29.4 %). A lot of the population aged between 25 and 64 is included in education and training in Sweden (29.4 %) and Finland (25.2 %). The average portion of EU28 countries is particularly decreased by Romania (1.1 %) and Bulgaria (1.7 %). Less than 5 % are registered in Poland (3.5 %), Slovakia (3.0 %), Greece (2.9 %) and Croatia (2.6 %).

Countries whose citizens aged between 25 and 64 are willing to participate in education and training (up to 15 %) are compared using Eurostat data about learning. We compare the following data: doing an online course in the last 3 months (Online course), uploading self-created content to a website for sharing purposes (Upload & share), consulting wikis to obtain knowledge (Wikis) and participating in social or professional networks (Networks) (Table 3).

Table 3. Using internet for acquiring knowledge (%)

Country	Online course	Upload & share	Wikis	Networks
EU28	6	29	45	52
Denmark	8	52	62	73
Sweden	8	38	62	69
Finland	13	28	77	60
The Netherlands	9	48	58	68
France	5	22	24	38
Luxembourg	11	42	78	69
UK	12	48	56	70

Source: Eurostat 2016a.

It is interesting that the French, despite having their own MOOC provider that provides MOOCs in French, are not willing to participate in online courses. The share (5 %) is below the EU28 average (6 %) (Table 3).

The first MOOCs were computer and programming oriented. Due to the fact that MOOCs came from traditional universities, students were the logical target group. A comparison was attempted between Eurostat data about using the Internet to take an online course among the population aged 24–65, ICT professionals and students (Fig. 1). In Finland and Sweden students are the most prepared to take online courses thus in Spain ICT professionals use the Internet for online learning the most. As we mentioned before MariadaX is one of the important MOOC providers that provide courses in Spanish. A lot of them are dedicated to ICT professionals.

The most recent data on organizing any type of continuing vocational training (CVT) in enterprises was collected in 2010 [10]. There are 55 % enterprises that organized any type of CVT in EU28. On the top of the scale are Danish (91 %), Austrian and Swedish (87 %) enterprises. There is a smaller possibility for employees to be trained at work in Poland (22 %), Romania (24 %) and Greece (28 %).

---

[22] Persons who are neither employed nor unemployed.

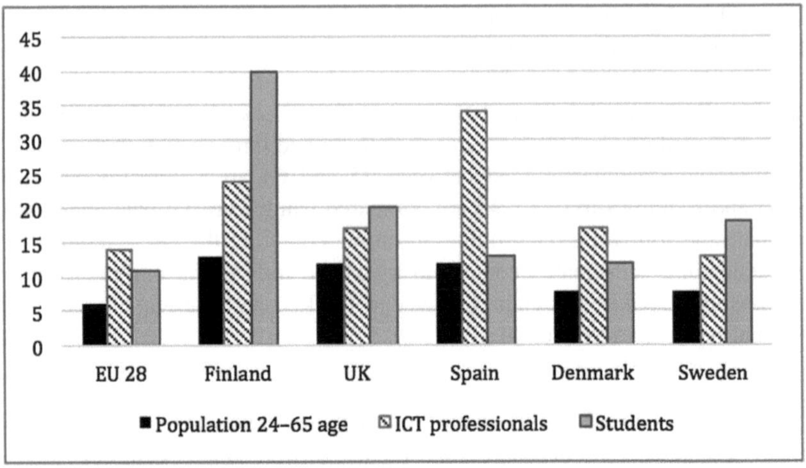

Fig. 1. Taking an online course (in %)

In EU28 countries 42.5 % of persons are looking for information about formal or non-formal learning and 30.7 % for informal learning.

Information on learning possibilities can be gathered from different sources. An average EU28 citizen prefers to use the Internet as a source of information (61.1 %), 29.7 % receive information from employers and 25.0 % from educational institutions. The career guidance provider (10.4 %), mass media (10.8 %) and books (9.9 %) are not useful information media about learning opportunities. Eurostat collected all data in 2011. Comparing the data on information searches on learning possibilities and data about willing participation in education and training showed that in countries with a large share of higher educated (5th level and up) people willing to learn found negative statistical significant correlations with using mass media (–0.40) and books (–0.49).

We tried to investigate if there are any correlations between data collected in 2015. It is obvious that more digital literate persons are more willing to participate in education and training. The correlation is high (0.72) and significant. We find that participation in education and training is statistically significant correlated to Online course (0.63), Upload & share (0.60), Wikis (0.66) and Networks (0.50). Using wikis to obtain knowledge on any subject further explain 42 % variability of participation in education and training (Sig. < 0.01)[23].

3.2 MOOCs for Training?

MOOCs have already shown their potential value for higher education students [6]. They can help students to prepare themselves for advanced placement exams. MOOCs can enable a potential student to become more familiar with the subject they would like to study and with higher education expectations before they enroll at university.

[23] ANOVA regression analyses (Stepwise method) was used.

They also help students to expand their horizons and intercultural experience (ibidem). But do the MOOCs have any potential as in-house company training solutions?

Meister [23] from Forbes saw the future for MOOCs in corporate learning more than in higher education. Pappas [26] exposed the benefits of MOOCs for in-house company training. MOOCs are accessible without any limit in time (24/7), place and number of participants. Employees are able to improve their skills or to acquire new knowledge that impact on company productivity without any additional cost for the employer.

Based on research that Future Workplace conducted among 195 corporate learning and human resource professionals, 70 % respondents saw opportunities in the integration of MOOCs into their learning programs [23]. MOOCs were firstly seen as additional content that can help learners to learn at their own pace and as a part of so-called flipped learning, where students learn at home and discuss about what they have learnt when they meet each other. Some USA companies see MOOCs as a way of filling skill gaps in their environment [14].

On eLearning Industry[24] employers can find links to several MOOCs providers that provide different courses. Some of these MOOCs are indented for people that would like to run their own business, others to leading staff at different management positions. Large organizations such as Microsoft and AT&T piloted their self-created MOOCs [24] thus the other tried to develop strategies that align available MOOCs to their own needs. Based on Future Workplace data 31 % of organizations are interested in creating MOOCs only for internal use, 22 % are only interested in curating external MOOCs and 44 % are interested in both strategies (ibidem). It is interesting that the greatest resistance for any of the above strategies comes from training and instructional staff (44 %), which is similar to faculty resistance to MOOCs at universities. Resistance in one third is noticed from IT departments and lines of business executives. Only one quarter of employees and less than one fifth of human resources staff resist MOOCs.

Staff resistance is not the only barrier that company faces. The Future Workplace exposes three of the most enhanced barriers [24]. Developing internal MOOCs demands a company learning budget or employed training staff that are skilled in preparing MOOCs. The technical and security issues are also highlighted.

We mentioned that English still dominates the MOOC market, so curating existing MOOCs for in-house company training in English speaking countries would not be as difficult as it is for companies from non-English speaking countries. Therefore, language issue may be a serious barrier for implementing MOOCs into company training strategy.

4 Conclusion

We have witnessed the growth of MOOCs in the last 4 years. MOOCs came from high-ranking US universities were study is payable and therefore MOOCs are presenting a great opportunity to acquire knowledge and certificates for free. This opportunity was

[24] http://elearningindustry.com/9-free-moocs-for-corporate-training.

accepted not only by American students but also by students from less developed regions of the world. EU responded to this global learning movement in 2013 with the initiative "Opening up education". This initiative is mainly oriented towards higher education institutions [9].

Modern companies of any size from any part of the world are doing their business online, mostly in the cloud. They are connected with their customers and partners in the global digital world. Higher education institutions are trying to do the same. The idea of a virtual university is not new and has been being discussed for a long time [27]. But is seems that MOOCs found a more suitable model of online learning that was met before. From open courses, providers are now making their own business models and trying to make a business from them. Although MOOCs are known as higher education courses more and more MOOCs are becoming seen as more suitable for corporate learning. Especially in English speaking countries and/or companies it is easy to find a suitable course and to adopt it to company-training programs.

From 2013 Europe launched their own initiative that try to find their own path toward implementing MOOCs in higher education. One of the results of this initiative is the portal OpenEducationEuropa[25], where MOOCs can be searched and found. Courses can be searched by different characteristic (subject, the educational level, language, license etc.). Science and technology is the most common MOOC subject followed by social science and humanities. The course structure on this portal is a bit different to other well-known MOOCs providers, but as mentioned the EU MOOC approach is not the same as the US MOOC approach.

The goal of this paper was to collect some data about MOOCs together and to present some data about how European citizens are willing to learn. The Internet is a common source of information and for learning. People in particular EU countries have been starting to participate in some MOOCs, more ICT professionals and students than others. In the last year FutureLearn from the UK and German Iversity are providing different MOOCs. Iversity recognized the potential of MOOCs for company training and they offer their resources to help them[26].

Curating external MOOCs for in-house company learning programs needs adequate strategies that have to take into account the barriers they will encounter.

References

1. ISCED 2011 – International Standard Classification of Education (2012). http://www.uis.unesco.org/Education/Documents/isced-2011-en.pdf
2. Baggaley, J.: Reflection MOOC rampant. Dist. Educ. **34**(3), 368–378 (2013)
3. Barba-Sánchez, V., del Pilar Martínez-Ruiz, M., Jiménez-Zarco, A.I.: Drivers, benefits and challenges of ICT adoption by small and medium sized enterprises (SMEs): a literature review. Prob. Perspect. Manage. **5**(1), 103–113 (2007)

[25] http://www.openeducationeuropa.eu/en/about_this_portal.

[26] http://business.iversity.org/en/#app-home-3.

4. Bates, T.: What do we mean by 'open' in education? (2015). http://www.tonybates.ca/2015/02/16/what-do-we-mean-by-open-in-education/
5. Blake, D.: The Rising Power of MOOCs: Now, everyone can learn at Harvard (2014). http://moocs.com/index.php/category/mooc-infographics/. Accessed 2 June 2015
6. Chung, C.: Five Reasons High School Students Should Consider MOOCs. Class Central's MOOC Report, 28 April 2015. https://www.class-central.com/report/five-reasons-high-schoolers-consider-taking-moocs/
7. Cusack, A.: MOOC INFOGRAPHICS. MOOCs – Think Massively (2014). http://moocs.com/index.php/category/mooc-infographics/. Accessed 8 Feb 2016
8. Devlin, K.: MOOCs and the Myths of Dropout Rates and Certification (2013). http://www.huffingtonpost.com/dr-keith-devlin/moocs-and-the-myths-of-dr_b_2785808.html. Accessed 11 July 2015
9. EADTU. Institutional MOOC strategies in Europe (2015). http://www.eadtu.eu/documents/Publications/OEenM/Institutional_MOOC_strategies_in_Europe.pdf
10. Eurostat. Education and training (2016a). http://ec.europa.eu/eurostat/web/education-and-training/data/database. Accessed 2 Mar 2016
11. Eurostat. Information Society (2016b). http://ec.europa.eu/eurostat/web/information-society/data/main-tables. Accessed 4 Mar 2016
12. European Commission, Directorate-General for Education and Culture. Opening up education - Education policy - EU Bookshop (2014). doi:10.2766/77543, http://bookshop.europa.eu/en/opening-up-education-pbNC0214816/?CatalogCategoryID=QN4KABste0YAAAEjFZEY4e5L
13. Fee, K.: Delivering e-learning. Kogan Page, London (2009)
14. Fitzgerald, M.: Companies Create MOOCs To Fill Skills Gaps. InformationWeek (2013). http://www.informationweek.com/education/online-learning/companies-create-moocs-to-fill-skills-ga/240155639
15. Haag, S.: Management Information Systems for the Information Age. McGraw-Hill, Irwin (2013)
16. Halawa, S.: MOOC dropouts – What we learn from students who leave. Št. 00328, 11 July 2014. http://www.universityworldnews.com/article.php?story=20140708163413797. Accessed 15 Oct 2014
17. Hislop, D.: Knowledge Management in Organizations. Oxford Universty Press, Oxford (2009)
18. Michael, B.H.: MOOCs for high school: unlocking opportunities or substandard learning. Educ. Next, 14(3) (2014). http://educationnext.org/moocs-high-school/
19. Jarvis, P., Holford, J., Griffin, C.: The Theory and Practice in Learning, 2nd edn. Kogan, London (2003)
20. Kolowich, S.: George Siemens Get Connected. The Chronicle of Higher Education – Technology (2014). http://chronicle.com/article/George-Siemens-Gets-Connected/143959/. Accessed 3 July 2014
21. Laudon, K., Laudon, J.: Management Information Systems: Managing the Digital Firm, 10th edn. Prentice Hall, Upper Saddle River (2006)
22. Marentič-Požarnik, B.: Psihologija učenja in pouka. DZS, Ljubljana (2010)
23. Jeanne, M.: How MOOCs Will Revolutionize Corporate Learning and Development, 13 August 2013. http://www.forbes.com/sites/jeannemeister/2013/08/13/how-moocs-will-revolutionize-corporate-learning-development/#db6d20c3e859
24. Jeanne, M.: MOOCs Emerge As Disruptors To Corporate Learning. Forbes, 10 June 2015. http://www.forbes.com/sites/jeannemeister/2015/06/10/moocs-emerge-as-disruptors-to-corporate-learning/

25. Oz, E.: Management Information Systems, 6th edn. Cengage Learning, Boston (2009). Course Technology
26. Pappas, C.: 6 Benefits Of Using MOOCs for Corporate Training (2015). http://elearningindustry.com/6-benefits-of-using-moocs-for-corporate-training. Accessed 3 June 2015
27. Robins, K., Webster, F. (eds.): The Virtual University? Knowledge, Markets and Management. Oxford Press, Oxford (2002)
28. Shah, D.: MOOCs in 2013: Breaking Down the Numbers (2013). https://www.edsurge.com/news/2013-12-22-moocs-in-2013-breaking-down-the-numbers. Accessed 3 Mar 2016
29. Shah, D.: MOOCs in 2014: Breaking Down the Numbers (2014). https://www.edsurge.com/n/2014-12-26-moocs-in-2014-breaking-down-the-numbers. Accessed 3 Mar 2016
30. Shah, D.: MOOCs in 2015: Breaking Down the Numbers (2015). https://www.edsurge.com/news/2015-12-28-moocs-in-2015-breaking-down-the-numbers. Accessed 3 Mar 2016
31. Smith, M.K.: Informal, non-formal and formal education: a brief overview of different approaches, the encyclopedia of informal education (2002). http://www.infed.org/foundations/informal_nonformal.htm. Accessed 08 July 2014
32. Thrun, S.: Self-Driving Education. The Huffington Post (2013). http://www.huffingtonpost.com/sebastian-thrun/selfdriving-education_b_4676484.html. Accessed 4 Feb 2014

Problem Solving and Knowledge Transfer

Designing Technology-Based Tasks for Enhancing Mathematical Understanding Through Problem Solving

Fernando Barrera-Mora and Aaron Reyes-Rodriguez(✉)

Mathematics and Physics Department,
Autonomous University of Hidalgo State, Pachuca, Mexico
fbarrera10147@gmail.com, aaron.reyes.rdz@gmail.com

Abstract. In this paper, we propose some organizing principles that can be useful for high schools or bachelor mathematics teachers when designing technology-based instructional tasks. It is widely accepted that tasks are the most important aspect to promote students' mathematical understanding, since tasks offer opportunities to attain relevant sensorial experiences fostering the construction of mental images as sources of meanings for mathematical concepts. In this vein, we reflect on the work developed by three bachelor mathematics teachers who participated in a problem solving seminar. The main points identified during task design involved recognizing how mathematical concepts are structured around the task, and which are needed to approach it, and proposing a hypothetical learning trajectory in which technology plays a role as amplifier and reorganizer of cognitive processes.

Keywords: Tasks design · Mathematical understanding · Technology

1 Introduction

Tasks design is important, since tasks orient the work that teachers and students develop in mathematics classrooms. Characteristics of tasks have a significant effect on levels of mathematical understanding that students can attain [1], since activities that students address in a classroom shape their mathematical view and influence the ways they behave when confronted with problem situations [2].

The main objective of mathematics educations is that students construct mathematical ways of thinking, as well as progressive levels of conceptual understanding. To achieve this objective, it is important that learning environments offer students opportunities to experience critical thinking and reasoning, and to develop specific skills through solving problems related to professional fields [3].

However, we generally observe passive and uninterested students in mathematics classrooms. We argue that it is due to the kind of tasks that are implemented in school, which are inadequate to enhance students' particular learning styles and potentiate their natural reasoning abilities. Alignment of mathematics learning with mathematical thinking is an important goal in school [4], which requires that teachers be able to design tasks based on mathematical principles. In this vein, it is relevant that teachers have a

L. Uden et al. (Eds.): LTEC 2016, CCIS 620, pp. 183–192, 2016.
DOI: 10.1007/978-3-319-42147-6_16

deep mathematical knowledge, knowledge about learning theories, mathematics pedagogy and brain functioning [5]. Related to the latter, teachers should know that sense making for mathematical ideas involves engaging learners in significant sensorial experiences (seeing, hearing, touching, moving, reasoning) and promoting reflection about those experiences as the source of meaning [6]. All the products of the mind come from the human body interactions with the world [7] and for this reason, sensible experiences help us to construct mental images to link previous and new knowledge [3] and as a consequence, attain higher levels of conceptual understanding.

Teaching new materials is often done without taking into account concepts or ideas related to a given context. Naaranoja and Uden [3] argue that there exists evidence that mathematical understanding requires constructions of relations between previous knowledge and new ideas, as well as clues to recover or reconstruct those links. People learn new material contextually fitting it into existing cognitive structures to develop robust conceptual networks. New information that cannot be linked to existing knowledge is not likely to be integrated into a robust network of concepts. No one can understand anything if it is not connected in some way to something they already know [7]. Additionally, once information is stored in the long term memory, cues in the form of mental images are required for recovering and mobilizing this knowledge.

2 Some Principles to Guide Task Design

One basic principle that supports this work is that intelligence is a product of the relation between mental structures and the actions we perform with tools provided by the culture. Tools help us transcend the biological limitations of mind [4, 8, 9] by externalizing the intermediate products of thinking through representations such as words, texts, graphs, tables, etc. These representations provide material records that are useful to organize thinking and reflect about our own thought processes [4].

From the previous arguments, it is important to consider and analyze the fundamental characteristics of learners' thinking that accompany the usage of these tools. What aspects of mathematical thinking can digital technologies enhance, catalyze or uncover? The dynamic and interactive media provided by digital tools make it possible to gain an intuitive understanding of the interrelations among several representations which are more accessible to learners.

An instruction based on problem solving that promotes the systematic use of digital tools helps mathematics becoming *functional*, since technologies prompt the development of mathematical thinking, and conceptual tools formation during the solution of tasks that represents an intellectual challenge for learners. Interactive technologies enhance construction of meaning and understanding, since they provide a means of intertwining multiple representations and the formation of mental images that help us organize and integrate conceptual, factual and procedural knowledge into a network of relationships [4].

In the same vein, construction of mathematical understanding requires learners to develop successive cycles of action, observation, formulation of conjectures and justification of results (Fig. 1). Each cycle is nurtured with the information and relations of the previous one. In this process, the learners' construction of progressive understanding

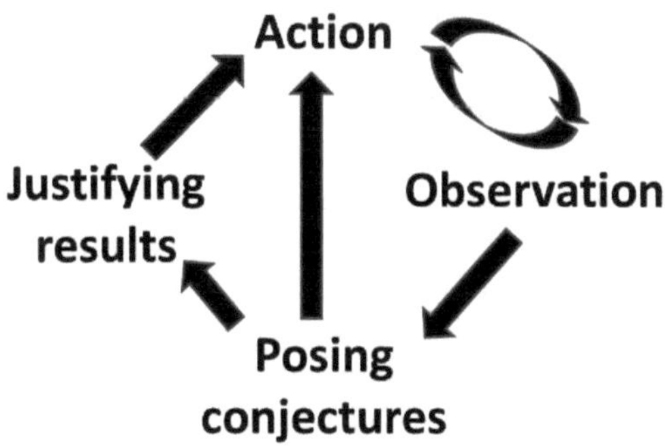

Fig. 1. Basic cycle to develop conceptual understanding during problem solving processes (Adapted from [7]).

levels is stimulated through problem situations which encourage acting on and integrating contents, resources and strategies in learners' problem solving approaches.

The action and observation phases are closely intertwined. In the action phase learners focus on representing the information and reflecting on the mathematical objects involved in a problem, in terms of its fundamental properties. At this stage, it is important to quantify some objects' attributes or adding auxiliary elements in order to get insights into the problem. During the observation phase, it is important that learners identify relationships among the elements considered in the previous phase. The posing conjectures phase is oriented so that learners can formulate their observations in mathematical terms. Some learners possibly need to go back to a new *action-observation-posing conjectures* cycle in order to gain better understanding of the problem, while others can go directly to the justification phase. This latter phase includes the use of visual, empirical and formal arguments, as well as extending and generalizing the task.

Addressing problem solving with digital tools demands that learners think about mathematical objects in terms of their basic properties, and that they consider problems as a set of dilemmas which should be approached by means of mathematical resources: How are the objects involved in a problem defined? Is there any relation between those objects? What are the characteristics, if any, of those relationships? A key element to promote the construction of connections among mathematical ideas is to take advantage of visualization and exploration affordances offered by digital tools to explore properties of mathematical objects, to formulate and justify conjectures, to communicate results and pose new problems [10].

It is well known that using different ways of representing data in a problem are crucial for the generation of solution routes, as are strategy selection, prior knowledge and the tools used to organize a solution path [11]. The more senses we use in an activity, the more fruitful the learning experience will become, since it increases the neuronal connections in students' brain and therefore the knowledge is more accessible and usable [6]. All students have prior knowledge that affects how they approach the activities that are proposed to them.

In this paper, a technology-based task is conceptualized as a guide to help teachers organize classroom activities by engaging learners in significant sensorial experiences (seeing, hearing, touching, moving, and reasoning) promoted by the systematic use of digital artifacts and reflection about those experiences. The experiences and reflection about technology based tasks have the aim to promote the construction of mathematical ways of thinking and mental images, which have a twofold function: structuring previous and new concepts into a network or mental schema and act as clues to recover and use the knowledge. The design of technology-based tasks rests heavily on a complex relationship between teacher knowledge about mathematics, learning, teaching, tool affordances and a kind of feedback offered by the tools [12]. A technology-based task has the objective of promote constructing new connections or relations between concepts, starting from students' prior knowledge, through sensorial experiences and reflection promoted during problem solving activity (Fig. 1).

The design of technology-based task involves determining the core mathematical concept that students must learn and reflect about the relations needed to structure prior and new knowledge, mental images that give meaning to the concepts, as well as the sensory experiences, and reflection activities useful to achieve such organization and structuration of mathematical ideas, considering potentialities and limitations of available tools.

3 The Research Context

The task proposed in this paper was discussed in a context of problem-solving seminar in which participated mathematics teachers, mathematicians and mathematics educators. The aim of this seminar is to promote the discussion and reflection about mathematics teaching and learning, specifically about how students develop progressive levels of mathematical understanding, reasoning and mathematical ways of thinking when they are engaged in problem solving activities.

In the seminar development, at the end of the first semester of the academic year 2015-2016, three mathematics teachers, who teach Precalculus courses to engineering students, solved a task using GeoGebra and reflected on the developed problem solving process from a didactic point of view with the aim to design a similar task to be implemented in their classrooms. All teachers have gained a bachelor degree in applied mathematics; two of them are enrolled in a master program in mathematics and one is a PhD mathematics students. GeoGebra is a Dynamic Geometry System that integrates different tools of geometry, calculus, and statistics, among other and can be used to explore different kind of mathematical problems from elementary school to university mathematics courses.

An important element in this paper is to explore how each question or reflection was posed and pursued during the seminar sessions. To this end, we identify some routes that the participants, as a group, identified as important and discussed while delving into the task. The departure point in each session was to conceptualize solving problems as an opportunity to understand the different ways that students think about and learn. Thus, our unit of analysis is what the group as a whole proposed and discussed during each of four sessions of an hour and a half.

Data included teachers' written records, electronic files, and video recordings of each session, which were transcribed. First of all, data analysis was mainly oriented to identify stages of basic cycle to develop conceptual understanding (Fig. 1). Based on these, we draw some organizing principles that might be useful to design instructional tasks.

The seminar discussion was oriented to determine some of the core mathematical concepts in a Precalculus course. Teachers agreed that one of the central concepts in calculus is the concept of function and that this is grounded on the idea of covariation of two quantities. Then, teachers suggested that some mental images to give meaning to this idea can be approached by posing problems related to uniform motion, filling liquid containers, population growth, simple and compound interest or problems of maxima and minima.

3.1 The Task

With the aim of promoting problem solving activities as well as didactical reflection, the research team proposed the teachers to solve the following problem: find the rectangle of maximum area that can be inscribed in a given triangle. The resources needed to approach the problem consisted of basic geometric ideas such as triangle, inscribed rectangle and area calculation. In a first approach, teachers proposed solving the task by means of standard calculus procedures, which include determining a function of one variable, calculate the derivate, solving an equation to obtain the critical points and so on. However, teachers were encouraged to think and reflect about the minimum mathematical requirements to approach the task and ways to promote construction of mental images about covariation of two quantities using GeoGebra and the basic cycle to develop conceptual understanding (Fig. 1). The use of Geogebra was suggested since dynamic characteristics of this tool are useful to explore phenomena of change and variation.

First Episode: Understanding the Problem and Gaining Insights about Students' Mathematical Action. In this phase teachers realized that to approach the task, students should know that inscribing a rectangle in a triangle means that the vertices of the rectangle must lie on the sides of the triangle. Teachers constructed the dynamic configuration easily, however to engaged them thinking how students could construct such a configuration required a deep reflection about problem solving activity. Teachers agreed that sketching a drawing on paper and pencil can be useful to organize the data of the problem, but the construction of the figure in GeoGebra also involves thinking about the inscribed rectangle in terms of mathematical properties such as perpendicularity and parallelism of lines. Additionally, teachers realized that using GeoGebra can allow students considering non-prototypical examples, which is useful to generate robust mental images associated with the idea of a triangle.

Some useful questions that teachers identified as important to promoting students' action are: For what kind of triangles are there two vertices of the inscribed rectangle on two sides of the triangle? Is it possible to inscribe a unique rectangle for any given triangle? Can each side of the triangle contain the base of an inscribed rectangle?

Teachers also considered that constructing several particular cases of rectangles inscribed in a given triangle could be useful as a first approach to note the covariation of two quantities (relating the change of some length and the area of the rectangle).

The teachers realized that dragging affordances of GeoGebra can be employed to direct students' attention to the construction of families of geometrical objects and to highlight the differences of area among elements of this family. During the discussion, teachers pointed out the importance that students communicate their observation about area variation orally or in writing form. Ideally, reflection about extreme cases could allow students to realize that there exists a rectangle of a maximum area. An important element that was also recognized is that students should identify some other variable quantities as well as possible ways to relate them.

Second Episode: Analyzing Problem Information as a Way to Observe Relations, Patterns and Invariants. This phase was oriented to formulate questions about the problem data as a means to detect relations, patterns and invariants among them. In this vein, teachers commented about the importance that students realize that translating the triangle on the plane does not change the area of an inscribed rectangle or other variables of the problem. This knowledge is a necessary antecedent to introduce a coordinate system as a tool for representing symbolically two variable quantities.

Teachers commented that using appropriately a coordinate system requires to relate points in a plane with ordered pairs of real numbers. On the other hand, managing and operating equations of loci requires that students approached previously sub-tasks that allow them to realize that the coordinates of loci satisfy some relations and that these relations can be generalized and represented in symbolic language. It is important that students identify those changes of position of a locus result in changes on the equation representing it. In this line of ideas, it is important that students realize that placing geometric objects in a suitable position can be useful to simplify equations that describe those geometrical objects.

Teachers expressed that students have several difficulties to explore the general case, and for this reason they proposed to explore particular cases of triangles with integer coordinates, for example triangle ABC whose vertices coordinates are A = (0,0), B = (8,0), C = (5,3). Students can be encouraged to develop an empirical route dragging point D (Fig. 2) to approach the rectangle of maximum area and then, the teacher could orient students' attention to observe some relation between vertex *C* and position of *D* that approximates the maximum area. Students might be able to conjecture that the x-coordinate of point D is a half of the x-coordinate of point C.

Some identified questions to promote posing of conjectures are: Is there any relationships between the area of the inscribed rectangle and the area of triangle *ABC, in particular when the area is maximized*? What is the ratio between the lengths of segments *AE* and *EC* and between the segments *CF* and *FB*? Are there any similar triangles in Fig. 3? Students could be oriented to recognize that some relevant ratios between lengths or areas are ½, 1/3, 2, 3, $\sqrt{2}, \frac{1}{\sqrt{2}}$, etc., and that significant relations have to do with midpoints, equality of lengths, areas or perimeters and so on. Observing the previous relationships can also be useful in the phase of justification of conjectures. In this case the main conjecture is that the maximum area of a rectangle is half of the area

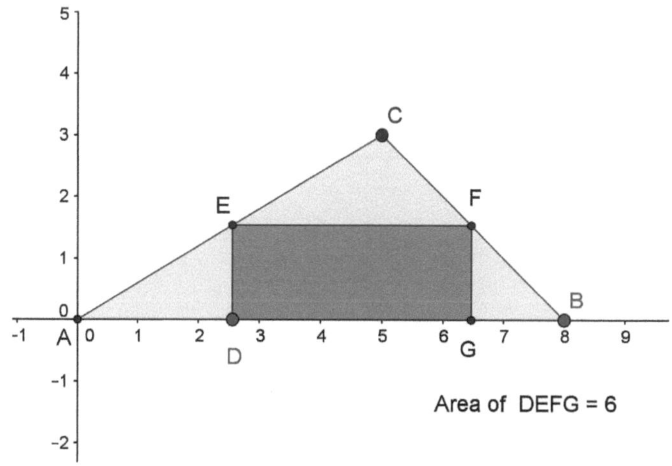

Fig. 2. Solution path based on particular cases.

of triangle *ABC*. Other related conjectures are that *E* is the midpoint of *AC*, *F* is the midpoint of *CB*, and that $AD + GB = (AB)/2$.

Continuing the analysis of particular cases, teachers considered as relevant that students relate graphically some variable quantities. For example, using the locus tool students can be oriented to observe that the relation between the area of the inscribed rectangles and length AD, is described by a parabola that opens downwards and that the vertex of the parabola provides information regarding the point where the inscribed rectangle reaches the maximum area. Teachers recognized that graphical representation highlights some relationships that are not readily observable in the numeric register, for example, that the maximum area is reached in a position such that the x-coordinate of point D is a half of the x-coordinate of point C, and that relation has to do with symmetry properties of a parabola.

Third Episode: Generalizing Results and Searching for Arguments. Teachers proposed that from observations about particular cases, students could be oriented to detect what are the similarities with the aim to generalize the results and to express those results in symbolic language. Teachers recognized as an important element that students should pay attention on relations between symbolic expressions and its concrete referents as well as to which letters represent fixed quantities in the context of the particular problem or which represents variable quantities.

Searching for arguments involves relating factual knowledge with results developed during problem solving processes. For developing this activity teachers consider relevant to look over digital content related to the concepts emerging during previous episodes (similarity of triangles, properties of a parabola, ratios and proportions) and those that are available on sites such as Wikipedia, GeoGebra tube or Khan Academy as a mean to promote connections between mathematical concepts and procedures, and develop a conception of mathematical content as tools to solve problems.

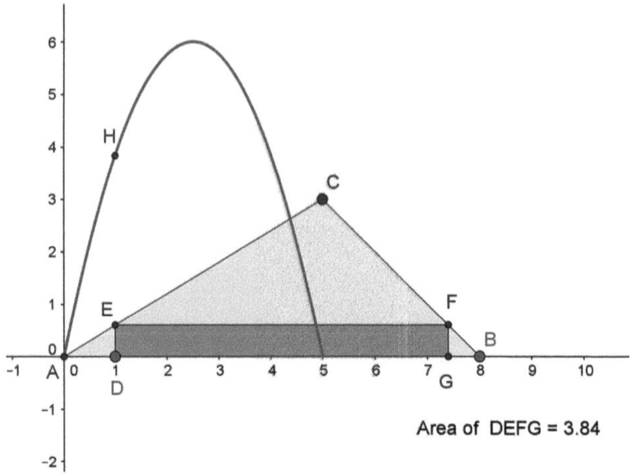

Fig. 3. Connecting several representations.

Fourth Episode: Searching for Alternative Solution Paths and Formulating New Problems. Searching for or discussing multiple solution paths has been recognized as a powerful strategy for students to engage in mathematical thinking and learning [13]. Teachers considered that an alternative route to solve the problem without employing a coordinate system is the following: the distance AD can be denoted by the expression r (AH), such that r is a real number in the interval (0,1) and H is the foot of the altitude of the triangle passing through vertex C (Fig. 4). Then, by similarity of triangles ABC and EFC, $EF = (1\text{-}r)(AB)$, and $ED = r(CH)$.

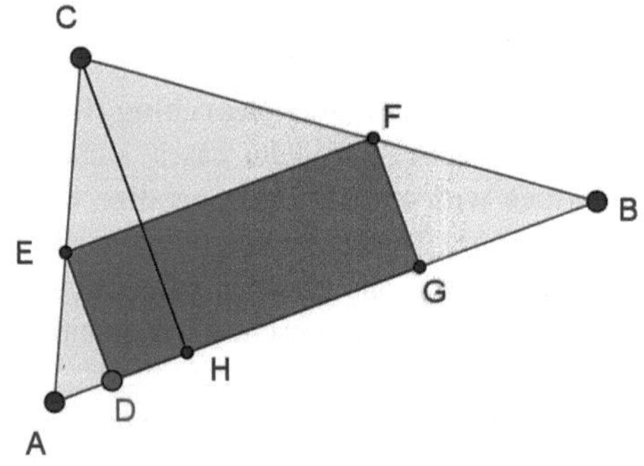

Fig. 4. Another solution route.

Based on the previous relations, the area of rectangle DEFG can be calculated to be (EF)(ED) = $r(1-r)(AB)(CH)$, since $(AB)(CH)$ is two times the area of the triangle ABC, which is a fixed quantity, then the maximum area is reached when $f(r) = r-r^2$, reaches its maximum value. The graph of this function is a parabola whose vertex has coordinates (½, ¼). Then, the maximum area is reached when D is the midpoint of segment AH, and the area of the rectangle is half of the triangle's area.

4 Final Remarks

Analyzing teachers' activities during the seminar allowed us to identify some elements that should be considered when designing technology-based tasks oriented to foster mathematical understanding.

First of all, interaction among member of a professional community is important to identify the core concepts that guide construction of conceptual mathematical structures (function concept and covariation). Secondly, teachers must define the possible contexts that can help students' to give meaning to those concepts (uniform motion, filling liquid containers, population growth, simple and compound interest or problems of maxima and minima). At this stage it is necessary to think about problems in a specific context that could contribute to structure core mathematical ideas, concepts and procedures. Textbooks constitute a relevant source to find problems; however the problems must be adapted in order to represent an intellectual challenge for students as pointed out by the problem solving approach [14].

Another important activity during tasks design involves defining the minimum resources needed to approach the problem (concepts of triangle and inscribed rectangle and area calculation), the mental images useful to structure the prior and new knowledge (quantities changing together), and the sensorial experiences or reflection activities useful to construct those images, based on potentialities and limitations of available tools (construction of a family of inscribed rectangles whose area depend of the position of a point that can be dragged).

An important resource for tasks design is the basic cycle to develop conceptual understanding (Fig. 1), since it describes important processes that allow students to connect previous knowledge with the new core concepts. We would like to point out specifically the interaction between action and observation phases in which technology affordances play a crucial role. In the discussed task, different dynamical visual representations (changing images and changing numerical data) help to identify some patterns (the rectangle of maximum area is reached when two vertices are located on the midpoints of two sides of the triangle).

A central point during the interaction between observation and posing conjectures phases is related to identifying general results and their formulation in mathematical symbols, which possess meaning through the particular cases explored.

We would like to highlight that designing technology-based tasks involve several complex elements that should be explored and reflected within a professional community in order to provide a wider range of opportunities to promote students learning.

References

1. Watson, A., Minoru, O.: Themes and issues in mathematics education concerning task design: Editorial introduction. In: Watson, A., Ohtani, M. (eds.) Task Design in Mathematics Education: An ICMI Study 22, pp. 3–18. Springer, Cham (2015)
2. Schoenfeld, A.H.: Mathematical Problem Solving. Academic Press, Orlando (1985)
3. Naaranoja, Marja, Uden, Lorna: Eight R's – case study. In: Uden, L., Liberona, D., Welzer, T. (eds.) LTEC 2015. CCIS, vol. 533, pp. 67–76. Springer, Heidelberg (2015)
4. Pea, R.D.: Cognitive technologies for mathematics education. In: Schoenfeld, A. (ed.) Cognitive Science and Mathematics Education, pp. 89–122. Erlbaum, Hillsdale (1987)
5. Jensen, E.: Teaching with the Brain in Mind, 2nd edn. Association for Supervision and Curriculum Development, Alexandria (2005)
6. Beard, C., Wilson, J.P.: Experiential Learning: A Handbook for Education, Training and Coaching. KoganPage, London (2013)
7. Zull, J.A.: The Art of Changing the Brain: Enriching the Practice of Teaching by Exploring the Biology of Learning. Stylus, Sterling (2002)
8. Vygotsky, L.S.: Thought and Language. MIT Press, Cambridge (1962)
9. Vygotsky, L.S.: Mind in Society: The Development of the Higher Psychological Processes. Harvard University Press, Cambridge (1978)
10. Santos-Trigo, M., Reyes-Rodriguez, A., Espinosa-Perez, H.: Musing on the use of dynamic software and mathematics epistemology. TEAMAT **26**(4), 167–178 (2007)
11. Polya, G.: How to Solve it. Princeton University Press, Princeton (1945)
12. Leung, A., Bolite-Frant, J.: Designing mathematics tasks: the role of tools. In: Watson, A., Ohtani, M. (eds.) Tasks Design in Mathematics Education, pp. 191–228. Springer, Cham (2015)
13. Santos-Trigo, M., Reyes-Rodriguez, A.: The use of digital technology in finding multiple paths to solve and extend an equilateral triangle task. Int. J. Math. Educ. Sci. Tech. **47**(1), 58–81 (2016)
14. Santos-Trigo, M.: La Resolución de Problemas Matemáticos: Fundamentos Cognitivos. Trillas, México (2007)

Digital Technologies and a Modeling Approach to Learn Mathematics and Develop Problem Solving Competencies

Manuel Santos-Trigo(✉), Isaid Reyes-Martínez, and Daniel Aguilar-Magallón

Mathematics Education Department, Centre for Research and Advanced Studies, Cinvestav-IPN, Av. IPN 2508, San Pedro Zacatenco, 07360 Mexico City, Mexico
msantos@cinvestav.mx

Abstract. This study is framed within a conceptual approach that integrates modeling, problem solving, and the use of digital technologies perspectives in mathematical learning. It focuses on the use of a Dynamic Geometry System (GeoGebra) to construct mathematical models as a means to represent and explore mathematical relationships. In particular, we analyze and document what ways of reasoning high school students exhibit as a result of working on a mathematical task in problem solving sessions. Results show that the students rely on a set of technology affordances to dynamically visualize, represent and explore mathematical relations. In this process, the students' discussions became relevant not only to explain their approaches; but also to contrast, and eventually refine, their initial models and ways of reasoning.

Keywords: Digital technologies · Modeling · Problem solving · Mathematics learning

1 Introduction

Significant developments and uses of digital technologies permeate the ways people communicate, share information, interact and carry out social events. Educational systems face a challenge to incorporate the use of several digital technologies in both the ways of structuring and approaching the content to be studied and in the design of learning scenarios for students to construct disciplinary knowledge. In the learning of mathematics, both multiple purpose (Internet, YouTube, Wikipedia, etc.) and ad hoc technologies (Dynamic Geometry Systems, WolframAlpha, etc.) are transforming the mathematics curriculum (all levels) and the design of learning scenarios. In this context, mathematical tasks are essential to analyze what changes the use of technology brings to the content and to document the type of thinking that learners develop or construct as a result of problem solving instruction. The National Council Teachers of Mathematics (NCTM) [15] recognize that tasks are the vehicle for high school students to engage in mathematical reasoning and making sense activities in order to understand mathematical concepts and to develop problem solving competencies. Similarly,

L. Uden et al. (Eds.): LTEC 2016, CCIS 620, pp. 193–206, 2016.
DOI: 10.1007/978-3-319-42147-6_17

Schoenfeld [18] stated that "… curricula could be enlivened with more interesting tasks, with a greater focus on sense making, and with a more coherent attempt to build problem-solving skills: not as "add-ons" but as a core component of mathematical activity" (p. 506). Thus, the design or selection of mathematical tasks is crucial for instruction to help and promote the students' construction of mathematical knowledge and a way of thinking that is consistent with mathematical practice. Cai [2] stated "[o] nly worthwhile problems give students the chance to both solidify and extend what they know and to stimulate their learning" (p. 252). It is also relevant to recognize that students' understanding of mathematical ideas is an ongoing process in which they gradually construct a network of concepts. Engelbrecht [5] mentioned: "the dynamic process of understanding new mathematics takes place in layers. With every layer you understand a little deeper" (p. 152).

English and Sriraman [6] argued that if students are to develop a problem solving approach in a productive way, they need to engage, during their interaction with the tasks, in iterative cycles of describing, representing, exploring, testing, and revising mathematical interpretation, as well as identifying, modifying, and refining mathematical concepts to be used in problem solving.

2 Conceptual Framework

The notion of "bricolage", taken as the convergence of several perspectives, is used to structure and frame the study. That is, "…rather than adhering to one particular theoretical perspective, we act as bricoleurs by adapting ideas from a range of theoretical sources" ([4], p. 29). To this end, the foundations, in this study, incorporate concepts associated with modeling approaches [1, 11]; and principles associated with problem-solving approaches and the use of digital technologies to support and frame the study [19, 21]. Simon [20] pointed out that "the availability of multiple explanatory theories and the use of multiple layers of analysis can, depending on the research, provide a richer set of constructs for accounting for observed phenomena" (p. 484). Under these frameworks and perspectives, the students' construction of mathematical knowledge is conceptualized as a process in which they gradually construct an interrelated network of concepts (conceptual comprehension); utilize different procedures and algorithms; participate in the process of formulation of questions and conjectures; propose various ways to explore, explain, and support mathematical results; and develop a disposition to solve problems and to exhibit reasoning habits[1] associated with mathematical thinking [9].

Kelly & Lesh [8] have recognized that researchers, teachers, and students rely on models to represent, organize, examine, and explain situations or phenomena. Thus, models are not only key ingredients and tools for researchers to explain the students' development of mathematical thinking; they also are essential for teachers to structure and promote their students' construction of mathematics knowledge. For instance,

[1] The NCTM (2009) stated that "a reasoning habit is a productive way of thinking that becomes common in the process of mathematical inquiry and sense making" (p. 9).

researchers construct models to analyze and interpret teachers and students' mathematical behaviors. Similarly, teachers use models to foster, describe, examine, and predict students' mathematical competencies. In this context, model construction becomes a crucial activity for students to describe, explain, justify, and refine their ways of thinking. Thus, modeling is essential for students to develop sense making and to use mathematics. Lesh and Sriraman [11] pointed out that "the subjects need to express their thinking in the form of some thought-revealing artifact (or conceptual tool), which goes through a series of iterative design cycles of testing and revision in order to be sufficiently useful for specified purposes" (p. 125). Thus, a model is conceived of as a conceptual unit or entity to foster and document both the teachers' construction of instructional routes and the students' development of mathematical knowledge. As Lester [12] pointed out, a perspective based on modeling might be considered as "a system of thinking about problems of mathematical learning that integrates ideas from a variety of theories" (p. 73).

The model construction process involves examining the situation or problem to be modeled in order to identify essential elements that need to be represented and scrutinized through operations and rules with the aim of identifying and exploring mathematical relations [16]. Mathematical models need to be contrasted and refined. That is, "models evolve by being sorted out, refined, or reorganized at least as often as they evolve by being assembled (or constructed)" ([10], p. 365). In addition, model construction relies on using diverse strategies to represent and explore patterns and relations. Schoenfeld [19] recognizes the complexity in selecting and implementing a particular strategy: "For example, to use the strategy "Make sense of the problem by looking at examples" one must (a) think to use the strategy, (b) know which version of the strategy to use, (c) generate the appropriate examples, (d) gain the insight needed from the examples, and (e) use that insight to solve the original problem" (p. 106).

Another crucial element of the framework is to explain the role played by digital technologies during the constructions and refinements of models associated with posed problems. Specifically, the use of the tools becomes relevant to sustain and promote students' mathematical activities and in this study the technology affordances offered the participants the opportunity to participate in activities for:

> …(a) gaining insight and intuition, (b) discovering new patterns and relationships, (c) graphing to expose mathematical principles, (d) testing and especially falsifying conjectures, (e) exploring a possible result to see whether it merits formal proof, (f) suggesting approaches for formal proof, (g) replacing lengthy hand derivations with tool computations, and (h) confirming analytically derived results (Borwein & Bailey, 2003, cited in [22], p. 1170).

The tool or artifact itself does not provide affordances needed for students to use it in problem solving activities; it requires an appropriation process in which the students transform an artifact into an instrument. Trouche [21] argued: "an instrument can be considered an extension of the body, a functional organ made up of an artifact component (an artifact, or the part of an artifact mobilized in the activity) and a psychological component" (p. 285). That is, the artifact or technology characteristics (ergonomics and constrains) and the schemata developed by the subjects during the activities are important for students to transform the artifact into a problem-solving instrument. Thus, the use of a dynamic geometry system plays an important role in constructing models of situations and tasks where the movement of particular elements can be examined and explained in terms of mathematical relations [17]. That is, models might involve configurations made from simple mathematical objects (points, segments, lines, triangles, squares, etc.) in which some elements of the models can be moved within the configuration in order to identify and explore mathematical relations. These relations and conjectures become a source that engages students in mathematical inquiry and reflection.

2.1 Participants, Research Questions, Design, and General Procedures

The study is part of an ongoing project that aims to analyze and document what ways of reasoning high school teachers and students develop as a result of systematically using various computational tools in problem solving environments [14, 17]. The project involves orienting high school teachers and students in using several digital technologies in problem solving approaches. The focus of this study is on analyzing the extent to which six volunteer senior high school students rely on technology affordances to reason and solve mathematical tasks. The participants worked on a set of mathematical tasks during three-hour weekly problem solving sessions for a full semester. In each session, the six students received a written statement of the tasks. Afterwards, they were asked to read and make sense of the problem individually, and later they worked on the problem in pairs. Then, each pair of students had the opportunity to present to the others their approaches to the problems. At this stage, all students and the teacher could ask for concept explanation or clarification. At the end of the session the teacher encouraged the students to contrast the different models used to solve the problems. In general terms, an inquiring approach to the task was key for the participants in eliciting individuals' ideas that later were refined in pairs and small group discussions. For example, when students introduced an idea or used a representation, the teacher questioned and encouraged them to reflect on their ideas and other related concepts. Similarly, when students ran out of ideas the teacher either oriented the discussion (through questions), or asked other students for suggestions to consider. The aim was to encourage the students themselves to formulate and then pursue the questions. In this perspective, the organization of the sessions is consistent with the activities that Mason and Johnston-Wilder [13] recommend for students to participate during problem-solving discussions. In particular, the authors identify four ways to organize students' participation to develop and discuss their mathematical knowledge:

> *Individual* work allows learners to review, consolidate, and develop their facility, as well as to reconstruct for themselves.
> Work in *pairs* allows learners to try out ideas on each other before offering them to a wider group; it also provides an opportunity for learners to consider something that has happened or been said, and to generate more ideas about this [the problem] than an individual is likely to produce when working alone.
> Work in *small groups* allows a multitude of ideas to be generated, and also allows a large task to be split up amongst several people; with discipline, small groups can provide a forum for discussing ideas, modifying conjectures, and coming to a consensus with supporting reasons and justifications.

> *Collective* and *plenary* work allows everyone to hear about novel ideas and approaches, and to see teachers or peers displaying their mathematical thinking (p. 52, italics in the original).

The research questions used to guide and structure the development of the study were:

1. What ways of reasoning did the participants exhibit to construct a model, including dynamic models, to represent and explore the problems? The students' previous knowledge and resources play an important role in representing and constructing models. Thus, it becomes relevant to document the extent to which the dynamic representation of mathematical objects shapes the students' ways of reasoning about the problems, and as a consequence their model construction process.
2. What were the stages or cycles of comprehension that students showed during the process of refining their initial models? According to Lesh & Sriraman [11] the students' model construction involves a series of iterative cycles where initial models are refined or transformed into powerful, shareable, and reusable entities. Thus, it is important to discuss the extent to which the use of the tools, the students' interactions, and group discussions help the participants move from the construction of partial or limited models to more robust ones.
3. What type of mathematical resources and strategies emerge during the students' construction of mathematical models associated with the phenomena? The goal here is to analyze the extent to which the use of a dynamic geometric system helps the participants retrieve conceptual knowledge that might appear when moving mathematical objects within the model. In addition, it is important to document the patterns of productive or nonproductive behaviors that students exhibit during their interaction with the tasks.

Each pair of students handed in for each session the computer files in which they showed their problem approaches. Additionally, all pairs' presentations and groups' discussions were videotaped and transcribed. Thus, sources of information came from the pairs' files, teachers' notes, and videotapes of the group discussions. The videotapes were analyzed during the research group meetings. The group includes a mathematician, two mathematics educators, and four doctoral students.

The analysis of the students' work was done by first focusing on individual contributions and pairs' presentations, and later by discussing the phases involved in the modeling process. A task that involves deciding the position of a camera to take a picture to capture a certain part of a mural was chosen to discuss ways in which students constructed their models. The problem is similar to those that were discussed throughout the sessions. The participants worked on this problem during two problem solving sessions (six hours total) held at the end of the semester. At this stage, the participants had developed a significant experience in the use of GeoGebra.

The Task. Alan wants to take a picture of a mural painting and sets his camera lens with a fixed horizontal viewing angle of 12 degrees. From his position, he focuses on a view of the mural that he wants to use as a reference to take the picture. That is, he wants to fit the viewing angle and an imaginary segment joining two points of the mural (Fig. 1). Are there other positions for the camera where Alan can fit the viewing angle and the mural segment to take the picture? (Justify your answer).

Fig. 1. Taking a picture of the mural by adjusting a fixed horizontal viewing angle to a bottom segment of the mural.

3 Presentation of Results

To present and discuss the approaches exhibited by the students during the problem solving sessions, we focus on relevant phases around the model construction. The conceptual framework discussed previously provided the structure to recognize model construction cycles that appeared during the students' work.

Comprehension and Making Sense of the Task. Students spent some time reading the problem individually and later they worked in pairs. In general, they initially focused their attention to the identification of key elements associated with the situation. Some questions that the students posed included: What does it mean that a camera has a fixed horizontal angle? Can that angle be changed? How can the camera position be adjusted to capture the view of the mural painting? What is the difference between focusing the camera on a point from focusing it on a segment of the mural? What does it happen to the view of the mural when the camera is moved closer or farther from the position where the angle fits the mural segment? These and similar questions were discussed during the initial session by all participants and were important for the students to identify and visualize relevant information for the task. At this stage, students commenced to address the problem in pairs. For example, Anna and Patricia, who used their mobile phone camera to capture a part of a wall, stated that for a point on the perpendicular bisector there should be a point where the horizontal fixed angle captures the view of the segment. The position was standing up in front of the picture.

- Anna: I want to use my phone to take a picture of that wall, but I don't see the angle I need to fix. I see the mural here (pointing at her phone screen).
- Patricia: Right… But if you get closer to the mural you will see different parts of the wall. The angle changes when you change your position.
- Anna: I see that, OK…
- Patricia: There, you move back and forth to fit the angle with the target, as the problem figure.

Problem Representation and Model Construction. Students observed that the camera horizontal angle vertex formed a triangle with the points that determine the segment located at the bottom of the mural (Fig. 1). Thus, their idea was to identify other positions for the camera in which they could fit the fixed angle with the mural bottom segment. The three pairs of students decided to use GeoGebra (a dynamic geometric system) to represent the task. Anna and Patricia first tried to draw by hand a segment and its perpendicular bisector to identify a point (vertex) where the angle was 12 degrees; but when they wanted to measure the angle for different positions of the vertex, they switched to the use of GeoGebra. Then, they drew segment AB (the mural bottom), its perpendicular bisector and chose point D on it. Then, they moved point C along the perpendicular bisector to identify a position where angle APD measured 12 degrees (Fig. 2). To this end, the students observed that the angle decreased when point D was further from the segment. So, they found a position for D where angle APD measured 12 degrees. They also noticed that when point P was located at the position C then angle ACB measured 24 degrees and they recognized that at this location point C was the center of a circle that passes by points A, B, and D (Fig. 2). Without providing any argument or explanation, they drew the circle with center at C and radius CA. Here, they sated that "the camera eye could be located at any point on the arc of the circle ADB."

Thus, Anna and Patricia reported that the camera lens could be located at any point on the arc of the circle ADB (Except points between A and B) because the angle to capture the segment AB was always the same (Fig. 2). However, their explanation was based on using the problem representation they had constructed.

Comment: Anna and Patricia model construction focused on identifying a point D on the perpendicular bisector of segment AB such that angle ADB was the desired angle (Fig. 2). Their empirical approach relied on using the software to measure the angle and moving point D along the perpendicular bisector to identify the position of D where the angle ADB measured 12 degrees. When they identified the position for D in which the angle was 12 degrees, then they also recognized that there was a point on the perpendicular where the central angles measured 24 degrees. Based on this information they drew a circle with center at C and radius CA and showed the camera could be situated at any point along the arc ADB. Thus, this empirical model was built in terms of recognizing the relationship that exists between the central and inscribed angles in a circle (although they never mentioned it). That is, *the inscribed angle in a circle measures half of the central angle measure*. Regarding the use of the tool, there is evidence that they thought of the problem in terms of moving a point on the perpendicular bisector and matching its corresponding angle measure with the desired value (12 degrees). That is, they relied on a functional approach in which a point on the bisector was associated with an angle value, but without explicitly defining that function.

Rob and Lionel (another pair of students) approached the problem by drawing segment AB to represent the bottom view of the mural. They drew a circle with center at point A and any radius AP (the circle is a heuristic to move a line on the plane) and chose point C on the circle to draw line AC. On line AC, they chose point D that represents the position of the camera and line DE was drawn by rotating line AD an angle of 12 degrees around point D (Fig. 3).

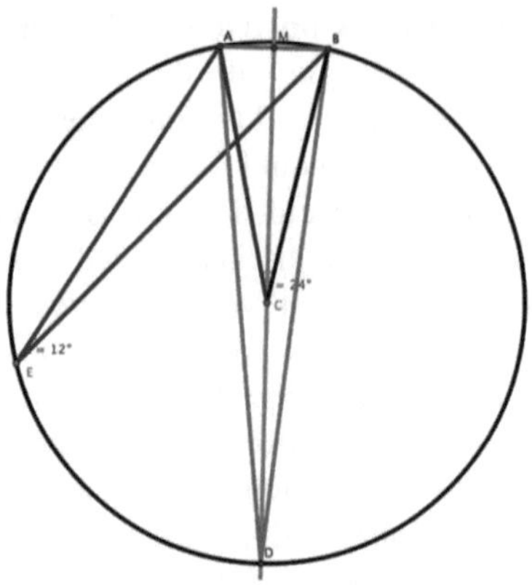

Fig. 2. Finding a position for P on the perpendicular bisector where angle APB measures 12 degrees.

Based on Fig. 3, the students noticed that the angle ADE did not capture the complete segment AB. Here, they started to move line AC (by moving point C along the circle) and found that for a certain position of point D the angle covered the segment AB (Fig. 4). This empirical model was constructed by adjusting the angle view to the length of segment AB. This partial solution allowed the students to identify triangle ADB and to think of drawing a circle that passes by its vertices.

- Lionel: Look, there is a triangle ADB(E) and we can draw a circle that passes through the three vertices, OK?
- Rob: why do we need to draw a circle if we got the solution already?
- Lionel: Because, if we draw it, we can find others…You know how can we find the center of the circle?
- Rob: I see it, we need to draw the perpendicular bisectors…

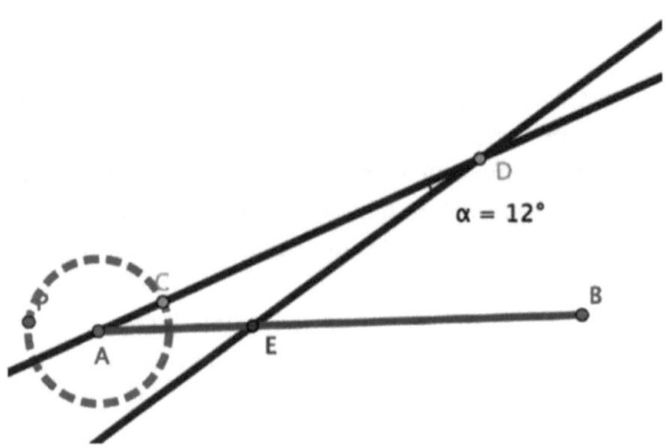

Fig. 3. A dynamic representation of the problem where point C can be moved along circle with center A and radius AC.

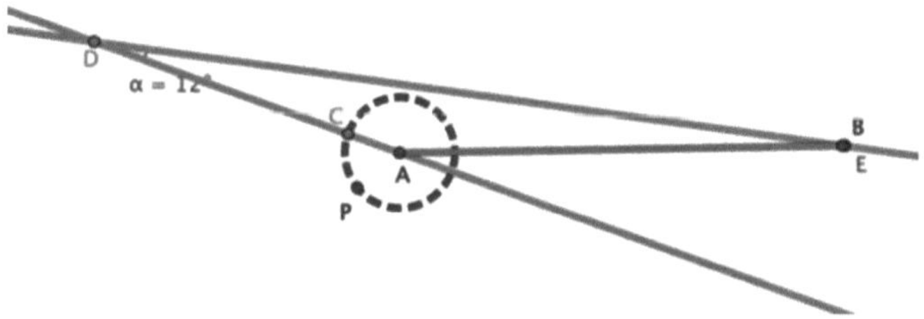

Fig. 4. For a certain position of point D, the angle includes segment AB.

Based on this visual approach, the students decided to identify the center of a circle that passes through points A, D, and B. Here they recognized that the Circumcenter of triangle ADB is the point where the perpendicular bisectors of its sides intersect (Fig. 5). Thus, this pair reported that they had solved the problem and were ready to present their solution to the class. That is, they wrote that the camera could be located at any point on the arc ADB (Fig. 5). They also mentioned that the camera could not be situated on the arc that completes the circle because from there they would observe the rear side of the mural.

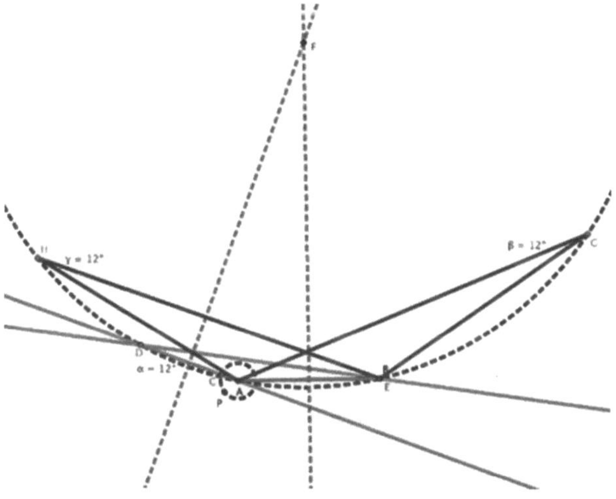

Fig. 5. Identifying different position for point D.

Comment: To construct this model, the students focused on drawing an angle with a side one of the extreme of the targeted segment. To draw the angle with the given measure, they used the command "rotate". The key component in this construction was that the angle could be moved (by moving line AC along the circle) without altering the angle measure. That is, by moving line AC, they observed that there was a position for point D (angle vertex) where the angle included the whole segment AB (Fig. 5). Again, when they found this position, then they recognized that points A, D and B formed a triangle and decided to find the circle that passes through the three vertices. Thus, this visual model was useful for students to identify relevant information needed to locate the camera position.

A Locus Model: Dianne and Petra (the last pair of students) also used the software to represent the problem dynamically (Fig. 6). They also represented the bottom view of the mural as segment AB. From A they drew a line AC (via a circle with center at A and radius AP) and rotated this line around D (D was a point on line AC) at an angle of 12 degrees. Thus, angle ADE measures 12 degrees. They noticed that angle ADE did not capture the whole bottom view (segment AB). And then they drew a parallel line to ED that passes through point B. This line intersects line AD at M. Here, they mentioned that angle AMB is congruent to angle ADE. Therefore, point M is the position where the camera can be situated to completely capture the segment AB (Fig. 6). They also observed that when line AD is moved (by moving point C along the circle with center A and radius AC) then point M describes a path or locus. With the help of the software, they recognized that the locus of point M when line AP is moved is a circle. Thus, these students reported that the camera could be situated at any point on the arc BMA (Fig. 6).

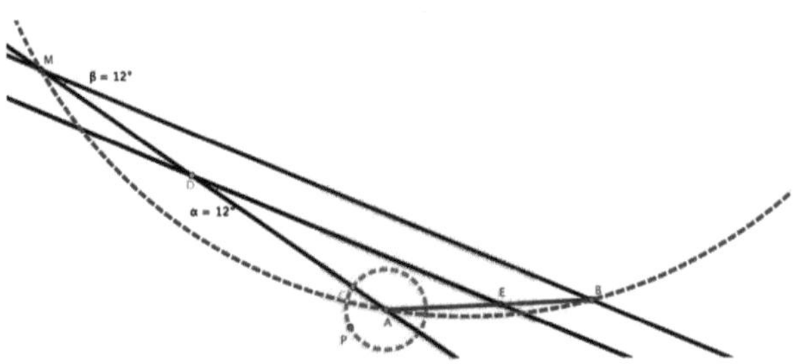

Fig. 6. What is the locus of point M when point C is moved along line the circle with center at A and radius AC?

- Dianne: Angle ADE does not fit the segment and if I move point D along line AC, then it seems that the angle (she is referring to angle ADE) can be moved to fit the segment.
- Petra: I see that line DE is parallel to the line that passes through point B.
- Dianne: Right, you mean that the parallel line to DE that passes through point B forms an angle BMA that is the same as angle ADE?
- Petra: Yes, line AD is transversal to both parallels, and they are corresponding angles.
- Dianne: OK… What about if we move line AC? …you see point M moves in a certain path.

Comment: In this model, an interesting feature is that the participants observed that point M followed a path when line AC is moved along the circle (Fig. 6). This path was determined with the help of the tool. These students showed evidence that they had a good appropriation of the tool. They were the only pair that introduced the *locus* concept to solve the problem. In addition, they asked the others pairs to complement their empirical approaches with more formal arguments.

Students' Model Presentations. Each pair of students presented its work to the whole group and had an opportunity to explain and defend each approach to the problem; but also an opportunity for the others to question and contrast their solutions. For example, when Anna and Patricia explained to the group their solution, they were asked about whether they could draw the inscribed angle without moving the point along the perpendicular bisector. To respond, they examined triangle ADB (Fig. 2) and argued that it was isosceles. Indeed, they mentioned that all the family of triangles that were generated by moving point D along the perpendicular bisector was isosceles. Therefore, the two congruent angles of triangle ADB (Fig. 2) would measure 78 degrees each. And they explained that to draw angle BAD with a measure of 78 degrees, it was sufficient to rotate 78 degrees segment AB around point A. Similarly, when Dianne and Petra presented their solution to the class, all agreed that the way how they identified the initial position of the camera did not depend on moving a particular point or line; rather, it was obtained by using parallel lines properties. However, they were questioned on why they thought that locus generated by point M when point C was moved along the circle was a circle (Fig. 6). Their argument was that the locus passed through points M, A, and B and these points were vertices of triangle MAB, and as a consequence, there is only one circle that passes through those points. Indeed, they mentioned that the center of that circle was the intersection point of the perpendicular bisector of two sides of triangle MBA. Rob and Lionel recognized that their solution was similar to what Dianne and Petra had presented. They mentioned that Dianne and Petra's approaches to find the camera angle to include the whole segment was more general than their construction. This was because in their model, Rob and Lionel moved the line (by moving point C on the circle) manually in order to identify the position for point D to match the angle with the given segment (Fig. 3). They also recognized that they focused on triangle ADB to draw the circle instead of determining the locus of point D. Thus, all recognized that Dianne and Petra's model does not rely on moving a point to identify a determined angle measure or moving a line to visualize the solution, rather it is based on relating properties of parallel lines to the angle position.

4 Discussion of Results and Remarks

The models constructed by the students while interacting with the task showed interesting mathematical features. Indeed, the students' use of the tools provides consistent information around the cycle nature of a problem solving approach [3]. Although two of these models (Anna and Patricia's and Rob and Lionel's) followed different paths, both relied on students' empirical reasoning to identify and relate key concepts to solve the problem. Anna and Patricia identified the vertex of the given angle by moving a point on the perpendicular bisector of the segment that represented the view of the mural. This point was obtained by observing the variation of the angle's measure to match the given value. Similarly, Rob and Lionel identified the position of the camera by moving a lined around a circle. In this case, they identified visually the point in which the angle included the entire segment. For both pairs, this stage was crucial to relate other concepts that they used to identify other camera positions to take the picture. Anna and Patricia relied on the relationship between the central and inscribed angles of a circle; while Rob and Lionel related the triangle to the construction of the circle that passed through its vertices. The third model also involved the construction of the given angle that later was translated to a position from where its vertex covers the segment. The translation was made by drawing a parallel line to one side of the initial angle that passes through one extreme of the segment (view of the mural). Here, the students observed that the vertex of the angle followed a path when one side of the initial angle is moved. They used the software to identify the locus of the vertex because they thought that the path was a circle. Although, at that moment they did not explain why that locus was circle, later on when these students presented their solution to the class, they were asked to justify that conjecture. In terms of problem solving behaviors there is evidence that the students grasped the structural relations associated with the situations and those relations were first identified and later explored with the help of the tool [7]. For example, the construction of a circle that passed by three points (vertices of a triangle) or finding the locus of a particular point became a crucial stage to find different positions for the camera.

During the group discussion, the teacher asked the students to identify the relevant content and processes that were important during the solution of the task. In terms of contents they identify the concept of perpendicular bisector, the relationship between inscribed and central angles in a circle, properties of triangles (isosceles, sum of interior angles), the circumcenter, parallel lines, and corresponding angles. They mentioned that the processes involved in their approaches included the construction of dynamic models, the visualization of relations, observing variation patterns, exploring functional relations, justification of conjectures, etc. From this perspective, students recognized that the use of the tool was relevant to initially construct a model to relate and explore the situation in terms of mathematical objects. That exploration led them to identify concepts and to look for relations to solve the problem. In addition, they recognized that their presentations and discussions within the whole group were important not only to acknowledge the work done by others, but also to refine their own models. It became evident that arguments based on geometric properties to justify their constructions were more formal and solid than those based on visual results. Here, they accepted that both types of arguments are important while exploring the situation. They also recognized that often visual explorations, together with empirical analysis, can lead the problem solver to identify interesting relations that are not easy to find in formal approaches.

Acknowledgement. The authors would like to acknowledge the support received from Conacyt (project reference 168543) during the development of this research.

References

1. Blum, W., Galbraith, P.L., Henn, H.-W., Niss, M. (eds.): Modelling and Applications in Mathematics Education. Springer, New York (2007)
2. Cai, J.: Commentary on problem solving heuristics, affect, and discrete mathematics: a representational discussion. In: Sriraman, B., English, L. (eds.) Theories of Mathematics Education, pp. 252–257. Springer, New York (2010)
3. Carlson, M.P., Bloom, I.: The cyclic nature of problem solving: an emergent multidimensional problem-solving framework. Educ. Stud. Math. **58**, 45–75 (2005)
4. Cobb, P.: Putting philosophy to work: coping with multiple theoretical perspectives. In: Lester, F. (ed.) Second Handbook of Research on Mathematics Teaching and Learning, vol. 1, pp. 3–38. Information Age Publishing, Greenwich (2007)
5. Engelbrecht, J.: Adding structure to the transition process to advance mathematical activity. Int. J. Math. Educ. Sci. Technol. **41**(2), 143–154 (2010)
6. English, L., Sriraman, B.: Problem solving for the 21st century. In: Sriraman, B., English, L. (eds.) Theories of Mathematics Education: Seeking New Frontiers, pp. 263–290. Springer, New York (2010)
7. Jackiw, N., Sinclair, N.: Sounds and pictures: dynamism and dualism in dynamic geometry. ZDM Math. Educ. **41**, 413–426 (2009)
8. Kelly, A.E., Lesh, R.A.: Handbook of Research Design in Mathematics and Science Education. Lawrence Erlbaum Associates, Mahwah (2000)
9. Kilpatrick, J., Swafford, J., Bradford, F. (eds.): Adding it Up: Helping Children Learn Mathematics. National Academic Press, Washington, D.C. (2001)
10. Lesh, R., Doerr, H.M.: Symbolizing, communicating, and mathematizing: key components of models and modeling. In: Cobb, P., Yackel, E., McClain, K. (eds.) Symbolizing and Communicating in Mathematics Classrooms: Perspectives on Discourse, Tools, and Instructional Design, pp. 361–383. Lawrence Erlbaum Associates, Mahwah (2000)
11. Lesh, R., Sriraman, B.: Re-conceptualizing mathematics education as a design science. In: Sriraman, B., English, L. (eds.) Theories of Mathematics Education, Seeking New Frontiers, pp. 123–146. Springer, New York (2010)
12. Lester Jr., F.K.: On the theoretical, conceptual, and philosophical foundation for research in mathematics education. In: Sriraman, B., English, L. (eds.) Theories of Mathematics Education: Seeking New Frontiers, pp. 67–85. Springer, New York (2010)
13. Mason, J., Johnston-Wilder, S.: Designing and Using Mathematical Tasks, 2nd edn. Tarquin, St Albans (2006)
14. Moreno-Armella, L., Santos-Trigo, M.: The use of digital technologies in mathematical practices: reconciling traditional and emerging approaches. In: English, L., Kirshner, D. (eds.) Handbook of International Research in Mathematics Education, 3rd edn, pp. 595–616. Taylor and Francis, New York (2016)
15. National Council of Teachers of Mathematics (NCTM): Focus in high school mathematics: Reasoning and sense making. NCTM, Reston (2009)
16. Santos-Trigo, L.: Problem solving in mathematics education. In: Lerman, S. (ed.) Encyclopedia of Mathematics Education, 1st edn, pp. 496–501. Springer, Netherlands (2014)
17. Santos-Trigo, M., Reyes-Rodriguez, A.: The use of digital technology in finding multiple paths to solve and extend an equilateral triangle task. Int. J. Math. Educ. Sci. Technol. **47**(1), 58–81 (2016)
18. Schoenfeld, A.H.: Bharath Sriraman and Lyn English: Theories of mathematics education: seeking new frontiers. ZDM Int. J. Math. Educ. **42**, 503–506 (2010)

19. Schoenfeld, A.H.: Reflections of an accidental theorist. J. Res. Math. Educ. **41**(2), 104–116 (2010)
20. Simon, M.A.: Amidst multiple theories of learning in mathematics education. J. Res. Math. Educ. **40**(5), 477–490 (2009)
21. Trouche, L.: Managing the complexity of human/machine interactions in computerized learning environments: guiding students' command process through instrumental orchestrations. Int. J. Comput. Math. Learn. **9**(3), 281–307 (2004)
22. Zbiek, R.M., Heid, M.K., Blume, G.W.: Research on technology in mathematics education. In: Lester Jr., F.K. (ed.) Second Handbook of Research on Mathematics Teaching and Learning, pp. 1169–1207. Information Age Publishing, NCTM, Charlotte (2007)

Knowledge Transference and Management Model for MSMEs Through the Pedagogical Strategy of Simulated Companies

Sandra Bonilla Cely[1(✉)], Leonor Rojas Marmolejo[1], and Victor Hugo Medina García[2]

[1] Learning Service SENA Risaralda, Pereira, Colombia
{sbonillac,lrojasm}@sena.edu.co
[2] Universidad Distrital "Francisco José de Caldas", Bogotá, Colombia
vmedina@udistrital.edu.co

Abstract. This is a model proposal for the improvement and strengthening of the training processes through management strategies and modern pedagogies, which energize and make the learning process more efficient, thus contributing to improve the processes and actions of the Micro, small and medium enterprises "MSMEs" of the region supplying their demand for knowledge.

In the research, existent world theories were analyzed related to the management and transference of knowledge as innovative approaches to better the performance and competitiveness supported within the human component as the most valuable resource of the organization. Also, the pedagogical strategy of simulated companies was analyzed as a worldwide experience that can expand the process of comprehensive professional training. The study was implemented in the Centre for Commerce and Services of the Colombian National Learning Service (SENA - Institution for technical training) in Risaralda in order to provide an opportunity to improve the quality of the training imparted by SENA, adding value by stablishing an approximation and a connection with the production environment, where the common and fundamental factor is the transfer of information between different parties.

Keywords: Management · Knowledge · Transfer · Model · Pedagogy · Didactics · Simulated · Cybernetics

1 Introduction

To achieve an improvement in the competitive Colombian business sector, the state commissions the National Learning Service to provide professional comprehensive training FPI, in order to prepare the human talent required by the business organizations according to the economic and social needs for the purpose of achieving higher productivity levels [1].

At the same time, the productive sector, specifically Msmes, search for strengthening their processes and strategies to be each time more successful within a constantly changing market in the middle of globalization.

L. Uden et al. (Eds.): LTEC 2016, CCIS 620, pp. 207–218, 2016.
DOI: 10.1007/978-3-319-42147-6_18

Accordingly, a proposal is generated, permitting the training institution and entrepreneurs to reach their objectives through management knowledge as an innovative approach that integrates the competence-based training methods, the simulated company as a pedagogical strategy based on the principles of action-based learning [2], and the project approach which parts from the necessities of the productive sector to cultivate education giving response through companies simulation. The proposed model transcends the pedagogical current model because it permits the intervention to companies during the complete training process, creating cooperative and interrelated ties between the educational system and productive sector by means of the generation and transfer of data [3].

2 The Problem

Msmes are considered of great importance in Colombian economic land-scape. They represent 96,4 % of the country′s industry, close to 63 % of employment, 45 % of manufacture production, 40 % of salaries and 37 % of added value [4]. The evident significance of these organizations has generated the passing of the 905 law of 2004 through which public policies were produced to stimulate the Msmes development.

The current economic conditions demand constant changes from companies to fortify their performance, make them competitive in the market and acquire knowledge to stay at the forefront which is the dominant need in an economy that is characterized by empowering innovation and competitiveness. Nevertheless, the difficulties prevail and Msmes continue dying on stage during the first years of creation [5].

In this manner, the educational public and private institutions require constant innovation and improvement on their pedagogical and administrative processes in a way that they can be oriented and motivated to supply the demand of knowledge through academic, and research studies, and strategies of cooperation to support the function, process, productivity, competitiveness and maintenance of these organizations.

3 Research Methodology

Using the methodology of holistic investigation, according to Hurtado de Barrera [6], an exploration and descriptive phase was started where the research question, justification and development of objectives are made. So, the question that leads the research project is: What adaptable management and knowledge transfer model for a training institution can improve the quality in the training processes and at the same time attends the necessities of the productive sector? Based on this question, the general objective of the investigation is created: To state a management and knowledge transfer model through the pedagogical strategy of project-based learning and simulated companies to improve the quality of creating processes and better the productive sector.

Then, the phases of comparison, analysis and explanation continue where a detailed document revision and dynamic integration of information related to the studied topic was made. Next, the predictive, projective, and interactive phases were put into action through which the type of investigation, the variables, samples, instruments and techniques for data analysis were stablished.

Finally, in the confirmation phase, the diagnosis of the current situation of the training center where the research was applied is stablished and at the same time, the model according to the outcomes and general objective is laid out, in order to obtain the results and conclusions in the evaluation phase.

4 Management and Knowledge Transfer Model

The pedagogies and dynamics that have laid the basis of comprehensive professional training which are part of the pedagogical model [7] proposed to ensure the quality of training processes [8] required to be renewed, updated with innovative contributions following successful models contributing to achieve the proposed strategic objectives. That is how it was proposed to the center of Commerce and Services, a management and knowledge transfer model that unites all the guidelines and institutional policies acquired through history, complementing and improving the current pedagogical model with simulated companies, bringing closer the apprentice to realities of work life by the means of experiences closer to real labor environment in a created company towards an instructive dynamic [9] end, but at the same time it helps to improve the conditions of the productive sector through consultancy and improvement proposals that are part of the formative project. Its origin is based on what it was known before as dynamic commercial companies with similar references since the 70 s in Germany, then in Latin America in countries such as Uruguay, Brazil, Argentina, and Salvador. These countries have applied this methodology as innovation in their training processes [10]. These educational practices in Argentina are called professional trainings and they are mandatory for the technical secondary education [11].

In SENA in Colombia, there are simulated enterprises known as didactic companies. In some centers like the Center of Commerce and Services of Risaralda since the year of 2004 and The Center of Administrative process in Bogotá D.C. since the year of 2009. These practices have been developed in a successful way [12], demonstrating a strong relation with the productive sector through the transfer of information [13].

The model, which was represented in a symbolic and schematic way is based on references and diverse authors such as: Intelect model, Nonaka and Takeuchi, Arthur Anderson, known in the modern theories of knowledge management [14].

The general model stablishes relations between three components identified in the following manner:

- *Knowledge Management Component:* It relates all the activities prone to improve and acquire the knowledge from the association of the organization by relating human capital as one of the principal elements and structural capital as part of people interaction with the methods, techniques, processes and other resources of the organization needed to fulfil the proposed objectives. This component leads to organizational learning.
- *Simulated Companies Component:* It is related to the structure of the pedagogical model based on the training of competencies and project-based learning along with

the philosophy of action-based learning and the activities prone to better the quality of the professional training which point towards the solution of the problems of the productive sector stated in the formative project. This component directs to knowledge appropriation.

– *Component MSMEs:* It is implicit in this component the relational capital and the transfer of knowledge that provides the improvement of management and performance of the organizations. The knowledge that the productive sector demands will be supplied by the simulated companies from the prior component during the learning time of each academic program.

These components have the tacit and explicit information as the fundamental axis with all their relations, which is transferred in cyclic shape and feedbacks as the process is developing in the individual and the organization (Fig. 1).

Fig. 1. Step and knowledge transference model Source: Authors

5 Method for the Execution and Control of the Model from Cybernetics and Future Works

The model requires for its functioning to do a follow up and control of the activities and processes related with the administrative management, just like pedagogical action in relation with strategic direction of the institution and knowledge transfer to the productive sector. Therefore, cybernetics was elected as the science that is in charge of the systems of control and communication in any system and it is based on feedback [15] to explain by figures like nodes and circles, rec-tangles and arrows the transgress from one place to another of information. Also, the principles of design, ludic evaluation and pedagogical didactics [16] were applied in the following manner:

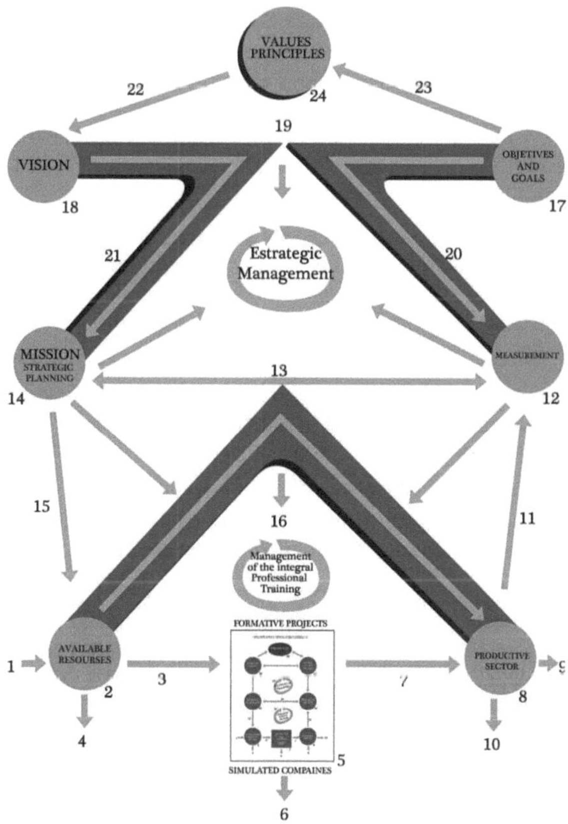

Fig. 2. Model cybernetic step knowledge Source: Authors

The Fig. 2 shows with numbers from one to twenty four the course of knowledge in the middle of processes and activities, since it acquires the human resource owner of knowledge to the final transfer which impacts the productive sector. When an arrow is seen, it means flow or movement from one place to the next, when a circle is viewed, it is because a control action is done, when a triangle is observed, it is be-cause a series of activities take place which generate more knowledge or changes and improves in itself, then it transforms following the flow or path to another circular node as a check point to complement the given process [17] (Table 1).

The only rectangle in Graphic two represents a series of activities in-side a process called execution of professional training. It explains the function of simulated companies as instructive scheme that transforms knowledge by the means of people´s learning and transfer it to the productive sector. For example, the process is initiated with the necessary resources for the management process, such as: the training program, the Project, the planning, the guide and the human talent. Then, the business with the needs to be fulfilled is chosen. The activities that are proposed in the project are developed, such as the diagnosis, information analysis and the specific proposal for the

Table 1. Explanation of Fig. 2: Nodes and Flows of movement

1	➡	The first flow of entries is represented by the resources available such as human and structural capital. It corresponds to people´s knowledge, experiences, abilities, education, strengths, values, attitudes and the structural capital that part from the processes, culture, pedagogic model, directional system and organizational management.
2	●	The first node is called resources available. It represents the knowledge process component, which is defined as the group of actions that tend to promote the creation, acquisition, diffusion or data generation from people and their organizational processes by the development of their activities.
3	➡	The exit flow of this node corresponds to the actions or progressions related to management and instructive schemes assimilated and fulfilled with the purpose of facilitating or expanding the methods and teaching procedures according to the pedagogic model proposed by the institution.
4	➡	The elimination flow denotes the resources that do not comply with the required specifications for the permanency or entry to the organizational process
5	■	The simulated company process symbolizes the key strategy together with project-based learning and the model of work competencies within the institution's pedagogic model promote the quality of forming methods and join the productive sector for problem solving that stresses a specific understanding
6	➡	The process flow of elimination represents some not assimilated procedures, obsolete knowledge and individuals not agreeing with the process.
7	➡	The Exit flow of the process is shaped by the transference of information between two units like the simulated enterprise as part of the foundational knowledge and Msmes of the real productive sector. All the activities are related that contribute to transgress course, communication and transferred understanding. This is part of innovation that helps to improve the management and performance.
8	●	The second node is named productive sector Msmes. It represents the use, the application and diffusion of transferred understanding to companies giving them value and answer to their necessities of human talent required for the improvement proposals and services offered during the training process.
9	➡	This flow shows the management improvement and performance of Msmes´ clients considering the use of the services and presented proposals just like the necessary adequate human talent training.

(*Continued*)

Table 1. (*Continued*)

10	➡	The Elimination flow embodies the activities or products that do not contribute to the improvement of management and performance of the Msmes in terms of pertinence, utility, cost, quality and the unsatisfied resources.
11	➡	The control flow, where the information and data leave node 8, are collected and processed to pass to the next measurement node
12	●	The third node called Measurement confronts the results facing the proposed objectives through established indicators
13	➡	Comparison flow between the objectives , assigned resources and obtained results
14	●	Fourth node is named Mission, it represents the social objective that includes the institution and prepared actions in the strategic plan.
15	➡	The comparison flow between the mission and the resources of assigned entry.
16	●	The fifth node denominated professional training exemplifies all the activities, experience, abilities, values, acquired and processed knowledge directed to the preparation for the work field oriented by formative projects along with the program and the world labor necessities according to regions vocation.
17	●	The sixth node named Objectives and institutional goals are related with the strategic plan
18	●	The seventh node called Vision signifies the projection of the organization in the long run
19	➡	The comparison flow relates the projection with the goals and objectives of the institution and its own vision
20	➡	The flow that associates the objectives and goals with the measurement that is made from the processes and maintains its own control by the means of institutional indicators.
21	➡	Flow that shows the link among long term vision and the permanent institutional mission
22	➡	This flow indicates the coherence between vision and the values of the organization stated as guide and support of the people´s conducts
23	➡	The objectives and goals are related in a direct flow between values and principles that manage the institution
24	●	The eight flow denominated values and principles direct all the organizational processes as successful guaranties of the existent human relations in all the procedures.

selected business. Then, some visits aimed to feedback the process with business owners and students are paid. The results are evaluated according to the goals considered in the learning pedagogy and the business owner's satisfaction is measured to stablish improvement actions for the pedagogical strategy. In this way, using cybernetics as control representation and specific follow up for the pedagogic strategy, Fig. 3 represents all the cycle of didactic companies.

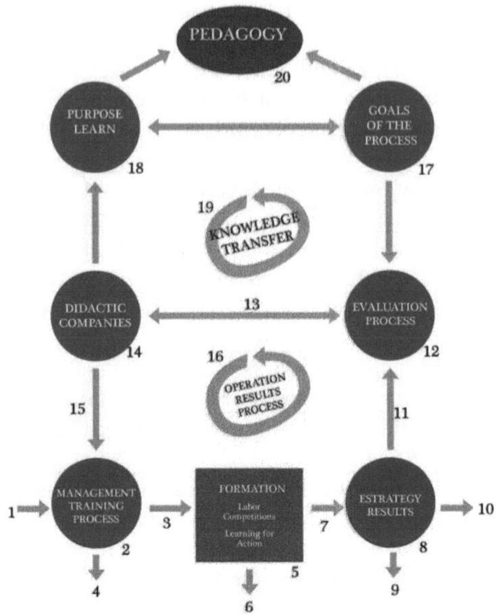

Fig. 3. Management model simulated enterprises Source: Authors

The Table 2 shows with numbers from one to twenty via arrows, circles and rectangles the transfer of knowledge from one side to the next and its transformations.

6 Stages for the Application and Development for the Execution and Control of the Model from Cybernetics

In order to start and develop constantly, the model is required to make a series of activities related with the enrollment and trimestral execution where all the proposed components unite with the respective coordination and team work required like this:

a. Planning.

- Conception and revision of current and new formative projects by instructors with the required profile through the assessment and aid of the trainer of trainers.
- Program the executor team. The directions based on the in-formation of programs, projects and programmed routes of each group elaborate the plan having in mind the human re-sources, physical resources, learning environment, times and institutional chronogram.
- Development of pedagogical planning for the trimestral formative project.
- Elaboration of interdisciplinary guides by the executor team.

Table 2. Explanation of Fig. 3: Nodes and Flows of movement

1	➡	It represents the entry of needed elements in order to have an adequate and satisfactory training process such as project, program, pedagogical planning, programming and learning guides
2	●	The first node denominated Management of training process makes reference to the group of used elements by the instructors in the strategy of simulated enterprises which allows the development of constructive project
3	➡	This flow makes a relation to entry step allied to elements, facts, selected and used conditions in the process of training through simulated company.
4	➡	This corresponds to the elimination of elements or conditions not convenient or not efficient that are removed in the process of the strategy
5	■	The transformation or operation in the process called Training Execution through the strategy by which the apprentice stores, generates and acquires knowledge, abilities and strengths for the work field by the living experience and the contribution to productive sector.
6	➡	Process Elimination or waste. It corresponds to the practices that do not contribute to learning process.
7	➡	The step exit vector relates to the results of the strategy, the subsequent satisfaction of the process of training which will be evaluated
8	●	The second node denominated Control corresponds to the expected results utilizing the strategy of simulated companies in the learning process. They are seen in the products stated by the formative project
9	➡	The overflow vector relates to the number of apprentices that do not acquire the necessary knowledge required to achieve the strategy objectives
10	➡	The Exit flow corresponds to the apprentices that finalize the process with a satisfactory result
11	➡	The Control vector that brings the result information from the didactic scheme to the evaluation node
12	●	The third node denominated Evaluation corresponds to examinations applied to identify the level of knowledge of apprentices which receive the data of the expected results and buy the goals as well as the purpose of the simulated enterprise strategy
13	➡	Corresponds to the comparison between the didactic strategy used and the evaluations
14	●	The Fourth node named simulated Enterprise relates to didacticism. It is part of the formative process. Once the strategy is defined, the plans and politics to follow are identified not only for the management of the simulated enterprise but also for the evaluation.
15	➡	This vector permits the transmission of information between the didactic scheme to be used and the management of the formative process

(*Continued*)

Table 2. (*Contined*)

16		The fifth node called resulting Operation is managed by each member of the team that participates in the strategy and it is used to obtain the best results of process. For this, the management information, expected results, evaluations and used strategy are used.
17		The sixth node named Goals analyzes the determined objectives for the learning process together with the results identifying the meaning and satisfaction
18		The seventh node denominated Purpose of learning has implicit the philosophy of educational projects for competencies and learning action.
19		The eighth node called Transference of knowledge presents the capacity to transmit and generate new information from the creativity, innovation and living experience
20		The nineth node named pedagogy represents the way how the strategy of simulated enterprise transmits the knowledge in a process of teaching learning by the means of the relation with all the represented nodes and flows of information linking all the elements

- Didactic company Conformation: It gives place to the creation complying with the existent knowledge networks which are constituted legally. In addition, it states the strategic direction.
- Creation of trimestral activities chronogram for customer service and the management of didactic company.
- Planning service offers through service package.
- Meeting gatherings of executor team for the control and follow up during the trimester.

b. Execution.

- Execution of learning activities within the specified times and the characteristics of the forming pedagogic process.
- Implementation of company management activities according to the assigned roles and stablished functions on top of the deadlines and stipulated requisites.

c. Evaluation and Improvement.

- Result and advances evaluation of the formative project.
- Assessment of knowledge and performance of didactic company apprentices.
- Examination of client satisfaction degree of companies in the productive sector.
- Trimestral management reports of company´s management considering corrective measures.
- Strategy Evaluation for management and assigned instructors considering corrective measures, new aspects to apply, and constant feedback of the experience by trimestral meetings.

7 Conclusions

The institute´s characteristics of training with their pedagogic model are given to make dynamic and innovative actions around the individual and collective capacities in a manner that the exposition to the management model and knowledge transference through pedagogic strategy of training for projects and simulated enterprises can improve the quality of formative processes and strengthen the productive sec-tor.

From the diagnosis of the processes, proceedings, strategies, activities, elements and variables that interact in the forming steps and knowledge transference, variables and conditions to improve were identified in the management and pedagogic processes.

The institutional model, politics, strategies, processes, didactic techniques, resources, environments and existent relations among them were analyzed. This allowed to integrate and generate significant changes in the management.

The adapted model was proposed by integrating the traditional institutional model, selected knowledge management model and simulated company model in order to attend the demand of the productive sec-tor.

It was proposed by stages to guarantee the effectivity and control of the process using tools of follow up and monitor to constant improvement.

References

1. General, D.: Planning and corporate management. SENA, Bogotá (2011)
2. Hansen, R.G. (s.f.).: Learning by action a beginning fot teaching general education and technical and vocational training. Development German cooperation GTZ, Germany
3. General, D.: SENA 2011–2014 Strategic Plan, Bogotá (2011)
4. Colombian enterprise portal: Centro de Estudios Latinoa-mericanos CELSA.com. (28 de diciembre de 2013). Obtained from Mipymes, Mypes and large enterprises (2012). http://www.mipymes.gov.co/
5. Anzola, O.M.C.: Determinants of management actions of pymes, microenterprises. Cargraphics, Digital Print-ing, Colombia (2007)
6. de Barrera, J.H.: Holistic Research. Fundacion Sypal, Caracas (2000)
7. Cruz Romero, J.E.: Pedagogical Models, Bogotá (2007)
8. General, D.: SENA vocational pedagogical training model, Bogotá (2012)
9. Mata Iglesias, J.A.: Programs Simulation of companies with educational purposes. ICT Board of Andalusia, 16 (2007)
10. Zinsmeister, K.: The simulated company. An innovative didactic strategy from technical high school from El Salvador. Sectoral network Mercosur and Andean countries, 97 (2000)
11. Do Pico, M.V.: Professionalizing practices. Association corporate Argentina, 51 (2013)
12. Bonilla, S.: Leadership report simulated companies, Bogotá (2013)
13. Bonilla, S.: Transfer of knowledge to human talent process of Mipymes by means of simulated companies. Memories CISTI 2014. Barcelona (2014)
14. European Committee for Standardization: European guide on good practices of knowledge management (2004)
15. Rocha Gonzalez, J.E.: Model of knowledge management based on Cybernetics from the productive chain of tanned leather in Bogotá. Master Thesis Bogotá DC (2012)

16. Arango Londoño Carlos, M.L.: Design and Evaluation of Games. Ludic Devices, Pedagogical and Didactic. A Proposal from Cybernetics of Third Order. Impregraf, Bogota (2014)
17. Bonilla, S.M.: Model management and transfer of knowledge through teaching strategy of simulated companies. SENA case Risaralda. Master Thesis Industrial Engineering, Bogotá D.C., pp. 89–100 (2015)

Knowledge Management Metamodel from Social Analysis of Lessons Learnt Registered in the Cloud

José López Quintero[1], Víctor Hugo Medina García[2(✉)], and Cristina Pelayo García[3]

[1] CUN - Corporación Unificada Nacional de Educación Superior, Bogotá, Colombia
Jose_lopezq@cun.edu.co
[2] Universidad Distrital Francisco José de Caldas, Bogotá, Colombia
vmedina@udistrital.edu.co
[3] Universidad de Oviedo, Oviedo, Spain
crispelayo@uniovi.es

Abstract. This article describes the development of a functional architecture for Personal Knowledge Management, defined from the lessons-learnt concept registered in a mass-use social network. This functional architecture applies, in practical manner, the implementation of a registry system of the personal lessons learnt in the cloud through a Facebook social network. The process starts by acquiring data from the connection to a non-relational database (NoSql) in Amazon's SimpleDB and to which a complementary analysis algorithm has been configured for the semantic analysis of the information registered from lessons learnt and, thus, study the generation of Organizational Knowledge Management from Personal Knowledge Management. The final result is the design of a functional architecture that permits integrating the Web 2.0 Application and a semantic analysis algorithm from unstructured information by applying machine learning techniques.

Keywords: Knowledge management · Tacit knowledge · Knowledge model · Organizational learning

1 Introduction

One of the trends in the study of Knowledge Management (KM) that has gained notoriety in recent years is Personal Knowledge Management (PKM), which is held as a process prior to Organizational Knowledge Management (OKM). This work focuses on the design and implementation of a functional architecture for Knowledge Management as a basic tool to integrate systems supported on cloud computing through social networks. The work seeks to show the possibility of a KM metamodel evidenced in a prototype of an application implemented in the Facebook social network, which demonstrates the possibility of doing OKM from PKM; the latter is developed from the base concept of the lessons learnt by individuals.

L. Uden et al. (Eds.): LTEC 2016, CCIS 620, pp. 219–232, 2016.
DOI: 10.1007/978-3-319-42147-6_19

The work was carried out in phases, with the first phase being the development of the conceptual aspects that define its structure. It starts with the conceptualization of the aspects that define and comprise a metamodel [1] and the stages that must be considered for its construction. Thereafter, the definitions of KM and PKM are presented. Regarding PKM, the work delves into and shares the new research trend that stipulates that flexible scenarios are required to support the knowledge generated by each human being [2]. At the end of this conceptualization phase, social network aspects will be worked on along with their support for the generation and socialization of knowledge, closing with the detailed concept of the lessons learnt as the type of knowledge that will be worked on in the metamodel developed as the proposal in this work.

The second part focuses on describing in detail the design, implementation, and verification of the prototype for Facebook. This will be implemented in the cloud through a non-relational database that will support the real registry of an undefined and random number of lessons learnt, which – in turn – apply and evidence the concept of flexibility of scenarios for PKM.

The final phase presents the second component of the applied model, which is the ontological analysis system, as tool and big data technique that verifies the real possibility of conducting OKM from PKM.

2 State-of-the-Art

2.1 Knowledge Management

Tacit knowledge as the first state of knowledge [3] has peculiarities characterized to define the strategies of its management. This knowledge can be divided into knowledge yet to be formalized and knowledge that cannot be formalized [4]. Knowledge that can be formalized and described explicitly is particularly characterized as *"know how"*, also called "Tacit Cognitive" knowledge and when it is specified through some tangible means, it becomes "Explicit Knowledge". Stemming from this concept, KM theories focus on the mechanisms that permit keeping knowledge within organizations [5] and in said evolution different models have been proposed, which now lead us to prefer working on the PKM concept, as one of the last work trends in this area.

2.2 Personal Knowledge Management

According to Razmerita, Kirchner, and Sudzina (2009), Miller (2005) and Pauleen (2009), PKM is a trend that manages to complement and rethink the dynamics of research and formalization of KM at organizational levels. These authors have delved into its conceptualization, highlighting the importance of PKM, as base nucleus of any greater magnitude process of KM, concluding on the need to for more experimental research on it. The first versions of KM systems have been mainly concerned with establishing integrated organizational systems that have often overlooked the basic parameters for "*the person*", who is the center of the generation of knowledge, to register, organize, and collaborate with the generation of new knowledge.

Also, PKM is supported on web 2.0 through a set of tools that permit individuals to create, encode, organize, and share knowledge, as well as socialize, broaden personal networks, collaborate in its organization, and create new knowledge [6, 7]. These authors base the characteristics of a system for PKM from the use of web 2.0 resources to avail of on-line communication and socialization mechanisms. For example, [8] proposes evolving in models that visualize performance indicators and PKM as objects and processes toward models based on an ecological view, which starts from the principles of socialization networks.

The interaction between the tacit and explicit dimensions of knowledge defines its nature by studying the source from where it is generated. A creation perspective exists related to the Knowing entity [3], which defines collective knowledge as an aggregation of individual knowledge. This aggregation cannot be generalized linearly as a sum of elements, given that its evolution generates a synergy that establishes that collective knowledge be a more complex process that integrates structures, dynamics, and relationships [9].

2.3 Lessons Learnt

Social capital has emerged as an adequate framework to explain knowledge exchange and transference mechanisms in organizations [10]. One of those mechanisms is denominated lessons learnt, which are defined as a type of explicit knowledge that results specifically from two main opportunities: i. *Errors and/or strengths obtained during any process of knowledge application or generation, and, ii. And from the possibility of innovation of an objective sought to be reached* [11].

These can also be defined as a type of knowledge that results from experience through complex, systemic, asynchronous, and individual reflection processes [12]. For knowledge transference to satisfy the needs of organizations, lessons learnt must be presented at the moment and within the adequate context, thus, defining the principle of opportunity. Thereby, knowledge generated can be reused [13].

Additionally, the conclusions of related works recommend that any process of generation of lessons learnt be supported on information systems with databases that permit diversity of models and objects of knowledge [12]. This seeks to facilitate precise location and rapid consultation of information required for knowledge to be subsequently distributed and accessed in timely maner by all those involved or interested in the context or situation being worked on [14].

In complementary manner, the opportunity to use lessons learnt also depends on systemic aspects that integrate, manage, and support an actual and closer concept of KM. Among these aspects, the following may be described: i. interested personnel; ii. a theme requiring their generation and consultation; iii. related experts; and iv. a system that supports the interaction and flow of said management [15].

2.4 Analysis of Social Behavior for Knowledge Management

Analysis of social behavior by applying semantic techniques is considered a new paradigm in OKM. Recently, the use of data and information extraction stemming from structured sources like Web 2.0 applications is gaining terrain in the study of the social web [16]. Cases of interest and publications have been reported in the field of social networks integration and their analysis. This new semantic approach permits the dynamic change of the semantic social network and establishment of knowledge management models from and toward people in organizations.

Modern organizations had never before had new needs and opportunities to use their knowledge more rapidly and efficiently from the implementations of applications supported on semantic analysis. Construction of sophisticated knowledge bases, decision support systems, as well as other intelligent systems often takes time and considerable economic resources [17]. Studies like those by [18] have implemented diverse web mining techniques to extract the semantics of the social structure underlying people's behavior, preferences, and tendencies; although it is important to analyze existing on-line social networks, the data and information extraction process related to profiles of users in applications supported on social web from structured sources, inevitably provokes a loss of the real semantics of the social system.

3 Methodology

3.1 Architecture Proposed

The KM metamodel applied herein was derived from the metamodel developed by [19]. Its structure is described through six entities: people, processes, documents, themes, tacit knowledge, and explicit knowledge. It abstracts essential entities from a domain of interest and its interrelations with the concepts of metamodels applied to KM and to software development.

For its dynamic part advanced processing techniques are included for application through the 'big data' technique, denominated 'latent semantic indexing (LSI)'. Figure 1 shows the flow or relationship among elements or entities that make up the metamodel proposed: data-information-knowledge. The metamodel proposal integrates entities in the following manner:

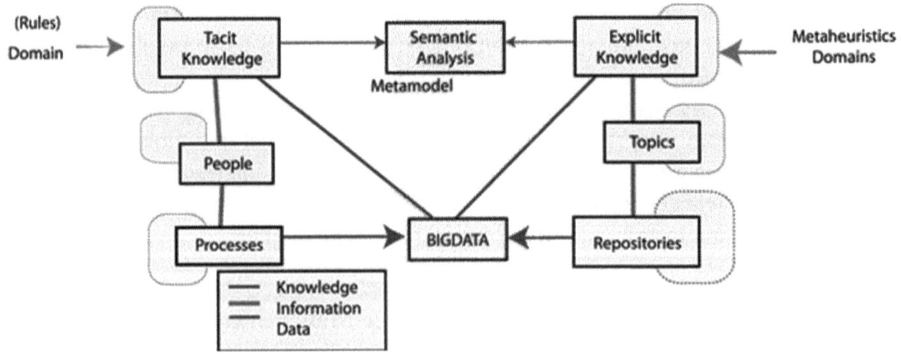

Fig. 1. Global architecture of the KM metamodel

The previous architecture is structured so that each of the components is interrelated for transmission within the chain of organizational data, information, and knowledge given through the following elements:

- *Processes:* The definition of necessary processes for the interaction of people and resources or platforms that comprise the system.
- *People:* The metamodel should be based on the interaction of tacit knowledge from the lessons learnt of each participant.
- *Repositories:* The opportunity to develop in the model and prototype the necessary documents and evidence of said lessons and of the model itself.
- *Topics (themes):* Represented in the possibility of defining categories and themes to generate knowledge from the different profiles of people who interact with the system.
- *Tacit knowledge:* Described and evidenced through the lessons learnt that exists in each human being.
- *Explicit Knowledge:* Reflected through the treatment of the lessons learnt in new forms of knowledge, using advanced processing techniques.
- *Semantic analysis*: The semantic analysis process is applied on an unstructured base, that is, sets of terms in a domain determined in text format. Each data analyzed behaves as taxonomy; the process is in charge of identifying key terms and classifies the terms the vocabulary contains within the database; this is to enable a simpler search for the system. The taxonomy gathers various terms around a set of concepts to then map and fraction these through the text mining flow implemented in Konstanz Information Miner (KNIME).

The metamodel uses the logical sequence of data, information, and knowledge. These three elements circulate through each of the entities of the model. The upper layer evidences the execution of a semantic analysis fed by sources of tacit and explicit knowledge. Tacit and explicit knowledge gather information from people and themes of interest, primarily. These, in turn, receive information from processes and repositories and, simultaneously, provide data to be processed by the Big Data LSI technique.

3.2 General Model - QIRISYA

The QIRISYA prototype, as the application will be identified ahead, was generated from the same conception of the model of lessons learnt within a social network environment. For its design, software has been developed to permit registering the lessons learnt by each user with a structure defined in three levels: Profile, Categories, and Subcategories. These can be established in personalized and flexible manner by each user. Given the vast amount of contributions expected, a non-relational database will be used to avoid the possibility of application saturation. The prototype can be seen in Fig. 2 with its explicit components: 1. User or knowing entity. 2. The application in the social network (Facebook). 3. The platform that supports the application: non-relational database; and 4. The semantic analysis system.

The user records the lessons learnt initially in the form of explicit knowledge, describing in text format the knowledge or experience acquired and recording it on the

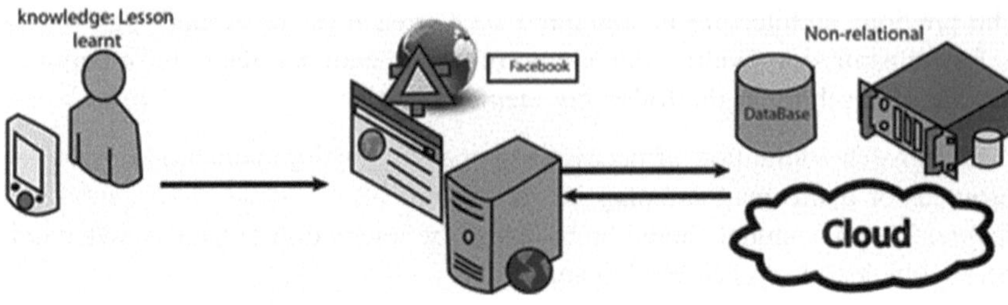

Fig. 2. General prototype diagram

profile, category and subcategory in which he/she seeks to relate it. These lessons do not have text limit, can be described as reflections, both simple on very punctual events and complex on the analysis on the participation in a project or on the reflection about another professional, personal, or educational activity.

To complement the prototype, a semantic analysis application was developed to permit precisely identifying and quantifying trends in the generation of knowledge, using key words and making the configuration for group analysis in the social network (Facebook). This facilitates the characterization of knowledge generation in work teams, *i.e.*, this last module permits bringing PKM in practical manner to an application of OKM.

To develop the functional application of lessons learnt, it was necessary to use different libraries that permit making structured connections and designs, these are: i. Facebook SDK PHP [20]: Used to make the communication of the external application with Facebook, defining the necessary permits and obtaining this platform's necessary data, like name, profile image, and identifying number of the user's account; ii. The FancyApps & Skarnelis [21] Used to manage the iframes on transparent backgrounds in the deployment of some of the notifications; iii. GoogChart [22]: Used to generate pie graphs and bar diagrams; iv. JQuery API [23]: It is a javascript framework used to give dynamism to html pages and it is used as base by different APIs; v. jsDatePick [24]: It is a javascript calendar that permits selection of dates upon defining the limits to generate graphics and vi. AWS SDK for PHP [25]: Used to establish communication between SimpleDB and the application, permitting manipulation of the necessary data through a development interface.

3.3 Design of the Functional Architecture and Semantic Analysis Algorithm

This section presents the development of the functional architecture that permits semantically analyzing lessons learnt from a data source defined and incorporated by each user onto the prototype (QIRISYA); crossing the structure of profile, categories, and subcategories defined by it. Semantic analysis on lessons learnt permits determining in an organization the current trends and behaviors that are a support for a foresight study of possible strategic planning goals, specifically in the management of human capital.

Given the large quantity of contributions expected, an unstructured data source is used that permits reducing the possibility of application saturation. Graphically, the architecture is shown in Fig. 3, where the flow is shown: data, information, knowledge through a logical sequence given among the application, the data source, and the segmentation of groups of people. The flow is guided from the social behavior of specific groups given by the social analysis process from the textual sources incorporated.

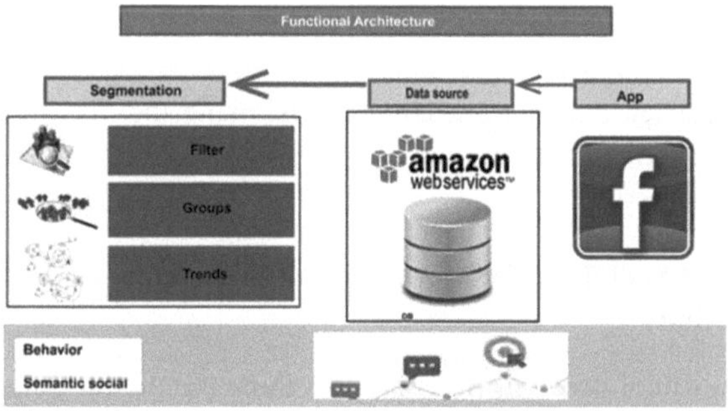

Fig. 3. General structure of the semantic analysis algorithm

The architecture proposes mechanisms for simple consultations seeking to facilitate support of decisions by connecting existing databases and corporate information systems through web services. The final result proposes the development of a comprehensive solution aimed at KM and whose objective is to establish the current state of the organization and its environment regarding the determination of work profiles and competencies. Implementation and use of this framework was conducted from several characterizations of users with different profiles and needs. Users selected followed the application's linking procedure and started to define their profiles and categories, permitting – in turn – to register lessons learnt in the application.

Figure 4 shows a chronological behavior of a user with his/her respective categories and profiles within the framework established by the application. Here, the system permits registering several lessons and, upon using the distinct options (like private and public records), information is managed from lesson-suppression operations, modification and visualization of statistics, and record of evidence of typifying the lessons learnt in the distinct profiles and categories.

Within the architecture proposed, the application of concepts requested by various authors is evident, when they state that further development is needed to facilitate PKM and which in this project has been visualized from the concept of the *"lessons-learnt typifying diagram"* through a social network (tacit knowledge → explicit knowledge), as shown in Fig. 1. Hence, it is permitted to profile each individual or groups of people, their generation of knowledge, showing the emphasis or progress of their lessons learnt in ranks or time periods defined by each user of the prototype. Finally, by applying an algorithm supported on textual analysis techniques at semantic level like LSI (Suarez & Salinas, 2009), we can inquire on trends and on the reality of the generation of

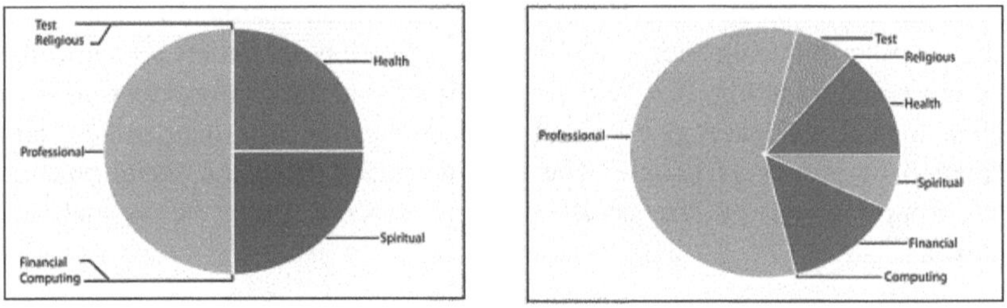

Fig. 4. Lessons-learnt typifying diagram

knowledge being carried out in work teams; thus, using the dissemination of lessons learnt from each of its members.

3.4 Semantic and Social Analysis Algorithm on Lessons Learnt in Web 2.0 Applications

Suppose the organization involves in its profiles three trends: (a) Project Management, (b) Knowledge Management, and (c) Management of Innovation and Technological Development. An analysis process of social behavior is of special interest for KM; especially, in dynamic environments where roles and profiles have to be analyzed by the members of an organizational unit. This is done to establish if a member has or does not have certain skills and/or knowledge; and, also, to analyze that other members should and can support other members of the organization in very particular or special roles. Thus, the question arises: how do you find the most suitable person for a given function, considering the social network? [26]. To answer said inquiry on the practical use of the prototype, a textual analysis algorithm is presented applied to the data source from the web 2.0 application. The algorithm is elaborated via a KNIME data environment that permits performing a predictive non-probabilistic social analysis from machine learning techniques to determine possible behaviors and social tendencies in lessons learnt in the QIRISYA web 2.0 application.

The algorithm elaborated through the KNIME flow permits determining, from machine learning techniques, a set of classifications, groups, and predictions on the current state of acquisition and KM on certain lessons learnt managed through the web service. Now, the data source correspond to nominal attributes and unstructured text sources that contain information about the classes, profiles, categories, descriptions, codes, dates of registry, and control, along with all the terminology appertaining to a set of lessons learnt in KM.

The characteristics of the data source include that in their totality they can be considered sequential multivariate data on time line. In the data cleansing and filtering process information is converted from text chain type to nominal attributes that facilitate follow up and interpretation of results, filtering of columns considered not having relevant information during the analysis process and, finally, a data balancing process was applied from the nearest-neighbor technique to give an oversampling to the minority class to mitigate deviations due to data still lacking. Figure 5 shows the result

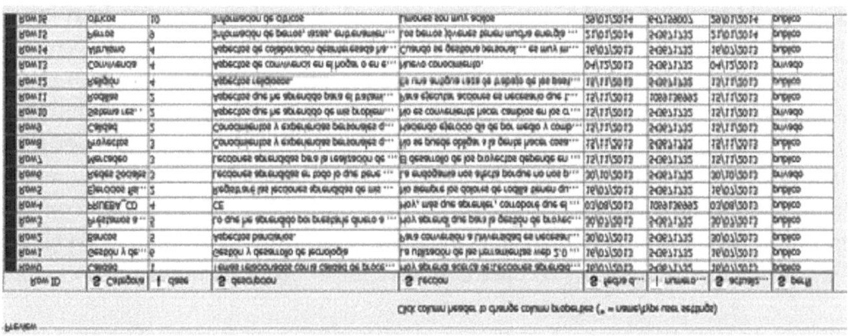

Fig. 5. Data set obtained

obtained of preliminary data cleansing and which will lead to the following data analysis phase.

The data source provided by the model comes specifically from a relational database embedded in a web service (Amazon web Services); this web service inter-operates with a web application (QIRISYA) aimed at management of web 2.0 lessons learnt.

During the information analysis process through machine learning, supervised analysis techniques were applied given that work was undertaken from a classification; for this the attribute *"profile class"* was determined as class; application of decision trees became a fundamental tool in the process. A type of gain ratio without pruning was implemented to the decision tree with 70 % training data and 30 % prediction data.

4 Results

As mentioned in previous sections, the repository analyzed corresponds to the information from the (QIRISYA) application database; the need to apply a cleaning and transformation process it was also determined to proceed to the analysis. The attributes analyzed correspond to information of lessons learnt within an organizational context in determined times, as observed in Table 1; the data stored in the database are finally categorized and synthesized, thus:

Table 1. Description of data-set attributes

Category	Class	Description	Lesson	Date of record	Record number	Profile update	Profile
Defines the category of lessons learnt	Identifies the profile classifier	Describes the type of profile	Determines the lesson learnt in a category	Indicates the date of in-corporation of the lesson	Record consecutive	Date of consolidation of lessons learnt	Public or private

The social analysis of the data source through the use of machine learning algorithms applies two experimental scenarios. The first scenario shows the correlation among the lessons learnt on a given theme and the profiles assigned to each category. In an exploratory scenario it can be noted how some skills are identified within the data set of lessons learnt; Fig. 6 permits graphically comparing the class behavior (profile) in distinct groups of lessons learnt; for example, for classes 2 to 5 we find the highest continuous concentration of lessons in a given time space. Within this context, an organization needs to use KM to guarantee successful implementation of change, as well as to maintain long-term competitive advantages from its intellectual capital.

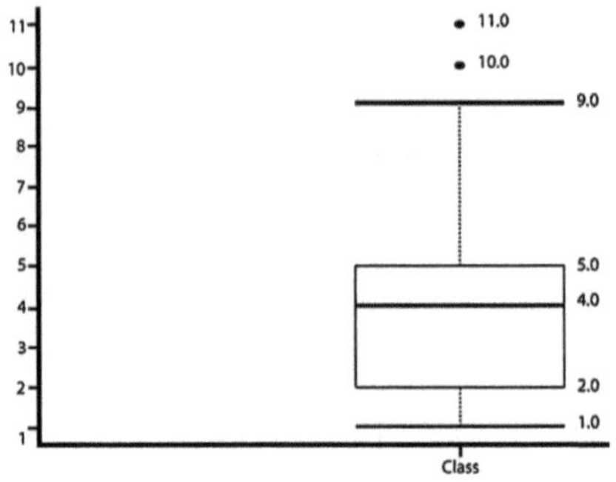

Fig. 6. Continuous distribution of the class attribute

The second scenario evidences the supervised classification criteria from decision trees that permit determining the tendencies and projections of the lessons learnt. The experimentation approached for the study of social behavior on lessons learnt in KM allows determining from a classifier (class) what the tendencies within a group in acquisition of knowledge from experience.

Observation of the results obtained for the sample of skills acquired from lessons learnt studied demonstrates that the model produces part of the lessons learnt and result in themes like *"health in the profession"* and *"experiences in the profession"*, originating a projection and tendency that can help to improve *"quality"*, *"professional skills"* and *"health conditions at work"*. Although, both *"health"* and *"profession or labor"* are different categories; semantically, the model determines that a direct relationship exists between the "labor activity" and "health" activities. Observing the decision tree in Fig. 7, which is generated in the machine learning process in the model developed, it can be identified that the initial node on the tree congregates nine of the 11 labor profiles controlled by the class attribute.

The decision tree provides an adequate structure to determine skills from the lessons learnt; it may be extrapolated as a multidisciplinary, dynamic, and non-probabilistic model to optimize performance, organizational learning, and organizational behavior, which are vital premises in the construction of KM systems. Herein, experiments are being conducted with a first multidisciplinary model of classical measures to unify

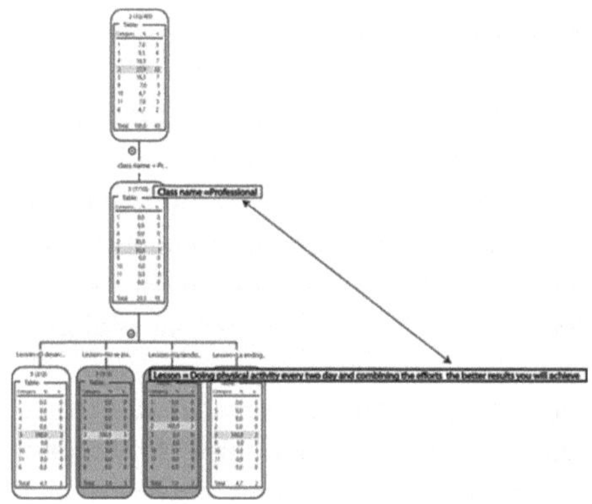

Fig. 7. Partial decision tree generated in the social analysis model

competencies, skills, and lessons learnt to bring them to the application of the analysis and engineering of knowledge, supported on machine learning techniques to provide and extract semantic relationships between concepts and propose as the following phase a meta predictive non-probabilistic model of broadened semantic social network analysis.

Also, three natural groupings emerge in the experimental study of the people who have relative knowledge and who provide different learning perspectives. A group is inclined to diminishing in uniform and weak manner its activity related to a knowledge domain, in the sense of applying lessons learnt in the *"pets"* and *"vehicles"* domain, while another natural group invites other profiles to consume significantly less knowledge to focalize on priority themes. It may be interpreted as a need of academic formation, or of a tutorial imparted by the individuals who already had the competency.

The third group, as shown by Fig. 8, represents a close social and semantic relationship among category, profiles, and lessons without regard to the time series, under three natural groups of profiles; in this scenario, the financial, religious, and labor profiles mark a mutual relationship with the health profile.

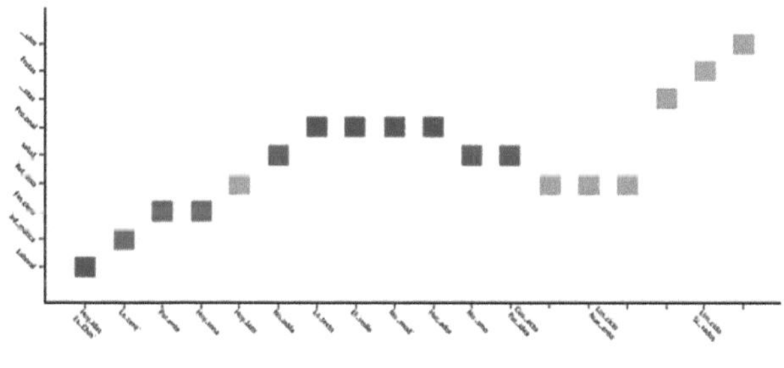

Fig. 8. Conformation of group profile (clusters)

5 Conclusions and Future Work

This work permits inferring that the development of empirical systems to apply PKM from algorithmic techniques supported by semantic social analysis are a latent, but real organizational alternative to manage knowledge and define improvement alternatives.

In particular, it is important to recognize that we successfully proposed an architecture that is applied and adapted to the world's most used social network and it is, likewise, supported on tools that facilitate their exponential growth, such as Amazon's Simple DB database.

This work has several extensions in its practical and research application, arising from each of its functional and structural modules, for example, from the functional point of view it would be important to continue delving into the systemic use of the application on knowledge generation routines for each person involved in the lessons learnt generation process. It may also be possible to delve into the dynamic generation of more lessons when including modules like early warnings in the use of the application. From the structural point of view, it would be necessary to verify the characterization in using the database to measure efficiency in its use, to reach a commercialization and massive-use process of the prototype at organizational levels.

In large volumes of data, a semantic analysis applied on a big data tool will permit asking a team or work group how their dynamic capacities are being generated for KM and what is the profile developed in it, from a systematic analysis of the individual or personal profiles of each of its members in a time line.

As stated by some authors referenced in this work, the work that needs to continue is the development of adequate and integral spaces where each person or individual feels comfortable and knowledge flow is facilitated that permits their self-recognition and, thus, generate the capacity to bring their tacit knowledge to explicit knowledge, which permits their collaboration with learning and development objectives within the contexts or environments in which they are developed. Finally, this model would be the first version to achieve a powerful version of a predictive non-probabilistic model of broadened semantic social networks analysis as basic component of the metamodel proposed in the functional architecture.

References

1. Montenegro Marín, C.E., Gaona García, P.A, Cueva Lovelle, J.M., Sanjuan Martínez, O.: Application of Model-Driven Engineering (MDA) for the construction of a tool for domain - specific modeling (DSM) and the creation of modules in Learning Management Systems (LMS) platform independent. Dyna, vol. 169, pp. 43–52 (2011)
2. Nasiri, S., Ansari, F., Fathi, M.: Dynamics of knowledge assets and change management perspectives. In: 2013 IEEE International Conference on de Electro/Information Technology (EIT) (2013)
3. Nonaka, I., Peltokorpi, V.: Objectivity and subjectivity in knowledge management: a review of 20 top articles. Knowl. Process Manage. **13**(2), 73–82 (2006)
4. Kakabadse, N.K., Kouzmin, A., Kakabadse, A.: From tacit knowledge to knowledge management: leveraging invisible assets. Knowl. Process Manage. **8**(3), 137–154 (2001)

5. Haas, M.R., Hansen, M.T.: Different knowledge, different benefits: toward a productivity perspective on knowledge sharing in organizations. Strateg. Manage. J. **28**(11), 1133–1153 (2007)
6. Razmerita, L., Kirchner, K., Sudzina, F.: Personal knowledge management: The role of Web 2.0 tools for managing knowledge at individual and organisational levels. Online Inform. Rev. **33**(6), 1021–1039 (2009)
7. Pauleen, D.: Personal knowledge management: Putting the person back into the knowledge equation. Online Inform. Rev. **33**(2), 221–224 (2009)
8. Chatti, M.A.: Knowledge management: a personal knowledge network perspective. J. Knowl. Manage. **16**(5), 829–844 (2012)
9. Spender, J.: Method, philosophy and empirics in KM and IC. J. Intellect. Capital **7**(1), 12–28 (2006)
10. Widén, G.: Social capital and knowledge sharing – lessons learned. In: Camarinha-Matos, L.M., Pereira-Klen, A., Afsarmanesh, H. (eds.) PRO-VE 2011. IFIP AICT, vol. 362, pp. 48–57. Springer, Heidelberg (2011)
11. Robertson, B., Beruvides, M.G., Daniel, B.: A software-based lessons learned management system: enhancing knowledge management in organizations. In: de IIE Annual Conference. Proceedings (2008)
12. Greer, S.: A lessons-learned knowledge management system for engineers: an organizational lessons-learned system facilitates the transfer of knowledge from one project team to another. (Engineering Practice), Chemical Engineering (2008)
13. Richter, M.M., Weber, R.O.: Knowledge Management, Case-Based Reasoning, pp. 487–505 (2013)
14. Cardenas, J., Spinola, M.: Role of knowledge management systems within the expertise transfer. In: Proceedings of PICMET 2013, de Technology Management in the IT-Driven Services (PICMET) (2013)
15. Fahey, D.F., Burbridge, G.: Application of diffusion of innovations models in hospital knowledge management systems: lessons to be learned in complex organizations. Hosp. Top. **86**(2), 21–31 (2008)
16. Schatten, M.: Knowledge management in semantic social networks. Comput. Math. Organ. Theory **19**(4), 538–568 (2013)
17. Breslin, J., Decker, S.: The future of social networks on the internet: the need for semantics. IEEE Internet Comput. **11**(6), 86–90 (2007)
18. Cantador, I., Castells, P.: Multilayered semantic social network modeling by ontology-based user profiles clustering: application to collaborative filtering. In: Staab, S., Svátek, V. (eds.) EKAW 2006. LNCS (LNAI), vol. 4248, pp. 334–349. Springer, Heidelberg (2006)
19. Ammann, E.: A meta-model for knowledge management. In: de Proceedings of the 5th International Conference on Intellectual Capital, Knowledge Management and Organisational Learning (2008)
20. Facebook, Facebook SDK PHP (2013)
21. FancyApps, T., Skarneli, J.: Fancybox API (2013)
22. Pettersson, L.: Googchart: PHP Google Chart Class (2008)
23. The jQuery Foundation, JQuery API (2013)
24. Arjuan, I., Walsh, P.: jsDatePick (2013)
25. Amazon Web Services, AWS SDK for PHP (2013)
26. Thovex, C., Trichet, F.: Static and semantic social networks analysis: towards a multi-dimensional convergent model. In: de COLLA 2011: The First International Conference on Advanced Collaborative Networks, Systems and Applications (2011)

27. Suárez Barón, M., Kathleen, S.: An approach to semantic indexing and information retrieval. In: Revista Facultad de Ingeniería Universidad de Antioquia, vol. 48, pp. 174–187 (2009)
28. Moon, H., Lee, C.: The mediating effect of knowledge-sharing processes on organizational cultural factors and knowledge management effectiveness. Perform. Improv. Q. **26**(4), 25–52 (2014)
29. Miller, R.: The Evolution of Knowledge Management: This Time It's Personal (2005)

Case Study

Teaching Information Literacy in Secondary Education: How to Design Professional Development for Teachers?

Sabine Seufert[1], Nina Scheffler[1(✉)], Katarina Stanoevska-Slabeva[2], and Severina Müller[2]

[1] Institute of Business Education and Educational Management, University of St. Gallen, St. Gallen, Switzerland
{sabine.seufert,nina.scheffler}@unisg.ch
[2] Institute for Media and Communications Management, University of St. Gallen, St. Gallen, Switzerland
{katarina.stanoevska,severina.mueller}@unisg.ch

Abstract. The networked information and media society provides us increasingly with digital information and knowledge. However, the effective and efficient use of information also requires a high level of information literacy (IL), the competent handling of information and the ability to do that from an early age. Despite this early beginning, the development of IL is considered an important goal of schoolteachers who are required to integrate IL into their daily teaching practice. One reason that IL has only been considered sporadically in education is the lack of a scientifically proven model to operationalize and measure IL. Furthermore, teachers are often uncertain when dealing with digital media pedagogically and need support and clarity in terms of how to evaluate IL in their specific subjects. In the implementation of formal educational efforts, the low practical feasibility in specific working contexts, time and financial aspects are criticized. The current contribution presents a 7i model for the conceptualization and measurement of IL. Furthermore, it provides alternatives to the dominant "training model" to develop the competence of teachers by combining formal and informal learning.

Keywords: Information literacy · Teachers' professional development · Informal learning

1 Introduction

One major benefit of the information age is the ubiquitous availability of information and knowledge from various information sources at our fingertips. However, the effective and efficient use of digital media requires information literacy (IL), which is the proficient handling of information [28]. For example, UNESCO considers IL as a major practical competence relevant for the 21st century networked society [32]. Other authors consider it a key competence that facilitates participation in society, a self-determined life and lifelong learning [8]. In general, IL refers to skills necessary to use information effectively and efficiently and is described as the ability to recognize

L. Uden et al. (Eds.): LTEC 2016, CCIS 620, pp. 235–249, 2016.
DOI: 10.1007/978-3-319-42147-6_20

problem-driven information needs, to select information sources, to access, evaluate and use information, and to reflect upon both the applied information searching and processing procedure, and the information resulting from it [2, 8, 28].

In the information age, children and pupils are being exposed to digital media and information and have to deal with them starting from early childhood [9]. Thus, it is becoming increasingly important to promote IL and create awareness of it. This is an important goal for schools [1]. Teachers are faced with the challenge to integrate IL into their learning environments. In order to achieve this goal, a scientifically sound and proven model to operationalize and measure IL is necessary. This would help teachers to define learning outcomes and to evaluate IL by themselves. Furthermore, formal training activities seem to be insufficient to foster teachers' competencies to use digital media pedagogically in their specific working contexts.

The paper at hand first shows the main obstacles preventing IL and digital media from finding their way into the classroom as yet. In a second step, the 7i Framework for measuring IL and the results of the empirical testing are presented and discussed. Finally, alternative approaches to support teachers' media educational skills are shown.

2 Problem and Research Question

In the so-called information age the goal to embed IL in schools has not yet been achieved, as has been outlined above. This can be explained by the inadequate integration of IL as a learning objective into existing curricula. To integrate IL, schools need two models in terms of curriculum development. One type is generic IL model to promote critical thinking, higher-order thinking, reflection and decision making by students for the competent use of digital information (integrated in ICT courses). The other is a discipline specific model to aid in further understanding of a particular school subject.

One reason for this is the lack of a scientifically sound and proven model to operationalize and [28] measure IL. Teachers need support and clarity in terms of how to evaluate IL in their subjects. This seems to be a critical point. The ability of teachers to use digital media pedagogically in the curriculum is still in its infancy [18, p. 159]. Moreover, teachers addressing new digital skills, such as the competent handling of online information, are often entering uncharted territory in their respective fields (media education). In this context, teachers are increasingly demanding the teaching of media-specific qualification goals. However, which skills teachers need to acquire remains rather unclear and these skills are largely limited to the use and operation of the ICT [4, p. 76]. In order to be able to plan and design suitable media education training measures for teachers, a concrete discussion and formulation of the required skills is required [21, p. 157].

The main research question of this paper focuses on this critical issue:

How to design professional development for teachers to develop information literacy skills in Secondary Education?

In order to pursue the leading research question, the following questions are important:

- How can information literacy in high schools be defined and operationalized (Student perspective on learning outcomes)?
- What are the necessary knowledge areas for teachers in terms of the TPACK model (Teacher perspective on instructional practice)?
- How can the competence of teachers be developed by combining formal and informal learning (as emerging alternatives to the dominant "training model")?

The paper is structured as follows: The next section states the rationale of the research project and composes the leading research question based on the problem identified. The third section explains the applied research methodology. The fourth section provides an overview of the findings: (1) the 7i framework for conceptualization and measurement of IL (student perspective of IL) (2) the required skill-set for teachers based on TPACK model (teacher perspective of IL) and (3) forms of competence development by combining informal and formal learning (emerging alternatives to the dominant "training model" of teachers' professional development). The last section concludes the paper by discussing the results and providing recommendations for future research.

3 Research Methodology

The main goal of the research presented in the paper at hand is to develop a conceptual framework for teachers' professional development focused on IL in secondary schools. In order to achieve this goal a two-year research project has been established in cooperation with a secondary school in the German-speaking part of Switzerland. The project is based on a methodological combination of literature analysis, model development and empirical model testing. The following are important:

1. To get an overview of existing IL research, a systematic literature analysis has been performed by focusing on the following research questions (see also [28]): Which terms associated with IL exist and how is IL defined in the literature? What are the salient conceptualizations and measurement models of IL? Which methods are applied in order to examine IL?
2. Based on the findings of the literature research, and by combining and extending existing models, the 7i Framework for measuring IL has been created.
3. The 7i Framework for measuring IL has been tested in five classes at a Swiss secondary school.

The results of the literature analysis and model development are presented in detail in [28, 29]. The most important results are presented in this paper to answer the first research question in order to operationalize IL as learning outcomes.

Further literature analysis has been conducted in the field of teacher education with a focus on digital competencies. One main model to develop the digital media skills of teachers is the TPACK model developed by Koehler and Mishara [15]. This model offers a framework to specify further the required skills to integrate IL into teaching practice. Empirical practice reflection within the research project mentioned and a thorough literature analysis are the main research methods for the design of teachers' professional development.

4 Results

4.1 Teaching Information Literacy Skills in Secondary Education Based on the 7i – Framework – the Learner Perspective

The starting point for teachers' professional development in the field of information literacy (IL) must be to clarify the required learning outcomes. The learner perspective defines what an information literate student needs to know and to do. Therefore, an IL framework has been developed to provide a basis for teachers to answer questions such as how students' learning processes can be scaffolded, how feedback can be given and how the IL performance can be evaluated and graded (for more detail see [32, 33]).

The proposed 7i Framework is shown in Fig. 1. It contains seven sub-competencies comprising knowledge, skills and attitudes: (1) Information needs; (2) Information sources; (3) Information access and seeking strategy; (4) Information evaluation; (5) Information use; (6) Information presentation; (7) Information process & finding reflection.

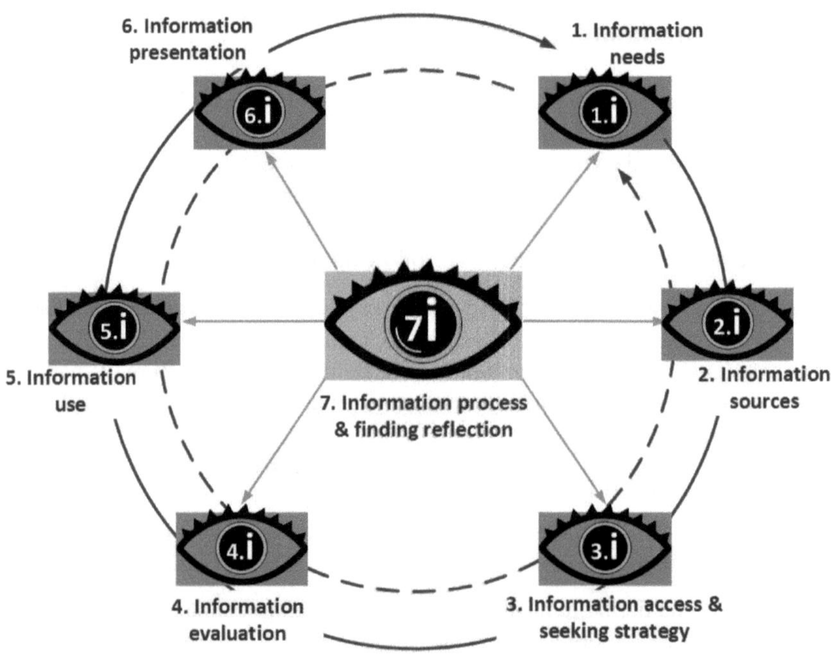

Fig. 1. 7i framework – students' information literacy

The Student who is information literate knows:

1. *Information needs:*
   How to determine information needs in the context of a given problem, i.e. to determine information needs in a problem-driven manner

2. *Information sources:*
   Identification of relevant information sources and of which information sources apply best to the information needs identified
3. *Information access & seeking strategy:*
   Identification of search strategy of information sources identified, and of which methods and search strategies suit best to access the selected information sources
4. *Information evaluation:*
   Evaluation of information sources and resulting information. Strategy for evaluating whether the sources and information are valid and reliable
5. *Information use:*
   Appropriate and problem-oriented use of the information found. This might also include a general understanding of ethical, legal and socio-political issues related to the information, or a subject- or problem-specific understanding of information and of how to use the information appropriately in order to solve the problem
6. *Information presentation:*
   Present the information geared to defined target groups
7. *Information process & finding reflection:*
   Reflect upon the information search and processing procedure and upon the information resulting from it and learn how to reflect the information search and processing procedure and the information resulting from it and to learn for future information search processes.

Based on this 7i framework a questionnaire was developed. The 7i measurement model results in two different scores in terms of IL. There is one objective score based on generic assignments, and one rather subjective score, based on self-assessment. Overall, the 7i Framework enables different approaches to measure IL: (1) the objective and self-assessed IL, (2) the separate measurement of the competence level in terms of each of the seven sub-competencies, (3) the interrelationship between the objective and self-assessed IL.

In cooperation with a Swiss high school the model presented has been empirically validated. To achieve this, data from 145 students from eight high school classes were collected using an online-based survey and the date was subsequently analyzed. The results demonstrate on the one hand, the students' objective IL (evaluated by using standardized criteria), and, on the other hand, the subjective IL (self-assessed by the students). The objective IL with a mean score of 29.12 (maximum possible score of 70 points) shows that the vast majority of students have a low level of IL. In the sample, the score ranged from 18 to 42 points and the maximum score measured is only slightly above 50 % of the maximum score possible. The highest score was achieved for sub-competence 5 (information use), while sub-competence 6 (information presentation) received the lowest score. Other results are detected in connection with the self-assessed IL of the students with a mean of 42.69 points - significantly higher than the objective IL.

Finally, the results show a discrepancy between the self-assessed IL score and the objective IL. While most of the students evaluated themselves as competent, the objective literacy is considerably lower. Furthermore, in the self assessed test, the students on average gave themselves high scores for all of the seven sub-competences, whereas the objective test unveils substantial differences among the seven sub-competences [29]. Consequently, a main challenge for teachers will be to sensitize and support students in their handling of online based information.

The 7i model allows teachers to assess their students' level of IL at different times and to support the process of IL development continuously. Furthermore, the measurement instrument provides a measure of the students' IL level in terms of the seven proposed sub-competences. On this basis teachers are able to identify learning needs for each phase and decide on further intervention.

Because of this, in the next section the teachers' perspective on how to integrate IL into their own teaching practice and subject areas will be analyzed.

4.2 Teaching Information Literacy Skills in Secondary Education Based on the TPACK Model – The Teacher Perspective

Schools face the challenge of how to ensure the permanent upskilling of teachers in the use of digital media and in particular to support information literacy in high school. In terms of the promotion of the digital media skills of teachers, one example is the TPACK model developed by Koehler and Mishara [15]. The model offers a framework for concretizing a required knowledge base for teachers if they want to use technologies meaningfully for teaching and learning. In the light of the observations in Shulman's pedagogical content knowledge (PCK) model [26, 27], the authors assume that the development of both technological pedagogical knowledge (TPK) and technological content knowledge (TCK) (together TPACK) is a prerequisite for successful technology-based teaching. The knowledge base (content, pedagogy and technology) form the core of the "technological, pedagogical and content knowledge" (TPACK), whereby the focus is particularly on the interaction and interfaces between the areas. The authors extend Shulman's model by the requisite technological knowledge and defined the following seven knowledge areas (Table 1):

In the light of the defined areas of knowledge in the TPACK model, the corresponding educational goals can be derived for describing a skills profile for teachers' professional development. The respective knowledge must be put in an application-specific context. The advantage of such an approach lies in the exact definition of the necessary knowledge base, skills and attitudes. This enables overlaps in the basic knowledge base to be avoided. The disadvantages include in particular the fact that teachers may not be able to derive any practical relevance for their lessons. Thus, for example, courses are often not geared towards the integration of technical knowledge into specific teaching situations. This therefore makes it difficult for teachers to apply a hands-on approach.

For this reason, teachers' professional development with a focus on digital skills and integrating IL into teaching practice has to be considered in new ways. The dominant "training model" focused primarily on expanding an individual repertoire of well-defined and skillful classroom practice is not adequate to achieve the ambitious visions of teaching and schooling embedding technology-based learning and integrating new learning outcomes such as IL. Therefore, the next section will highlight this issue.

Table 1. Areas of the TPACK-model with focus on information literacy (IL)

Knowledge area	Description	Guiding questions	Mastery information literacy
Content knowledge (CK)	Knowledge about the teaching subject and topic (theories, concepts, ideas etc.) of the respective subject area.	What content is relevant to understand the topic and should be covered in this lesson? Content for IL as interdisciplinary competences, specific content in the subject area.	Mastery of the IL content in the specific subject area, for example: Integration of IL into subject area "economics and law": google, amazon, apple, facebook as quasi-monopolists in a digitalized society.
Pedagogical knowledge (PK)	Knowledge about processes and methods of learning and teaching. This means an understanding of processes students use to gain new insights and how students could be stimulated or motivated.	What kind of pedagogical principles should be used in this lesson? Developing a personal learning environment to enable deep learning including IL.	Mastery of classroom strategies (inductive learning strategies), use of learning theories, different types of methods (active search as well as reflection methods), evaluation methods for IL, e.g. self-assessment tools, grading rubric
Technological knowledge (TK)	Knowledge, which is more than a pure application of knowledge. Rather it means a broad understanding of the opportunities for technology-based communication, information processing and problem solving.	Which technologies should be used in this lesson? Platform technology for classroom management, tools for specific learning phases along the IL competence model	Mastery of different kinds of technologies and ability to provide useful technologies for learning processes: e.g. using search engines, subject-related databases, tools for information use, reflection tools such as blogs

(*Continued*)

Table 1. (*Continued*)

Knowledge area	Description	Guiding questions	Mastery information literacy
Technological content knowledge (TCK)	Knowledge about the way technologies and content interact with each other. Furthermore, teachers need to know which specific tool is best for conveying the content.	Does the use of technologies support representing the content in multiple ways and will these technologies help to ensure a better understanding?	Use of technologies supports the understanding of content, for example to understand google as a quasi-monopolist using expert knowledge about the search engine.
Pedagogical content knowledge (PCK)	Knowledge about different opportunities to teach a specific content taking into account the students' prior knowledge, education guidelines on curricula and requirements.	Does the underlying pedagogical principles foster an understanding of the topic or stimulate a deeper learning?	Challenging problems as the starting point for deep internet research (knowledge not facts); adequate learning strategies (inductive learning strategies and reflection methods)
Technological pedagogical knowledge (TPK)	It needs an understanding of the drawbacks of technologies as well as the resulting pedagogic-didactic consequences within a disciplinary context.	Are the pedagogical principles and selected technologies well matched?	Focused on using technologies for learning and helping learners to use them in different ways. But the learning activities (IL integration in lessons) could take them away from actually learning content.
Technology, pedagogy, and content knowledge (TPACK)	Knowledge of the interaction and interfaces between content, technology and pedagogy in terms of the specific context. It needs an understanding of how these domains interact.	Do the selected technologies foster the underlying pedagogical principles and can the interaction between technologies and principles contribute to a better understanding of the content?	A masterful 21st Century classroom, which considers the learning content, based on good learning theories provided by digital media and using digital information.

4.3 Forms of Competence Development: Combining Informal and Formal Learning

Common teacher training practices are in themselves a major barrier to why the digital media teaching skills of teachers are only developing to a limited extent. Like their students, most teachers learn how to use digital media not so much in formal learning situations, but more informally, in practice. Teachers often simply lack the time to attend a course or to work on a self-learning program regularly [31, p. 3]. As numerous studies show, teachers generally seem to develop their skills predominantly informally in the context of their teaching practice, in an exchange with colleagues and through critical, individual reflection [12, 19]. Learning in informal contexts takes place alone or with others outside of institutionalized teaching environments. In contrast, learning under formal conditions takes place in training and further education institutions, where professional teachers endeavor to learn how to teach, assess and if necessary even to certify.

At voluntary further education events for teachers the fact that the individuals who generally attend usually already have a certain level of expertise is often criticized, and attendees often return to school disappointed because what they learned is difficult to put into practice because of a lack of time and money. In addition, school-based training courses (SBT) that are tailored to the needs of a school are very widespread. However, some research studies show that even formally organized school-based events also have a limited impact [14, 22]. Therefore, the international research literature on the education and training of teachers increasingly focuses on workplace-integrated learning, which takes informal learning into account more [12, 35]. One key finding is that formal and informal learning should be more closely interlinked to develop the skills of teachers. A promising approach would in particular appear to be the search for interfaces between learning in formal and informal contexts [7].

The following section focuses on the importance of the skills development of teachers in this context. Heise [10] particularly emphasizes the importance of largely self-directed further education in this professional field. To support and strengthen these desired informal learning activities, it would appear absolutely essential to create an environment conducive to communication within the school organization. The targeted encouragement of professional discussions before classes begin or during breaks and the use of free periods for detailed reflection, for example on critical practical situations, can make an important contribution to triggering and promoting informal learning among teaching staff [10]. However, not all teachers will be willing or able to collaborate with their colleagues on the preparation and follow-up of the classes. On the contrary, a certain proportion of teachers usually work alone. This might make a different kind of support necessary than would be required for teachers that already cooperate or collaborate with one another [12]. A concept to promote informal learning tailored individually to the aims and objectives of teachers could therefore generate added value for curriculum and school development.

In the field of information literacy, for example, the pressure on teachers to seek further education has increased immensely because of constant and rapidly advancing technological development.

A main question for schools to address is how skill development measures for teachers which integrate learning in informal contexts be structured in practice. Some examples are outlined below (see following illustration): (Fig. 2)

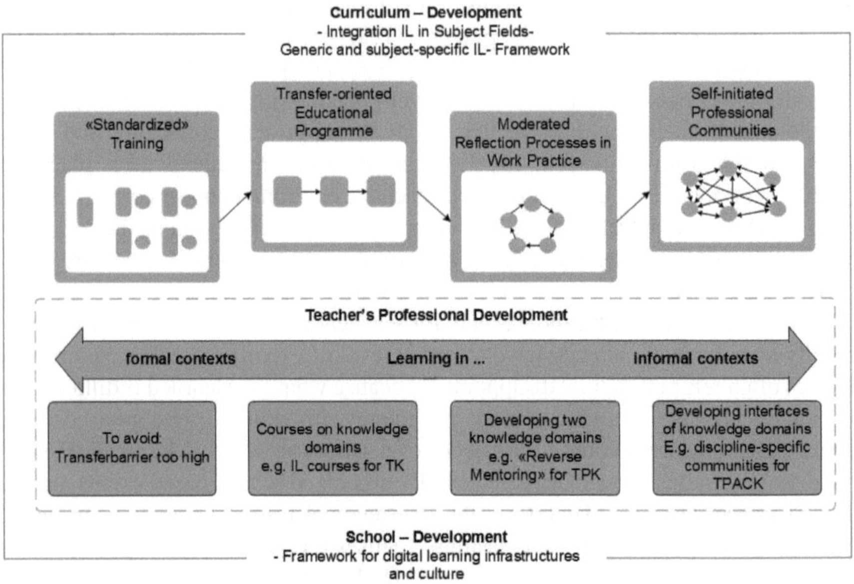

Fig. 2. Teacher's professional development in formal and informal learning settings and based on TPACK-model.

Transfer-Oriented Training. School-based training (SBT) is basically nothing new. However, it is now often combined more than was the case in the past with measures that support the transfer of what has been learned (such as preparatory phases and follow-ups). Effective results can for example also be achieved with more open learning environments, such as Engestrøm's Change Laboratory® [7]. In such a framework it would be possible to re-design courses at a professional association and hence combine the skills development of teachers with innovative strategies for curriculum development in schools [7, p. 12]. Whether or not the transfer of training or further education into the everyday life of teachers succeeds largely depends on individual factors [12]. An open mind towards new ideas and the willingness to adopt and implement innovative proposals are prerequisites for initiating and implementing change processes in school routine. How teachers learn informally differs from one individual to the next [12]. This aspect should be borne in mind when developing further education concepts and should lead to a sense of openness with respect to the curriculum, so that it is possible to adapt learning processes to the individual's needs. One significant advantage provided by the required openness is the ability to obtain feedback on the progress of learning. For example Zwart et al. [35], suggest providing teachers with a "peer coach", who can help them reflect upon what has been learned [12].

Moderating the Reflection Processes Regarding Teaching Practice. Critical, individual reflection upon one's own teaching basically represents a central impetus for the skills development of teachers [19]. A change in thought structures and hence upskilling is possible especially when the teacher experiences cognitive dissonance, i.e. inconsistencies between their own perception and how they actually experience critical teaching phases [17, p. 410]. This raises the question of to what extent such learning options can be promoted in order to initiate appropriate reflection processes. The findings of the group led by Zwart et al. [35, p. 990] show that informal talks with students from the perspective of an observer offer a valuable learning option. Other examples involve mentoring programs in which students act as trained mentors and assist the teacher in teaching with notebooks. "Reverse mentoring" is currently enjoying growing popularity even in business. Trainees who are familiar with digital media and able to use it critically act as mentors for senior managers and help them find their way in the new digital world. It remains to be seen whether this is merely a short-term fad, or whether it will become established as an element of a changing learning and management culture. Reverse mentoring could also be an approach for a school's learning environment to compensate for any lack of media skills on the part of teachers by using the potential of the digital natives. In this way the students' resources could contribute to the informal skills development of the teachers.

Furthermore, other forms of mentoring, such as near-peer shadowing, are capable of triggering reflection processes among teachers and thereby promoting informal skills development [19] Experimenting with new teaching methods (whether adapting a theoretically recognized concept, copying a colleague's method or developing one's own new idea) and even the immediate feedback from a colleague contribute substantially to the informal learning of teachers [12, 19, p. 90]. In this regard, mentoring programs can be orchestrated in different ways, i.e. the proportion of informal and formal elements of the learning process vary greatly [5]. The degree of refinement of the framework, such as the concrete learning setting, the place of learning or the general process, influences the "predictability of chance" in the further education of teachers and generates an added value for the school organization and the learners.

Self-Initiated Learning in Communities of Practice. The idea of near-peer mentoring entails a practice-oriented community of people (community of practice according to Wenger [33], who are informally linked with one another, are faced with similar tasks, and shape the practice in this community through a self-organized exchange. "Professional Learning Communities" in the teaching profession have long been a popular research field [13, 30], but the effects of professional learning communities have yet to be researched in detail [17, p. 408]. The basic consensus in the literature seems to be that community-internal characteristics – such as high motivation for self-development and student focus – are required in order to obtain a deeper level of reflection on the part of teachers than the level obtained at a conventional training seminar [17, p. 408]. The literature on collegial reflection illustrates the added value of such working relations [12, 19]. Communities of practice increase the circle of possibilities for reflection and, provided the aforementioned conducive group characteristics exist, are another instrument for the informal skills development of teachers

A beneficial environment for the successful interplay within the community of practice, such as the time window for the professional exchange, must be provided by the school.

Not only networking internally within the teaching staff, but also the search for forms of more intensive cooperation between learning locations, are fields that are still relatively young in Switzerland and have yet to be implemented systematically [6]. Schneider and Mahs [24] provide one example of a concept of continuous self-qualification and cooperative self-organization for the skills development of teams of trainers (trainers, teachers, professional services). Here, team meetings represent an important measure, in the course of which training modules and further education per se can take place in a self-organized way through the multiplier principle [24, p. 300]. More recent examples support learning cooperation using Web 2.0 to bridge the gap between learning locations [3]. However, experience with knowledge forums [16, p. 416] reveals that work within the forum has so far encountered considerable problems. There is often a lack of motivation to cooperate at the various locations. The formation of networks in relation to the outside world thus also has a bearing on the internal relationship between the participating organizations, ("which is why knowledge forums cannot become bridges between the organizations, yet bridges are built without ensuring the access," [16, p. 416]. Even when using Web 2.0 applications, the relevant prerequisites for success are therefore not so much technological as cultural factors that represent incentives for participation in the community of practice. The above-mentioned promotion of a climate that is conducive to cooperation within the school influences the informal learning activities of the teachers [11]. The availability of time and virtual and real rooms fosters proactive action by the practical community [20].

In the light of on the above examples, it is clear that the combination of formal and informal learning is possible, in particular by using two different approaches. "This can be done independently by the learner (e.g. through documentation, checklists, learning diary) and/or with support (e.g. learning process support, group discussions). By means of constructive and critical reflection on one's own experiences, the mere "gaining of experience becomes an effective learning experience that supports one's own skills development" [23, p. 77]. Alternatively, however, significance is attached to the structuring of the self-organization of learning processes on the continuum between formal and informal. With this approach, self-organized learning is promoted in daily school routine through staffing, methodological or medial structuring aids. This makes it possible to tap into the experience of organized forms of learning gained in the course of everyday teaching practices for the acquisition of skills (for example through the combining of project and learning tasks or observational tasks to focus the attention of the students).

5 Discussion and Future Perspectives on Professional Development for Teachers

This contribution posits a problem of "fit" between new requirements in terms of digital skills such as IL and prevailing configurations of teachers' professional development. It argues that the dominant "training model" of teachers' professional development focused primarily on expanding an individual repertoire of well-defined and skillful classroom practices is not adequate to realize the ambitious visions of teaching and schooling that embeds digital skills such as IL.

Emerging alternatives to the training model, though small in scale, embody assumptions about teacher learning and the transformation of schooling that appear more fully compatible with the complex demands of teaching digital skills.

The skills development of teachers, in particular in order to test and learn new teaching concepts, is inextricably linked to curriculum and school development. As already stated in the introduction, school routine is currently dominated by traditional forms of teaching, in which innovative educational approaches are almost impossible to realize. Such teaching practices are therefore the central impediment to the integration of digital media in everyday school life [34, p. 38].

Teachers' professional development in terms of the competent use of digital information therefore requires considerable efforts in the schools. Consequently, it is certainly not enough to organize a new training course for teachers. Such courses are usually held as a one-off events. Hence, a new further education course will continue to be out of place in the school. On the contrary, it appears all the more important that support initiatives for the skills development of teachers are based on this context and are simultaneously embedded in innovation strategies and quality development processes in schools [24, 25]. As a result, curriculum development, staff training and school development measures must be coordinated in order to implement education reforms [30]. The development of a school culture in which students and teachers alike attach great importance to learning together and from one another is of central importance [13, 30].

Developing a learning-conducive school culture can be regarded today as one of the key challenges for the successful implementation of educational innovation and continuous quality improvement processes. To enable technology to become firmly established as a method and a subject in school routine in the long term, appropriate framework conditions are required at the organizational level. In this context, an appropriate learning culture must be established. This would promote learning with and from one another, and would promote the testing of new forms of teaching with digital media.

References

1. Argelagós, E., Pifarré, M.: Improving information problem solving skills in secondary education through embedded instruction. Comput. Hum. Behav. **28**, 264–270 (2012)
2. Balceris, M.: Medien- und Informationskompetenz: Modellierung und Messung von Informationskompetenz bei Schülern. Dissertation, Freie Universität, Berlin (2011)
3. Beiling, B., Fleck, A., Schmid, C.: Lernortkooperation mit dem Web 2.0 - ein neues Mittel für eine alte Herausforderung? Berufsbildung in Wissenschaft und Praxis (BWP) **3**(41), 14–17 (2012)
4. Blömeke, S.: Medienpädagogische kompetenz. In: Frey, A., Jäger, R.S., Renold, U. (eds.) Berufspädagogik. Kompetenzdiagnostik. Theorien und Methoden zur Erfassung und Bewertung von beruflichen Kompetenzen, vol. 5, pp. 76–97. Empirische Pädagogik e.V, Landau (2005)

5. Colley, H., Hodkinson, P., Malcolm, J.: Formality and Informality in Learning. Learning and Skill Research Centre, London (2003)
6. Dubs, R.: Schweiz. In: Euler, D. (ed.) Handbuch der Lernkooperation. Theoretische Fundierungen, vol. 1, pp. 564–579. Bertelsmann, Bielefeld (2003)
7. Engestrøm, Y.: New forms of learning in co-configuration work. J. Workplace Learn. **16**(1/2), 11–21 (2004)
8. Gapski, H., Tekster, T.: Informationskompetenz in Deutschland - Überblick zum Stand der Fachdiskussion und Zusammenstellung von Literaturangaben, Projekten und Materialien zu einzelnen Zielgruppen. Landesanstalt für Medien Nordrhein-Westfalen, Düsseldorf (2009)
9. Gust von Loh, S., Henkel, M.G.: Information and media literacy in kindergarten. In: Kurbanoğlu, S., Špiranec, S., Grassian, E., Mizrachi, D., Catts, R. (eds.) ECIL 2014. CCIS, vol. 492, pp. 253–262. Springer, Heidelberg (2014)
10. Heise, M.: Professionelles lernen jenseits von fortbildungsmassnahmen. Zeitschrift für Erziehungswissenschaft **10**(4), 513–531 (2007)
11. Heise, M.: Informelles Lernen bei Lehrkräften. In: Bodowski, M., Devers-Kanoglu, U., Overwien, B., Rohs, M., Salinger, S., Walser, M. (eds.) Informelles Lernen und Bildung für eine nachhaltige Entwicklung. Beiträge aus Theorie und Praxis, pp. 255–264. Budrich, Leverkusen/Opladen (2009)
12. Hoekstra, A., Korthagen, F., Brekelmans, M., Beijaard, D., Immants, J.: Experienced teachers' informal workplace learning and perceptions of workplace conditions. J. Workplace Learn. **21**(4), 276–298 (2009)
13. Hord, S.M.: Professional learning communities: Communities of continuous inquiry and improvement. Southwest Educational Development Laboratory, Austin (1997)
14. Jurasaite-Harbison, E.: Teachers' workplace learning within informal contexts of school cultures in the United States and Lithuania. J. Workplace Learn. **21**(4), 299–321 (2009)
15. Koehler, M.J., Mishara, P.: What is technological pedagogical content knowledge? Contemp. Issues Technol. Teacher Educ. **9**(1), 60–70 (2009). Accessed 01 July 2015
16. Kremer, H.: Wissensforum als Instrument der Lernortkooperation. In: Euler, D. (ed.) Handbuch der Lernortkooperation. Praktische Erfahrungen, vol. 2, pp. 411–418. Bertelsmann, Bielefeld (2003)
17. Lipowsky, F.: Theoretische Perspektiven und empirische Befunde zur Wirksamkeit von Lehrerfort- und -weiterbildung. In: Terhart, E., Bennewitz, H., Rothland, M. (eds.) Handbuch der Forschung zum Lehrerberuf, pp. 398–417. Waxmann, Münster/New York/ München/Berlin (2011)
18. Ludwig, L., Narr, K., Frank, S.: Abschlussbericht Initiative Lernen in der digitalen Gesellschaft - offen, vernetzt, integrative Internet & Gesellschaft Collaboratory (2013). Accessed 07 Oct 2013
19. Meirink, J., Meijer, P., Verloop, N., Bergen, T.: How do teachers learn in the workplace? An examination of teacher learning activities. Eur. J. Teacher Educ. **32**(3), 209–224 (2009)
20. Overwien, B.: Schulorte und Raumgefüge informellen Lernens. In: Böhme, J. (ed.) Schularchitektur im interdisziplinären Diskurs. Territorialisierungskrise und Gestaltungsperspektiven des schulischen Bildungsraums, Wiesbaden (2009)
21. Petko, D., Döbeli Honegger, B. (2011). Digitale Medien in der schweizerischen Lehrerinnen- und Lehrerbildung: Hintergründe, Ansätze und Perspektiven. Beiträge zur Lehrerbildung, 29(2). Retrieved June 18, 2015
22. Richardson, V.: The dilemmas of professional development. Phi Delta Kappan **85**(5), 401–411 (2003)

23. Rohs, M.: Zur Theorie formellen und informellen Lernens in der IT-Weiterbildung, Universität der Bundeswehr Hamburg, Hamburg (2015). https://www.deutsche-digitale-bibliothek.de/binary/MV7JDGZH33VAWF6S5DLYV3JCETEVKDFK/full/1.pdf. Accessed 28 August 2015
24. Schneider, P., Mahs, C.: Kontinuierliche und Kooperative Selbstqualifikation und Selbstorganisation (KoKoSS) der Ausbilder. In: Euler, D. (ed.) Handbuch der Lernortkooperation. Theoretische Fundierungen, vol. 1, pp. 298–312. Bertelsmann, Bielefeld (2003)
25. Seufert, S., Lehner, M., Tödtli, M.: Didaktisierung des informellen lernens. In: Seufert, S., Metzger, C. (eds.) Kompetenzentwicklung in unterschiedlichen Lernkulturen. Festschrift für Dieter Euler zum 60. Geburtstag, pp. 487–507. Eusl., Paderborn (2013)
26. Shulman, L.: Those who understand: knowledge growth in teaching. Educ. Res. **15**(2), 4–14 (1986)
27. Shulman, L.: Knowledge and teaching: foundations of the new reform. Harvard Educ. Rev. **57**(1), 1–22 (1987)
28. Stanoevska-Slabeva, K., Müller, S., Seufert, S., Scheffler, N. (eds.) The 7i framework – towards a measurement model for information literacy. In: Proceedings of the American Conference on Information Systems (AMCIS), Fajardo (2015a)
29. Stanoevska-Slabeva, K., Müller, S., Seufert, S., Scheffler, N.: Modelling and measuring information literacy in secondary education. In: International Conference on Information Systems (ICIS), Fort Worth, Texas (2015b)
30. Stoll, L., Bolam, R., McMahon, A., Wallace, M., Thomas, S.: Professional learning communities: a review of the literature. J. Educ. Change **7**, 221–258 (2006)
31. Weiss, R.: Medienkompetenz als neue Kulturtechnik. Berufsbildung in Wissenschaft und Praxis (BWP) **41**(3), 3 (2012)
32. UNESCO: Outcome Document – World Summit on the Information Society (2013). http://www.itu.int/wsis/implementation/2013/forum/inc/doc/outcome/S-POL-WSIS.OD_FORUM-2013-PDF-E.pdf. Accessed 05 Aug 2015
33. Wenger, E.: Communities of Practice: Learning, Meaning, and Identity. Cambridge University, Cambridge (1998)
34. Wilbers, K.: Entwicklung der Kompetenzen von Lehrkräften berufsbildender Schulen für digitale Medien. Berufsbildung in Wissenschaft und Praxis (BWP) **3**, 38–41 (2012)
35. Zwart, R., Wubbels, T., Bolhuis, S., Bergen, T.: Teacher learning through reciprocal peer coaching: an analysis of activity sequences. Teach. Teacher Educ. **24**(4), 982–1002 (2008)

Can K-12 Students Learn How to Program with just Two Hours?

Kadri Umbleja(✉)

Tallinn University of Technology, Ehitajate tee 5, 19086 Tallinn, Estonia
kadri.umbleja@ttu.ee

Abstract. This paper presents results of analyzing almost 1500 students', from ages 6 to 18, feedback and test results to a two hour long programming workshop using LEGO Mindstorms kits. Students had very little or no previous programming experience. At the end of the workshop they were asked how the workshop affected their interest towards engineering in general, robotics and programming. They were also asked list of theoretical question about concepts and ideas learned during the workshop. Students' answered were analyzed according to genre, age and school type. As a result, it can be concluded that two hours of intense programming workshop gives students similar basic understanding about programming concepts as other students with previous experience have. Primary school students were most excited about the workshop and stated highest positive change as a result of the workshop. On the other hand, they lacked ability to understand programming concepts. Therefore students between ages 11–12 and 16–18 benefit most from the workshop as they have high interest and they also are able to comprehend theory. Type of school student attends does not affect the results. Girls have lower previous interest towards three considered fields before the workshop and they have slightly lower results than boys.

Keywords: Programming · K-12 · Lego Mindstorms · Outreach · ICT education

1 Motivation

Due to current demographical trends, the number of 18–19 years olds in Estonia is decreasing. This trend is set to continue and bound to get worse in time. Public universities are funded by the government depending on the number of students they have. Potential undergraduate students tend to prefer more "softer" curriculums despite many attractive career opportunities for STEM (Science, Technology, Engineering and Math education) course graduates. For example, ICT (information and communication technologies) sector is one of the fastest developing sectors of Estonian economy that has been described of having a big cap between required and available workforce.

Estonia is a country that has put a lot of emphasis on ICT education, especially for K-12 students [1]. Since 2012, program ProgeTiger has been introduced in selected schools where programming is taught from first grade (age 7) [2, 3]. There have been hopes that introducing programming for students in early ages makes them more

L. Uden et al. (Eds.): LTEC 2016, CCIS 620, pp. 250–264, 2016.
DOI: 10.1007/978-3-319-42147-6_21

affirmative towards STEM subjects and encourages them to consider ICT curriculums in higher education and therefore narrow the workforce cap in ICT sector.

Importance of early ICT education has been widely covered [4–6] but there have been few comprehensive studies about its impact and how well are students capable of learning programming that covers the whole range of age groups in K-12. No studies have been previously published about the unique situation in Estonia.

2 Workshop

For the current study, two hour intense programming workshops with Lego Mindstorms EV3 kits were developed and conducted [7]. No code was written by the students. Instead visual programming software offered by Lego was used that "hides" all programming complexity. Students only needed to drag and drop blocks and change their modes and parameters in order to solve the task. Students participated in the workshops in pairs of two. Workshop used simple two wheeled robot with third ball wheel for balance.

Workshop started with a short introduction of robotics, followed by 30 min spent on finishing the robot by adding sensors. Afterwards, short lecture about programming followed. After the programming blocks were introduced and students were familiarized with the programming environment, the workshop's assignment was introduced. It was a simple line following exercise. Robots start to move after a touch sensor has been pushed and use gyro sensor to turn 180 degrees. Then, using a color sensor, they track the edge of the black line until they reach the finish, marked with yellow. Robots use sound to notify that they have reached the end.

Teams had around 20 min to come up with an initial program and to start doing test runs. Then they were encouraged to try different parameters on blocks controlling robot's movement to make the robot go faster. By trial and error they changed their program and tried different types of movement programming blocks until they found what they thought to be the fastest solution. Usually programming part of the workshop with testing took around an hour. Workshop ended with a race between teams – it was not used so much for finding the best team but to remind them that with two hours they all managed to make robot move and race.

This version of workshop was attended mostly by students who had very limited or no previous experience with robotics or programming. For verification purpose another workshop was implemented for students with previous experience.

3 Feedback

The workshop concluded with a feedback form. It include questions about student's background, school, and interest before and after the workshop. Also multiple choice questions about programming blocks and what they do, were included. In total 15 questions were asked – 8 about programming concept and 7 about robot movement. All the blocks used in the assignment were covered, few of them doubled for verification purposes (to identify students who randomly select answers and might have got "right" answer due to luck). Choices for each question contained multiple "correct" answers with few obviously wrong ones. The choices were designed so that some reflected understanding of the block in current task's context; others reflected more comprehensive understanding of the programming concepts. Also, option of "do not know" was offered. There was around 10 % of students who chose "Do not know" for majority of questions.

4 Analysis

Almost 1500 students have filled out comprehensive online questionnaire. Their age distribution can be seen in Fig. 1. 36 % of them were girls and 64 % of them were boys.

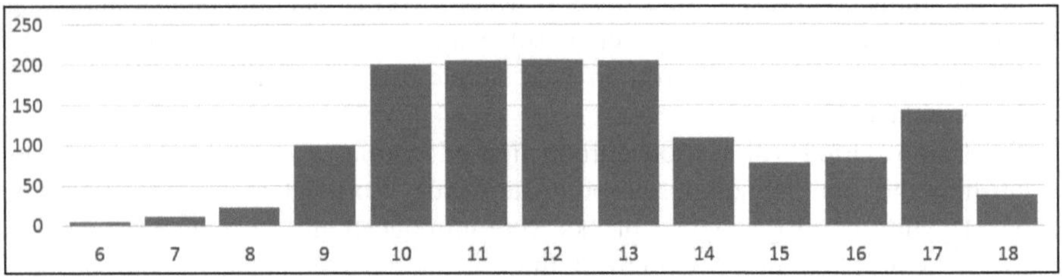

Fig. 1. Participants' age

33 % stated that they had previous programming experience while 31 % said they have had some kind of encounter with robotics. Most of the stated experience by the students was very minimal and superficial. Most popular statements were in after school courses in robotics or in Scratch. Main previous contact with robotics was in after school robotics courses or attending robotics fair "Robotex".

When looking at students' interests it can be seen that in general, students had highest interest (77 % said they had high or very high interest) towards engineering in general and lowest towards programming as largest percentage of students (14 %) stated they had low or very low interest towards programming. In general, the differences between different topics of interests were within 8 % as can be seen in Fig. 2.

As a result of the workshop, students' interest towards engineering in general rose the most as 69 % of students stated that they their interest towards engineering rose or rose a lot. Robotics was the field where most students (28 %) stated that their interest remained the same as before while around half said it rose. Students' interests towards programming saw different changes. More than half said they are now more interested towards the field but also more than quarter said that their interest dropped or dropped a lot.

4.1 Analysis by Genre

In the main group, 60 % of participants who filled the feedback form were boys and 40 % girls. The genre cap came mainly from teachers who usually pre-selected boys to participate in the programming workshop. Sometimes, girls convinced their teachers so

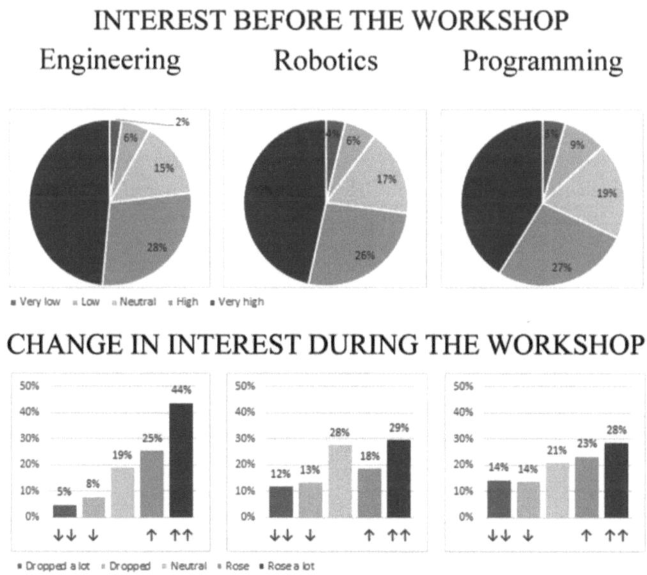

Fig. 2. Participants' interests before the workshop and how the workshop affected them (Color figure online)

that they could also participate in the programming workshop. Therefore, important reason why there is so few girls entering university in engineering majors might be forced role behaviors from early age.

31 % of them had some kind of programming experience and 30 % some kind of experience with robotics. Majority of the previous programming experience consisted of robotics or programming after school classes they have taken. Some students specified that they have learned Scratch. In addition, some of the students had attended other kind of Lego robotics workshops during other projects (for example, sumo robots workshop). Robotics experience consisted some students having previous or this version of robot at home or attending very popular robotics fair "Robotex".

Girls, on the other hand, had less previous experience. 14 % of them had previous programming and only 11 % had previous robotics experience. Most popular previous programming experiences came from computer lessons in school. Also, with girls, many said that their family member has learned programming or works in IT field and they have learned from them. Robotics experience mostly consisted of visiting robot's fair or having being able to see robots. Very few had real practical hands on experience.

As can be seen in Fig. 3, in both cases, engineering has highest interest. Girls are less likely to states highest than boys but with second highest grade also taken into account the percentages are only slightly less than boys.

Students were also asked to grade how they apprise changes in their interest towards three fields considered during the workshop. There were big differences between boys and girls. Girls were more likely to say their interest remained the same.

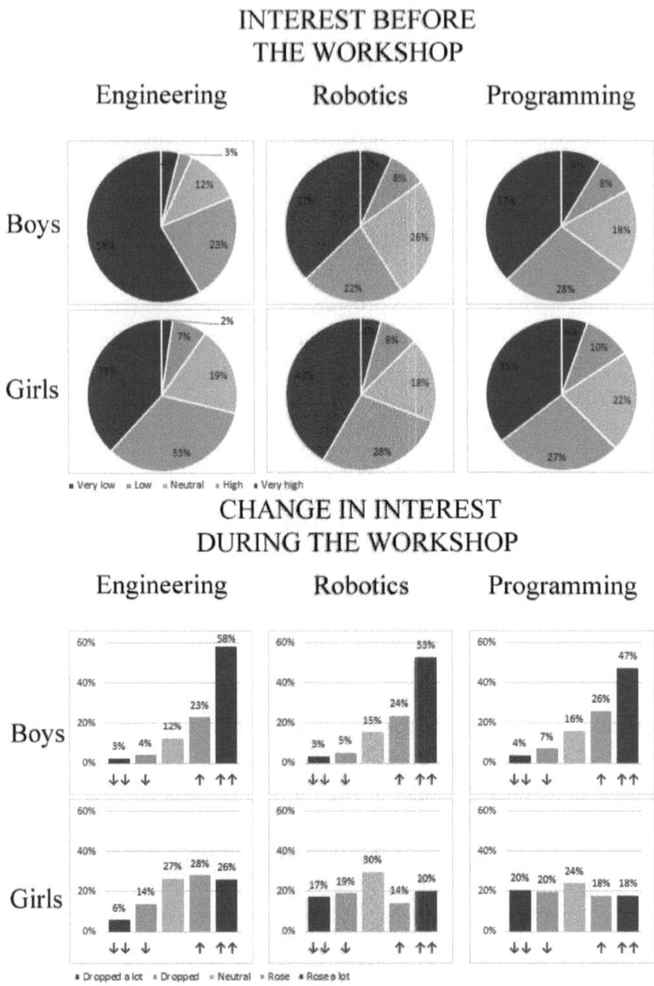

Fig. 3. Students' interests by genre before the workshop and how workshop affects them. (Color figure online)

They also had most positive rise in interest towards engineering as general where half said their interest grew or grew a lot. Programming and robotics saw around 36–40 % of students saying their interest actually decreased or even decreased a lot.

Boys, on the other hand, said in more than 50 % of cases that their interest towards engineering and robotics grew a lot during the workshop. Programming saw slightly lower rise.

When looking at the results, girls were more likely (26 % vs 21 %) to choose "Do not know" option. They had similar percentage of wrong answers (21 %). Girls were more likely to choose correct answer in current task sense where boys showed more conceptually higher level of understanding. Easiest questions for boys and girls were the same-parallel action, wait and sound. Girls were more likely to give correct answer to programming concept questions when boys showed better results with movement questions.

4.2 Analysis by Age Group

When looking at the age groups, as can be seen in Fig. 1, 16 % were up to age 10 (included). 33 % belonged to age group 11–12. 29 % were between ages 13–15 and 22 % were 16 and older. First group corresponds to ages in primary school. Second group corresponds to grades 5 and 6 with third group corresponding to grades 7 to 9 in middle school. Last group consists of students studying in high school.

6–10 years Olds. This group consisted of 58 % of boys and 42 % of girls. 23 % of them have had previous experience with programming and 25 % with some kind of connection with robotics. Most of the previous programming and robotics experience comes from school. Scratch was mentioned by students. Also, visiting robotics' fair "Robotex" was very popular option for this age group. Also, many students mentioned different programs (like "ProgeTiger") that has been implemented for children in order to introduce programming for them.

When looking at results, on average, 31 % of cases "Do not know" was chosen. 21 % of cases wrong answer was selected. In 14 % of cases, students choose answer that reflected highest level of understanding. Easiest questions for youngest age group were about parallel action (despite very few choosing answer reflecting conceptual understanding), wait and sound.

11–12 years Olds. This group consists of 64 % of boys and 36 % of girls. 31 % of them had previous programming experience and 37 % of them had some kind of previous robotics experience. Most of the previous experience consisted of robotics classes in school or after school courses. Also owning Lego robots at home was mentioned often by this age group.

When looking at their results, they showed improvement compared to youngest group. On average, 22 % of cases, "Do not know" was chosen and in 21 % of cases, wrong answer was chosen. Also, percentage of conceptually correct answer rose to 19 %. More questions were also given generally correct answers. Easiest questions were same to younger age group with loop and switch receiving noticeable rise in correct and conceptually correct answers.

13–15 years Olds. This group consisted of 70 % of boys and 30 % of girls. 32 % of them had previous experience with programming and 29 % had previous experience with robotics. Again, robotics and programming classes in school and after school activities were most popular options for previous experience. Also, having own Lego Mindstorms (EV3 or older) at home was mentioned frequently. Some students stated that they have built apps or participated in courses teaching them that.

Older secondary school students got wrong answer in 21 % of cases, same as other two age groups. Percentage of "Do not knows" dropped to 15. There is slight rise in answers reflecting highest level of understanding (from 19 % to 21 %) but the difference is much smaller than between first two groups. Easiest questions are the same as with other age groups. Surprisingly, question about two wheel movement that saw rise in correct answers with younger secondary school students, dropped for this age group noticeably. Also, it was noticeable with this age group that if they had question were both correct answer on current task based was available with conceptually correct answer, they preferred choose current task based answer.

16–20 years Olds. This group consisted of 59 % of boys and 41 % of girls. 40 % of them had previous programming experience while 30 % of them had some kind of experience with robotics. Most popular previous experience was school computer classes and studying programming on their own. Many student mentioned that they know popular high level programing languages like Java, C and Phyton.

On average, 14 % of cases, "Do not know" was chosen. In 19 % of cases, smallest percentage of all age groups, wrong answer was chosen. For this age group, the easiest questions were about sound, wait and large motor with two wheels. Also, loop and interrupt saw many students give them conceptually correct answers. As could be expected, oldest age group showed best conceptual understanding with 27 % cases conceptually correct answer was chosen.

Students' Interests. When looking at students' interests, as can be seen in Fig. 4, differences between ages groups are emerging.

Elementary school students states that they have largest high interest towards all three considered fields before the workshop. They state especially elevated interest towards robotics with 65 % saying that they have very high interest in that field.

Second group of students, aged 11–12, have also quite high interests towards engineering and robotics but they are less likely to state that their interest is very high. The interest has specially dropped, in programming, compared to elementary school students.

Third group, older students in middle school, have less students with very high interest in robotics and programming. Around 35–38 % only chose this option with more students saying that they have neutral feelings towards those feels.

High school students are even less likely to state that they have very high interest towards engineering in general. Their interest towards programming and robotics see rise in students who have neutral feelings or who state they have low or no interest at all.

As a result of the workshop, youngest participants are the ones stating that their interest rose or rose a lot. Workshop affects the engineering in most positive way while robotics and programming see less gain. Also, robotics and programming see much higher drop in interest than engineering. Older middle school students have highest percentage of students with negative change in interest due to the workshop in programming. They also recorded highest percentage of students stating that their interest remained the same with robotics. High school students have noticeable less students stating positive change in interest towards engineering than younger age groups – probably due to the fact that they have already developed their preferences by that age.

Overall, it looks like the youngest participants were most eager about three fields considered and had most positive impact due to the workshop. One reason for that kind

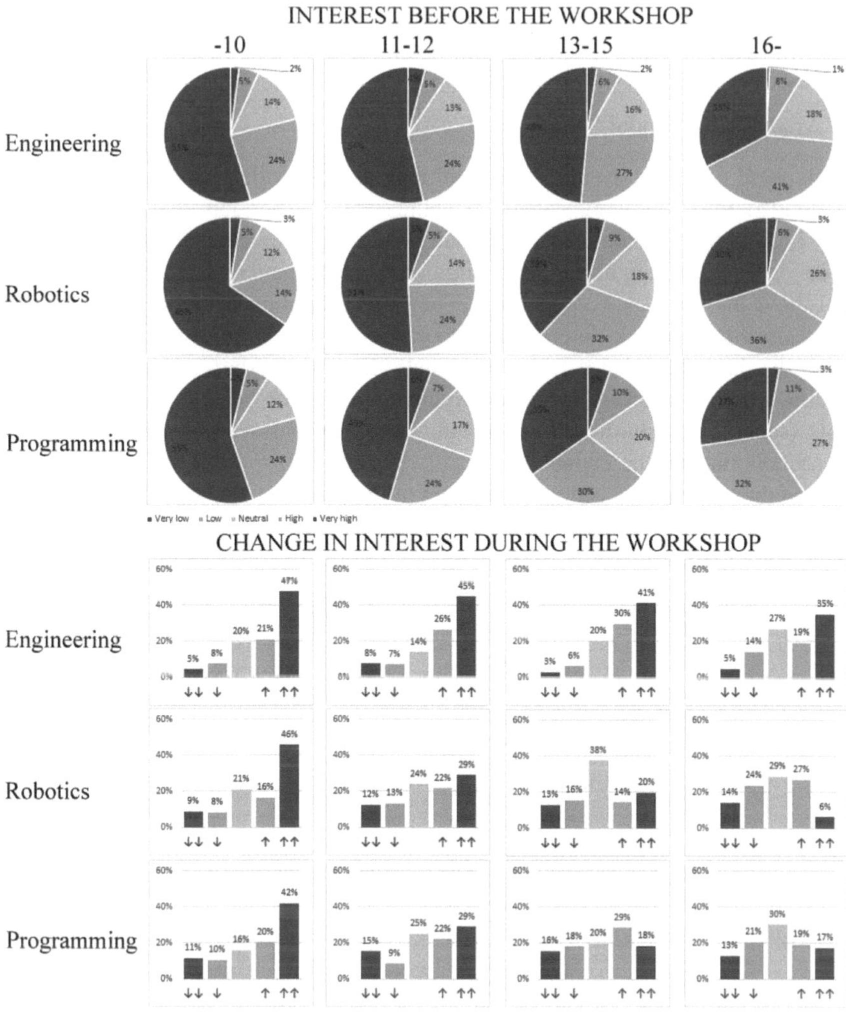

Fig. 4. Students' interests before the workshop and change during the workshop by age (Color figure online)

of answers might be that they may not have specific idea what those fields consist or they are most likely excited about making their robot move.

Students with lowest interest towards all considered fields were older middle school students who were also most likely to have drop in interests due to the workshop. It might be cause due to their age and attitude as this age group contains teenagers. Furthermore, participating in the workshop is decided by the teacher and students may not have had any say in it. Also, there seems to be clear pattern that with age students are less likely to state highest interest towards fields considered – also, implication that older students have well developed ideas what they like and what they do not like.

Therefore, it seems that workshop seems to have most positive impact to younger age groups who have not yet developed full picture of their interests.

4.3 Analysis by School Type

Students were asked to specify the school they are currently studying. Then, schools were divided into following categories: elite schools (Schools that have stand out having high national exam results. Usually they have specific theme (for example, Science or English language) with additional special-interest classes. Also, those schools have high entrance competition. They are still public schools and free to attend but they are likely to ask parents to support special-interest classes), private schools (schools that have attendance fee), vocational school (secondary or higher educational institution where in addition to general education a specific vocation is taught), special schools (schools for children with specific needs), usual schools within capital and usual schools outside the capital.

Out of those 6 types of schools 4 of them (elite, private, usual schools within capital and usual schools outside the capital), as can be seen in Fig. 5, have had enough students participating in the workshops to have statistical relevance.

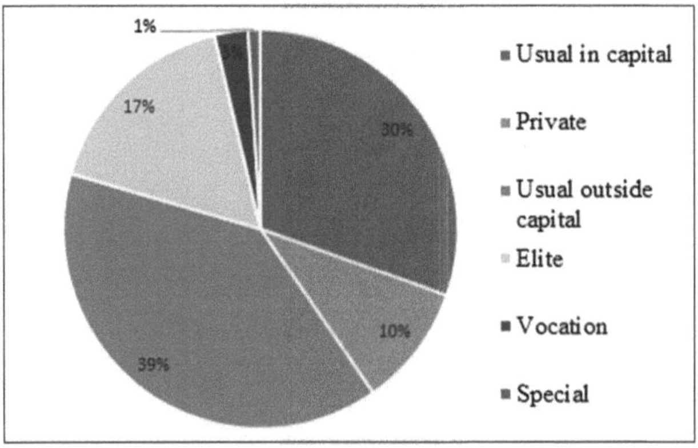

Fig. 5. School types of students who answered feedback form (Color figure online)

Usual Schools within the Capital. This group has 39 % girls and 61 % of boys. 98 % of them have had some kind of connection with Legos. 31 % of them have had previous programming experience and 33 % have previous experience with programming. Main connection with robotics and programming came from after school activities and computer classes in school. Robotics fair Robotex was also very popular as it is hold in capital. Some students said that they have learned higher level programming languages on their own.

In 21 % of cases, students choose not to answer. 22 % they got the wrong answer. This group showed good conceptual and higher level understanding – matching their counterparts in usual school outside the capital with highest scores. Easiest questions were sound, parallel action, interrupt and loop.

Usual Schools Outside the Capital. This group had almost equal percentage of boys and girls (53 % vs 47 %). 98 % of them had some kind of previous experience with Legos. 28 % of them had previous programming experience and 26 % had previous experience with robotics. Those numbers are lower than for their counterparts in capital.

Most of the previous experiences were connected with school activities – computer classes and after class activities in school. Many students said that there have been different organizations and lecturers from universities and companies have come to their school to speak about information technologies. Also, some students marked that they have gained experience in programming on their own, with Phyton and Scratch being the most common examples. Also many of them who had previous experience in programming, had tried building web sites.

This group showed best result with 6 % of students answering all questions correctly or making only one mistake. They also had high percentage of answers showing higher level of understanding. In 22 % of cases, they got answer wrong and in 22 %, also, they tended not to answer. Easiest questions for this group were sound, parallel action, wait and loop.

Elite Schools. This group had 72 % of boys and only 28 % of girls participating in the workshops. 97 % of them have had any kind of previous experience with Legos. 32 % of them had previous programming experience and 33 % had previous experience with robotics, same as students in usual schools in capital.

Previous experience consists of school related activities. Many of those who had previous experience had programming or robotic class in school as part of their curriculum. Many said they had after school robotics activities.

This group, surprisingly, recorded lowest results. They also lacked students reflecting higher level of understanding. They got wrong answer in 22 % (similar to other groups) and did not answer in 23 % of cases. Easiest questions for them were sound, parallel action, wait and loop.

Private Schools. This group had 55 % of boys and 45 % of girls. All of them have had some kind of connection with Legos before. 32 % of them had previous experience with programming and 29 % of them had previous experience with robotics. 41 % of students preferred building with Legos with exactly the same percentage of students preferring only to program in the workshop, highest percentage for all groups.

Majority of previous experience consisted of after school activities in robotics. Some had also attended after schools programming courses. Also, more than with other school types, having previous experience with (and owning) Lego robots were mentioned.

This group got answer wrong in 19 % but decided not to answer in 30 % of cases. Easiest questions for them were sound, parallel action and robot movement with two wheels. They also showed better than average understanding of robot movement questions.

Overall, it can be concluded that school type does not affect the results much. It was unexpected that students from private schools were so much more likely to deciding not to answer than students from other type of schools. Also, it could have been assumed that students from elite schools may have higher results due to many extra curriculum activities and better level of education, usually ascribed to elite schools, but results did not reflect that hypothesis.

Students' Interests. Students' interest by school type can be seen from Fig. 6. Students from usual schools in capital had higher than average interest towards three considered fields. Noticeably, towards engineering. Their preference towards robotics and programming was almost the same. Students from outside the capital were more likely to declare very strong interest towards robotics and had less interest towards programming.

Elite schools stood out due to the fact that students from this school type had highest number of students with low interest towards three fields under consideration. They were also less likely to choose highest interest in considered fields than students from other types of schools.

Private schools students have higher than average percentage of students with very high interests towards robotics and programming (girls, actually had higher interests towards programming than boys!).

As a result of the workshop, students from usual schools had similar pattern with highest rise in engineering. Programming sees highest drop.

Elite schools had highest percentage of students who stated drop in interest due to the workshop. It is intriguing that girls in elite schools have similar pattern with girls in usual schools. Boys are the ones who have noticeably more negative perception of three fields under consideration.

Private school students have most positive change due to the workshop– almost 60 % of students' state rise in their interest in programming and robotics. It can also be noted that private school students have high interest towards robotics beforehand and after the workshop the interest rose even further.

4.4 Control Group

The purpose of the study was to see how students without any or with very limited previous experience gain knowledge about robotics and programming through workshop lasting just two hours. To verify the learning and see how their result different from students with experience, another workshop was conducted for students who had previous programming and/or robotics experience. Around 250 students participated in control group.

Due to implementation limitation and students' interest it was not possible to conduct the exact same workshop for this group as majority of them had already solved line following exercise during their previous experience. More advance and challenging workshop was requested by participants. The workshop consisted of 7 sophisticated tasks. Most of them required complicated path calculation, used different sensors, required making choices according to information received from sensors, for example. Students were free to choose which tasks they wanted to solve. On average, students managed 3 tasks with 2 h.

26 % of the participants on the control group were girls with rest being boys. Majority of the students in the control group were between ages 10–12. Around three quarter of them have had adequate previous experience with programming and robotics. Girls were slightly less likely to have adequate previous experience. After school and extra

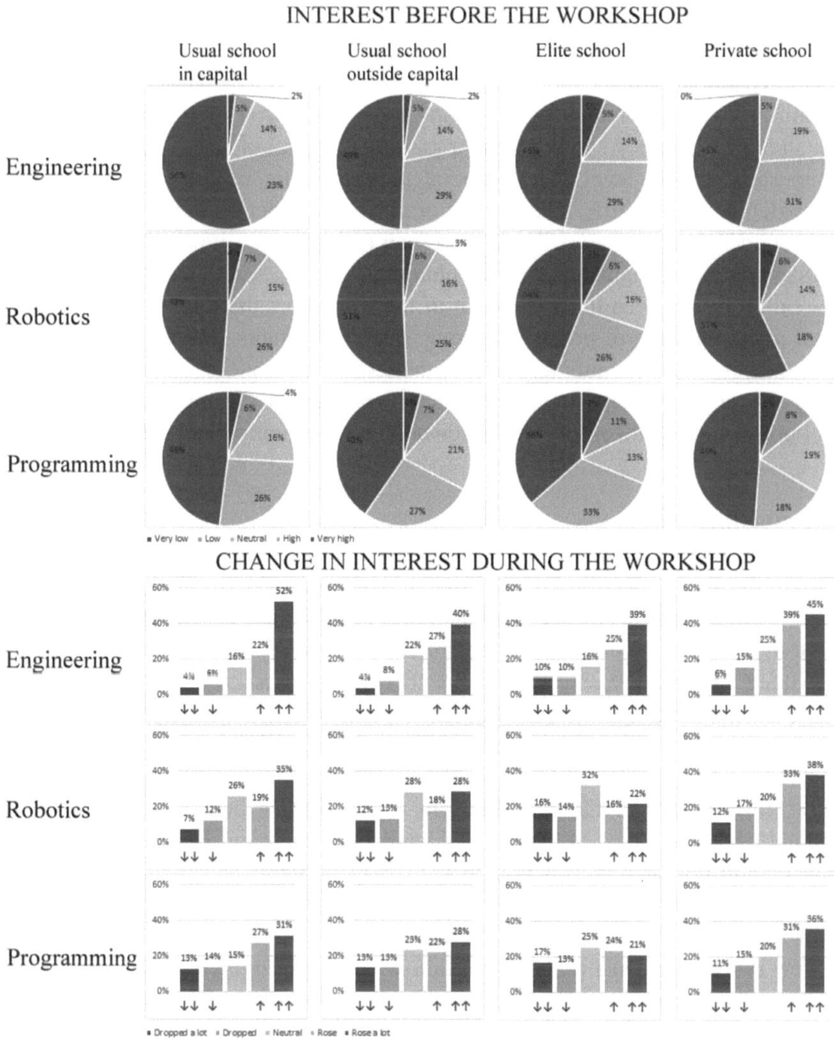

Fig. 6. Students' interests before the workshop and change during the workshop by school type (Color figure online)

curriculum activities were also very popular for previous programming experiences. Many students had attended programming camps or participated in workshops organized by the university. First Lego League was also mentioned by students.

Their interest before workshop were similar to main group participants but they stated more positive change due to the workshop than main group. Girls, in the control group, state much higher positive change due to workshop than girls in the main group. In main group, it was the engineering that saw most rise, but for girl in control group, all three fields saw significant rise.

Control group also had similar feedback form with 15 questions. As expected, control group was less likely to choose wrong answer. It would have also been expected that students show more conceptual understanding (higher level taxonomies) than main group but, in reality, both groups actually showed similar levels conceptual understanding. Also, they showed similar pattern as the main group that boys are more likely to show higher level of conceptual understanding of programming concepts (loop, switch etc.) than girls. The control group showed better understanding of robot movement questions on the feedback form than main group – it could be explained by all 7 tasks contained sophisticated path planning.

Overall, it can be seen that as a result of the workshop, there is no clear differences between main and control group. For some questions, main group shows better conceptual understanding (assumingly due to the lecture during the workshop). For other questions, the control group shows better high level grasp (assumingly from experience). Control group showed clearly better understanding of moving blocks than main group.

5 Discussion

The aim of the study was to see if students are able to experience programming simple (but still exciting) task with just two hours and evaluate if they are able to learn from this kind of intense workshop. At the beginning of the study there were many questions like if young students are able to understand what is asked of them, are they able to complete the task with just two hours, will they understand what they are doing. Also, there was a worry if a word "programming" would scare them away before they have even started.

Now, it can be said that despite their age, younger participates were able to understand what was asked of them. They were very eager and very excited – some of them just could not keep their hands off the robots while lecture part of the workshop was given. They wanted to see and try what robots can do instantly. There were also very few instances when younger participants were having trouble with the feedback form. Few times a students asked to explain what field "engineering" means. It never happened with "programming" or "robotics". The aspect of the feedback from that was not examined was how different age groups understood those three fields they indicated their interest. It can be expected that despite younger participants stating highest interest, they actually lack genuine understanding what those field fully cover.

It could be little surprising that it was actually hardest to get older secondary school students to participate in the workshop. Asking additional questions those students who were showing reluctance to participate, it came out that they think they are in age where "playing" with Legos hurts their "imago". They stated that Lego is a toy and they do not want to play with toys anymore. That was interesting as it was first observed from other studies and similar projects in university that if you would try to teach programming with other means (for example, pure code writing) they are very likely to get scared and assume it is hard before even trying. Lego was therefore assumed to be a great tool to encourage students not to be afraid. For the majority, it worked – there were lot of positive comments towards Lego robots from students from different age groups and genre. For example, from the free space in the feedback form, 17 year old boy wrote: "I hadn't played with Legos for a long time. This workshop reminded me how I used to love it. I am glad I could connect my childhood passion with something exciting as programming." 12 girl wrote: "I did not know this kind of Legos existed. I loved how the robot started to move. I want to build more! This Lego robot goes to my Christmas wish list". So, leaving out teenagers who had problem with "playing with Legos", it could be confirmed from the observation of students during the workshop that they do not feel threatened from Legos and that makes it easier for them to get into programming than pure code writing would. Also, the way students react when they first manage to make robots move is priceless – some are really surprised, others are hyper excited. Some are very proud. Others just cannot stop after that. Seeing how their program produces observable reaction seems to be the great motivation for students.

The topic of girls in engineering curriculums have been covered widely but it came as a surprise for lectures implementing the workshops that the school teachers are doing preselection for students attending the workshop based on genre. There were few cases when the girls, who were not able to participate in programming workshop, saw what their male classmates were doing and then cadged their teacher to return to university so that they could also program Lego robots. Also, it became clear that girls are less likely to have any previous experience – even if there are after school activities available in their schools, they are encouraged, again by their teachers, to enroll more in art or music activities rather than programming.

From those observations, it could be concluded that in order to solve the low enrolment of female students in engineering curriculums, the solution may lie changing school teachers assumption of genre roles and stopping them to enforce those assumed genre roles from early age. It is much harder to encourage girls in secondary school to get excited about programming if they have always been told that this is something only boys do. It is much easier to give primary school (or younger secondary school) female students change to try programming and other engineering related activities and let them make the decision if they like it by themselves.

Even though this study only looked how different age groups are able to learn programming with two hours, the underlying goal also was to give many students, who had no previous programming experience, change to try programming by themselves and get them excited. It seemed to work as many groups came back to university for more advance workshops. Also, university developed, due to the demand, special courses for school children (mostly age 10–14) for programming and other activities connected to engineering. Those courses have been always filled quickly by both boys and girls.

6 Conclusion

To sum up, it can be said that only with 2 h, students can learn basics about programming and later reflect on those newly learned knowledge, mostly in the context of current task done. It is easier for students to find correct answer if it is given in the same context as it was used in the workshop, reflecting the ability to copy information (lower levels of learning taxonomy) that they came across during the workshop. They are less likely to analyze or evaluate (higher levels of learning taxonomy) concepts behind the programming and movement blocks used during the workshop.

The workshop seems to be most suitable for younger middle school students (age 11 to 12) and to high school students. Primary school students recorded the highest interest in engineering, robotics and programming but due to their age, they are not fully able to comprehend programming principles or the theory taught during the workshop despite also recording highest positive change in interest due to the workshop. Younger middle school students also have high interest and rise in all three considered fields but they are better at acquiring new knowledge and understanding what is taught during the workshop. Furthermore, they are in age where they have not yet fully developed their interest and therefore this workshop may inspire them to try more activities connected to engineering. Older middle school students have lowest interest before and after the workshop. This age group has stated that it is "uncool" for them to play with Legos. High school students, on the other hand, have very specific already developed interest.

When there were clear differences between age groups, then type of school student studies does not have huge impact. Despite society having assumption that students in elite schools have better preparation and are more capable, elite school students actually record lowest interest and workshop seemed to lower their interest even further.

Workshop was mostly visited by boys, due to preselection by the schools. Therefore it could be assumed that genre gap in engineering in universities comes from early age assumed role behaviors influenced by schools. Boys, on average, had higher interest than girls and workshop also had higher impact on their interest. Boys also seemed to reflect better levels of understanding, mainly about robot's movement. Girls, on the other hand, outperformed boys in questions connected to programming concept blocks.

Acknowledgments. This study has been supported by "Study IT" program.

References

1. Mansel, T.: How Estonia became E-stonia. http://www.bbc.com/news/business-22317297. Accessed 20 April 2016
2. Olson, P.: Why Estonia has started teaching its first-graders to code. http://www.forbes.com/sites/parmyolson/2012/09/06/why-estonia-has-started-teaching-its-first-graders-to-code/. Accessed 20 April 2016
3. #Hitsa: ProgeTiger Programme. http://www.hitsa.ee/it-education/educational-programmes/progetiger. Accessed 20 April 2016
4. Barr, V., Stephenson, C.: Bringing computational thinking to K-12: what is Involved and what is the role of the computer science education community? ACM Inroads **2**(1), 48–54 (2011)
5. Grover, S., Pea, R.: Computational thinking in K–12 a review of the state of the field. Educ. Researcher **42**(1), 38–43 (2013)
6. Kalelioğlu, F.: A new way of teaching programming skills to K-12 students: code. org. Comput. Human Behav. **52**, 200–210 (2015)
7. Umbleja, K.: The first year experience of using LEGO Mindstorms robots in the Tallinn University of Technology outreach program for secondary and primary school learners. In: New Technologies and Innovation for Global Business: ICEE 2015 International Conference of Engineering Education, pp. 741−748 (2015)

Course Implementation: Value-Added Mode

Vello Kukk(✉)

Tallinn University of Technology, Ehitajate tee 5, 19086 Tallinn, Estonia
vello.kukk@ttu.ee

Abstract. This paper introduces a new learning control method – 'value-added mode'. This mode is based on counting credits for only new knowledge learned whereas 'old' knowledge is taken into account with low weight. The need for such mode appears when background of students starting a course is very varying. This situation becomes more and more frequent, because of globalization, personal study tracks etc. In this paper we describe how this mode is implemented and also describe an application Build-Your-Course.

Keywords: Course · Adaptive · Credits · Compiling course

1 Introduction

This paper considers the case when a course has with very varying input meaning that background of the students starting the course is very different. This situation is more and more frequent because of several reasons, including globalization, MOOCs, varying study paths which are becoming very personal. The problem is not new and one solution has been using some introductory or preparatory actions where potential students pass some special training with expected leveling of their abilities. However, after passing a course the students are again unleveled – grading is clear sign of it. Facing such situations, some teachers have split course into two ones (may be more?) to meet different audiences. However, this may cause further splitting and therefore less efficiency.

Another view on the problem is when we ask for what a learner is paying? If answer is 'to get a certificate' then this is not the case. If the answer is 'to get smarter' then this is just the case: there is no reason to pay for something I know; I agree to pay only for new knowledge.

We describe how 'value-added mode' has been implemented and which problems arise when using this mode. Value-added mode is related to calculation of credit units as formal outcome and is intended to make amount of knowledge really learned and credit units awarded to match each other. So, credit units are not considered as evaluation of average time wasted but as a measure of knew knowledge. It is known that amount of work needed for acquiring the same material differ more than 5 times and therefore CUs can be used as estimated time only for averages. However, we also give some evaluation of amount of work done in an example below.

This approach may be compared with Advance Placement activities [1]. Getting deeper into learning processes can be discovered in many recent studies; however, this is rather for external applications, for example for prediction of expected exam

L. Uden et al. (Eds.): LTEC 2016, CCIS 620, pp. 265–273, 2016.
DOI: 10.1007/978-3-319-42147-6_22

results [3]. We include very detailed information directly into real learning process closing feedback loop with minimal time delay.

We also discuss generating personal courses. Similar problems are discussed at the level of curricula with courses as elements in [4] and involving students in curricula development [5]. Extraction of knowledge and assigning credit value from course documents is described in [6]; however, this is formal calculation and does not consider learning process.

This new mode can be implemented only when we have detailed structure of the knowledge available in the course. Our case is based on very low-level competencies with an important conditions: measuring how they are acquired by a learner must be determined and preferably done automatically. Basic constructions used in the system are described in [10, 11].

2 Elementary Competencies - Comps

Our model is based on low-level competencies or 'comps' - entities which have among other attributes **ability**, measured in some scale (from 0 to 1 or weak to strong etc.). Student's ability levels are determined during learning process and are comparable, for example, with probability of correct answer in Item Response Theory [2]. The scale which is used is not important, in our case it is integer values from 0 to 127 (non-negative values of one-byte numbers). Considering the value as probability, it could be in [0, 1]. Ability levels are changing during learning process, depending on results of problem solving and additionally, decreasing as forgetting [7, 8] model is applied to all comps [9].

Learning is considered as sequence of solving tasks and correcting ability levels through processing of solutions results. Every task has several comps assigned to it which are to be used when solving the task. Processing of the solution results modifies ability levels of connected comps (parameters of forgetting model are also updated). Number of comps related to a task vary from 1 (very rare) to 10 (also rare) and are of two types: input and output comps. For example, a task *T* may have 3 input comps $\{A_1, A_2, A_3\}$ and 2 output comps $\{P_4, P_5\}$. In this case, all A_i-s can be used for activation of task and as a rule, corresponding abilities are updated. Output comps, here P_k –s, may be evaluated but may be not depending on solution. There is no strict rule for the choice of type but designer must keep in mind that input comps will be used for (automatic) selection of tasks.

This model has been used for learning over 5 years (with continuous modification, of course). Primary areas have been electric circuits, some software courses, nanotechnology, microprocessors, partial implementations in civil engineering, language learning etc.

A course is a set of comps and every comp of this set has the weight – amount of credit units, usually measured in mCU (milli credit units, integer values only). So, for learner every comp has two attributes: amount of mCU (fixed for the course) and ability level (variable). In this two-dimensional plane, the goal of a student is to reach high values in both dimensions. Therefore the grade available is determined by area formed by mCU*Ability products for all comps [11]. If official credits for the course are for example CU (1000*CU in mCU) then max area is Amax = 127*1000*CU and grading thresholds are from 60 % to 92 % of that value.

The courses in active use have quite varying number of comps included: from 32 to 238 comps; the last number is just in the master course having the largest extension (Sect. 3 below). The basic ideology when designing courses is compiling i.e. all comps must be ready and the only additional action is assigning weights (mCU) to comps (they may be and must be different in different courses). Note that experimental assignments (labs) are very important in engineering and there are comps which appear only in practical tasks.

Usually, total available area has been kept about 15 % bigger than formal amount of CUs meaning that highest grade can be achieved even when some comps have not brought to sufficiently high level.

Example. We describe here a simple task which however allows to show almost all aspects appearing (Fig. 1).

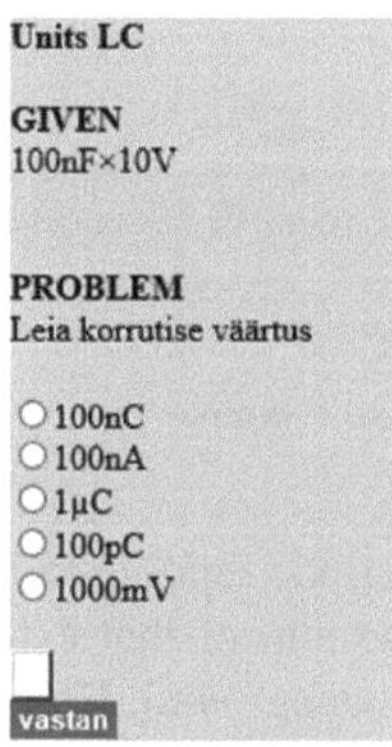

Comp	Answer		
	1μC	100nA	100pC
Volt	1	-1	1
Farad	1	-1	1
Coulomb	1	-1	1
nano	1	-1	-1
Amper		-1	
Volt			
micro	1	-1	-1
pico			-1

Fig. 1. An example of simple task eft and processing for some answers

There is only one correct answer 1μC. Such task may have the following input comps: Volt (V), Farad (F), nano (n), and micro (μ). Depending on (wrong) answer passive comps (ampere, volt, and pico) can be also evaluated.

This is a simple task but shows how productive may be using even such elementary tasks. And the practice shows that these tasks are needed and not too simple. The system includes more than 20 types of tasks, including such where processes must be laid out, writing and testing programs, measuring frequency responses, allocating sensors etc. In case of lab experiments measurement errors and other factors are taken into account producing results between −1 and +1.

3 Extension of the Set of Comps in the Course

First extension of comp set was originally assigned to a master course because the students who registered to the course had very varying background. First, local students which had a semester or two ago completed some BSc courses which have been considered as prerequisite. Second, students coming from other universities, countries, or even from the same university but from other faculties. The course that was tuned for the first type of students, appeared to be too complicated for students of the second type. Therefore content of the course was extended towards BSc course to give to students of the second type possibility to pass the course (Fig. 2). The result was that for the first type students the course was too easy as they had recently passed the parts located in lower extension. Note that the variety of learners is even bigger as some students have passed corresponding BSc prerequisite but several years ago and their abilities were downgraded by some extent by forgetting model.

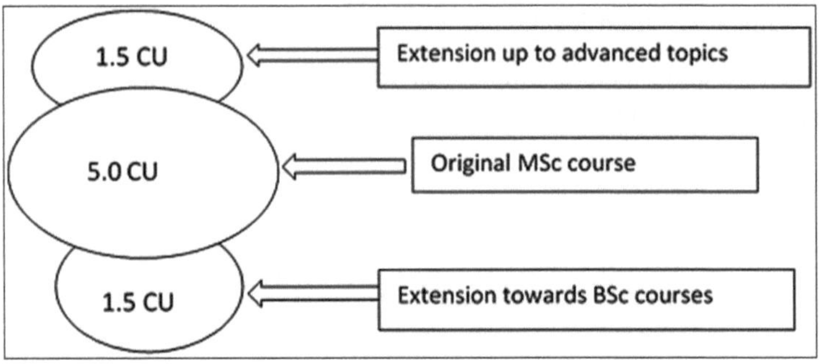

Fig. 2. Extensions to regular course

The next extension was made into upper direction – adding more content that was missing in the original version of the course. The aim of that extension was to give possibility to learn more for students with wider background. However, as they could reach easily good grade in the lower part, motivation to do so was not great.

This experience was the main argument for introducing 'value-added mode' meaning that learned area which determines final grade is formed mostly by new comps, or that only added value is granted.

4 Value-Added Mode

Implementation of that mode is the following. For the first date of starting the course (declaration in this university), the system evaluates levels of abilities for all comps included in the course. Part of them may have non-zero values (even very high values) when the student has passed some course which included corresponding comps. Most of ability values are equal to zero, either because they are new or have been not studied or have downgraded by forgetting model of the system. So far, we can use only data from courses supported by our system as extracting detailed information form courses passed by student is almost impossible. However, it seems that storing and making available more detailed information of studies is increasing trend.

Starting learning, the student has all comps open for task activation but there are different modes which could be used and were used before. The first mode is 'starting from scratch' when it is assumed that a learner has no previous knowledge about the course content and all ability levels are set to zero. This is a standard approach but not fare because some students may have very good background, even having 'almost passed' a course or similar earlier (the same course in other institution).

The second mode is starting from the state that is extracted from some database. This is somewhat opposite to the previous case and may need less work as certain parts may be 'pre-passed' and in extreme situation nothing is to be done to obtain a grade.

The third is just new 'value-added' mode when state at the start is taken into account but with some weight to build compromise.

During first pass of this new mode several versions were considered. We shall not discuss all of them and present here the final decision only. Obviously, the states that have ability levels (and credits) more than zero should be downgraded somehow. Acceptable version is to assign lower values of credits for those comps that have nonzero ability levels at start. Then nothing is to be changed in learning control but weight of that comp in final 'area' is less and so this models 'value-added' principle. In other words, if one starts from high level of a comp then it is easy to obtain highest level but added value is small which seems to be correct approach when we want to evaluate work done (or new knowledge acquired).

After considering several approaches, the following model was introduced. If a comp C*i* has assigned credits CU_i and initial ability level A_i then when calculating area for this comp the following modified amount of credits is used:

$$C_i^* = (1 - \frac{A_i}{224})C_i \tag{1}$$

This expression can be interpreted as follows. If ability level A_i is 0 (new comps have this value) then $C_i^* = C_i$ that is obvious. For maximum value of ability equal to 127, weight is minimal and equal to 127/224 = 0.566. For example, when $C_i = 50$ mCU (typical value) then it is downgraded to 28 (always rounded to integer value). A learner may not touch this comp at all and then area will remain 127*28. Obviously, this ability level may change when solving a task where this comp is passive forgetting downgrades ability level. However, amount of mCU-s remains 28.

The constant 224 was chosen during analysis of real situations in the first course where the mode was implemented. It is assumed that the constant may be different (in different courses) determined by analysis of real learning processes but so far it remains the same.

Let us consider some examples. First, in spring semester of 2016 the model was in several courses and here we take a look on a BSc course. On Fig. 3 we show the areas (mCU*level) for some of them who completed the course early.

Let us compare two students who obtained highest grade 5: call them *Left* and *Right* (second and fourth on Fig. 3). The *Left* had almost half of his final area from previous studies as the *Right* had only 10 % (DIFF in Fig. 3). They added almost equal area (ADD) and obtained the same (the highest) grade. Their data is presented in Table 1 where initial areas (credit*ability products) are shown. Total number of active comps is 181. Difference in columns NQ and NL (numbers of solved tasks) shows effect from value-added mode: both students obtained max grade but *Left* had to do more work

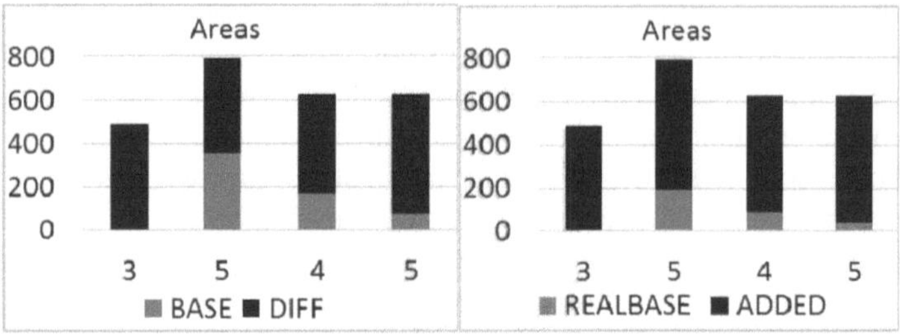

Fig. 3. Comparing 4 students with different backgrounds. The left picture shows total area and area at start (grey). The right one shows which part in final state is weighed from start and which is added during learning. Final grades are shown as labels on horizontal axes.

Table 1. Comparison of two students

Name	BASE	DIFF	Total	ADD	NQ	TQ	NL	TL	NZ
Left	354	438	792	600	1147	15.0	139	8.17	22
Right	72	555	627	589	927	15.8	75	3.25	24

than *Right* (total number of comps is 214 and 186, respectively) because his initial level was much higher (354 vs 72).

Columns NQ and NL show the amount of tasks solved,'theoretical tasks' NQ and experiments (labs) NL. TQ and TL show the time in hours used for solving tasks. These numbers demonstrate that amount of work is almost the same for both students except labs where student *Right* had more experience from previous life. In the last column the number of comps NZ with zero ability is shown (about 10 %).

The course has totally 224 comps from which 181 are active and 31 % of them (57) can activate some lab task. Some comps have very low number of attached tasks and they may be blocked for some time (last 5 solutions must contain different tasks). The number of comps that may activate only theoretical tasks is 116.

5 Problems

5.1 Obtaining Initial Data

How to obtain initial data for student, is a real problem. In case above and other courses that are active now, the data was available from the system where students had passed courses. Those (local) students could learn something in other courses from which we do not have information, however, no remarkable distortion was discovered (some small parts might be too easy for them). For students with zero background data, the courses seem to be still a little bit difficult.

We can compare the situation with having introductory tests (as well AP) as part of learning process itself. We do not have information about inclusion of the results of pretests into course 'live' but what is done in value-added mode can be interpreted just as that.

5.2 Parallel Courses

More difficult is the case when a student starts two (or more) coupled courses in parallel. Coupled means here overlapping which is not very small (say, more than 10 %). We do not have solution for this case – simply both will start from their own. First cases are underway and one of students in example above (*Right*) passed two courses successfully. His initial state (very small area - 72) was obtained just from parallel course. We did not face any problem and the student passed both courses.

5.3 Starting Date

Starting date may be critical when a student has the only goal to get credit units. In this case he/she may try to downgrade ability levels. However this may work against student's intentions. Opening those comps which are overpriced by forgetting model and giving intentionally wrong answers change forgetting parameters as well. We have not detected any such attempts so far. Probably, students feel by default that it is not useful for them.

Our practice has also shown that we face the need to extend course to 'upper end' as students may not have enough comps. This happened in case of MSc course discussed above when we had to extend the 'barrel' by about 1.5 CU up. The same need appeared one BSc course. In other courses we see the same and it is obvious that next year further extensions are needed as students will have higher starting levels.

In real life, forgetting may become very important because even if training is in some very practical field, rehearsing in certain elementary topics may be needed (mathematics, for example). As obtaining data that could help to form current knowledge model may be impossible, it seems natural to include elementary comps into course content. Practice shows that teacher tend to overestimate knowledge of people not vice versa. If abilities are at levels high enough there is no problem to pass through those parts and what is important, this process helps to build personal knowledge map for future.

6 Build Your Course (BYC)

There are several reasons for building person's own course. In formal education system, it may appear (appears in the university we refer to) that a student has to obtain small amount of credits to meet some formal conditions. Instead of waiting for proper semester and choosing some small course, one could try to build personal course that will extend his/her abilities in the major field of studies. If the set of comps available is more than used in the courses passed by the student he/she may choose comps (or sets of them called skills in the system) that are based on current knowledge portrait. The system helps allowing two modes for selection: lowest level, choosing comps, and higher level, choosing sets of comps (skills). In both cases, amount of CU-s that can be obtained is shown. As skills have closed set of comps and tasks, this mode is simpler. On the lowest level, selection of one comp automatically includes comps that are most closely related to the selected one. Close relationship here means that selection of comp

C_i means that tasks that can be activated from that comp include some other comps. Including those comps must guarantee that on formed set, tasks can be activated. This process is used for compilation of regular courses anyway with one important difference: this process works on the smaller set of comps and must take into account personal status of the person. Adjustment of conventional course means adjustment on large set of comps (usually 100–250) where depending on coverage by tasks may mean including, excluding, assigning active or passive attributes. In case of personal BYC at every step, possible outcome in credits and areas are estimated.

Formal basis is implemented as defining open content courses having 1, 2 or 3 CU with general course description and remark that real implementation is built by student (suggestions based on previous cases may be given).

Obviously, procedures that exist and that will be developed for BYC could be used for generating regular courses. Those procedures may be also used for analysis of the course, for example, for finding connections with other courses and holes in the course under development.

Probably the most important application of BYC is in continuing education. There are two key aspects that must be considered. First, how to get information about learners abilities. The second is finding which basic comps are relevant for particular course (its set of comps). This is not easy task and our experience has shown that proper information can be obtained only from analysis of real learning processes. The main reason is that teachers tend to make unbiased assumptions about abilities of learners, usually overestimating students' knowledge.

An example of iteration process:

1. Select a comp C_i to be added to the current set
2. Evaluate how this comp can be served (is number of tasks for all levels more than zero)
3. If this condition is not met then finding which additions are to be included; for that purpose, consider task having comp C_i as input and determine adding of which comps solve the problem making this task accessible.
4. Repeating the process for new comps imported in step 3 or go to 1.

One modification which may be needed when solving the problem on level 2.is as follows. For every task and connected input comp, a difficulty level is assigned (currently number of levels is 4). Difficulty levels have been determined by processing results of real learning process (usually 1-2 times a year). In case of problem with number tasks, assigned levels can be corrected manually. This has been practiced in a number of cases, however better solution is to create new tasks with proper characteristics.

7 Conclusion

Introducing of value-added mode has been an idea for some time, hoping that this may help to solve problems related to variety of students starting learning a course. It was implemented in 2015 and experience from the first applications appeared to be positive, helping to achieve better motivation for students and generating further ideas of implementation and different applications. Therefor from 2016 this mode is implemented in all courses (implementation means simply adding some general procedures and they are working always).

The need for BYC appeared just when first results of application of value-added mode were obtained. We foresee more wide application of BYC in the near future. Note that small courses derived as parts from regular ones did not appear to be popular. One reason could be that when student wanted to choose one of them, the request was declined because the student had too large part of it covered by some previous course (s). We cannot predict future of BYC but we are optimistic that this may better meet real needs.

The final note is that value-added-mode is not the must for just learning. It is relevant when learning is based on courses or one has to pay for learning.

References

1. De Urquidi, K., Verdin, D., Hoffmann, S., Ohland, M.W.: Outcomes of accepting or declining advanced placement calculus credit. In: Frontiers in Education Conference (FIE), pp. 1–6. IEEE (2015)
2. Rasch, G.: On general laws and the meaning of measurement in psychology. In: Proceedings of Fourth Berkeley Symposium on Mathematical Statistics and Probability, vol. 4, pp. 321–333. University of California Press (1961)
3. Kaur, K. Kaur, K.: Analyzing the effect of difficulty level of a course on students performance prediction using data mining. In: Proceedings of 1st International Conference on Next Generation Computing Technologies, Dehradun, India, pp. 756–761 (2015)
4. Tao, J., Wu, G.: An application of undergraduate academic growth path on the credit system based on data mining. In: Proceedings of 12th International Conference on Fuzzy Systems and Knowledge Discovery, Zhangjiajie, China, pp. 789–794 (2015)
5. Fernandez, A., Delgado, E., Montoya, Y., Gonzalez, R., Vaughan, M.: Student led curriculum development and instruction of introduction to engineering leadership course. In: Frontiers in Education Conference (FIE), pp. 1–8. IEEE (2015)
6. Wang, M., Zheng, J., Wang, S.: A new automatic knowledge extraction method for course documents applied in the web-based teaching system. In: Proceedings of 12th International Conference on Fuzzy Systems and Knowledge Discovery, Zhangjiajie, China, pp. 1620–1625 (2015)
7. Wozniak, P.A.: Two components of long-term memory. Acta Neurobiol. Exp. **55**, 301–305 (1994)
8. Wixted, J.T., Carpenter, S.K.: The Wickelgren power law and the ebbinghaus savings function. Psychol. Sci. **18**(2), 133–134 (2007)
9. Kukk, V., Umbleja, K.: Analysis of forgetting in a learning environment. In: 13th Biennial Baltic Electronics Conference, Tallinn, Estonia, pp. 335–338, 3–5 October 2012
10. Kukk, V.: Student's behavior in free learning environment and formal education system. In: Uden, L., Sinclair, J., Tao, Y.-H., Liberona, D. (eds.) LTEC 2014. CCIS, vol. 446, pp. 187–194. Springer, Heidelberg (2014)
11. Kukk, V., Umbleja, K., Jaanus, M.: Two-dimensional knowledge model for learning control and competence mapping. In: Uden, L., Liberona, D., Welzer, T. (eds.) LTEC 2015. CCIS, vol. 533, pp. 16–27. Springer, Heidelberg (2015)

Establishing Meta-Learning Metrics When Programming Mindstorms EV3 Robots

Michael Vallance(✉)

Department of Media Architecture, Future University Hakodate,
116-2 Kamedanakano, Hakodate, Hokkaido 041-8655, Japan
michael@fun.ac.jp

Abstract. Recently, wider issues of social relationships, contexts, feelings and personal goals have been recognized as impacting upon learning. Moreover, as the Higher Education paradigm appears to be shifting towards students as consumers, there is added pressure on academics to ensure students evaluate and subsequently 'make sense' of their educational experiences. This has been termed 'meta-learning' but there has been little research on meta-learning compared to the more recognized cognitive science term of metacognition. The paper describes a project in a Japanese university where meta-learning was promoted among first-year Systems Information Science students learning to program LEGO Mindstorms EV3 robots. Students were engaged in a collaborative, creative cycle termed TKF (*Tsukutte* つくって- Create)/*Katatte* かたって- Share)/*Furikaeru* ふりかえる- Reflect) to build and program robots to solve systematic problems. This paper will demonstrate that learners actively engaged in iteratively challenging robot-mediated interactive tasks can develop generic, declarative and epistemic competencies, with a consequential development of meta-learning.

Keywords: Competencies · Meta-learning · Programming · Systems Information Science · Robots

1 Introduction

In the 1960 s and 70 s learners were thought of as 'intelligent systems' and the term 'metacognition' (awareness and control of thinking processes) fell in line with the 'brain as computer' metaphor. However, studies in neuroscience reveal that learning is far more complex. Recently, wider issues of social relationships, contexts, feelings and personal goals have been recognized as impacting upon learning [1–3]. Meta-learning is an additional cycle in the learning process through which metacognitive knowledge about learning is constructed. Meta-learning is essentially 'making sense' of one's experience of learning. Just like any other knowledge, it is pieced together from organized, and sometimes fragmented, information and personal experiences. Students with meta-learning awareness realize 'what' is learned (termed declarative knowledge) and 'how' something is learned (termed 'procedural knowledge'). Students advanced in meta-learning capabilities additionally realize 'why' something is learned (termed

L. Uden et al. (Eds.): LTEC 2016, CCIS 620, pp. 274–288, 2016.
DOI: 10.1007/978-3-319-42147-6_23

'metacognitive knowledge'). This will be discussed in the context of learning to program at a Higher Education Institute.

When learning to program in a Systems Information Science (*aka* Computer Science) course a number of relevant observations have been made. In 1987 Cafolla [4] suggested there was a relationship between programming success and Piaget's 3 stages of cognitive development [5]. This was tested much later in 2013 by Gluga *et al.* [6] who found, in general, the following: students considered at the pre-operational stage could follow code but could not write code; students considered at the concrete stage could write code related to prior examples; students considered at the formal stage could reason logically, reflect on one's own reasoning, and deal with the hypothetical and unfamiliar when writing code. Morra *et al.* [7] similarly discovered that successful programming requires increasingly abstract forms of reasoning. This was later supported by Lau *et al.* [8] and Chen [9] who concluded that the cognitive characteristics of logical cognition dealing with procedural and abstract conditions, in addition to being open to experiences and creativity, are important factors for success at programming.

White *et al.* [10] went as far as suggesting particular programming languages are acquired by specific learners, based upon some early EEG scans of the brain: visual, procedural programming such as Visual Basic favored left-cognitive hemisphere thinkers while C ++ was hemispheric friendly (left and right). Doubt has been cast on this assumption though as recent discoveries of the brain and how we learn suggest that the left and right hemispheres are so interconnected that one cannot assume an either/or dichotomy. For instance, Siegmund *et al.'s* [11] fMRI research provides "... new evidence that programmers are using language regions of the brain when understanding code and found little activation in other regions of the brain devoted to mathematical thinking." This may be in contradiction to the findings of Katz *et al.* [12] who determined that a SAT math score was a predictor of a student's programming level; which may also be the perception among many academics in Computer Science. Alas, recent neuroscience research may prove this not to be the case.

In a broader context, Higher Education nowadays is seeking to enact a more holistic, multi-disciplinary education. Mima *et al.* [13] and Honey *et al.* [14] suggest that even within the context of Science, Technology, Engineering and Mathematics (STEM), Design-based Learning engages students as critical thinkers to solve challenges. Additionally, the emerging Maker Movement is informed by Piaget's approach to learning where learners personally, and sometimes collaboratively, construct solutions thereby gaining experience and, over time, calling upon their own embedded heuristics [14]. Subsequent 'cognitive engagement' thus supports students' psychological investment and effort directed toward learning and understanding, whilst mastering knowledge, skills or craft that the academic work is intended to promote. This leads to a more self-determined learner who becomes more autonomous through the development of his/her meta-cognitive knowledge [15]; i.e. they are becoming better at meta-learning. Such independence though can appear in conflict with the desire of universities that wish to focus on content delivery and quantitative assessment. However, Turkle and Papert [16] have argued for 'epistemological pluralism' where multiple ways of learning and knowing are valued.

A literature review by Martin *et al.* [17] deduced possible metrics of learning can be represented by a learner's competencies: generic, declarative and epistemic.

Generic competencies are expected of graduates and are linked to what Goodyear [18] calls transformative potential: willingness to learn, have new ideas, and consolidate previously studied information. This can be simplified by the question: What are your capabilities? Declarative competency is considered to be the application of knowledge in problem solving; a process sometimes referred to as the acquisition of "academic competence" [18]. This can be simplified by the question: How are you using your capabilities (what you know)? Epistemic competency can be displayed by evidence of increased flexibility in the utilization of knowledge [19] such as making connections, reflecting on what is known, and pragmatically applying theory to unique situations. This can be simplified by the question: Why are you using your capabilities?

In conclusion, meta-learning is essentially 'making sense' of one's experience of learning. Overall it was found that there has been little research on meta-learning compared to the more recognized cognitive science term of metacognition. The aim of this research therefore was to promote meta-learning with Systems Information Science students involved in collaboratively programming robots to solve specific tasks. To implement instances of meta-learning, Resnick's Creative-Thinking Model was employed: Imagine – Create - Play – Share – Reflect – Imagine [20]. To locate the research in Japan, a comparable creativity spiral by academics Mima and Yamauchi [13] and Ueda [21] called TKF (T (*Tsukutte* つくって) is Creating/Making; K (*Katatte* かたって) is Sharing/Talking; F (*Furikaeru* ふりかえる) is Reflecting/Discussing) was adopted. In addition, students' generic, declarative and epistemic competencies were then measured to determine instances of meta-learning.

2 Research Hypothesis

Hypothesis 1: Learners actively engaged in iteratively challenging robot-mediated interactive tasks develop generic, declarative and epistemic competencies.

Hypothesis 2: Increased meta-learning is associated with the development of generic, declarative and epistemic competencies.

The research was not about acquisition of particular knowledge (e.g. content) but attempts to learn more about the processes of acquiring knowledge (e.g. competencies/knowledge put into action).

3 Implementation

To implement a Design-based learning approach in a Japanese educational context, an interpretation of Mitch Resnick's Creative-Thinking Model, or Creativity Spiral, called TKF (T (*Tsukutte* つくって) is Creating/Making; K (*Katatte* かたって) is Sharing/Talking; F (*Furikaeru* ふりかえる) is Reflecting/Discussing) was utilized (see Fig. 1).

- T (*Tsukutte* つくって) is Creating/Making.
  When people use their hands and body, they can gain a deep awareness through embodiment of the artifact. The subsequent artifact creation process and/or a product can be the context for sharing (*Katatte*) and reflecting (*Furikaeru*).

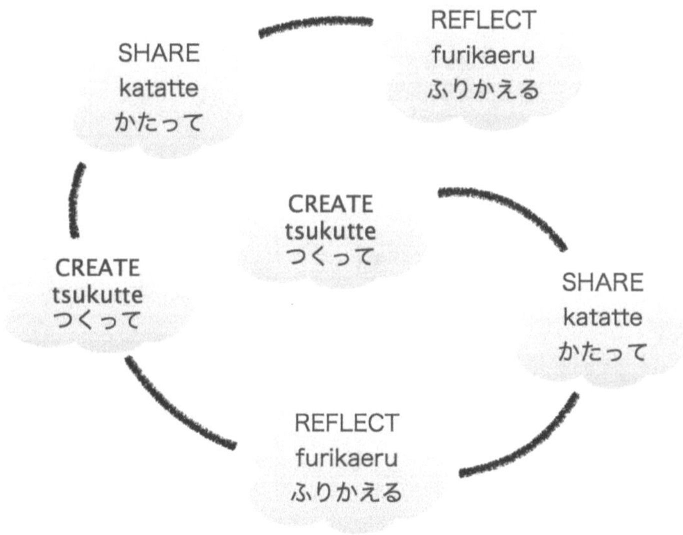

Fig. 1. TKF model.

- K (*Katatte* かたって) is Sharing/Talking.
  People can verbalize their intentions for making things. They can give significant information with actions and they become conscious of their actions.
- F (*Furikaeru* ふりかえる) is Reflecting.
  People share and discuss about their actions and there is a pressure for changing thoughts relative to previous thinking. This results in reflective thinking, and it can change their attitudes and deep realizations.

To test the efficacy of the TKF model to determine metrics of meta-learning, six Japanese male university undergraduate students studying Systems Information Science were recruited. The purposive sample was limited by the lab size and unfortunately no female students volunteered to join the project. Although considered technically literate, no student had prior experience programming robots at school or in prior after-school activities. Moreover, closed and highly defined tasks needed to be designed in order to provide the necessary comparability and empirical data to determine the success of task completion from tangible and quantifiably measured outcomes.

To satisfy these criteria, the programming of a LEGO Mindstorms EV3 robot to navigate mazes of measurable complexity was adopted [22]. LEGO Mindstorms is often thought of as simply a toy for children interested in building robots. LEGO markets Mindstorms for children aged 10 and over. But this downplays the enormous versatility LEGO Mindstorms has to offer learners of all ages. The programming of a LEGO Mindstorms robot (see Fig. 2) begins with the drag and drop graphical user interface (see Fig. 4) that enables commands to be downloaded from a computer to the 'brick' (a programmable micro-computer with a processor, Flash memory and Linux operation system). At the beginning this allows new users to appreciate the concept of procedures. Adding sensors to a robot requires learners to then consider sensor values,

Fig. 2. EV3 Mindstorms robot

variables, arrays and logic. Learners become engaged in testing and adjusting their programs in attempts to succeed in their desired outcomes. LEGO Mindstorms is not only for school children but for any aged learner starting out in programming or any STEM discipline. Research by Lui *et al.* [23] used LEGO Mindstorms with university Computer Science students to promote self-directed learning. Popelka *et al.* [24] utilized LEGO Mindstorms as a simulation of robotic systems using the programming language C#, a PID controller, Visual Studio software and MonoDevelop Framework; tools far beyond the level of a 10-year old and certainly more appropriate for university undergraduates. They concluded that, "Based on discovered facts LEGO Mindstorms can be considered for low-cost and capable kit to simulate real robotics systems" (p. 1128). Catlin *et al.* [25] adopted LEGO Mindstorms to promote Computational Thinking which involves mathematical modelling, inductive thinking and experimentation. Turner *et al.* [26] used LEGO Mindstorms as a prerequisite for teaching Java programming at a university. They focused on problem-solving and robot maze emulation. Lew *et al.* [27] used LEGO Mindstorms on an Advanced Software Engineering course utilizing the leJOS firmware replacement for Java programming. They concluded that there were sufficient technical challenges with the use of LEGO Mindstorms that they will continue to be used in this course in future semesters. To sum up this small sample of literature, due to its versatility LEGO Mindstorms is misrepresented as a simple toy and can be as powerful a robotic tool as any child, adult or Computer Science student wishes to imagine.

In this project a physical environment was set up to observe students communicating the programming of the distinct challenges set for the robot (see Figs. 2 and 3). Ten tasks were conducted once a week in a 2 h period for 10 consecutive weeks over

Fig. 3. Students programming the EV3 robot to navigate a circuit

one semester. Each task had a clear goal but the TKF process of the solutions were completely determined by the students.

1. Students confirmed the task with the instructor and one another to be absolutely sure of the task goal;
2. Students discussed, drew and planned possible solutions on paper;
3. Students divided up the workload such as robot construction and EV3 programming;
4. Students tested their robots and made required modifications to both physical robot and the EV3 program;
5. During the task the instructor observed and recorded student interactions, in addition to the EV3 Mindstorms program solutions (see Fig. 4);
6. Once complete, students completed the post-task survey and discussed their solutions, the problems encountered, and explained what they had learned (e.g. robot components such as a new sensor; EV3 programming such as use of data wires; and team communication);

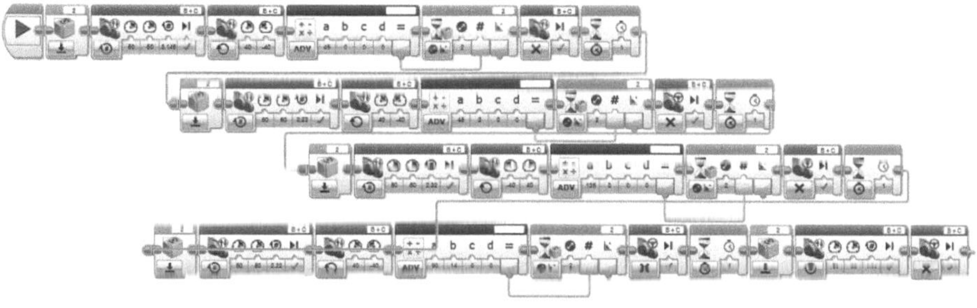

Fig. 4. An example EV3 Mindstorms program

7. Also, plenty of time was allocated for post-task reflections. It was important that the post-task surveys and discussions were not rushed.

The instructor designed ten tasks where students had to program a LEGO EV3 robot to navigate a circuit. After each task the students participated in a survey in order to collect data about their actions during the task and their reflections after the task. The survey (see Table 1) and subsequent data (see Figs. 5, 6 and 7) were organized into the TKF schema, and by competency: generic (memory, new ideas, decision), declarative (viewpoints, explain, problem) and epistemic (understand, apply, reflect) [17].

Table 1. Post-task survey

TKF and Competency statements	SA	A	D	SD
I used some experiences from previous tasks or class. (K•F) MEMORY				
I found new functions in EV3 today. (T•K) NEW IDEAS				
I had a new idea today. (T•K) NEW IDEAS				
I had to think deeply and analyze today's task. (K) UNDERSTAND				
I had to explain something to another student or my instructor. (K• F) EXPLAIN				
I had to solve a technical problem (hardware or software or circuit). (T) PROBLEM				
I implemented the EV3 program successfully. (T)				
I had fun. (F)				
I learned about different viewpoints of my colleagues VIEWPOINTS				
I can reflect on my learning REFLECT				
Feel free to write anything about today's activities.				

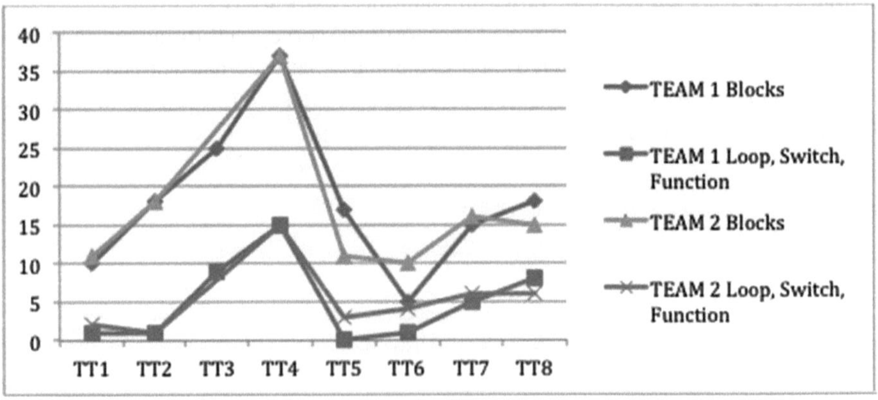

Fig. 5. Number of EV3 blocks programmed ordered by Teacher task difficulty.

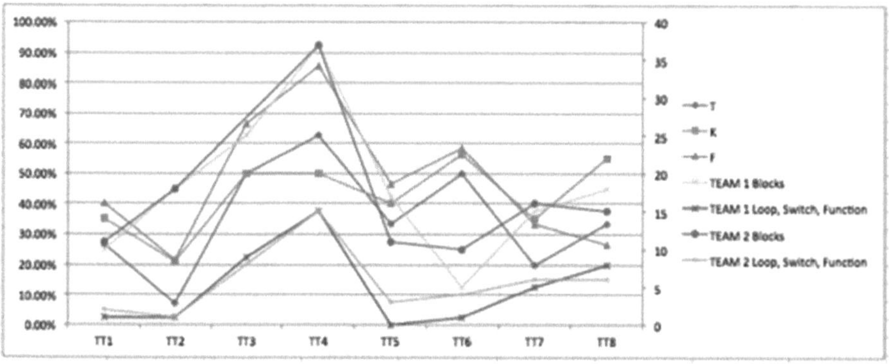

Fig. 6. Number of EV3 program blocks programmed transposed onto TKF data. (Color figure online)

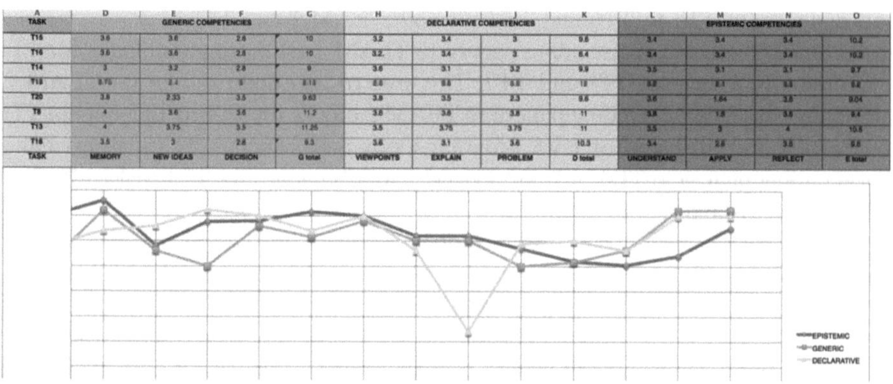

A	D	E	F	G	H	I	J	K	L	M	N	O
TASK	GENERIC COMPETENCIES				DECLARATIVE COMPETENCIES				EPISTEMIC COMPETENCIES			
T15	3.6	3.6	2.8	10	3.2	3.4	3	9.6	3.4	3.4	3.4	10.2
T16	3.6	3.6	2.8	10	3.2	3.4	3	6.4	3.4	3.4	3.4	10.2
T14	3	3.2	2.8	9	3.6	3.1	3.2	9.9	3.5	3.1	3.1	9.7
[illegible]	[illegible]	2.4	3	[illegible]	[illegible]	[illegible]	[illegible]	12	[illegible]	[illegible]	[illegible]	[illegible]
T20	3.8	2.33	3.5	9.63	3.8	3.5	2.3	9.6	3.6	1.64	3.8	9.04
T8	4	3.6	3.6	11.2	3.8	3.8	3.8	11	3.8	1.8	3.8	9.4
T13	4	3.75	3.5	11.25	3.5	3.75	3.75	11	3.5	3	4	10.5
T18	3.5	3	2.8	9.3	3.6	3.1	3.6	10.3	3.4	2.6	3.8	9.8
TASK	MEMORY	NEW IDEAS	DECISION	G total	VIEWPOINTS	EXPLAIN	PROBLEM	D total	UNDERSTAND	APPLY	REFLECT	E total

Fig. 7. Competency totals.

Once the task commenced, the instructor observed and made notes of the procedures and communication of the student participants. Photos and video captures of robot solutions were collected periodically for post-task discussions. Upon successful completion of the task, the students were asked to immediately reflect upon their experiences by answering a survey available as a Google Doc on provided iPads. The survey instrument was designed to capture TKF and competency data using a 4-point Likert scale (see Table 1). All data can then be summed appropriately and compared using the Pearson's Chi Square Test (see Sect. 4). The post-task survey and subsequent interviews were designed to elicit student thinking and post-task reflections.

An additional 10 tasks were implemented with the same participants in Semester 2, though due to later tasks resulting in multiple solutions, the focus on these latter tasks was on capturing data related to competencies.

The next section will summarize the results from the two sets of data: the TKF data and the Competency data.

4 Results and Discussion

4.1 TKF Data

It was hypothesized that Creating/Making (T) and Sharing (K) metrics can be determined by the programming of the LEGO EV3 robot undertaken by the students. First, looking at each EV3 Mindstorms task solution, the number of programmed blocks and loops and switches were totaled. Figure 5 illustrates the number of blocks per task in Task difficulty order as determined by the instructor. There were two teams of students participating in each task (Team 1 and Team 2). Looking at Fig. 5 it can be seen that even though the teams produced different programming solutions, the number of blocks and loops utilized were comparable. The EV3 program block data per task was then transposed onto the TKF data (see Fig. 6).

In Fig. 6 it can be observed that T (Creating/Making) has a corresponding pattern to TEAM 1 EV3 program blocks and TEAM 2 EV3 program blocks for TT1 to TT7. Also, T (Making) has a corresponding pattern to utilization of EV3 program loop/switches for TT1 to TT6 and TT8 for both TEAM 1 and TEAM 2.

K (Sharing) has a corresponding pattern to TEAM 1 EV3 program blocks for TT1 to TT5 and TT8, but not TT6 and TT7. This pattern was quite similar for TEAM 2. K (Sharing) has a corresponding pattern to TEAM 2 blocks for TT1 to TT5 but not TT6 to TT8. For the inclusion of EV3 program loops and switches, K (Sharing) has a corresponding pattern to TEAM 1 and TEAM 2 loop/switches for TT1 to TT5 for TT1 to TT5 and TT8, but not TT6 and TT7.

Finally, F (Reflection) has a corresponding pattern to TEAM 1 EV3 program blocks for TT1 to TT5 but not TT6 to TT8. This is quite similar to TEAM 2 where F (Reflection) has a corresponding pattern to TEAM 2 blocks for TT1 to TT5 and TT8 but not TT6 to TT7. For the inclusion of EV3 program loops and switches, F (Reflection) has a corresponding pattern to both TEAM 1 and TEAM 2 loop/switches for TT1 to TT6 but not TT7 to TT8.

To summarize, Fig. 6 illustrates that in both participant teams in this project, the EV3 programmed blocks and students' TKF data corresponded with one another. From the comparably patterned data it may be stated that '*Tsukutte* - Create/*Katatte* - Share/*Furikaeru* – Reflect' are 'potentially' valid indicators of learning, and that such an approach can be adopted by instructors not only to encourage a more participatory learning environment but also as a valid means of evaluating students' meta-learning. This motivated the research to further collect data related to specific competencies and meta-learning.

4.2 Competency Data

A further 10 tasks of increasing complexity, as determined by the Circuit Task Complexity (CTC) values [28], were undertaken by the same participants in the second semester. Competency data was collected for all 20 tasks (see Fig. 7). The Likert scores of each competency were summed for each task. The totals for Generic, Declarative and Epistemic were then correlated with Reflect values using a Pearson's Chi Square Test.

Using the iNZight statistics application [29] the totals were also subset by each Circuit Task Complexity (CTC) value. This 'three-variable' data illustrated where specific tasks (as determined by its CTC value) were located 'within' the Reflect versus Competency data (see Figs. 8, 9 and 10).

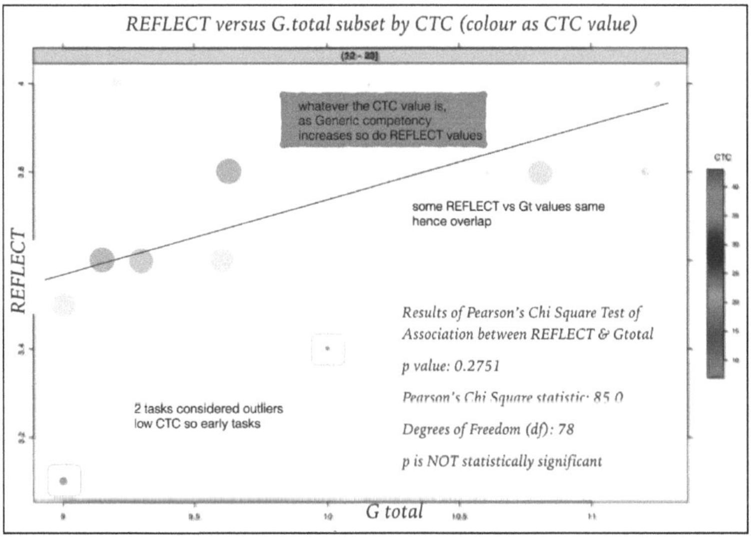

Fig. 8. Graph of Reflect versus Generic competencies (Color figure online)

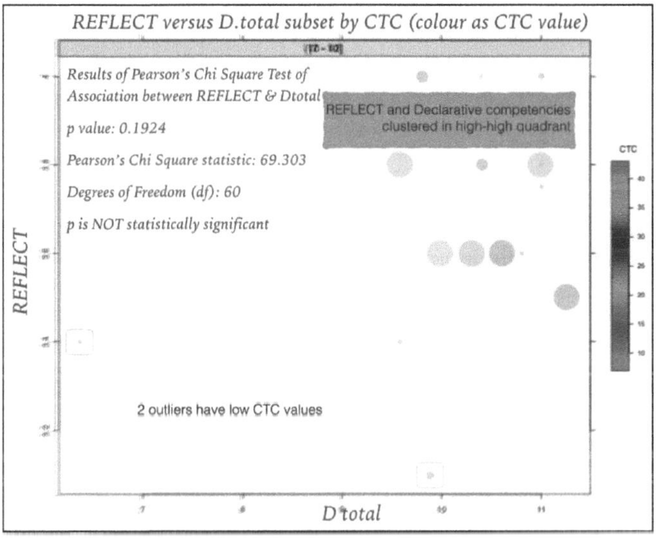

Fig. 9. Graph of Reflect versus Declarative competencies (Color figure online)

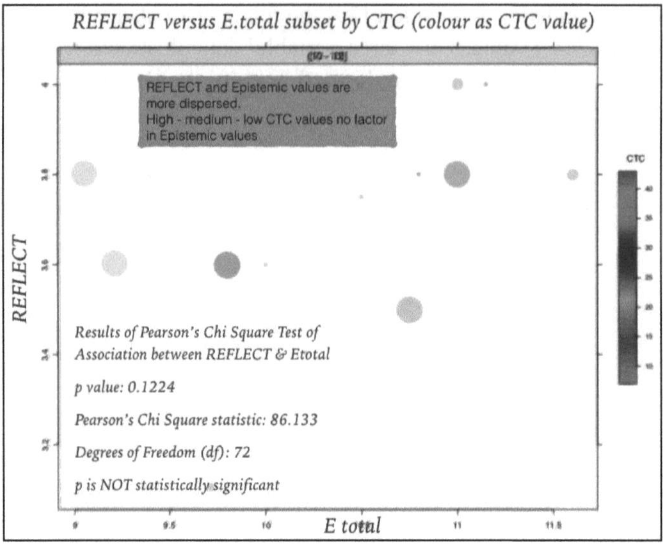

Fig. 10. Graph of Reflect versus Epistemic competencies (Color figure online)

From these graphs a number of observations can be made. It was found that irrespective of a task's complexity, as generic competency increases so do Reflect values (see Fig. 8). Declarative competency and Reflect values are clustered in the high-high quadrant which suggests that meta-learning is most prevalent when declarative competency is high (see Fig. 9). However, the data for Epistemic competency was dispersed suggesting that the value of task complexity has no impact on a student's capability to transfer his knowledge to other situations (see Fig. 10). This seems at odds with 'common sense' as it would be expected that learners who have a high meta-learning capability would be able to transfer their knowledge to unique situations. Turning to Table 2, the feedback reveals students' more pragmatic reflections and does not show any examples of students' awareness of capabilities which can be used in other situations such as in their Final Year projects or Programming courses. This may be due to their current inability to explicitly associate one learning scenario to another possible scenario in a different context. This remains a challenge to advocates of meta-learning and multi-disciplinary teaching.

4.3 Research Hypothesis Summary

4.3.1 Hypothesis 1

Learners actively engaged in iteratively challenging robot-mediated interactive tasks develop generic (G), declarative (D) and epistemic (E) competencies.

The data has revealed that generic, declarative and epistemic competencies are mostly patterned per task. Students' comments were categorized as being flexible (E), thinking differently (G), being creative (G), taking risks and being aware of taking risks (E), comparing ideas and others' points of view (D), perseverance (E). The hypothesis can be considered partially true.

Table 2. Students' post-task feedback summary

Challenges	Students' comments
Being flexible	When I saw other solutions, I felt that flexibility can be so helpful and important to make smart solutions. There are various ways to make robot turn, such as using time, sensors, number of rotations, and so on. But they can be easily affected by some conditions, like friction, structure of circuits, sensor's feeling Thinking differently, being creative, taking risks and being aware of taking risks. I tried to make several parts that were quite different from what I usually make Seeing different idea in same task was very interesting and impressive for me! This would absolutely make us more productive because the more challenges we do, the more ideas we can see, get, and make!
Comparing ideas and other points of view	Through this challenge, I talked and had communication with foreign students for the first time. Then I could see different views and ideas from them. When it comes to the solution for today's task, I got interesting idea from my partner. He thought and said that moving a robot in entire circuit to find balls can be done by moving it, like drawing smaller circles or spirals. This was quite different idea from mine. I could see another point of view
Perseverance: start again and remake	I and Keitaro mainly organized the circuit. We could do that well, but making proper one wasn't easy to do. We tried to make it according to our first plan. But we needed add some changes to move our robot smoothly. Our robot is a little bit big, so it requires, kind of, big space to go around. We measured distances to make enough spaces, made sure walls are tall enough, tried to choose proper stuffs for circuits, such as blocks, boxes, and boards. It was difficult to make a robot which attached any sensors. I may be going to remake that robot
Communication	I had to explain about our solution, what we tried to do, and functions of our robot to foreign students, not only our members. That was quite difficult for me because situations seemed to be so different. I wasn't sure whether I could tell them well. Actually I was kind of worried

4.3.2 Hypothesis 2

Increased meta-learning is associated with the development of generic, declarative and epistemic competencies.

Whatever the CTC value, as generic competency increases so do reflect values; though not statistically significant. Declarative competency and reflect values are also not statistically significant. However, with high CTC values, declarative competency and reflect values are high. Epistemic competency and reflect values are also not statistically significant. High - medium - low CTC values have no impact on epistemic competency.

Students did reflect but there was little evidence of understanding and applying new knowledge in their reflections. Therefore, the hypothesis can be considered partially true for generic and declarative competencies but not true for epistemic competency.

5 Limitations and Future Research

It is acknowledged that there are a number of limitations in this research which future iterations will attempt to overcome. More participants and Control versus Experiment groups are the most obvious but this is difficult given time for each task (120 min) and initial Mindstorms EV3 teaching time. Also, more reliable psychometrics need to be utilized. In addition, an explicit attempt of transfer should be sought by linking tasks to the university's programming, design and math curricula.

6 Conclusion

The Design-based TKF learning model has encouraged students to create physical solutions for robot related tasks, participate in the communication and sharing of their solution processes, and finally reflect upon their actions and perceived learning. Vallance *et al.* [22] hypothesized and demonstrated that if the Mindstorms EV3 program blocks represent a student's solution in solving a given task problem, then the subsequent Mindstorms EV3 program can be a proxy metric of the student's learning outcome. This paper has subsequently determined that the LEGO Mindstorms EV3 program solutions can 'potentially' be used as a metric to establish students' meta-learning as characterized by TKF. To support this supposition, the competencies of students were additionally measured. Consequently, this paper has shown that learners actively engaged in iteratively challenging robot-mediated interactive tasks can develop generic, declarative and epistemic competencies, and that a development of meta-learning can be associated with increased generic, declarative and epistemic competencies. However, the results are inconclusive and further research is, of course, recommended.

Acknowledgments. Yuta Goto for his initial research on TKF [30], and students in the iVERG lab @ FUN, Future University Hakodate, Japan.

References

1. Papert, S.: Mindstorms. Children, Computers, and Powerful Ideas. Basic Books, New York (1993)
2. Vygotsky, L.: Thought and Language. MIT Press, Cambridge (1986)
3. Dede, C.: The evolution of distance education: Emerging technologies and distributed learning. Am. J. Distance Educ. **10**(2), 4–36 (1996)
4. Cafolla, R.: The Relationship of Piagetian formal Operations and other cognitive factors to computer programming ability. Dissertations Abstr. **A47**(7), 2506 (1987)
5. Piaget, J.: Intellectual evolution from adolescence to adult. Hum. Dev. **15**, 1–12 (1972)

6. Gluga, R., Kay, J., Lister, R., Kleitman, S.: Mastering cognitive development theory in computer science education. Comput. Sci. Educ. **23**(1), 24–57 (2013)
7. Morra, S., Gobbo, C., Marini, Z., Sheese, R.: Cognitive Development: Neo-Piagetian Perspectives. Lawrence Erlbaum Assoc Inc., Abingdon (2007)
8. Lau, W.W.F., Yuen, A.H.K.: Exploring the effects of gender and learning styles on computer programming performance: implications for programming pedagogy. Br. J. Educ. Technol. **40**(4), 696–712 (2009)
9. Chen, L.: Web based learning programs: used by learners with various cognitive style. Comput. Educ. **54**(4), 1028–1035 (2010)
10. White, G., Ploeger, F.: Cognitive characteristics for learning visual basic. J. Comput. Inform. Syst. (JCIS) **44**(3), 58–66 (2004)
11. Siegmund, J., Kastner, C., Apel, S., Parnin, C., Bethmann, A., Leich, T., Saake, G., Brechmann, A.: Understanding Understanding Source Code with Functional Magnetic Resonance Imaging, ICSE 2014, May 31–June 7, Hyderabad, India (2014)
12. Katz, S., Albritton, D., Aronis, J., Wilson, C., Soffa, M.L.: Gender, achievement, and persistence in an undergraduate computer science program. Database Adv. Inform. Syst. **37** (4), 42–57 (2006)
13. Mima, N., Yamauchi, Y.: Design for Learning Environments: Space, Activity and Community. University of Tokyo Press, Tokyo (2005)
14. Honey, M., Kanter, D.E.: Design, Make, Play: Growing the Next Generation of STEM Innovators. Routledge, New York (2013)
15. Hase, S.: Learner defined curriculum: heutagogy and action learning in vocational training. Southern Institute of Technology Journal of Applied Research. http://sitjar.sit.ac.nz/SITJAR/Special. Accessed 27 Aug 2014
16. Turkle, S., Papert, S.: Epistemological pluralism and the revaluation of the concrete. In: Harel, I., Papert, S. (eds.) Constructionism, pp. 161–191. Ablex Publishing, Norwood (1991)
17. Martin, S., Vallance, M.: The impact of synchronous inter-networked teacher training in Information and Communication Technology integration. Comput. Educ. **51**, 34–53 (2008)
18. Goodyear, P.: Psychological foundations for networked learning. In: Steeples, C., Jones, C. (eds.) Networked Learning: Perspectives and Issues. Springer Verlag, London (2001)
19. Morrison, D., Collins, A.: Epistemic fluency and constructivist learning environments. In: Wilson, B.G. (ed.) Constructivist learning environments: Case studies in instructional design, pp. 107–119. Educational Technology Publications, Englewood Cliffs (1996)
20. Resnick, M.: All I Really Need to Know (About Creative Thinking) I Learned (By Studying How Children Learn) in Kindergarten. In: ACM Creativity & Cognition Conference, Washington DC (2007)
21. Ueda, N.: ワークショップ—新しい学びと創造の場 (Workshop – new learning and creation of place). Iwanami Shoten, Japan (2011)
22. Vallance, M., Naamani, C., Thomas, M., Thomas, J.: Applied information science research in a virtual world simulation to support robot mediated interaction following the fukushima nuclear disaster. Commun. Inform. Sci. Manage. Eng. (CISME) **3**(5), 222–232 (2013)
23. Lui, A.K., Ng, S.C., Cheung, H.Y., Gurung, P.: Facilitating independent leaning with LEGO Mindstorms robots. ACM Inroads **1**(4), 49–53 (2010)
24. Popelka, M., Nožička, J.: Lego mindstorms as a simulation of robotic systems. Int. J. Comput. Control Quantum Inform. Eng. **8**(7) (2014)
25. Catlin, D., Blamires, M.: The principles of educational robotic applications (ERA). In Constructionism 2010: Constructionist Approaches to Creative Learning, Thinking and Education: Lessons for the 21st Century, Proceedings for Constructionism 2010: The 12th EuroLogo Conference, Paris (2010)

26. Turner, S.J., Hill, G.: Robotics within the teaching of problem-solving. ITALICS Innov. Teach. Learn. Inform. Comput. Sci. **7**(108), 119 (2008)
27. Lew, M.W., Horton, T.B., Sherriff, M.S.: Using LEGO MINDSTORMS NXT and LEJOS in an advanced software engineering course. In: 23rd IEEE Conference on Software Engineering Education and Training (CSEE&T), Pittsburgh, pp. 121–128 (2010)
28. Vallance, M., Martin, S., Naamani, C.: A situation that we had never imagined: post-Fukushima virtual collaborations for determining robot task metrics. Int. J. Learn. Technol. **10**(1), 30–49 (2015)
29. iNZight. https://www.stat.auckland.ac.nz/~wild/iNZight/index.php
30. Vallance, M., Goto, Y.: Learning by TKF to promote computational participation in Japanese education. In: Proceedings of 43rd International Conference on Engineering Pedagogy, 20–24 September, Florence, Italy (2015)

Three Curriculum Maturing Cycles in Academic Curriculum Management Systems

Kai Pata[1(✉)], Kairit Tammets[1], Vladimir Tomberg[1], Mohammad Al-Smadi[2], and Mart Laanpere[1]

[1] School for Digital Technology, Narva Road 25, 10120 Tallinn, Estonia
{kpata,kairit.tammets,vtomberg,martl}@tlu.ee
[2] Computer Science Department, Jordan University of Science and Technology, P.O.Box: 3030, Irbid 22110, Jordan
maalsmadi9@just.edu.jo

Abstract. The top-to-down and bottom-to-up processes in the semantic competence management of curriculum development in higher education context were investigated based on different semantic systems for curriculum management. As a result the paper proposes the framework and the three interrelated curriculum maturing cycles of (i) standards maturing, (ii) curriculum maturing and (iii) personal competence maturing in semantic systems for academic organizations.

Keywords: Curriculum management · Academic systems · Curriculum maturing

1 Introduction

Curriculum design and management is one of the most challenging and least automated areas in education where semantic technologies seem to have unrealized potential because they enable encoding meanings and defining relationships between resources with machine-readable ontologies (Brewster and O'Hara, 2007). Recently, semantic technologies play a salient role in learning systems (Devedzic, 2006; Bittencourt et al., 2009) to define, share, and maintain common and reusable understanding of leaning domains (Brewster and O'Hara, 2004), to provide easy-access and retrieval of learning resources (Devedzic, 2006; Lee et al., 2008), and facilitating the modeling of learning objectives, competences, and appropriate assessment methods (Friedler and Shneiderman, 2008; He et al., 2009). However, each example from research with semantic technologies in curriculum management processes provides only partial views to the curriculum management possibilities and there is the need for mapping these studies to provide the generalized framework.

Several authors (Ronchetti and Santi, 2007; Dexter and Davies, 2009; Paquette, 2007; Vaquero et al. 2009; Barrera et al., 2012; Lu, 2009; Karunananda, et al., 2012; Cameron and Brickett, 2012; Spreckelsen, et al., 2013; Pata, et al., 2013) have investigated the possibilities of semantic technologies in curriculum design, management and evaluation highlighting the problems like updating and evolving the curricula, addressing curricula match with standards, working with multiple partially

L. Uden et al. (Eds.): LTEC 2016, CCIS 620, pp. 289–300, 2016.
DOI: 10.1007/978-3-319-42147-6_24

overlapping ontologies and the collaborative semantic curriculum maintenance, achieving the linkages of competences with resources, allowing collaboration in curriculum development, and the reuse of other curricula in this process, getting overviews of the curricula for evaluation purposes or for planning personalized learning tracks based on curricula, handling the self-directed learning.

In this paper we propose the general framework for semantic curriculum management systems that addresses the gap of ontology-based mapping of top-to-down and bottom-up processes in curriculum development and management. The article is organized as follows: In Sect. 2, we present the background of the curriculum development in higher education. Section 3 introduces briefly the methodology. In Sect. 4, based on the analysis of existing systems' and generalizations we propose the framework. In Sect. 5 we propose the three interrelated maturing processes in the semantic curriculum management systems in academic organizations.

2 Competence Management in Curriculum Development

2.1 Curriculum Development Concepts

In June 1999, representatives of the Ministers of Education of 29 European countries convened in Bologna, Italy, to formulate the Bologna Declaration, which aimed at establishing a common European Higher Education Area (EHEA) (Kennedy, Hyland and Ryan, 2006). The Bologna process spells out a number of 'action lines' in which learning outcomes play an important role (Adam, 2006). One of the decisions was that education in higher education institutions throughout the EHEA should be based on the concept of learning outcomes, and that curricula should be redesigned to reflect this. *Learning outcome* is an expression of what a student will demonstrate on the successful completion of a course. Learning outcomes are related to the level of the learning; indicate the intended gain in knowledge and skills that a typical student will achieve and should be capable of being assessed. Outcomes tend to be formulated as competences (Paquette, 2007; Dexter and Davies, 2009; Cameron and Brickett, 2012). Sampson and Fytros (2008) define *competences* as personal characteristics (e.g. skills, knowledge, attitudes) that an individual possesses or needs to acquire, in order to perform an activity within a specific context, whereas performance may range from the basic level of proficiency to the highest levels of excellence. Paquette (2007) defines competencies as statements that link together skills and attitudes to knowledge required from a group of persons and more generally, from resources. Thus he suggests that competences serve to annotate resources, human as well as media resources, giving them semantic meaning as to the knowledge and skills they own or contain. *Learning activities* are activities performed to achieve learning outcomes. *Assessment methods* are used for measuring learning outcomes. *Learning resources* are various resources that are used for developing the competences and knowledge in the domain.

Curriculum is made up of a number of parts, what in general fall under the broad headings of content, learning experiences, objectives and assessment (van der Horst and McDonald, 1999). Broader concept of curriculum defines it as a plan for learning (Child, 2004) that specifies how learning takes place, considers central rationale, the aims and objectives, content, organization, and evaluation of learning (Taba, 1962). It may contain a sophisticated blend of educational strategies, course content, learning outcomes, educational experiences, assessment, the educational environment and the individual students' learning style, personal timetable and the program of work (Walker, 2003). The learning outcomes defined as competences are the foundation for decisions about the curriculum, instruction, assessment, staff development and so on. *Course* is a subset of a program of study (equivalent to a module or unit of study) within a curriculum. Typically, course design starts with the definitions of the competences that must be met at the end of the course.

Nationally outcomes based education (OBE) has been implemented through the requirements in the *National Higher Education Standards*. These standards are obligatory when designing curricula and courses in higher education institutions, and are used in the curriculum evaluation process. Van der Horst and McDonald (1999) noted that one of the problems of OBE lies in the teachers' ability to translate the imprecisely worded outcomes into their teaching and learning practice. Besides the learning outcomes from National Standards, *competence models* for certain work domain and the *domain ontologies* influence curriculum development. Paquette (2007) suggests that semantic indexing of educational resources, actors and activities should be the combination between domain ontologies and competence ontologies that consider mastery level as prerequisites.

Often the curriculum design is hindered by the lack of shared vocabulary among different stakeholders (such as curriculum board and the teachers who prepare the courses) to communicate about the curriculum. Such shared vocabularies relate with *ontologies* of domain-related concepts, teaching-related concepts (learning activities, assessment methods) and learning resources, but rather represent the *user-generated ontologies*.

2.2 Two Processes in Curriculum Development

Curriculum is not something static, and permanent change is one of its key features. Lu (2009) has detected that it is not easy to keep track of the curriculum evolution – *the* information of the curriculum design may get lost when interpreted by different stakeholders. Developing a university curriculum and keeping it up to date is guided by two counter-directional processes:

I. The stabilizing process: Mapping the curriculum goals and the course goals to the existing standards in certain domains.

Hsiao et al. (2001) have suggested three stages to develop a practical competency oriented curriculum: the first is the planning stage; the second is designing stage and the third stage is to choose the representative subjects in this program, to develop the teaching materials and to proceed with the experimental instructions. In the first stage the curriculum board discusses and analyzes, which courses should be taught and what competences required for labor market. In the next stage the development and design of the curriculum takes place. Informed and intentional curriculum design is guided by a vision, what considers university and national strategic plans, policies, priorities and quality processes, external accreditation processes and domain knowledge and competences.

The national and international competence models in this domain area serve as the main guiding factors in the goal development, enabling standardization of learning goals, and the further evaluation of curricula, based on these standards.

The head of the curriculum and the curriculum board should define overall goals and aims for the curriculum, stating specific measurable knowledge, skill/performance, attitude, and process objectives for it, and defining how these goals might be achieved in different course modules. Learning goals and outputs for every course and subject should be compatible with those criteria but would be developed by teachers as the course developers.

II. The change process: Advancing the existing competence conceptualizations and creating new competences.

Boud (2003) points out that it's the courses not the narrow top-to-down operational competency-based approach that is guided only by curriculum learning outcomes that gives an educational approach to the curriculum. Furedi (2004) argues that curriculum objectives should be flexible enough to allow 'individual scholars to pursue their passionate interests' within the curriculum objectives, however, very few course developers examine the full curriculum document or take guidance from national standards (Tammets and Pata, 2013).

If the curriculum board would be willing to bring in the change factor into the curriculum development, the course developers need to be provided with the freedom creating new learning outcomes for course programs and proposing these to be integrated to the curriculum learning outcomes. Thus, after the curriculum goals have been defined at competence level, the initiative should be given to the course developers who must take responsibility for developing the particular course goals.

Roche (2001) have also indicated that collaboration between the curriculum designers and academics in curriculum development process is an efficient strategy that promotes creating curriculum ownership (Dexter and Davies, 2009; Spreckelsen et al., 2013). Assuming that each course developer is an expert in this domain, and is involved into the international research and development besides teaching, would guarantee that they could embed this front-line knowledge and expertise into their courses. It is highly unlikely that the existing competence descriptions, derived from the normative standards into the curriculum would cover all the required competences needed at the courses. The course developers must define new learning goals for their courses that do not appear in competence standards, and backward mapping to the curriculum and standard must be conducted. Zervas and Sampson (2007) have described that both the available and required competences for a certain role, job or function should be kept updated in formal standards. In the curriculum development process, it means that mapping new emerging competences, searching, mapping and filtering them, is needed. The new learner-directed approach to curricula also suggests considering and integrating learner-defined outcomes to the course outcomes, that proposes yet another bottom-up approach to curriculum development.

3 Methodology

Angelov et al. (2012) propose using publications of existing systems as the input for developing the reference framework, which we followed in this paper. We compared the relationships at the activity-, competences-, and competence *management* ontologies from different research papers and mapped as the final result as the concept map (see Sect. 4.1). We iteratively analyzed several studies (Ronchetti and Santi, 2007; Dexter and Davies, 2009; Paquette, 2007; Vaquero et al., 2009; Barrera et al., 2012; Lu, 2009; Karunananda et al., 2012; Cameron and Brickett, 2012; Spreckelsen et al., 2013) that support managing curricula using the semantic approach. From this literature review we summarized the framework elements: users, assets and processes and their interrelations (see Sect. 4.3).

4 Results

4.1 The Conceptual Framework for Semantic Curriculum Management Systems

The relationships at the activity-, competences-, and competence management ontologies from IntelLEO ontology framework (IntelLEO, 2011), the competency definition model (Paquette, 2007), the concept map of curriculum evolution (Lu, 2009), the model of tagging competencies (Dexter and Davies, 2009) and the set of ontologies related with competence management (Vaquero et al., 2009) were compared and complemented for mapping the semantic curriculum management concepts (Fig. 1).

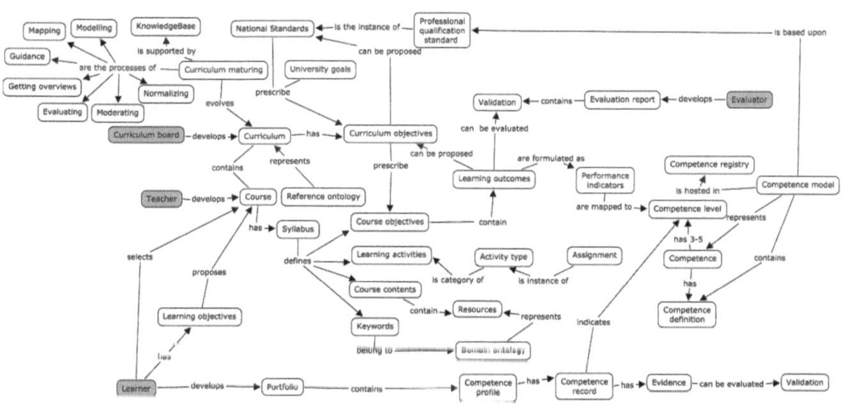

Fig. 1. Conceptual model for semantic curriculum management

4.2 Overview of the Existing Semantic Curriculum Management Systems

We *summarize* in this chapter the findings from the papers about the design of curriculum management systems using the vocabulary from Fig. 1.

Three aspects may be summarized based on the system examples:

The targets for semantic curriculum management tools are mainly academic staff – standard and curriculum managers – the boards, teachers as course designers, the evaluators of the curricula. Few studies (Dexter and Davies, 2009; Cameron and Brickett, 2012) suggest that the users for new type of curriculum development tools may target also self-directed learners and may be helping them to search across the curriculum, providing them with the enacted curriculum output in their portfolios.

The semantic curriculum management tools are mainly meant for *Mapping*, *Modeling*, *Evaluating* and *Getting Overview* of curriculum or its modules, courses or resources based on competences, learning activities or assessment methods. *Moderating*, *Normalizing* and semantic *Guiding* options of the curriculum are less frequent in the systems (see for more details in the chapter below). Most of the tools focus on managing the curriculum from its narrower perspective (managing curriculum competences). Few systems support also focusing on curriculum content and learning experiences, and conceptualize learning program development as an assembly-and-coordination system, using competencies to define the structure, learning cases and the resources of the program (Ronchetti and Santi, 2007; Dexter and Davies, 2009; Paquette, 2007). Some systems target rather the courses (Vaquero et al., 2009).

The ontology support is provided for the following purposes: *domain ontologies* catch the central concepts and relations of a domain and have been used for mapping courses and resources from the curriculum (Ronchetti and Santi, 2007; Dexter and Davies, 2009; Cameron and Brickett, 2012; Spreckelsen et al., 2013); *competence models* may serve as templates or cases for modeling new curricula (Paquette, 2007; Vaquero et al., 2009; Barrera et al., 2012; Karunananda et al., 2012; Pata et al., 2013); *reference ontologies* or example *curricula as ontologies* for the curriculum have been used for managing learning outcomes (Karunananda et al., 2012; Spreckelsen et al., 2013), or dealing with curriculum management aspects and phases (Lu, 2009).

4.3 The Framework Elements for Curriculum Management Systems

For developing reference frameworks three dimensions should be mapped (Angelov et al., 2012): (i) *Goals* has the sub-dimension *Why*; (ii) *Context* has the sub-dimensions of *Where*, *Who* and *When*, and (iii) *Design* has the sub-dimensions *How* and *What*.

In our study we generated and generalized the framework based on the system examples (Paquette, 2007; Vaquero et al., 2009; Dexter and Davies, 2009; Ronchetti and Santi, 2007; Karunananda et al., 2012; Lu, 2009; Cameron and Brickett, 2012; Spreckelsen et al., 2013; Pata et al., 2013) summarized in Sect. 4.2. The concrete examples from systems to illustrate the framework elements have not been provided due to lack of space, but overview of these systems may be found in (Pata et al., 2013).

Goals

Why? Designing semantic curriculum management systems has the following goals: (i) Managing curriculum and course development (to address coherence within the curriculum courses, to maintain traceability of curriculum linkages with resources for planning and updating it, to address coherence within the course competences, activities and resources, to manage and update case-based activities and resources dynamically across the curriculum); (ii) Managing curriculum and standard evolution (using standards such as competence models, domain ontologies and similar curricula as reference ontologies for modeling the curriculum and evolving the standards); (iii) Managing internal and external evaluation of curricula based on academic analytics and getting overviews; (iv) Managing shared vocabulary development, collaboration and "ownership taking" in curriculum development; (v) Managing student-centered approach to learning with personal portfolios in the curriculum development (to use the curriculum as the "underground map" for planning learning for competences, finding learning resources for personalized learning experiences, proposing learner's expected learning outcomes, activities and resources to the courses and the curriculum).

Context

Where? The usage contexts are: (i) Standards and curriculum maturing: Top-to-down and bottom to up semantic curriculum development and evaluation processes; (ii) Semantic resource provision for curriculum management; (iii) Personal competence maturing: Managing student-centered approach to learning with semantic curriculum management tools.

Who? The users of the systems are: *curriculum/standards managing boards, course developers (teacher), curriculum evaluators, students.*

When? Standards maturing and curriculum/course maturing cycles may take several years or are conducted annually.

Design

What? The main assets according to concept map (see (Fig. 1) are: (i) Curricula/Courses/Resources/Portfolios; (ii) Competence models/Domain ontologies/ Reference ontologies; (iii) Competences/Activities/Assessment/.

How? The main curriculum maturing processes are *modeling, mapping, evaluating, moderating, normalizing, guiding, getting overviews* and using the *knowledge base.*

Modeling is a process denoting the development of the schematic description of a system, theory, or phenomenon that accounts for its known or inferred properties and may be used for further study of its characteristics. All the aforementioned assets can be modeled. The variants of *Modeling* are developing the model from scratch and modifying the existing models. *Modeling* is based on the idea that user-communities develop and generally *Mature* shared knowledge structures. *Modeling* is described by the following set of processes for developing/modifying the model elements (model components, relationships, attributes and values): (i) Add new element (component/ relationship/attribute/value); (ii) Add new sub-element; (iii) Remove selected element; (iv) Compose the hierarchy of components; (v) Group the components; (vi) Add annotation to the component; (vii) Add/modify the description to the component; (viii) Add roles (who can use, whom it concerns) for the component; (ix) Form user-community based on grouping (e.g. group of curricula, curriculum, module);

(x) Add context to the component; (xi) Add prerequisites to the component; (xii) Add priorities to the component; (xiii) Add incentives to the component.

Mapping is a process denoting the activities to adapt or suit the models so that a balanced or harmonious result is achieved; cause to correspond, coupling. *Mapping* may result in discovering complete match, partial match, mis-match between assets. *Mapping* can happen (i) between similar components across systems or (ii) purposefully related components within a system (such as learning outcomes – activities/assignments – assessment). *Mapping* is described by the following set of processes: (i) Acquiring model components from another model into a temporal store; (ii) Accepting model components from another model; (iii) Proposing model components to another model; (iv) Mapping the extent of match of the component name between models (uni- or bidirectional); (v) Mapping the extent of match of the component description between models (uni- or bidirectional); (vi) Mapping the extent of match of prerequisites between models (uni- or bidirectional); (vii) Mapping the extent of match of annotations (tags) between models (uni- or bidirectional); (viii) Adding comments about acquired/proposed model component; (ix) Sharing comments about acquired/proposed model component (across systems, within a system).

Evaluating is considered in the reference framework as a process that is supported especially by *Mapping*, *Getting overviews* and *Guiding*. It comprises: (i) Formative evaluation of curricula or courses; (ii) Summative evaluation (accreditation); (iii) Assessment of students' competences (or learning outcomes).

Moderating is used while *re-Modeling* the assets and involves processes done among different stakeholders in order to establish the common ground about the state of the new normative of an asset: (i) Negotiating about structuring, sequencing, grouping, describing and annotating components (*re-Modeling*); (ii) Negotiating about combining components to extend or merge different models (*Mapping*).

Normalizing is a process for bringing the assets to the normative condition and accepting the asset.

Guiding is a process of providing support about the assets and supporting collaboration on curriculum management. In this reference framework *Guiding* is constrained to the *Knowledge base* provided support. *Guidance* is based on the idea of semantic and user-community developed ontologies that can best provide guidance for each community member in curriculum management activities. The usage of such knowledge structures for guidance-provision is threefold – (i) The *Guidance* can provide semantic support for *Modeling* and *Moderating* as it helps to discover the relevant or related items (such as competences, activities, assessment, resources); (ii) the *Guidance* that provides support for *Mapping* and *Evaluating* can use *Overviews* in order to see the matches between similar components in standards, curriculum and courses or (iii) the *Guidance* for *Mapping* and *Evaluations* can use *Overviews* to see the purposefully related components within a system (such as mapping competences – activities – assessment – resources in the courses or across the curriculum).

Guiding is described by the following set of processes: (i) Provision of semantic guidance about single model components; (ii) Provision of guidance in the form of analytical model *Overviews* about mutually related model components (mapping data with standards, mapping data within a course).

Getting overviews is a process by which analytical overviews about the assets are generated and visualized for *Mapping* or *Evaluating* the curriculum, its modules or the course, for self-diagnosing or tracking the learning paths, for tracking the topics or resources etc.

Getting overviews is described by the following set of processes: (i) Collecting automatically data about *Modeling*, *Mapping*, *Moderating* and *Guidance* into the *Knowledge base;* (ii) Sorting data by group (such as group of curricula, curriculum, course module, topic, competence) for *Modeling*, *Evaluation* and *Moderating*; (iii) Sorting data hierarchically for *Modeling, Evaluation* and *Moderating*; (iv) Comparing two time-related sets of model components for *Evaluation*; (v) Comparing the match between two models from different systems for *Evaluation*; (vi) Estimating the coverage of models based on data (how courses cover the curriculum, a coverage between the set of actual and target competences etc.) for *Evaluation*; (vii) Visualizing *Overviews* (quick overviews, detailed overviews): e.g. drill-down the hierarchies; drill-down the charts (pie, bar, stacked columns), grids; (viii) Storing the *Overviews* for later usage in *Modeling* and *Moderating*.

Knowledge base tackles the semantic curriculum management based on the aforementioned reference framework components. *Maturing* comprises all the processes related to the evolvement of assets toward or reaching full development. *Maturing* concept relates with all the assets (models) described above. *Maturing* can be described in terms of the changes in model elements within the Knowledge base. *Maturing* is related with time and user interaction. *Maturing* happens as a result of input from *Modeling*, *Mapping, Evaluation, Moderating* and *Guiding*. *Maturing* can be detected by *Getting overviews* of the *Normalized* assets. Results of *Maturing* are the key assets used for processing *Guiding*.

5 Discussion: Three Maturing Cycles in Semantic Curriculum Management Systems

Finally, we used the concepts in modeling the curriculum maturing cycles (Fig. 2). The semantic curriculum management systems can be applied for Standards Maturing (National level), Curriculum Maturing (University Level), and Personal Competence Maturing (Learner level). Figure 2 illustrates the cycles of maturing in semantic curriculum management.

The ontological approach represented by the knowledge bases in the Fig. 2 enables stakeholders to manage the curriculum as follows:

(i) **Standards maturing** is an (inter)national level cycle that gets feedback through the loops of Curriculum maturing and Personal competence maturing. The *Mapping* of standards to the evaluated curricula enables to discover mismatch between the bottom-up grown needs and the existing Standard version. The curricula may also directly propose certain changes to the Standard during *Mapping*. Both activities bring the Standard to the *reModeling* state, which requires support from the *Knowledge base* – new contributions are proposed and *Guidance* may be received based on *Overviews* of academic analytics

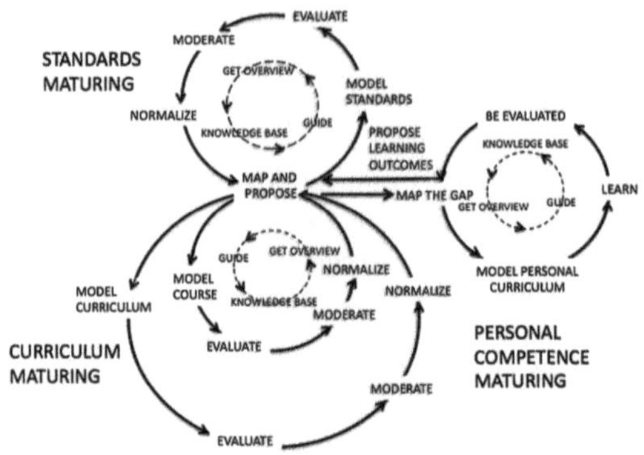

Fig. 2. Three maturing cycles in semantic curriculum management

in this system. Finally after *Evaluations*, and *Moderations* the new matured version of the Standard is *Normalized* and made accessible for curriculum developers.

(ii) **Curriculum maturing** is an annual cycle that starts from accessing the normalized set of National Standards (such as professional qualifications, nationally expected outcomes etc.) which prescribe for curricula certain norms. National Standards are *Mapped* to the University Standards and to the curricula. In the curriculum *Mapping* phase the bottom-up propositions can be made to the National Standards based on normalized Curricula. *Mapping* process takes the previous normalized curriculum to the *reModeling* state, and is supported by the university *Knowledge base* that collects data about the domain models, reference ontologies and domain ontologies, composes *Overviews* based on academic analytics, and provides semantic recommendations' in terms of *Guidance* to the curriculum board. The *Overviews* enable the curriculum board to internally evaluate the implemented curriculum or allow the external evaluators estimating the match between the curriculum and the National Standards as part of the curriculum accreditation. *Moderation* of the curriculum comprises negotiations among the curriculum board members and the evaluators about how to change the curriculum as a result of *Evaluation* findings. The curriculum is finally *Normalized* and proposed for the Course development.

The Course development targets the following types of *Mapping*: *Mapping* course learning outcomes to the curriculum learning outcomes; *Mapping* the learning outcomes, -activities and assessment within the course; *Mapping* the learning outcomes and -resources; and *Mapping* the personal learning outcomes of students to the course learning outcomes. The Course maturing gets input from the Personal Competence maturing cycle. The courses are annually mapped and remodeled, which is also supported by the university *Knowledge base.* The course developers can use *Overviews* and contribute and get semantic *Guidance* for *Modeling*, *Mapping*, *Evaluating* and *Moderating* the courses. The normalized courses are stored into the knowledge base and used for *Getting overview* of the curriculum in the curriculum *Evaluation* phase. The data from normalized courses are also used in the *Mapping* phase to propose missing learning outcomes to the curriculum.

(iii) **The Personal competence maturing cycle** enables students to plan learning in a self-regulated way – using the personal portfolio they can propose their personal learning outcomes, map their knowledge gap, identify the courses that they plan to attend, model the personal curriculum, collect evidences of their learning while following the curriculum, and be evaluated based on these evidences. The feedback about learning analytics may be collected as well and used for improving the courses. The personal competence maturing enables students to contribute to and get guidance based on academic analytics from the knowledge base. Personal competence maturing cycle enable learners to maintain their social identity and to seek support from others in their networks as well as form communities of practice.

The *Map* and *Response* process placed in the heart of our framework is the main process that bridges the gap between the top-down (driven by inter/national standards and communities) and the bottom-up (driven by learners and teachers) approaches. Using the knowledge bases on the three levels to maintain a common understanding and alignment among stakeholders, it provides easy to access knowledge, and feeds the *Guide* processes through overviews based on learning, academic and social analytics.

References

Adam, S.: An introduction to learning outcomes. In: Froment, E., Kohler, J., Purser, L., Wilson, L. (eds.) EUA Bologna Handbook. Raabe, Berlin (2006)

Angelov, S., Grefen, P., Greefhorst, D.: A framework for analysis and design of software reference architectures. Inf. Softw. Technol. **54**, 417–431 (2012)

Barrera, M., Montaño, N., Ramos, E.: An Ontological approach to support design competency-based curriculum. In: 2012 XXXVIII Conferencia Latinoamericana. En Informatica (CLEI), 1–5 Oct 2012, pp. 1–6 (2012)

Bittencourt, I., Costa, E., Silva, M., Soares, E.: A computational model for developing semantic web-based educational systems. Knowl. Based Syst. **22**, 302–315 (2009)

Boud, D.: Creating a work-based curriculum. In: Boud, D., Solomon, N. (eds.) Work-Based Learning: A New Higher Education?. SRHE and Open University Press, Buckingham (2003)

Brewster, C., O'Hara, K.: Knowledge representation with ontologies: the present and future. IEEE Intell. Syst. **19**, 72–81 (2004)

Brewster, C., O'Hara, K.: Knowledge representation with ontologies: Present challenges-future possibilities. Int. J. Human Comput. Stud. **65**, 563–568 (2007)

Cameron, I., Brickett, G.: A curriculum design, modelling and visualization environment. In: Proceedings of the 2012 AAEE Conference, Melbourne, Victoria (2012)

Child, D.: Psychology and the Teacher, 7th edn. Continuum, Suffolk (2004)

Devedzic, V.: Semantic Web and Education. Springer, Heidelberg (2006)

Dexter, H., Davies, I.: An ontology-based curriculum knowledgebase for managing complexity and change. In: Ninth IEEE International Conference on Advanced Learning Technologies (2009)

Friedler, S.A., Shneiderman, B.: Enabling teachers to explore grade patterns to identify individual needs and promote fairer student assessment. Comput. Educ. **51**, 1467–1485 (2008)

Furedi, F.: Where have all the Intellectuals Gone: Confronting 21st Century Philistinism. Continuum International Publishing, Suffolk (2004)

He, Y., Hiu, S., Quan, T.: Automatic summary assessment for intelligent tutoring systems. Comput. Educ. **53**, 890–899 (2009)

Hsiao, H.C., Chen, C.S., Huang, K.K.: Practice based curriculum development for technical institute. In: School International Conference on Information Technology Based Higher Education and Training, Kumamoto. Japan, pp. 451–457 (2001)

IntelLEO project's ontology framework (2011). http://intelleo.eu/index.php?id=183

Karunananda, A.S., Rajakaruna, G.M., Jayalal, S.: Using ontology for curriculum design and revision. In: Advances in ICT for Emerging Regions (ICTer) 2012, pp. 137–144 (2012)

Kennedy, D., Hyland, A., Ryan, N.: Writing and Using Learning Outcomes: A Practical Guide. In: Bologna Handbook C 3.4-1 (2006). http://www.bologna.msmt.cz/files/learning-outcomes.pdf

Lee, M., Tsai, K.H., Wang, T.I.: A practical ontology query expansion algorithm for semantic-aware learning objects retrieval. Comput. Educ. **50**, 1240–1257 (2008)

Lu, W.: Ontology-aware course management for curriculum evolution process in higher education. In: VERITE 13 March 2009 (2009)

Paquette, G.: An ontology and a software framework for competency modeling and management. Educ. Technol. Soc. **10**(3), 1–21 (2007)

Pata, K., Tammets, K., Laanpere, M., Tomberg, V.: Design principles for competence management in curriculum development. In: Hernández-Leo, D., Ley, T., Klamma, R., Harrer, A. (eds.) EC-TEL 2013. LNCS, vol. 8095, pp. 260–273. Springer, Heidelberg (2013)

Roche, V.: Professional development models and transformative change: a case study of indicators of effective practice in higher education. Int. J. Acad. Dev. **6**(2), 120–129 (2001)

Ronchetti, M., Santi, J.: Curriculum Management and Review: an ontology-based solution. Technical report # DIT-07-021 (2007)

Sampson, D., Fytros, D.: Competence models in technology-enhanced competence-based learning. In: Adelsberger, H.H., Kinshuk, J., Pawlowski, M., Sampson, D. (eds.) International Handbook on Information Technologies for Education and Training, 2nd edn. Springer, Heidelberg (2008)

Spreckelsen, C., Finsterer, S., Cremer, J., Schenkat, H.: Can social semantic web techniques foster collaborative curriculum mapping in medicine? J. Med Internet Res. **15**(8), e169 (2013)

Taba, H.: Curriculum Development: Theory and Practice. Harcourt, Brace & World, New York (1962)

Tammets, K., Pata, K.: The trends and problems of planning outcome-based courses in elearning. In: Saar, E., Mõttus, R., Bern, E. (eds.) Higher Education at a Crossroad: The Case of Estonia, pp. 281–301. Peter Lang Publishers House (2013)

van der Horst, H., McDonald, R.: Outcomes Based Education: A Teacher's Manual. Kagisto Education Publishers, Cape Town (1999)

Vaquero, J., Toro, C., Martín, J., Aregita, A.: Semantic enhancement of the course curriculum design process. In: Velásquez, J.D., Ríos, S.A., Howlett, R.J., Jain, L.C. (eds.) KES 2009, Part I. LNCS, vol. 5711, pp. 269–276. Springer, Heidelberg (2009)

Walker, D.F.: Fundamentals of Curriculum: Passion and Professionalism. Lawrence Erlbaum Associates, Mahjah (2003)

Zervas, P., Sampson D.: The TEN competence observatory: an enabling technology for common description of competences. In: Proceedings of the 7th IEEE International Conference on Advanced Learning Technologies, Niigata, Japan (2007)

Is a Virtual Learning Environment a One-Size-Fits-All Solution? A Survey of Cognitive Styles Within a University Student Population

Russell Barton and Jonathan Foster(✉)

Information School, University of Sheffield, Regents Court, 211 Portobello Street, Sheffield S1 4DP, UK
j.j.foster@sheffield.ac.uk

Abstract. Over the last decade, the large-scale introduction of Virtual Learning Environments (VLEs) into higher education has been a boon to learners and teachers alike. VLEs enable students to have ready access to digital materials before, during, and after classes; and to a platform for subsequent discussion. Over a number of years a body of evidence has emerged, suggesting that learners differ in their cognitive styles in significant ways; and that the matching/mismatching of instructional design with these styles can affect both how learners interact with materials and perform tasks, and learning outcomes. A survey based on a revised version of the Study Preferences Questionnaire [4] was distributed to students at a UK university in order to identify their style. 229 students returned the questionnaire. Of the respondents, 140 students were categorized as holists, 73 as serialists, and 16 as versatile. The implications of the prevalence of holists for instructional design are discussed. In a conclusion, it is suggested that research attention be given to a structure/structuring criterion as a way of exploring the matching/mismatching hypothesis; while the development of versatile rather than optimal information processing may also be a more productive educational goal.

Keywords: Virtual learning environments · Cognitive styles · Learning styles · Holists/serialists · Matching/mismatching · Information processing

1 Introduction

Since the 2000s universities have overseen the large-scale introduction of virtual learning environments. The term Virtual Learning Environment (VLE) refers to an online space specifically designed for use by students and staff, in order to further educational goals. Typically, VLE's are seen as an extension to the classroom, providing asynchronous methods of communication that allow students to access, manage, learn and edit material in their own time [2]. More recent developments, e.g. *Adobe Connect,* have enabled users to engage in real-time interaction with and around the materials. In short, VLEs enable the asynchronous and synchronous continuation of the face-to-face instructional environment, in different places and at different times;

L. Uden et al. (Eds.): LTEC 2016, CCIS 620, pp. 301–308, 2016.
DOI: 10.1007/978-3-319-42147-6_25

enabling the pursuit of educational goals outside of organized contact time between learners and teachers.

In a VLE the teacher is often not directly present, and the individual learner needs to navigate their way through the materials, without direct instruction from the teacher. Under these self-regulated learning conditions, it is considered beneficial to cater for individual learners' different cognitive styles when designing the learning materials. A cognitive style is a "person's typical or habitual mode of problem solving, thinking, perceiving and remembering" [14]. Therefore a person's learning style can be described as the typical or habitual mode of problem solving, thinking, perceiving and remembering that the individual learner displays within an educational setting. In each case research is concerned with the form of thinking, perceiving and remembering, and not the content of what is thought, perceived, and remembered.

2 Cognitive/Learning Styles

Research into cognitive styles differentiates a learner's typical or habitual mode of cognition along two basic dimensions. These dimensions are: wholist/analytic and verbalizer-imager. When addressing the wholist/analytic dimension, individual learners can be differentiated according to their capacity for adopting either a description building or a procedure building style, when approaching tasks and situations. The former involves "building a description of how elements in a topic interrelate, that is, forming an understanding of internal structure" [15], while the latter involves "building operations, that is, manipulating the underlying interrelationship between concepts in a topic" [15]. These styles are the cognitive styles as defined by the works of Pask and Scott [12, 13], in which they identified categories of individuals by their preferred approach to learning. An individual with a tendency to adopt a description building approach to tasks is known as a "holist", whereas individuals with a preferred procedure building approach are labelled "serialists". When no preference for adopting either approach is indicated, the individual is known as "versatile". Cognitive or learning styles can be viewed as a structure, as a process, or as a combination of both. When styles are viewed as a structure then attention is given to its "stability over time; as such, style is a 'given' in a training or an educational setting. Once the style in the setting is identified, the training material can be adapted or 'matched' to the individual's cognitive style" [14].

Since the 1970s a body of research has emerged around the concept of matching [12]. The concept of matching refers to how learning and teaching is considered most effective when the design of materials and instruction matches the cognitive style of the learner [3, 4, 6, 7, 9–13]. For example, in an experimental study conducted by Pask the "matched consistently performed better than the mismatched, for example, the mismatched holists needed 4 to 7 iterative repetitions in contrast to 1 to 3 for matched serialists" [11]. It was also found that learning in matched conditions was more enjoyable, quicker, and much less disruptive than in mismatched conditions. This places emphasis on the fact that in order for high quality education to occur, matching must be taken into account in the classroom. Further empirical studies support this conclusion, and highlight the fact that matching styles is greatly beneficial to education, and to interacting with sources of information [1, 3–5, 7]. A number of studies have established the positive effects of presenting information in way that matches with a user's or learner's cognitive style. For example, Ford and Chen [7] explored the effect on learning outcomes, of instructional materials presenting information matched and mismatched with students' field-dependent/field-independent style. Under matched conditions, i.e. holists presented with instructional materials presenting information 'breadth-first' and serialists presented with instructional materials presenting information 'depth-first', students achieved a significantly higher gain score or increase in conceptual knowledge. Chen et al. [1] also explored field-dependent (FD), intermediate, and field-independent (FI) learners' perceptions of a flexible interface design to three Web directories. Among their findings, they were able to establish that in the majority of cases cognitive style predicts a preference for organizing and presenting information in a way matched with the learners' cognitive style. When the screen returned results in response to a search task, 65 % of FD users preferred the items organized and presented in subcategories first, before viewing specific results; while 71 % of FI users preferred viewing specific results first, before viewing the information organized and presented into sub-categories. Within the cultural heritage domain, Goodale et al. [8] found that users with a holist/analytic style differed systematically in how they searched, explored, and interacted with a digital library. For example, holists took longer than analytics to complete their information-seeking tasks, required more prompting, and also took longer to complete a separate path creation task. Holists also made greater use than analytics of the tag-cloud feature. Each of the findings can be interpreted in terms of the holist's initial need for an initial global overview as a way of orienting themselves in a novel environment.

3 Methods

The paper reports findings from the first part of a two-part study exploring students' cognitive styles, and their interaction with a VLE instructional design. The aim of the first part of the study was to survey the cognitive styles present in a student population. The aim of the second part of the study was to identify and explain any matching/mismatching of students' different styles via a VLE usability study. The questionnaire used is a revised version of the Study Preferences Questionnaire [4]. The questionnaire determined the tendencies of individuals to adopt description-building and procedure-building styles when approaching tasks and situations. These styles are the cognitive styles as defined by the works of Pask and Scott [12], in which they identified categories of individuals by their preferred approach to learning. An individual with a tendency to adopt a description building approach to tasks is known as a "holist", whereas individuals with a preferred procedure building approach are labelled "serialists". When no preference for adopting either approach is indicated, the individual is known as "versatile". Therefore, the questionnaire was used as a way of categorising students as either holist, serialist or versatile with regards to their cognitive style. Data on individuals' cognitive styles have been collected using many different methods. These range from lengthy and difficult to administer experiments [12, 16], to short self-assessment forms [3, 4, 14]. Since this study is focused around the theoretical framework of cognitive styles, as defined by Pask and

Scott [12], the questionnaire must be able to distinguish between description building and procedure building. Time constraints, and the associated difficulty with repeating experiments, ruled out methods used for identifying cognitive styles as developed by Pask and Scott [12] and Witkin [16]. The 'Cognitive Styles Analysis' designed by Riding and Cheema [14], is also a very well respected instrument for testing cognitive styles but combines the wholist/analytic dimension with the verbal/imagery dimension. Since the conceptual approach to matching for this study consists of the serialist/holist dimension, it would not make sense to include the verbal/imagery dimension and a Cognitive Styles Analysis was ruled out for this study. Entwistle's [3] approaches to studying inventory was also considered, since cognitive styles can be inferred from the results of assessing other deep, surface, and strategic learning strategies. Ford's [4] 'Study Preference Questionnaire', which revises Pask and Scott [12], was selected; since it directly tests for the presence of holistic and serialist tendencies among the cognitive styles of study participants.

The Study Preference Questionnaire consists of 16 questions, each containing 2 statements. The participant is required to indicate which statement they most agree with by selecting a number between 1 and 5; a selection of 1 indicates total agreement with the statement on the left and 5 indicates total agreement with the statement on the right. Only 10 of the questions are relevant for determining cognitive styles with 6 included as decoy questions. Of these 10 remaining questions, 5 are designed to calculate a value for description building tendencies, and 5 are designed to calculate a value for procedure building tendencies. For example, a question such as "If I likened the way I put an essay together to painting a wall, I tend to put a first thin coat of paint over the whole area, then put on more layers until it's done" tests a tendency for description-building; while a question such "I like to deal fairly thoroughly with the particular aspect I'm working on before going on to study" tests a tendency for procedure building.

The value returned for description building, and for procedure building, can then be used to determine the preferred cognitive style of the individual by subtracting one from the other. If the value for procedure building is subtracted from the value for description building, and the resulting number is positive, then a holistic style is present, whereas if the resulting number is negative, then a serialist style is present [4]. The questionnaire generates a spectrum of final scores between −20 and +20, with a score of 0 indicating no preferred tendency and therefore classifying the individual as versatile. A higher numerical value indicates a stronger tendency towards that style. For example, an individual with a score of +15 is much more holistic than an individual with a score of +5, whereas a score of −15 indicates much more of a serialist tendency than that of −5.

The questionnaire was distributed to all undergraduate students at a UK University of Sheffield via an email broadcasting system. The questionnaire was designed as a Google Form, which meant that responses from participants were instantly collected and stored in a password-protected responses sheet. No names were saved, making the determination of each individual's cognitive style anonymous and not personally identifiable. Analysis of the quantitative data from the questionnaire enabled the determination and identification of the presence and distribution of different cognitive styles among a sample of the university student population; while also enabling the generation of hypotheses to be tested in a subsequent usability study conducted with volunteering students.

4 Findings

The questionnaire provided the original set of quantitative data that required analysis for this project. It was designed to calculate a student's cognitive style by generating a representative numerical score via calculations made on the student's responses. The questionnaire received responses from 229 students, generating a numerical score that represents the cognitive style present in each case. The response rate to the questionnaire was satisfying, returning a relatively large sample size, which in turn provides reliability of data [4]. Figure 1 illustrates the distribution of cognitive styles across the university students who participated, indicating that the most common score is +4. On the basis of the data returned, 140 students were categorized as holists, 73 as serialists, and 16 as versatile. Therefore, it can be asserted that 61 % of students at the university exhibit a holistic style, 32 % display a serialist style, and 7 % exhibit a versatile style. What is immediately surprising is that there are nearly twice the number of learners present in the population who display a holistic style, than those with a serialist style. While this distribution may seem surprising, Entwistle [3] provides a possible explanation for this distribution. When discussing "deep" and "surface" learning, he draws parallels between

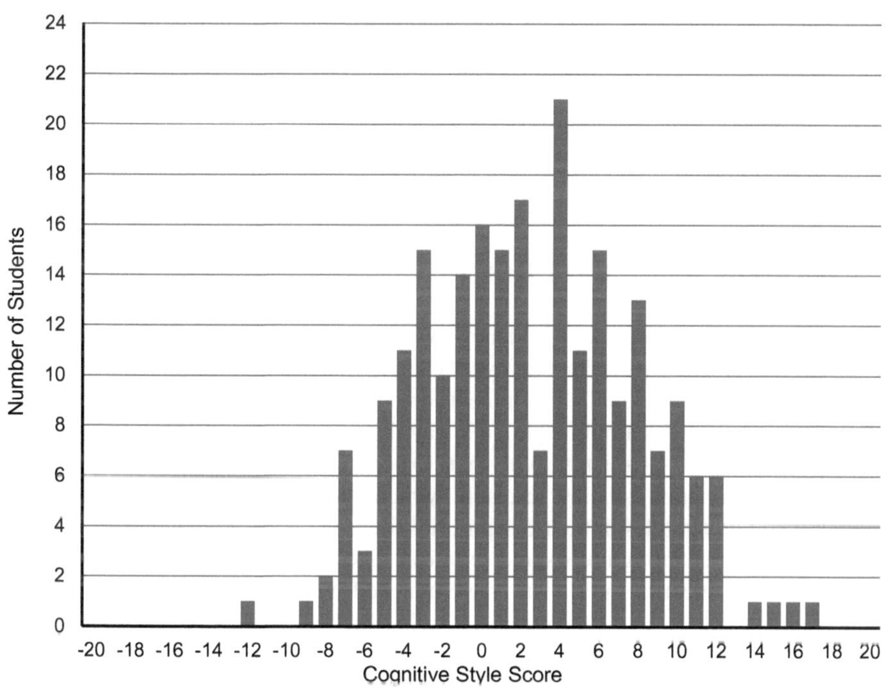

Fig. 1. Cognitive style score by student number

"deep" learners and a holistic style, and "surface" learners and a serialist style; proposing that university education requires a deeper approach to learning, and that those able to adopt a deeper approach will perform better. A university population may then naturally contain more learners with a description-building holistic learning style.

5 Discussion

The skew in distribution between students with a holist style and those with a serialist style is potentially significant, when gauging the matching/mismatching of students' cognitive styles with a VLE. In principle a VLE should enable individual learners to interact with tasks and materials in their own preferred style. In doing so an equally satisfactory learning experience is delivered to each and every learner. However, as the results from the survey highlight, differences and biases do exist. Knowing the tendencies in cognitive style that exist in a university's student population, will help to assess the relevance and significance of the impact of any bias intentionally or unintentionally designed into the VLE, and interactions with specific educational implementations of the VLE.

Is a VLE a one-size-fits-all solution? On the basis of the study conducted here, combined with those from previous studies, there are a number of possible answers. In the face-to-face educational arena Entwistle (1981) proposed that instructors should aim to accommodate all styles, and to avoid biasing instruction to any one specific style. In practice this will take a versatile teacher, who has the ability to vary his/her own style to accommodate those in his/her audience. An alternative, and more satisficing approach, based on the findings from this study, is to anticipate a broad description-building approach and an holistic style in one's university audience, and to deliver instruction appropriately. A further approach would be to adopt a holistic teaching strategy, while tailoring and personalizing where appropriate to a significant minority of serialists.

6 Conclusion and Future Research

This study identified a prevalent tendency towards an holistic style of thinking within the university student population surveyed. Clearly this has implications for the design of VLEs, and an instructional environment aimed at matching content and interaction with students preferred learning style, in a way that is educationally effective. In doing so students' levels of satisfaction with their experience can be raised.

Current information studies research, which has sought to accommodate and respond to cognitive styles in their designs, has focused on the global/analytic criterion as the factor differentiating holists and serialists' interaction with information systems. With the global aspect of the holist's style matched with breadth-first overviews, and the local or analytic aspect of the serialist's style matched with depth-first presentations of information. An alternative rationale for investigating the matching/mismatching hypothesis, that hasn't received so much attention, would be to differentiate between holists and serialists on the basis of the structure/structuring criterion. While holists appear, at least initially, to look for a map that structures the field, and thereby aids comprehension of the ensuing topic(s) to be learnt; serialists appear to have a preference for and be adept at structuring content, at least initially, via the concatenation of discrete items of information. In other words, holists appear to some degree to be comfortable with an externally imposed structure; while serialists prefer presentation of information and facilities that enable internal structuring of the content.

An alternative path for future research is to question the very assumption that learning needs to be matched. This path could be followed in at least two ways. To place less emphasis on the relative differences of holists and serialists, and to explore the conditions under which the same learner may display different strategies in response to different learning situations, e.g. breadth-first followed by depth, or depth-first followed by breath etc. This points to a further emphasis on the development of the versatile learner; and underpinning this a different educational philosophy that points less towards optimality in cognitive information processing, and more towards versatility in information processing as a response to the needs or demands of the learning environment encountered.

References

1. Chen, S., Magoulas, G.D., Dimakopoulos, D.: A flexible interface design for web directories to accommodate different cognitive styles. J. Am. Soc. Inf. Sci. Technol. **56**(1), 70–83 (2005)
2. Dillenbourg, P., Schneider, D., Synteta, P.: Virtual learning environments. In: Dimitracopoulou, A. (ed.) 3rd Hellenic Conference "Information and Communication Technologies in Education", Rhodes, Greece, pp. 3–18. Kastaniotis Editions, Greece (2002)
3. Entwistle, N.J.: Styles of Learning and Teaching. Wiley, London (1981)
4. Ford, N.: Learning styles and strategies of postgraduate students. Br. J. Educ. Technol. **16** (1), 65–77 (1985)
5. Ford, N.: Levels and types of mediation in instructional systems: an individual differences approach. Int. J. Hum. Comput. Stud. **43**(2), 241–259 (1995)
6. Ford, N.: Cognitive styles and virtual environments. J. Am. Soc. Inf. Sci. **51**(6), 543–557 (2000)
7. Ford, N., Chen, S.Y.: Matching/mismatching revisited: an empirical study of learning and teaching styles. Br. J. Educ. Technol. **32**(1), 5–22 (2001)
8. Goodale, P., Clough, P.D., Fernando, S., Ford, N., Stevenson, M.: Cognitive styles in an exploratory search system for digital libraries. J. Documentation **70**(6), 970–996 (2014)
9. Pask, G.: Conversation Theory: Applications in Education and Epistemology. Elsevier, Amsterdam (1976)
10. Pask, G.: Final report of SSRC Research Programme HR2708. Richmond, Surrey: System Research Ltd. (1979)
11. Pask, G.: Learning strategies, teaching strategies, and conceptual or learning style. In: Schmeck, R.R. (ed.) Learning Strategies and Learning Styles, pp. 83–99. Plenum Press, New York (1988)
12. Paskand, G., Scott, B.C.E.: Learning strategies and individual competence. Int. J. Man Machine Stud. **4**(3), 217–253 (1972)
13. Paskand, G., Scott, B.C.E.: CASTE: a system for exhibiting learning strategies and regulating uncertainty. Int. J. Man-Machine Stud. **5**, 17–52 (1973)

14. Riding, R., Cheema, I.: Cognitive styles—an overview and integration. Educ. Psychol. **11** (3–4), 193–215 (1991)
15. Riding, R., Rayner, S.: Cognitive Style and Learning Strategies: Understanding Style Differences in Learning and Behaviour. Routledge, Oxford (2012)
16. Witkin, H.A.: Perception of the upright when the direction of the force acting on body is changed. J. Exp. Psychol. **40**(1), 93 (1950)

Author Index

Aguilar-Magallón, Daniel 193
Aho, Anne-Maria 90
Alexiou, Aikaterini 39
Al-Smadi, Mohammad 289
Amado-Salvatierra, Hector R. 139
Augustin, Tobias 122

Barrera-Mora, Fernando 183
Barriga, July Katherine Díaz 77
Barton, Russell 301
Becker, D'Arcy 112
Bouta, Hara 39

Camacho-Machín, Matías 3
Cely, Sandra Bonilla 207
Chavez, Jorge 25
Chen, Whai-En 162
Creixell, Werner 61

Díaz, Yesid 51
Drum, Dawna 112

Ferro, Roberto 51
Florjančič, Viktorija 168
Foster, Jonathan 301

Ganter, Cristóbal 61
García, Cristina Pelayo 219
García, Víctor Hugo Medina 207, 219
Giannakou, Ioanna 39
Gütl, Christian 139

Hernández, Rocael 139

Jaramillo, Claudia 25

Kaplan, Jonathan 103
Kukk, Vello 265

Laanpere, Mart 289
Liberona, Dario 25

Marmolejo, Leonor Rojas 207
Molano, José Ignacio Rodríguez 77
Morales, Miguel 139
Moreno, Mar 3
Müller, Severina 235

Ortiz, Nancy Yurani 15

Paraskeva, Fotini 39
Pata, Kai 289
Pernsteiner, Aimee 112
Pirker, Johanna 139
Puentes, Jorge Leonardo 15

Quintero, José López 219

Reyes-Martínez, Isaid 193
Reyes-Rodriguez, Aaron 183
Rodriguez, José Ignacio 15
Romero, Christian David Gómez 77

Santos-Trigo, Manuel 3, 193
Sarmiento, Dacarth 51
Scheffler, Nina 235
Seufert, Sabine 235
Siemsen, Sabine 150
Sinclair, Jane 90
Stanoevska-Slabeva, Katarina 235

Tammets, Kairit 289
Tomberg, Vladimir 289

Umbleja, Kadri 250

Vallance, Michael 274

MIX
Papier aus verantwortungsvollen Quellen
Paper from responsible sources
FSC® C105338
www.fsc.org

If you have any concerns about our products,
you can contact us on
ProductSafety@springernature.com

In case Publisher is established outside the EU,
the EU authorized representative is:
Springer Nature Customer Service Center GmbH
Europaplatz 3, 69115 Heidelberg, Germany

Printed by Libri Plureos GmbH
in Hamburg, Germany